1000 Paintings of Genius

Authors: Victoria Charles
Joseph Manca, Megan McShane, Donald Wigal

With the dedicated support of Klaus H. Carl, Thu Nguyen, Marie de Roujoux, Trang Nguyen, Eliane de Sérésin, Cornelia Sontag, Elodie Vasseur, Maïté Vicedo, Thai Vo, Elisabeth Woodville.

Designed by: Baseline Co Ltd, 127-129A Nguyen Hue, Fiditourist Building, 3rd Floor District 1, Ho Chi Minh City, Vietnam

This edition published by Barnes & Noble, Inc., by arrangement with Sirrocco, London, UK.

2006 Barnes & Noble Books

M 10 9 8 7 6 5 4 3 2 1
ISBN 0-7607-7216-9

1000
Paintings
of Genius

BARNES & NOBLE

NEW YORK

CONTENTS

INTRODUCTION

For the sixteenth-century Italian writer and painter Giorgio Vasari, a dark period in human history ended when God took pity on humankind and brought about a reform of painting. Vasari wrote in his *Lives of the Artists* of 1550 that the naturalism of Tuscan painters like Giotto di Bondone in the early fourteenth century was a miracle, a gift to humankind to bring about an end to the stiff, formal, unnatural Byzantine style that had held sway before that time. Today, we recognise that it was hardly by chance or divine mercy that such a change occurred in artmaking. The development of crisp, effective narrative, convincing spatial representation, and the introduction of corporeal, realistic figures possessing physical presence are all aspects of painting echoing the changes in European culture that were beginning to take hold by the fourteenth century and later, and which found their most forcible expression in Italy. Set against a social revolution in which traders, manufacturers and bankers were gaining in prominence, painters were responding to the growing demand for clear, naturalistic representation in art. The monumental works of the Florentine Giotto and the elegant, finely wrought naturalism in the paintings of the Sienese Duccio di Buoninsegna were but one part of a larger cultural movement. It also comprised: the moving, vernacular writings of Dante, Petrarch, and Boccaccio; the vivid travel-adventure of Marco Polo; the growing influence of nominalism in philosophy, which encouraged real, tangible and sensate knowledge; and the religious devotion of Saint Francis of Assisi, who found God's presence not in ideas and verbal speculation but in the chirping of birds and the glow of the sun and moon.

What the *primi lumi*, the 'first lights', in the art of painting had commenced by the fourteenth century was continued in the fifteenth century with ever greater sharpness and thoroughness, and with a new historical sense that caused them to look back before the Middle Ages to the world of the classical civilisations. Italians came to admire, almost worship, the ancient Greeks and Romans, for their wisdom and insight, and for their artistic as well as scholarly achievements. A new kind of intellectual, the humanist, fuelled a cultural revolution in the fifteenth century. A humanist was a scholar of ancient letters, and humanism

was the broader attitude they fostered: a belief in the value of a thoughtful study of Nature, a faith in the potentiality of humankind, and a sense that secular, moral beliefs were necessary to supplement the limited tenets of Christianity. Above all, the humanists encouraged the belief that ancient civilisation was the apex of culture and one should be in a dialogue with the writers and artists of the classical world. The result was the Renaissance, the rebirth, of Greco-Roman culture. The panels, paintings and murals of Masaccio and Piero dell Francesca captured the moral firmness of ancient Roman sculptural figures, and these artists strove to show their actors as part of our world: the Renaissance perspective system is based on a single vanishing point and carefully worked out transversal lines, resulting in a spatial coherence not seen since antiquity, if ever. Even more clearly indebted to antiquity were the paintings of the northern Italian prodigy Andrea Mantegna. His archaeological studies of antique costumes, architecture, figural poses, and inscriptions resulted in the most thoroughly consistent attempt by any painter up to his time to give new life to the vanished Greco-Roman civilisation. Even a painter like Alessandro Botticelli, whose art evokes a dreamy spirit that had survived from the late Gothic style, created paintings with Venuses, Cupids, and nymphs that responded to the subject matter of the ancients and appealed to contemporary viewers touched by humanism.

It would be better to think of 'Renaissances' rather than a single Renaissance. This is demonstrated no more clearly than by looking at the art of the leading painters of the High Renaissance. Giorgio Vasari saw these masters as all setting out to create an art greater than Nature, as idealists who improved on reality rather than imitating it, and who thoughtfully suggested reality rather than delineating it for us in every particular detail. We recognise in these painters different embodiments of the cultural aspirations of the time. Leonardo da Vinci, trained as a painter, was equally at home in his role as a scientist, and he incorporated into art his research into the human body, plant forms, geology, and psychology. Michelangelo Buonarroti, trained as a sculptor, turned to painting and expressed his deep theological and philosophical beliefs, especially the idealism of Neoplatonism. His muscular, over-scaled and intense heroes could hardly differ any more from the graceful, smiling, supple figures of Leonardo. Raphael of Urbino was the ultimate courtier, whose paintings embody the grace, charm and sophistication of life at Renaissance courts. Giorgione and Titian, both Venetian masters, expressed with their colourism and free brushwork an epicurean sense of life, their art finding no better subject matter than in luxurious landscapes and sumptuous female nudes. All the sixteenth-century painters tried to improve on Nature, to create something greater or more beautiful than nature itself. Titian's motto *Natura Potentior Ars*, 'Art More Powerful than Nature', could be the philosophy of all the sixteenth-century artists.

Among the achievements of the Italian Renaissance painters was that they had established their intellectual credentials. Rather than being considered as mere handicraftsmen, artists – some of whom, such as Leon Battista Alberti, Leonardo da Vinci, and Michelangelo, were themselves writers on this subject – made a bid to be considered on a par with other thinkers of their time. The profession of painting experienced a sharp rise in its critical fortunes in Renaissance Italy. Michelangelo, for example, was called *Il Divino*, 'the Divine', and a kind of cult sprang up around leading painters and other artists of the time. Already in 1435, Alberti urged painters to associate themselves with men of letters and mathematicians, and this paid off. The present-day inclusion of "studio art" in university curricula has its origins in the new attitude to painting that arose in Italy during the Renaissance. By the sixteenth century, rather than only commissioning particular works, art patrons across the peninsula were happy to get their hands on any product of the great individual artists: acquiring 'a Raphael', 'a Michelangelo', or 'a Titian' was a goal in itself, whatever the work in question.

While the Italians of the Renaissance had turned to highly organised spatial settings and idealised figural types, the northern Europeans focused on everyday reality, on optical sensations, and on the variety of life on earth. No painter has ever surpassed the Netherlandish painter Jan van Eyck in his close observation of surfaces, and no one has ever seen and captured more clearly and poetically the glint of light on a pearl, the deep, resonant colours of a red cloth, or the glinting reflections that appear in glass and on metal. Scientific observation was one form of realism, while another was the intense interest at the time in the bodies of saints and on the anatomical details of the Passion of Christ. This was the age of religious theatre, when actors, dressed as biblical characters, acted out in churches and on the streets the detail of Christ's suffering and death. It is not coincidence this was also the period when masters such as Netherlandish Rogier van der Weyden and German Matthias Grünewald painted, sometimes with excruciating clarity, the wounds, streams of blood, and pathetic countenance of the crucified Christ. The northern masters carried out their pictorial research with a skilled use of oil painting technique, a medium in which they remained in the forefront in European art until the Italians joined them only in the later fifteenth century.

Spanning north and south during the Renaissance period was the art of Albrecht Dürer of Nuremburg. He followed the Italian penchant for canonical measure of the human body and perspective, even if he retained a form of sharp expressionism of line and emotional representation that was widespread in German art. While he shared the artistic optimism of the idealistic Italians, many other northern painters retained a sense of pessimism about the human condition. Giovanni Pico della Mirandola's essay on the *Dignity of Man* presaged Michelangelo's belief in the perfectibility and essential beauty of the human body and soul. For their part, Erasmus's *Praise of Folly* and Sebastian Brant's satiric poem *Ship of Fools* were part of the same northern European cultural milieu that produced the fantastic follies of humankind shown in Hieronymus Bosch's *Garden of Earthly Delights* triptych and Pieter Brueghel's raucous peasant scenes. There was hope for humankind in Paradise, but little consolation on earth for beings consumed by their passions and caught in a cycle of desire and fruitless yearning. Northern humanists, like their Italian counterparts, called for the classical virtues of moderation, restraint, and harmony and the pictures of Brueghel represented the very vices against which they warned. Unlike some of the contemporary Romanists, who had travelled from the Netherlands to Italy and been inspired by Michelangelo and other artists of the time, Brueghel travelled to Rome around 1550 but remained largely untouched by its art. He turned to local inspiration and staged his scenes amidst humble settings, earning him the undeserved nickname of "Peasant Brueghel". He was a herald of the realism and bluntness of the northern European Baroque.

The great intellectual revolt set in motion by theologians Martin Luther and John Calvin in the sixteenth century led to an attempt by the Catholic Church to respond to the challenge of the Protestants. Various Church Councils called for a reform of the Roman Catholic Church. In the arts, the participants at the Council of Trent declared that art should be simple and accessible to the broad public. A number of Italian painters, however, whom we know as Mannerists, had instead been practising an artistry that was complex in subject matter and style. Painters eventually responded to ecclesiastical needs as well as to the ennui that necessitated a response to Mannerist stylistic formulae. We call this new era the age of the Baroque, which was ushered in initially by Caravaggio. He painted what he saw in front of him, in the most realistic if dramatically dark and theatrically concentrated manner possible, and he gained a following among the popular masses as well as with connoisseurs and even with Church officials, who were at first sceptical of his overly realistic treatment of sacred subject matter. Caravaggism swept across Italy and then the rest of Europe, and a host of painters came to adopt and adapt his chiaroscuro and his suppression of flashy colouring; his earthy and sincere actors struck a chord with viewers across the Continent who had tired of some of the artificialities of sixteenth-century art.

In addition to the Caravaggism of the early Baroque, another form of painting later called the High Baroque soon developed; the most dramatic, dynamic, and painterly of styles hitherto developed. Many of its painters built on the foundation laid by the Venetians of the sixteenth century. Peter Paul Rubens, an admirer of Titian, painted huge canvases with fleshy figures, rich landscapes, broken brushwork, and flickering light and dark. His pictorial experiments were the starting points for the art of his countrymen Jacob Jordaens and Anthony van Dyck, the latter of whom had a great following among the European elite for his noble portrait manner. Rubens brought back the world of antiquity, painting on his canvases ancient gods, goddesses and human sea creatures, but his style was anything but classical. He found a ready market for his works among the European aristocrats, who liked his bombastic flattery, and among Catholic patrons of religious art, who found in his extroverted sacred scenes another weapon in Counter-Reformation ideology. In Rome itself, the sculptor Bernini was Ruben's counterpart, as the Catholic Church had in these two champions of Faith a means to show the power and majesty of the Church and the Papacy. The Italian Baroque painters let loose a torrent of holy figures on the ceilings of the churches of Rome and other cities, with the skies opening up to reveal Heaven itself and God's personal acceptance of the martyrs and mystics of the world of Catholic sainthood. The Spanish painters Velásquez, Murillo, and Zurburán took up the style in their native land, perhaps calming the physical

movements and open brushwork, but sharing with the Italians a mystical sense of light and the Catholic iconographic subject matter.

How different from all this were the paintings of seventeenth-century Holland! Having effectively freed themselves from Habsburg Spain by the 1580s, the Dutch practised a tolerant form of Calvinism, which eschewed religious iconography. A growing middle class and an increasingly wealthy upper class were present to buy the delightful variety of secular paintings produced by a host of skilled painters, with individual artists specialising in moonlit landscapes, skating scenes, ships at sea, tavern scenes, and a great variety of other subjects. From this large school of artists several individual painters stand out. Jacob van Ruisdael was the closest we have to a High Baroque landscape painter in Holland, his dark and sometimes stormy landscapes evoking the drama and movement so widespread in European art of the time. Frans Hals' painting, with flashy, quick strokes of the brush and exaggerated colouration of skin and garments, also, like Ruisdael's, approaches a more pan-European sensibility of the High Baroque. In contrast, Jan Steen typified the widespread realism and local quality of most Dutch art of the Golden Age, and he added a moral slant in his depiction of households in disarray and misbehaving peasants. Finally, the paintings of Rembrandt van Rijn stand alone, even from the Dutch. Raised as a Calvinist, he shared some beliefs with the Mennonites, and he was happy to depart from the Calvinist stricture against representing biblical scenes. His later paintings, with their quiet introspection, make the perfect Protestant counterpart to the showy, dynamic, Roman Catholic paintings of Rubens. While working early on in a tighter technique influenced by the Dutch "fine painters," Rembrandt developed a broad, shadowy manner derived from Caravaggio but expressed with much greater pictorial complexity. This style fell out of favour among the Dutch, but Rembrandt held his ground, going bankrupt though leaving a legacy that would be admired by Romantics and those modernists with a penchant for painterly abstraction. Rembrandt also stood out because of the universality of his art. He was steeped in knowledge of other styles and in literary sources. Although he never travelled to Italy, he was an artistic sponge, and he included in his works bits inspired by the late Gothic artist Antonio Pisanello and the Renaissance masters Mantegna, Raphael and Dürer. He constantly evolved, and he had the broadest artistic mind and deepest understanding of the human condition of any painter of his age.

Clearly, just as there were many 'Renaissances' in art, there were many forms of the Baroque, and the High Baroque was challenged by the Classical Baroque, which had its philosophical roots in ancient thought and its stylistic basis in the paintings of Raphael and other High Renaissance classicists. Annibale Carracci had embraced a classical approach, and painters like Andrea Sacchi challenged the supremacy in Rome of High Baroque painters like Pietro da Cortona. However, the most quintessential classicist of the seventeenth century was the Frenchman Nicolas Poussin, who developed a style perfectly suited to the growing ranks of philosophical Stoics in France, Italy, and elsewhere. His solid, idealised figures, endowed with broad physical movements and firm moral purpose, acted out a range of narratives, both sacred and secular. Another Frenchman developed a different form of classicism: the epicurean paintings of Claude Lorrain at first seem to differ sharply from those of Poussin, as Claude's pictures melt edges away, his waters ripple subtly, and hazy views into infinity appear in the distance. Yet, both painters conveyed a sense of moderation and balance, and appealed to similar kinds of patrons. All these painters of the seventeenth century, whether classical in temperament or not, participated in the explosion of subject matter of the time; not since antiquity had artmaking seen such a diversity of iconography of both sacred and profane subjects. With the exploration of new continents, contact with new and different peoples across the globe, and novel views offered by telescopes and microscopes, the world seemed to be a changing, evolving and fractured place, and the diversity of artistic styles and pictorial subject matter reflected this dynamism.

Louis XIV (d. 1715), the self-designated Sun King who modelled himself after Apollo and Alexander the Great, favoured the classical mode of Poussin and of painters such as his court artist Charles Le Brun, who, in turn, favoured the king with a number of murky paintings glorifying his reign. There arose in the end of the seventeenth century and the beginning of the eighteenth century a debate over style in which painters allied themselves with one of two camps, the Poussinistes and the Rubénistes. The former favoured classicism, linearity, and moderation, while the latter group declared the innate primacy of free colouring, energetic movement, and compositional dynamism. When Louis XIV died, the field in France was open, and the Rubénistes took the lead, bringing forth a style we call Rococo, which – roughly translated – means "pebblework Baroque," a decorative brand of the painterly Baroque. Rather than being a continuation of the style of Rubens, the manner of Antoine Watteau, Jean-Honoré Fragonard and François

Boucher conveyed a lighter mood, with more feathery strokes of the brush, a lighter palette, and even a smaller physical size of works. Erotic subject matter and light genre subjects came to dominate the style, which found favour especially among the pleasure-loving aristocrats of France, as well as their peers elsewhere in Continental Europe. The Rococo painters thus carried forward the debate between line and colour that had emerged in practice and in art theory in the sixteenth century: the argument between Michelangelo and Titian, and then between Rubens and Poussin, is a struggle that would not go away, and would return in the nineteenth century and later.

Not every artist succumbed to the Rococo. A focus in the eighteenth century on particular social virtues – patriotism, moderation, duty to family, the necessity to embrace Reason and study the laws of Nature – were themselves at odds with the subject matter and hedonistic style of the Rococo painters. In the realm of art theory and criticism, Diderot and Voltaire were unhappy with the Rococo style flourishing in France, and the days of the style were numbered. The humble naturalism of the Frenchman Chardin was based in Dutch still-life artistry of the previous century, and the Anglo-American and English painters, including John Singleton Copley of Boston, Joseph Wright of Derby and Thomas Hogarth painted in styles which, in different ways, embodied a kind of fundamental naturalism we recognise as fitting for the spirit of the age. A number of artists, such as Elisabeth Vigée-Lebrun and Thomas Gainsborough, incorporated into their paintings some of the lightness of touch that characterized the Rococo, but they modified its excesses and avoided some of its artificial and superficial qualities, however delightful those are.

A leitmotif of Western painting has been the persistence of classicism, and here the Rococo found its fiercest opponent. The essentials of the classical style – a dynamic equilibrium, an idealised naturalism, a measured harmony, a restraint of colour and a dominance of line, all operating under the guiding influence of ancient Greek and Roman models – reasserted themselves in the late-eighteenth century in response to the Rococo. When Jacques-Louis David exhibited his *Oath of the Horatii* in 1785, it electrified the public, and was applauded by the French including the King, and an international viewership. Thomas Jefferson happened to be in Paris at the time of the painting's exhibition and he was greatly impressed. The popularity of Neoclassicism preceded the French Revolution, but once the revolution occurred, it became the official style of the virtuous new French regime. The Rococo was associated with the decadent *Ancien Régime*, and its painters were forced to flee the country or change their styles. A later Neoclassicism remained in vogue in France through the Napoleonic age, and the elegant linearity and exotic attitude of Jean-Auguste-Dominique Ingres took the place of the works of David, who had softened his style later in life to create a copious, more decorative form of classicism suitable for the less bourgeois character of the French Empire.

If the eighteenth century was the Age of Reason and the Enlightenment, there was, developing at the same moment, an intellectual trend towards interest in the irrational and the emotional. A group of painters, sometimes regarded together under the term Romantics, flourished in the late-eighteenth century and the first half of the nineteenth century. Many of these painters co-existed chronologically with the classical artists, and there was a certain amount of rivalry between them. Some of the European painters from the last half of the eighteenth century to the first half of the nineteenth century were explicitly interested in the irrational, as was Henry Fuseli in his *Nightmare* and Francisco Goya in some of his violent or black paintings and their scenes of death and madness. Théodore Géricault explored medical insanity in some of his smaller paintings and the themes of death, cannibalism, and political corruption in his massive and turgid *Raft of the Medusa*. More subtle were the painters in this period who explored the emotional effects of landscape art. John Constable's flickering light and careful study of clouds and the sunlight on trees in the English countryside yielded strikingly emotive results. The German Caspar David Friedrich conveyed the religious mysticism of the landscape, while the American Hudson River School painters, such as Thomas Cole, represented the warm autumnal colours and desolation of a wilderness in the New World that was quickly disappearing. J.M.W. Turner's paintings of seascapes, landscapes, and historical scenes seemed to his contemporaries to be made of "tinted steam," and he edged towards modernism in his abstractness. The most influential and acclaimed of the French Romantic painters was Eugene Delacroix. He turned to the High Baroque painter Rubens for artistic inspiration and painted canvas after canvas of tiger hunts, Passion of Christ imagery, and – for contemporary taste – the exotic world of Arab warriors and hunters in northern Africa. Like the Baroque masters before him, he used zooming spatial diagonals, cut-off compositional elements, and bravura colourism with great effect. Delacroix gained the artistic and even personal enmity of Ingres, and contemporaries recognised in their art the timeless struggle of line versus colour.

The kind of anti-Romantic realism in Flaubert's *Madame Bovary* found expression in the art of the school of Realist painters. Gustave Courbet's unadorned representation of Nature and of village life stands as his attempt to show us the world without elaboration. His statement "show me an angel and I will paint one" is the sentiment which led to the creation of his monumental *Burial at Ornans*, a carefully composed work that he and critics of the time convinced themselves was little more than raw *réalité*. More traditional, but also based on close observation of nature, were the paintings of Jean-François Millet and the Barbizon School painters, led by Theodore Rousseau. Among the other Realists were Honoré Daumier, who concerned his efforts with contemporary urban life and in depicting the folly of civic officials and lawyers, the natural goodness of labourers, and the weariness of the poor. Contemporary in time with the French Realists were the English Pre-Raphaelite painters, who turned their backs on the artful idealism they associated with the Academy; they found inspiration instead in the detailed particularism and 'honesty' of painting in Italy before Raphael and the High Renaissance. Dante, Gabriel Rossetti and Edward Burne-Jones found solace in exotic stories of the Middle Ages, in accounts of early British history, and in all manner of moralising tales and parables. They painted with oils, but with the care of tempera paints, without the broad treatment of the brush, the scumbling of the colours across the canvas, and the rapid glazing technique that the oil medium makes possible. They would not be the last painters in the West to reject the pictorial possibilities of oil paint, or to defy the conventions of the academies of art from the sixteenth to the nineteenth centuries.

As urbanism and industrialism advanced in nineteenth-century Europe, a new and unexpected development occurred in painting with the rise of Impressionism. Claude Monet, Auguste Renoir, Camille Pissarro and others in their circle painted with rapid strokes and with an insubstantiality never before seen in painting. Sometimes capturing the idylls of the countryside and at other times capturing the light, smoke, colour, and movement of urban scenes, they turned their backs on the historical and concentrated instead on conveying the evanescence of present appearances. Rejected at first by critics and the public because of their insouciance with academic rules, the Impressionists had a lasting impact on art. As their styles developed, the modernity of their art became even more apparent. Monet's canvases became extremely abstract, and he came to finish his pictures, not in front of the visual source, but in his studio, sometimes long after contact with the natural model. Renoir eventually sought to represent the firm linearity he had discovered in Italian art, and his works became ever more planned in design, firmly based on figural models, and sugary sweet in colouring. The traditionalist painters Jean-Léon Gérôme and William Bouguereau in France and Ilya Repin in Russia achieved worldly success and acclaim with their more academic and conservative approaches, but the Impressionists had the greatest impact on the development of modernism, and their artistry soon inspired new branches of painting.

The Post-Impressionists were a group of artists who understood the potentialities of the way the Impressionists used the brush. Paul Cézanne was determined to make "something permanent" of the art of the Impressionists, endowing his pictures with the compositional solidity he found in classicism. He was intent on "redoing Poussin after Nature," and he developed a rough kind of classicism that, at the same time, broke down barriers by obscuring the edges of things and by making the paint surface an end in itself, with its own lighting, texture, and colouring. Vincent van Gogh built on Impressionism and imbued it with his mystical spirit. Paul Gauguin sought subject matter in the primitive areas of France and the South Pacific and painted with patches of sometimes barely mediated colours. Georges Seurat's art theory returned to some of the rhetoric of early Impressionism, as he set out to give an impression of reality through his novel technique. In his case, it was based on points of colour and optical mixing of colours to create the sense of reality, except that, like Cézanne, he gave his figures an almost neoclassical calm, presence, and moral *gravitas*.

The explosion of styles that had set in during the later nineteenth century continued in the twentieth century. The freedom and individualism of modernism found expression in a riot of painting styles. Thinkers in a number of fields in the early-twentieth century discovered the essential instability of form and existence: atonalism in music, the theory of relativity in physics, and the destabilising tendencies of psychoanalysis all pointed to a world of subjectivity and shifting viewpoints. For their part, the Cubists, led by Pablo Picasso and Georges Braque, systematically broke down ("analysed") reality in their Analytic Cubism, almost eliminating colour, direction of light, texture, and even the singularity of viewpoint and, for a while, they turned completely away from narrative in favour of immobile subjects of still-life and portraiture. In the history of styles, it can be said that the Cubists

demolished the Renaissance project – a project accepted by the Academic painters of the nineteenth century – of constructing a spatial box in which meaningful events unfold with convincing space, colour and light. Never painting in a pure, non-representational abstraction, the Cubists relied for artistic success on the tension between what one sees and what one expected to see. Picasso, who had earlier painted in an academic narrative manner as a youth and in poetic and rather representational Blue and Pink periods, later experimented almost endlessly, at times dabbling with Primitivism, Neoclassicism, and Surrealism. Not since Giotto had a single painter done more to change the field of his art. The works of the French painter Fernand Léger and the *Nude Descending a Staircase* by Marcel Duchamp were by-products of the styles of Picasso and Braque, an expansion of an idea into more dynamic settings of figures in an architectural environment.

Picasso's art was often witty and clever. A good deal of twentieth-century painting was more serious, and works like Picasso's *Guernica*, portraying the tragedy of war, were his own advance away from the playfulness of his early Cubist styles. Surrealist art, such as the dream paintings of Salvador Dalí, or the forbidding settings of the works of Giorgio de Chirico, capture some of the alienation and psychological intensity of modern life. The Futurists, Italian painters beholden to the Cubists, turned to dynamic, even violent movement in their paintings, and their art presaged the unpleasant mixture of modernism, urbanism, and aggression that, not by coincidence, fuelled the Fascist regime of Benito Mussolini. Quite unlike the outwardly intense Futurists, some modernists of the late-nineteenth and early-twentieth centuries included a group of painters set on exploring inner subjectivity, and the period of civilisation that gave us Freud and Jung was bound to include a group of painters willing to explore the psychological states of the human race. Edvard Munch's psychological insight and expressionism were matched in their intensity perhaps only by those of the German painters Ludwig Kirchner and Emil Nolde. A religious sentiment, also deeply emotive, flourished during this time in the abstracted art of the Catholic Georges Rouault and the Jewish Marc Chagall.

Modernists rejected tradition in architecture, literature and music, and painting was no different. The rise of abstraction has been much heralded, but it is arguable that no such thing is possible. The Dutchman Piet Mondrian saw in his abstractions various theological, gender, and existential categories, and his *Broadway Boogie Woogie* is suggestively titled. Kasimir Malevitch's abstract, geometric paintings carried ontological and divine connotations, while Wassily Kandinsky's abstractions are fraught with mysticism and secret messages. Jackson Pollock's Abstract Expressionist drip paintings contained in them a strong human presence in the very kinesthetic style itself, and he labelled his works with telling titles such as *Autumn Rhythm* and *Lucifer*. The Dutch-born Willem De Kooning's canvases are filled with an explosive and frantic application of the paint, often illustrating highly charged subject matter. Mark Rothko's fields of bleeding colours sprang from the artist's philosophical notions, and he wanted his viewers to be deeply moved by his pictures. Colour and shape had come to fill the gap left by the departure of the Virgin Mary and martyred saints, classical gods and triumphant generals of earlier artmaking. The older technique of oil painting was supplemented in the twentieth century with new or reborn substances: acrylic, aluminum paints, encaustic, enamel, and other binding agents, with the occasional quotidian object mixed in or glued onto the surface for good measure.

A reaction to the psychological intensity of the Abstract Expressionists was inevitable, and it took two forms. One was in a new objectivity and minimalism, championed by sculptors such as Donald Judd and David Smith, but also painters such as Ellsworth Kelly and Frank Stella, who set out to take a good deal of the human emotion, mysticism, and moral subjectivity out of painting. Another response was found in Pop Art, which vividly brought back the represented object, often in mirthful ways. Andy Warhol's soup cans, the collages of Richard Hamilton, and the comic book style of Roy Lichtenstein, works often carried in large scale, were serious in their intents. The commercial products of modern societies come spilling out on to the canvases of the Pop Artists, who ask us to consider the nature of consumerism and mass production as well as issues of artistic representation.

In the end, painting has triumphed in Western art over a host of opponents. In the Renaissance, the debate raged over the *paragone*, that is, the comparison of the visual arts, and Michelangelo and his camp proclaimed that sculpture was more real, more literally tangible, and less deceptive than painting. Leonardo and others fought back, with words and deeds, and one can argue that painting remained the preeminent art from the Renaissance to the twentieth century. It is telling that the average viewer can only name a few prominent sculptors of the Renaissance, but might easily name a small army of painters from that period. The same is true of the nineteenth century: in the nineteenth-century French context, for example, beyond Rodin, and perhaps Carpeaux and Barye, the sculptors are paled by the schools of painters who came forth with innovative ideas. Painting has overcome the cheap supply of prints that flooded the markets beginning in the fifteenth century, the attempts by some Baroque artists to merge painting with other visual arts, the promise of greater verisimilitude claimed by photography in the nineteenth century, and the competition offered by moving pictures in the twentieth. Digital media threaten a challenge once again in the early twenty-first century. But painting is too powerfully present, too flexible in results, and too rooted in our sensibilities to give way easily to upstarts. Even in practical terms, paintings can be rolled up and shipped, or when not in use they can be stacked, while, on the other hand, they can fill a blank wall or a ceiling with great effect. You cannot turn a painting off with a switch or an easy click of the mouse. They are flat, like the pages of our books and the screens on our computers, and can be reproduced in a compatible, two-dimensional format, without necessitating the difficult decisions of lighting called for in the reproduction of sculpture or with the questions of viewpoint as in the photography of architecture. Renaissance thinkers said a painter can exercise divine powers and, like God himself, create an entire world, and thousands of different pictorial worlds have been created since then.

The works chosen for this book demonstrate the variety of great painting to be found in our public museums. Surely, painting continues to have a lasting appeal in a changing world. Will the field continue to produce masterpieces? That is a more difficult question to answer. The works collected here indicate that physical craftsmanship is an important component of successful painting. It is also clear that painters succeed when they "stand on the shoulders of giants" and respond to art of the past, be it in admiration or in rebellion. Perhaps the world is awaiting the next great painter who, like Raphael, Rembrandt, and Picasso is steeped in the art of the past, and has the knowledge, sincerity, and technical skills to create something new and outstanding. If painters of the future produce works that are little more than sarcastic one-liners, or are by nature ephemeral in form and meaning, or disdain or ignore the whole of the history of art, the field of painting has little hope of success. However, manual skill and a determination to create a novel yet savvy work of art can go a long way towards preserving the art form. The pages of this book contain, without setting out to do so, a blueprint for painting's future.

— *Joseph Manca*

1

13th CENTURY

Following the Romanesque period, the Gothic period emerged in northern France. The centres of religious and intellectual authority moved from a rural-monastic environment to urban centres.

The Gothic ribbed vault, because it was light and thin, allowed for a new aesthetic to develop in which *lux nova* defined the new architecture. "New light" was communicated through the uplifting vaults and the stained glass that illuminated the new lofty spaces made technologically possible by flying buttresses on the exterior that provided support for the thin walls. Phillip II (r.1180-1223) built Paris into the capital of Gothic Europe. He paved the streets, embraced the city with walls, and built the Louvre to house the royal family.

Thomas Aquinas, an Italian monk, came to Paris in 1244 to study at the renowned university. He began, but never finished, the Summa Theoligica in the Scholastic model being taught in Paris. Based on Aristotle's system of rational inquiry, Aquinas used a model in his treatise that organised the work into books, then questions within the books, and articles within the questions. Each article then included objections with contradictions and responses, and answers to the objections became the final element in the model. Aquinas's work is a foundation of Catholic teaching.

When King Louis IX (1215-1270) assumed the throne, the Parisian "court style" of Gothic was at it height. Paris was not only revered for its university faculty and architects, but also for its manuscript illuminators. In Dante Alighieri's (1265-1321) *Divine Comedy* he noted Paris as the capital of the art of book illumination.

The rest of Europe tried to emulate the Gothic style of the Île-de-France, but the German and English traditions did not emphasise the soaring height in the way that the cathedrals of Reims or Amiens did. England's great achievements in the thirteenth century were political, including the *Magna Carta* (1215), generally thought by later generations to be a guarantor of human rights for all, and the establishment of Parliament during the reign of Edward I (1272-1307).

The crusades were in full force by the thirteenth century, but the battles were largely defined by Muslim counterattacks. The Fourth Crusade (1202-1204) was mainly played out in Constantinople and served to discredit the crusading trend, as Christians attacked Christians, and the schism between the Eastern Orthodox Christians and the Roman Catholics widened.

These military ventures did, however, create long lasting cultural exchanges. New foods and luxury items such as silks and brocades entered into circulation. Italian traders particularly benefited from this merchant exchange with the East, even expanding its reaches.

The famous Venetian explorer, Marco Polo (1254-1324), travelled from Europe to Asia and spent seventeen years in China developing Merchant contracts. While Italians used timber beams rather than high stone vaults to roof their structures, thereby limiting the height of their churches, they did soar in the arena of international trade, setting the stage for the "golden age" of the Renaissance.

1. **Bonaventura Berlinghieri**, 1205/10-c. 1274, Gothic Art, Italian,
   St Francis and Scenes From his Life, 1235, Tempera on wood, 160 x 123 cm,
   San Francesco, Pescia

2. Master of the Crucifixion, Gothic Art, Italian,
Crucifixion and Eight Stories of the Passion of Christ,
late 12th c. – early 13th c. Tempera on panel, 250 x 200 cm,
Galleria degli Uffizi, Florence

2

3. Tuscan Master, Gothic Art, Italian,
Crucifixion and Six Stories of the Passion of Christ, 1240-1270
Tempera on panel, 277 x 231 cm, Galleria degli Uffizi, Florence

3

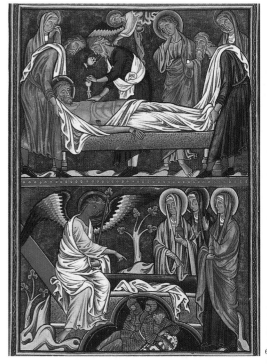

Cimabue (Cenni di Pepo)
(c.1240 Florence – 1302 Pisa)

After learning the art of making mosaics in Florence, Cimabue developed in the medieval Byzantine style, advancing towards more realism. He became the first Florentine master. Some of his works were monumental. His most famous student was Giotto. He painted several versions of the Maestà, "majesty, enthroned in glory", traditionally referring to Mary in setting, that show some human emotions, such as *Madonna and Child Enthroned with Angels and Prophets*.

4. Master of St Mary Magdalen, Early Renaissance, Italian,
St Mary Magdalen and Eight Stories from her Life, 1265-1290,
Tempera on panel, 164 x 76 cm, Galleria degli Uffizi, Florence

5. Workshop of Louis IX, Early Renaissance, France, Danish,
Joshua Stops the Sun and Moon, From the Psalter of Louis IX of France, c. 1258-1270,
Manuscript illumination, 21 x 14.5 cm, Bibliothèque Nationale, Paris

6. Workshop of the Ingeborg, Early Renaissance, Danish,
Embalming of the Body of Christ and the Three Marys at the Empty Tomb,
From the Psalter of Queen Ingeborg of Denmark, c. 1213,
Manuscript illumination, 30.4 x 20.4 cm, Musée Condé, Chantilly

7. Master of San Gaggio, Early Renaissance, Italian, *Madonna and Child
Enthroned with Ss. Paul, Peter, John the Baptist and John the Evangelist*,
Tempera on panel, 200 x 112 cm, Galleria degli Uffizi, Florence

8. Cimabue (Cenni di Pepo), 1240-1302, Early Renaissance, Italian,
S. Trinità Madonna, c. 1280, Tempera on panel, 385 x 223 cm,
Galleria degli Uffizi, Florence

*Cimabue painted this altarpiece for the Holy Trinity church in Florence, which is
unprecedented, albeit at first it appears very similar to other of his works of the
previous decade. It is smaller than his Maestà (1260), to which it can be contrasted
on several key points. The differences are important as the artist moves himself and
the art world beyond the rigid poses of the Byzantine icons to more three-
dimensionality. While there remains a strict symmetry of figures, the intentional
distortion of figures as in his earlier art is abandoned for more natural animation.
It is seen in each of the fourteen figures, including the prophets (left to right)
Jeremiah, Abraham, David and Isaiah, as they apparently find apposite scriptural
references.*

9. Cimabue (Cenni di Pepo), 1240-1302, Early Renaissance, Italian,
Madonna and Child Enthroned with Two Angels and Ss. Francis and Dominic,
Tempera on panel, 133 x 82 cm, Galleria degli Uffizi, Florence

10

12

Duccio di Buoninsegna
(1255 – 1319 Siena)

Duccio di Buoninsegna, originally a carpenter and manuscript illuminator, was influenced by Cimabue and the Sienese school of painting. With Giotto, he was one of the transitional artists between the Gothic and the Renaissance ages, showing Byzantine elements throughout. Also a profound innovator, he painted his figures with greater weight and solidity, and more characterisation than had been seen previously in Siena. He is considered as one of the seminal artists in the development of the Sienese school.

10. Duccio di Buoninsegna, 1255-1319, Sienese School, Florence, Italian, *Madonna and Child Enthroned with Six Angels (Rucellai Madonna)*, 1285, Tempera on panel, 450 x 290 cm, Galleria degli Uffizi, Florence.

Duccio's Madonna is seated on an elaborate throne. Although Our Lady and her child appear to be three-dimensional and realistic, the surrounding environment is stylised, disregarding the principles of perspective. Hierarchic scale, often used in medieval times, is featured, depicting the most important subject, Mary, as the largest. The symmetrical distribution of the six angels, three on each side of the Madonna, may be symbolic of the order that Mary, as Mother Church, imposes on her subjects. Yet above all she remains the loving mother.

11. Anonymous, French, *The Rheims Missal*, c. 1285-1297, Manuscript illumination, Stolen from the Library St. Petersburg, St. Petersburg

12. Gautier de Coinci, 1177-1236, French, *Life and Miracles of the Virgin*, late 13th c., Manuscript illumination, Stolen from the Library St. Petersburg, St. Petersburg

Illustration of the death of a money lender whose soul is taken away by the devil, and a beggar woman to whom the Virgin and the Holy virgins appear.

13

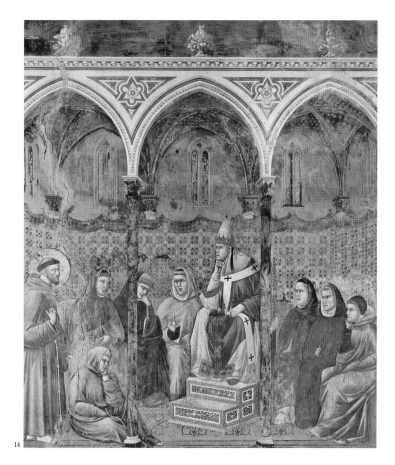

13. Giotto di Bondone, 1267-1337,
Early Renaissance, Florentine School, Italian,
The Demons are Cast out of Arezzo (detail),
1296-1297, Fresco, Upper Church of San
Francesco, Assisi

14. Giotto di Bondone, 1267-1337,
Early Renaissance, Florentine School, Italian,
*Legend of St Francis: St Francis
Preaching before Pope Honorius III,*
1296-1297, Fresco, Upper Church of San
Francesco, Assisi

14

Giotto di Bondone
(1267 Vespignano – 1337 Florence)

His full name was Ambrogiotto di Bondone, but he is known today, as he was in his own time, by the contraction, Giotto, a word which has come to stand for almost all the great things that art has accomplished. In his own day Giotto's fame as a painter was supreme; he had numerous followers, and these *Giotteschi*, as they were styled, perpetuated his methods for nearly a hundred years. In 1334, he designed the beautiful *Campanile* (bell tower), which stands beside the cathedral in Florence, and represents a perfect union of strength and elegance, and was partly erected in his lifetime. Moreover, the sculptured reliefs which decorate its lower part were all from his designs, though he lived to execute only two of them. Inspired by French Gothic sculpture, he abandoned the stiff presentations of the subjects as in Byzantine styles and advanced art towards more realistic presentation of contemporary figures and scenes so as to be more narrative. His breakthrough influenced subsequent development in Italian art. His significant departure from past presentations of the Maestà, starting around 1308 (in *Madonna di Ognissanti*), brought to it his knowledge of architecture and its perspectives. However, the disproportion of subjects in the presentation is a device intended to rank the subjects by their importance, as was done in Byzantine icons.

Thus, architect, sculptor, painter, friend of Dante and of other great men of his day, Giotto was the worthy forerunner of that galaxy of brilliant men who populated the later days of the Italian Renaissance.

14th Century

The fourteenth century is viewed as a transitional period from the Medieval to the Renaissance. The Catholic Church experienced disruptions, contributing to social chaos. In 1305 a French Pope, Clement V, was elected. He settled in Avignon rather than Rome, as did subsequent popes, causing the election of two popes in 1378, one in Avignon and one in Rome. This became known as the Great Schism. Not until forty years later in 1417, was the crisis resolved with the election of a new Roman Pope, Martin V, whose authority was accepted by everyone.

At this time, Italy was a group of independent city-states and republics, ruled mostly by an aristocratic elite. Dominating the international trade that connected the Europe with Russia, Byzantium, as well as the lands of Islam and China, Italy expanded trade and commerce through highly organised economic activity. This prosperity was brutally disrupted by the Black Death, or bubonic plague, in the late 1340s. In just five years at least twenty-five percent of the population of Europe, and upwards of sixty percent in some areas, were killed. Economic turmoil and social disruption ensued in Europe, while the Ottoman Empire and the Islamic states were far too strong to notice the expansion or decline of the European economic initiatives of the fourteenth century.

In the secular sphere, a great shift occurred with the development of vernacular, or everyday, literature in Italy. Latin remained the official language of Church and state documents, but intellectual and philosophical ideas became more accessible in the common language, which was based on Tuscan dialects from the region near Florence. Dante Alighieri (1265-1321), Giovanni Boccaccio (1313-75), and Francesco Petrarch (1304-74) all helped to establish the use of vernacular language. Dante's *Divine Comedy* and *Inferno*, as well as Boccaccio's *Decameron* enjoyed a wider audience because they were written in the vernacular.

Petrarch described ideas of individualism and humanism. Rather than a philosophical system, humanism referred to a civil code of conduct and ideas about education. The scholarly discipline humanists hoped to advance was based on human interests and values as separate from religion's otherworldly values, but not opposed to religion. Humanism enveloped a separate set of concerns than religious scholarly disciplines based not on faith but on reason. Latin classics from Greco-Roman antiquity helped to develop a set of ethics governing civil society including service to the state, participation in government and in the defence of the state, as well as duty to the common good, rather than self interest. The humanists translated Greek and Roman texts that had been neglected in the Middle Ages, but they also composed new texts devoted to the humanist's cult of fame. Just as sainthood was the reward for religious virtue, fame was the reward for civic virtue. Boccaccio wrote a collection of biographies of famous women and Petrarch wrote one of famous men who embodied humanist ideals.

15. **Giotto di Bondone**, 1267-1337, Medieval, Florentine School, Italian, *Flight into Egypt*, 200 x 185 cm, 1303-05, Fresco, Cappella Scrovegni (Arena Chapel), Padua

16

17

16. Giotto di Bondone, c. 1267-1337,
Early Renaissance, Florentine School, Italian,
*Scenes from the Life of Joachim: Meeting at
the Golden Gate*, 1303-05, Fresco, Cappella
Scrovegni (Arena Chapel), Padua

17. Giotto di Bondone, c. 1267-1337,
Early Renaissance, Florentine School, Italian,
*Scenes from the Life of the Virgin:
Presentation of the Virgin in the Temple*,
1303-05, Fresco, Cappella degli Scrovegni
dell' Arena, Padua

18. Master of St. Cecilia, Early Renaissance,
Italian, *Saint Cecilia Altarpiece*, after 1304,
Tempera on panel, 85 x 181 cm,
Galleria degli Uffizi, Florence

19. Duccio di Buoninsegna, 1255-1319,
Early Renaissance, Sienese School, Italian,
Christ Entering Jerusalem, 1308-11,
Tempera on panel, 100 x 57 cm,
Museo dell'Opera del Duomo, Siena

20. Duccio di Buoninsegna, 1255-1319,
Early Renaissance, Sienese School, Italian,
The Maestà, (back panel), *Stories of the
Passion: Peter's First Denial of Christ Before
the High Priest Annas*, 1308-11,
Tempera on panel, 99 x 53.5 cm,
Museo dell'Opera del Duomo, Siena

18

19

20

21

SIMONE MARTINI
(1284 SIENA – 1344 AVIGNON)

A Sienese painter, he was a student of Duccio. Influenced by his master and by the sculptures of Giovanni Pisano, he was even more influenced by French gothic art. First painting in Sienna, he worked as a court painter for the French Kingdom in Naples where he started to incorporate non-religious characters in his paintings. Then he worked in Assisi and Florence where he painted with his brother-in-law Lippo Memmi.

In 1340-41 Simone Martini went to Avignon in France, where he met Petrarch, illustrating a Virgil codex for him. His last works were created in Avignon where he died. Simone Martini gave a great sweetness to his religious compositions while, at the same time, he was the first who dared to employ his art for purposes not wholly religious.

21. Giotto di Bondone, c. 1267-1337, Early Renaissance, Florentine School, Italian, *Ognissanti Madonna (Madonna in Maestà)*, 1305-10, Tempera on panel, 325 x 204 cm, Galleria degli Uffizi, Florence

22. Simone Martini, 1284-1344, Gothic Art, Sienese School, Italian, *Maestà* (detail), 1317, Fresco, Palazzo Pubblico, San Gimignano

In this painting, the traces of Byzantine influence remain such as in the style of throne and stacking of figures as if on tiers. But overall the influence of the Gothic painters Duccio and Giotto are in greater evidence. Several of the saints carry symbols of themselves, often the instruments of their martyrdom. Each pole supporting the canopy is held by one of the saints. While the size of each figure is somewhat uniform, the Byzantine tradition of sizing figures in proportion to their importance still remains. This piece is the artist's earliest known work. The transparency of the angelic gowns is not an accidental effect from top layers fading over the years, but rather the effect is the result of a clever technique. Only seven years after its competition it had to be restored because of water damage. The fresco is surrounded by a frame decorated with twenty medallions depicting the Blessing Christ, the Prophets and the Evangelists and with smaller shields containing the coat-of-arms of Siena.

22

23. Jean Pucelle, c. 1300-55, Gothic Art, French, *The Betrayal of Christ and Annunciation*, from the Hours of Jeanne d'Evreux, 1325-28, Tempera and gold leaf on parchment, 8.9 x 6.2 cm (each page), The Metropolitan Museum of Art, New York.

23

24

24. Francesco Traini, active 1321-63, Early Renaissance, Italian,
The Triumph of Death (detail), c. 1325-50, Fresco, Campo Santo, Pisa

25. Taddeo Gaddi, 1300-66, Early Renaissance, Florentine School, Italian,
Life of the Virgin, c. 1330, Fresco, Baroncelli Chapel, Santa Croce, Florence

*According to Cennino Cennini, Taddeo Gaddi worked twenty-four years in Giotto's
workshop. The very personal style of the artist appears in the frescos of the* Life of the
Virgin, *in Santa Croce, although still very related to Giotto's manner.*

25

Taddeo Gaddi
(1300 – 1366 or 1368 Florence)

Son of the painter and mosaicist Gaddo Gaddi (c. 1260-
1332/33), he was Giotto's most important student and
collaborator for more than twenty years. In his frescos his
figures were still stiff, but he advanced perspective. He is
known to have been number one on a list of the best living
painters, compiled in 1347, to choose a master to paint a high
altarpiece for Pistoia Chapel. After his death, his son and
student Agnolo continued his workshop.

26. Ambrogio Lorenzetti, c. 1290-1348, Early Renaissance, Sienese School, Italian, *Scenes of the Life of St Nicholas: St Nicholas Offers Three Girls Their Dowry*, 1327-32, Tempera on panel, 96 x 53 cm, Galleria degli Uffizi, Florence

27. Ambrogio Lorenzetti, c. 1290-1348, Early Renaissance, Sienese School, Italian, *Scenes of the Life of St Nicholas: St Nicholas Is Elected Bishop of Mira*, 1327-32, Tempera on panel, 96 x 53 cm, Galleria degli Uffizi, Florence

29

28. Ambrogio Lorenzetti, c. 1290-1348, Early Renaissance, Sienese School, Italian,
The Presentation in the Temple, 1327-32,
Tempera on panel, 257 x 138 cm, Galleria degli Uffizi, Florence

29. Simone Martini and Lippo Memmi, 1284-1344 and 1317-47,
Early Renaissance, Sienese School, Italian, *Altar of The Annunciation*, 1333,
Tempera on panel, 184 x 210 cm, Galleria degli Uffizi, Florence

*Simone Martini comes from the same school as Duccio. He followed the Pope to
Avignon, in 1344, during the Schism. The frame of this painting was added in the
nineteenth century. The Virgin is represented without volume; she is more spirit
than substance and can be compared on that point to Duccio's virgins. Looking for
beauty and the depiction of details, the painter moves away from the works by
Giotto. Simone Martini uses a much nuanced game of colours (gold, browns and
pinks). He introduces depth in the foreground, using an edge that gives emphasis
to the distance and that obliges the viewer to step back. His study of perspective
from nature is made obvious on the depiction of the vase in the centre.*

30

30. Simone Martini, 1284-1344, Gothic Art, Sienese School, Italian, *Equestrian Portrait of Guidoricco da Fogliano* (detail), 1328-30, Fresco, 340 x 968 cm, Palazzo Pubblico, Siena

31

31. Ambrogio Lorenzetti, c. 1290-1348, Early Renaissance,
Sienese School, Italian, *Allegory of the Good Government*, 1338-39,
Fresco, Palazzo Pubblico, Siena

*The artist's view of his entire town and countryside are captured as large frescos
in the Sala della Pace, Palazzo, Siena, the town's city hall. This fresco is a
political propaganda, celebrating the virtues of the Administration of the
Commune. The Bad Government is illustrated by the devilish figure of
Discordia, and the Good Government is personified by the diverse emblems of
Virtue and Concordia. The reproductions of the frescos are rarely from the
visitor's floor level point of view. However, from that vantage point the
perspectives was more as intended, with the small figures in the foreground and
often the larger figures higher on the wall but apparently further in the distance.
Ambrogio's amazing sense of space was mastered later by his brother Pietro in
his* Birth of the Virgin *(1342).*

32. Bernardo Daddi (Attributed to), c. 1290-1350, Early Renaissance, Florentine
School, Italian, *Crucifixion*, c. 1335, Tempera on panel, 36 x 23.5 cm,
The National Gallery of Art, Washington, D.C.

*Daddi is believed to have been Giotto's student and his work strongly shows his
influence. Daddi, on his side, influenced Florentine art until the second half of
the century.*

33. Ambrogio Lorenzetti, c. 1290-1348, Early Renaissance, Sienese School,
Italian, *Madonna and Child Enthroned with Angels and Saints*, c. 1340,
Tempera on panel, 50.5 x 34.5 cm, Pinacoteca Nazionale, Siena

AMBROGIO LORENZETTI
(C. 1290 – 1348 SIENNA)

Ambrogio Lorenzetti, like his brother Pietro, belonged to the
Sienese School dominated by the Byzantine tradition. They
were the first Sienese to adopt the naturalistic approach of
Giotto. There is also evidence that the brothers borrowed tools
from each other. They were both major masters of naturalism.
With the three-dimensional, Ambrogio foreshadowed the art
of the Renaissance. He is well known for the fresco cycle
Allegory of the Good and Bad Government, remarkable for
their depiction of characters and of Sienese scenes. The frescos
on the wall of the Hall of Nine (Sala della Pace) in the Palazzo
Pubblico are one of the masterworks of their secular programs.
Ghiberti regarded Ambrogio as the greatest of Sienese
fourteenth-century painters.

34

35

36

34. **Master of Kaufmann**, Early Renaissance, Bohemian,
   The Crucifixion of Christ, c. 1340, Tempera on panel, 76 x 29.5 cm,
   Gemäldegalerie, Alte Meister, Berlin

35. **Hohenfuhrth Master**, Early Renaissance, Bohemian, *The Agony in the Garden*,
   c. 1350, Tempera on panel, 100 x 92 cm, Narodni Galeri, Prague

36. **Master of the Berlin Nativity**, Early Renaissance, Bavarian, *Nativity*, 1330-40,
   Tempera on panel, 33 x 24 cm, Gemäldegalerie, Alte Meister, Berlin

37

37. Ambrogio Lorenzetti, c. 1290-1348, Early Renaissance, Sienese School, Italian,
Birth of the Virgin, 1342, Tempera on panel, 188 x 183 cm,
Museo dell'Opera del Duomo, Siena

38

39

38. **Andrea di Cione Orcagna**, c. 1320-68, Gothic Art, Florentine School, Italian,
The Redeemer with the Madonna and Saints, 1354-57, Tempera on panel,
Strozzi Chapel, Santa Maria Novella, Florence

*It was originally the altarpiece of the Strozzi Chapel of Santa Maria Novella, Florence.
In this painting Orcagna reverted from a more naturalistic style to the Byzantine remote
and monumental figural type with resplendent colours and lavish use of gold.*

39. **Bohemian Master**, Gothic Art, Bohemian, *Death of the Virgin*, 1355-60,
Tempera on panel, 100 x 71 cm, Museum of Fine Arts, Boston

40. **Master of the Eichhorn Madonna**, Gothic Art, Bohemian,
Eichhorn Madonna, c. 1350, Tempera on panel, 79 x 63 cm, Narodni Galeri, Prague

40

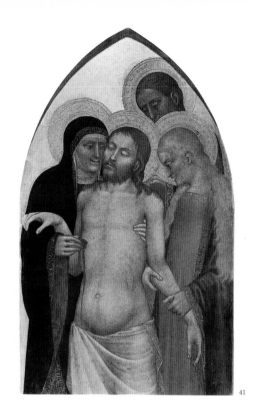

41

43

42

44

45

41. Giovanni da Milano, active 1346-69, Gothic Art, Italian, *Pietà*, 1365, Tempera on panel, 122 x 58 cm, Galleria dell' Accademia, Florence

42. Andrea di Cione Orcagna, c. 1320-68, Gothic Art, Florentine School, Italian, *St Matthew and Four Stories from his life*, 1367, Tempera on panel, 291 x 265 cm, Galleria degli Uffizi, Florence

43. Giottino, c. 1320-69, Gothic Art, Florentine School, Italian, *Pietà of San Remigio*, c. 1360-65, Tempera on panel, 195 x 134 cm, Galleria degli Uffizi, Florence

44. Tommasso da Modena, c. 1325-79, Gothic Art, Italian, *The Departure of St Ursula*, c. 1355-58, Tempera on panel, 233.5 x 220 cm, Museo Civico, Treviso

45. Matteo di Pacino, active 1359-94, Early Renaissance, Italian, *St. Bernard's Vision of the Virgin with Saints*, Tempera on panel, 175 x 200 cm, Galleria dell'Accademia, Florence

46

46. Agnolo Gaddi, c. 1345-96, Early Renaissance, Florentine School, Italian, *Madonna of Humility with Six Angels*, c. 1390, Tempera on panel, 118 x 58 cm, Galleria dell'Accademia, Florence

47. Melchior Broederlam, Early Renaissance, Dutch, *The Dijon Altarpiece: Annunciation and Visitation; Presentation in the Temple and Flight into Egypt*, 1394-99, Tempera on panel, 167 x 125 cm, Musée des Beaux-Arts, Dijon

48

48. Named after Wilton House, International Gothic, French,
The Wilton Diptych, Richard II presented to the Virgin and Child by his Patron
Saint John the Baptist and Saints Edward and Edmund, c. 1395-99,
Egg tempera on oak panel, 57 x 29.2 cm, National Gallery, London

The anonymous artist of this diptych is a Sienese painter, contemporary of
Giotto, renewer of the Sienese School. The Wilton Diptych was painted as a
portable altarpiece for the private devotion of King Richard II; the outside
bears his arms and his personal emblem of a white hart (a young deer) chained
with a crown around its neck.

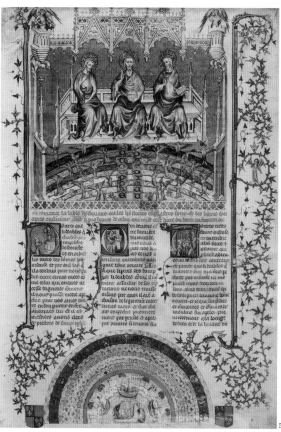

49. Anonymous, Early Renaissance, French, *Book of Hours of the Use of Rome*, late 14th c.- early 15th c., *Manuscript illumination*, Stolen from the Library St. Petersburg, St. Petersburg

50. Guyart des Moulins, Early Renaissance, French, La Bible Historiale, Third quarter of the 14th c., *Manuscript illumination*, Stolen from the Library St. Petersburg, St. Petersburg

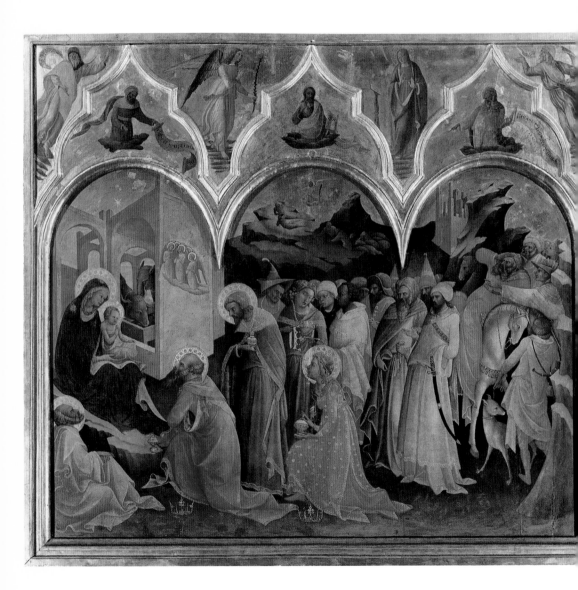

15th Century

Bridging the fourteenth and the fifteenth centuries was the Hundred Years War. This war contributed to instability and strife across the entire continent, even though the primary conflicts were between France and England, it also involved Flanders. After Philip the Bold (1342-1404) married the daughter of the count of Flanders, he was able to add these counties from the Netherlands to his realm as the Duke of Burgundy. Philip the Good (1396-1467) ruled next in secession, in what would then become known as the Burgundian Netherlands. Bruges, an important city for trade in Flanders, now lent enormous economic power to the newly acquired territory, making the Burgundian Netherlands a rival of France. Later, in a period of decline towards the end of the fifteenth century after Charles the Bold (1433-1477) had died at the battle of Nantes in 1477, the Burgundian lands were reabsorbed into France and the Netherlands became a part of the Holy Roman Empire.

This is an important time for the development of European capitalism. Big families throughout Europe developed international trade, such as the Medici of Florence. The French word for stock market, *bourse*, is derived from another big family of international traders, the van der Breuse family, who centred their enterprise in Bruges. Along with the increasing wealth from trade came a new opulence in materials for art. It is at this time that painters turned from using egg-based paint, or tempera, to oil-based paint. Oil had been used for many centuries, but it was not until the fifteenth century that it became widely popular, first in the north and then spreading to the south.

The development of manuscript illumination flourished at this time. The duc de Berry (1340-1416) was one of the greatest art patrons of the time. He had over one hundred lavish manuscripts among his rare jewels and works of art.

While exquisite hand-illuminated books were being created for the very wealthy, in the 1440s Johann Gutenberg (1398-1468) was able to expand on the block printed books of the fourteenth century by creating moveable type and modifying presses used for making wine to develop a more efficient and less expensive system for printing.

Other innovations of the time included Filippo Brunelleschi's (1377-1446) development of one point perspective for painting. This system allowed for greater illusionism in two-dimensional paintings, creating the impression of three-dimensional space. This was a breakthrough from the flattened, awkward pictures of the Middle-Ages.

This period was also known as the dawn of the Age of Exploration. Christopher Columbus (1451-1506) sailed across the Atlantic for the Americas in 1492 under the flag of Castille. While the Portuguese explorer, Pedro Alvares Cabral (1467-1520), later would claim Brazil for Portugal in 1500.

The Portuguese explorer, Vasco da Gama (1469-1524), also sailed to India in 1498 around Africa's Cape of Good Hope, which had been explored by Bartholomew Diaz in 1487. These sea routes would lead to tremendous expansion of European wealth and power through international trade.

51. Lorenzo Monaco, c. 1370-1424, International Gothic, Italian, *Adoration of the Magi*, 1421-22, Tempera on panel, 115 x 170 cm, Galleria degli Uffizi, Florence

52

52. Konrad von Soest, active 1394-1422, Northern Renaissance, German,
The Wildunger Altarpiece, c. 1403, Oil on panel, 158 x 267cm,
Church of Bad Wildungen, Bad Wildungen

53. Frater Francke, 1380-c.1430, International Gothic, German,
Pursuit of St Barbe, 1410-15, Tempera on panel, National Museum, Helsinki

54. Limbourg Brothers, International Gothic, Flemish,
The Very Rich Hours of the Duc of Berry: January, 1412-1416,
Illumination on vellun paper, 22.5 x 13.6 cm, Musée Condé, Chantilly

*These three Flemish brothers were the most famous illuminators of late Gothic.
The Very Rich Hours of the Duc de Berry in January is considered their greatest
work and an outstanding example of International Gothic art. The miniatures are
by common consent masterpieces of manuscript illumination for their masterful
rendering of space and their use of unusual colours.*

53

54

55. Gentile da Fabriano, 1370-1427, International Gothic, Italian,
   Adoration of the Magi, 1423, Tempera on panel, 303 x 282 cm,
   Galleria degli Uffizi, Florence

*The large, beautifully gilded Altarpiece for the Strozzi Chapel of The Holy
Trinity in Florence presents the Epiphany event. In its three lower panels, with
details like that of Dutch miniatures, it also shows three other related events
from the New Testament: The Nativity, the Flight into Egypt, and the
Presentation of Jesus in the Temple. The elegantly dressed three kings and their
large entourages, with horses and a large dog nearly dominate the scene.
Gentile's subjects in subsequent paintings, such as Golden Alms of
St. Nicholas (1423), become more natural as if anticipating the masters of
Italian Renaissance painting.*

GENTILE DA FABRIANO
(1370 FABRIANO –1427 ROME)

Fabriano was a leader of Italian late Gothic. His works were
religious, characterized with elegant gold gilding. His masterpiece
is the Altarpiece, *Adoration of the Magi* (1423). Shortly
afterwards he showed new insight into perspective with
foreshortening of his subjects as in *Golden Alms of St. Nicholas*
(1425).

56. Tommaso Masaccio, 1401-1428, Renaissance, Florentine School, Italian, *The Expulsion of Adam and Eve from the Garden*, 1425, Fresco, 208 x 88 cm Brancacci Chapel of Santa Maria della Carmine, Florence

This scene represents the expulsion of Adam and Eve following the Original Sin. Rays coming from the gate of Paradise represent the Voice of the Creator. The source of light, however, is to the right, as can be seen from the shadows. The Archangel Gabriel with his symbolic sword hovers above. The breakthrough element in the fresco is the depiction of human emotion by way of the body language and facial expressions of the couple. The important comparison to be made here is between this work and that of Michelangelo's treatment of the same biblical moment in his larger The Expulsion of Adam and Eve from the Garden on the Sistine Chapel ceiling. The latter was done only seventy-five years after the Masaccio, yet there is a leap ahead towards realistic, albeit monumental, rendering of the human forms of the couple. The figure of the angel in the Michelangelo expresses more depth and aggression. However, few months before the Michelangelo, Dürer's Adam and Eve (1509) gives the couple even more realistic shape, yet the infamous fig leaves are used and the poses are rather lifeless, compared even to the Masaccio.

57. Frater Francke, 1380-c.1430, International Gothic, German, *Christ Carrying the Cross*, 1424, Tempera on panel, 99 x 88.9 cm, Kunsthalle, Hamburg

58. Tommaso Masaccio, 1401-1428, Renaissance, Florentine School, Italian, *Madonna and Child with St Anne Metterza*, c. 1424, Tempera on panel, 175 x 103 cm, Galleria degli Uffizi, Florence

Masaccio was deeply influenced by Giotto's work. This work doesn't show superfluous decoration. Its bare aspect, and the treatment of perspective, prove how Masaccio changed drastically the traditional pictorial expression.

56

58

59   61

59. Tommaso Masaccio, 1401-1428, Renaissance, Florentine School, Italian,
The Tribute Money, c. 1428, Fresco, 255 x 598 cm, Brancacci Chapel of
Santa Maria della Carmine, Florence

Before they were written down as gospels, the oral tradition of the early church passed along fascinating stories about the life of Jesus, including miracles, miraculous healings, and other spectacular events. One such miraculous moment in the life of St. Peter, the most dominant of the apostles of Jesus, recalls when The Master told Peter, formerly a fisherman, to pay a tax collector with a coin that Peter would find in the mouth of a fish. This fresco shows Peter on the left catching the fish. On the right he gives the coin to the tax collector. In the middle of the work, Jesus is discussing matters with his apostles and the same tax collector. Jesus is mid-way in the vertical and slightly to the left of the horizontal mid-point. Masaccio shows a great master of perspective in this work. The characters are put in circle (not in the disposition of a frieze) and the grounds are depicted behind each other, terracing each other. The character in the foreground is all in volumes, with a strong modelling of his legs. His back to the viewer, he closes the composition and inserts depth into the painting.

60. Robert Campin (Master of Flémalle), c. 1375-1444, Northern Renaissance, Flemish,
Annunciation: The Merode Altarpiece, 1425-30, Oil on panel, 64.3 x 62.9 (central
panel); 64.5 x 27.4 cm (side panels), The Metropolitan Museum of Art, New York

Three names have been suggested to identify the master: Jacquet Daret, Rogier van der Weyden and Robert Campin. The work shows his taste for anecdotal details.

61. Tommaso Masaccio, 1401-1428, Renaissance, Florentine School, Italian,
Holy Trinity, c. 1428, Fresco, 667 x 317 cm, Santa Maria Novella, Florence

This painting is a great example of Masaccio's use of space and linear perspective; the first steps in the development of illusionist painting. The forms of architecture are borrowed from antiquity as well as from the Early Renaissance such as the coffered barrel vault.

Tommaso Masaccio
(1401 San Giovanni Valdarno –1427 Rome)

He was the first great painter of the Italian Renaissance, innovating with the use of scientific perspective. Masaccio, originally named Tommaso Cassai, was born in San Giovanni Valdarno, near Florence. He joined the painters' guild in Florence in 1422.

His influences came from the work of his contemporaries, the architect Brunelleschi and sculptor Donatello, from whom he acquired the knowledge of mathematical proportion he used for scientific perspective, and the knowledge of classical art that led him away from the prevailing Gothic style.

He inaugurated a new naturalistic approach to painting that was concerned less with details and ornamentation than with simplicity and unity, less with flat surfaces than with the illusion of three-dimensionality.

Together with Brunelleschi and Donatello, he was a founder of the Renaissance. Masaccio's work exerted a strong influence on the course of later Florentine art and particularly on the work of Michelangelo.

62

62. Fra Giovanni Angelico, 1387-1455, Early Renaissance, Florentine School, Italian, *The Coronation of the Virgin*, 1430-1432, Oil on wood, 213 x 211 cm, Musée du Louvre, Paris

Painted for the convent church of San Domenico, Fiesole, the theme of The Coronation of the Virgin *is taken from apocryphal texts largely spread during the thirteenth century by Jacobus de Voragine's* Golden Legend.

63. Jan van Eyck, c. 1390-1441, Northern Renaissance, Flemish, *Adoration of the Lamb (Ghent Altarpiece, central panel)*, 1432, Oil on panel, 350 x 461 cm (wings open); 350 x 223 cm (wings closed), Cathedral of St Bavo, Ghent

Jan van Eyck was the first popular oil painter. Being the most famous work of Jan van Eyck, the Ghent Altarpiece brings together twelve panels initially realised for St John's Church in Ghent. The central panel shows a life-sized Christ and a great deal of attention is given to the depiction of precious brocade (in the tradition of international style) and in the rendering of light. The three central panels show a triple portrait: of Mary-Sophia, of God the Father/Jesus, and of John the Baptist. Mary-Sophia is depicted enthroned, wearing the gem-encrusted golden crown of the divine Queen of Heaven, her dark blue robes adorned with a golden trim. The book she reads bears the symbolism of the Madonna as Holy Wisdom (Hagia Sophia). The blending of Mary with Sophia, the feminine aspect of God, was still acceptable in art during the early Renaissance, even as the patristic Church began to strongly discourage this line of thinking.

63

Jan and Hubert van Eyck
(c. 1390 near Maastricht –1441 Bruges)
(c. 1366?–1426 Bruges)

Little is known of these two brothers; even the dates of their births being uncertain. Their most famous work, begun by Hubert and finished by Jan, is the Altarpiece, *The Adoration of the Lamb*. Jan, as perhaps also Hubert, was for a time in the service of Philip the Good, Duke of Burgundy. He was entered in the household as ˝varlet and painter˝, but acted at the same time as a confidential friend, and for his services received an annual salary of two horses for his use, and a ˝varlet in livery˝ to attend on him. The greater part of his life was spent in Bruges.

Their wonderful use of colour is another reason of the fame of the van Eycks. Artists came from Italy to study their pictures, to discover what they themselves must do in order to paint so well, with such brilliance, such full and firm effect, as these two brothers. For the latter had found out the secret of working successfully with oil colours. Before their time, attempts had been made to mix colours in the medium of oil, but the oil was slow in drying, and the varnish added to remedy this had blackened the colours. The van Eycks, however, had hit upon a transparent varnish which dried quickly and without injury to the tints. Though they guarded the secret jealously, it was discovered by the Italian Antonello da Messina, who was working in Bruges, and through him published to the world. The invention made possible the enormous development in the art of painting which ensued.

In these two brothers the grand art of Flanders was born. Like ˝the sudden flowering of the aloe, after sleeping through a century of suns,˝ this art, rooted in the native soil, nurtured by the smaller arts of craftsmanship, reached its full ripeness and expanded into blossom. Such further development as it experienced came from Italian influence; but the distinctly Flemish art, born out of local conditions in Flanders, was already fully-grown.

64

65. Robert Campin (Master of Flémalle), c. 1410-1475, Northern Renaissance, Flemish, *A Woman*, c. 1435, Tempera on oak, 40.6 x 28.1 cm, National Gallery, London

Campin, long identified as the 'Master of Flémalle', painted three-dimensional figures with details of the face made clearly visible. This portrait was a pendant to a Portrait of a Man (London, National Gallery), presumably the husband of the woman represented.

65

FRA GIOVANNI ANGELICO
(1387 Vicchio – 1455 Rome)

Secluded within cloister walls, a painter and a monk, and brother of the order of the Dominicans, Angelico devoted his life to religious paintings.

Little is known of his early life except that he was born at Vicchio, in the broad fertile valley of the Mugello, not far from Florence, that his name was Guido de Pietro, and that he passed his youth in Florence, probably in some *bottegha*, for at twenty he was recognised as a painter. In 1418 he entered in a Dominican convent in Fiesole with his brother. They were welcomed by the monks, and, after a year's novitiate, admitted to the brotherhood, Guido taking the name by which he was known for the rest of his life, Fra Giovanni da Fiesole; for the title of *Angelico*, the "Angel," or *Il Beato*, "The Blessed," was conferred on him after his death.

Henceforth he became an example of two personalities in one man: he was all in all a painter, but also a devout monk; his subjects were always religious ones and represented in a deeply religious spirit, yet his devotion as a monk was no greater than his absorption as an artist. Consequently, though his life was secluded within the walls of the monastery, he kept in touch with the art movements of his time and continually developed as a painter. His early work shows that he had learned of the illuminators who inherited the Byzantine traditions, and had been affected by the simple religious feeling of Giotto's work. Also influenced by Lorenzo Monaco and the Sienese School, he painted under the patronage of Cosimo de Medici. Then he began to learn of that brilliant band of sculptors and architects who were enriching Florence by their genius. Ghiberti was executing his pictures in bronze upon the doors of the Baptistery; Donatello, his famous statue of *St. George* and the dancing children around the organ-gallery in the Cathedral; and Luca della Robbia was at work upon his frieze of children, singing, dancing and playing upon instruments. Moreover, Masaccio had revealed the dignity of form in painting. Through these artists the beauty of the human form and of its life and movement was being manifested to the Florentines and to the other cities. Angelico caught the enthusiasm and gave increasing reality of life and movement to his figures.

66

67

68

66. Jan van Eyck, c. 1390-1441, Northern Renaissance, Flemish,
Man in Red Turban (Self-Portrait?), 1433, Oil on panel, 26 x 19 cm,
National Gallery, London

67. Jan van Eyck, c. 1390-1441, Northern Renaissance, Flemish, *The Arnolfini
Portrait*, 1434, Oil on oak panel, 82.2 x 60 cm, National Gallery, London

*One of the most discussed of all paintings, van Eyck's masterpiece of natural
symbolism presents objects which have been given special meaning apposite
to this couple's marriage, yet the same objects are appropriate to the scene in
themselves. The work is, in effect, a visual in how one can find synchronicity
and deeper meaning in everyday circumstances. The lines between the neatly
groomed dog and the pairs of discarded shoes create a triangle. The dog
(symbolising loyalty) complements the shoes (also symbolising domesticity).
The man's feet are firmly in the middle of the lower triangle, indicating his
vow of stability. The faces of the married couple and their clasped hands form
the same size-and-shape triangle. The couple stands hand-in-hand as their
other hands wear wedding rings, as if their love is authentic and
complemented by, rather than caused by, their wedding vows. In the middle
of that triangle is a mirror in a circular shape recalling eternity. Ten of the
'Stations of the Cross' are symbolised around the frame of the mirror. Prayer
beads hang on the wall to the left of the stations-mirror. The reflection of the
mirror shows the couple from the mirror's point of view, as if creating a circle
of time and space. A statue of a saint on the bedpost is crushing a dragon
(symbolising evil). The elaborate signature of the artist is on the wall below
the mirror. The chandelier holds a single, lit candle. A superstition at the time
suggested that a single, lit candle near the wedding bed would assure fertility.*

68. Jan van Eyck, c. 1390-1441, Northern Renaissance, Flemish,
Portrait of Jan de Leeuw, 1436, Oil on panel, 25 x 19 cm,
Kunsthistorisches Museum, Vienna

*Considered the founder of western portraiture, van Eyck depicts here Jan de
Leeuw, member of the Goldsmith Guild in Bruges.*

69

69. Stefano di Giovanni di Console Sassetta, 1392-c. 1450, Early Renaissance, Sienese School, Italian, *The Mystic Marriage of Saint Francis with Chastity*, 1437-1444, Tempera on panel, 95 x 58 cm, Musée Condé, Chantilly

Sassetta's work shows certain conservatism, especially in the architectural structures of International Gothic design. However, his figures are set in the unity of Renaissance pictorial space.

70. Rogier van der Weyden, 1399-1464, Northern Renaissance, Flemish, *Deposition*, c. 1435, Oil on panel, 220 x 262 cm, Museo Nacional del Prado, Madrid

The life-sized figures and the gold background recall the influence of Campin on van der Weyden as the composition imitates the low-reliefs from Tournai (where the artist came from).

71. Antonio Puccio Pisanello, 1395-1455, International Gothic, Italian, *Portrait of a Princess of the House of Este*, c. 1435-1440, Oil on panel, 43 x 30 cm, Musée du Louvre, Paris

Pisanello is regarded as the preeminent master of the International Gothic style in Italian painting, but most of his major works have perished. This portrait of a young woman (assumed to be Ginevra d'Este) is flat – due to the use of medieval patterns in a 'modern' way, and its flowers and butterflies, though drawn from nature, seem like ornamental patterns from French or Flemish tapestries.

71

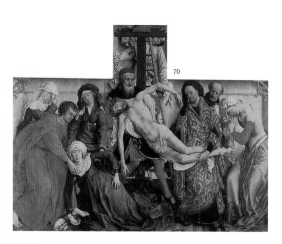

70

72. Fra Giovanni Angelico, 1387-1455, Early Renaissance, Florentine School, Italian,
The Deposition (Pala di Santa Trinita), 1437-1440, Tempera on panel, 176 x 185 cm,
Museo di San Marco, Florence.

*This painting was originally an Altarpiece in the sacristy of the church Santa Trinita
in Florence. The main panel figures the Deposition and the pilasters on each side
represent different saints. Fra Angelico was officially beatified by the Vatican in 1984
but he has long been called Beato Angelico (The Blessed Angelico).*

73

73. Paolo Uccello, 1397-1475, Early Renaissance, Florentine School, Italian, *The Battle of San Romano (Full title 'Niccolò Mauruzi da Tolentino at the Battle of San Romano'),* 1438-1440, Egg tempera with walnut oil and linseed oil on poplar, 181.6 x 320 cm, Galleria degli Uffizi, Florence

74. Antonio Puccio Pisanello, 1395-1455, International Gothic, Italian, *The Vision of Saint Eustace,* 1438-1442, Tempera on panel, 54.8 x 65.5 cm, National Gallery, London

Pisanello has carefully studied the animals in this painting, using both drawings from pattern books as well as studies from life.

74

Paolo Uccello
(1397 – 1475 Florence)

Paolo di Dono was called 'Uccello' because he loved birds and the Italian word for bird is *uccello.* As well as painting on panel and in fresco, he was also a master of mosaics, especially in Venice, and produced designs for stained glass. We can feel the influence of Donatello especially in a fresco representing the *Flood and the Recession,* whereas the figures in this work is reminiscent of Masaccio's frescos of Brancacci chapel. His perspectives studies are very sophisticated, recalling the Renaissance art treatises of Piero della Francesca, da Vinci or Dürer. He was a major proponent of the Renaissance style. However, if his masterwork *The Battle of San Romano* (1438-40) has Renaissance elements, Uccello's gold decorations on the surface of his masterpieces are indebted to the Gothic style.

75. Giovanni di Paolo, 1403-1482, Early Renaissance, Sienese School, Italian, *Madonna of Humility*, c. 1442, Tempera on panel, 62 x 48.8 cm, Courtesy of Museum of Fine Arts, Marie Antoinette Evans Fund, Boston

76. Fra Giovanni Angelico, 1378-1445, Early Renaissance, Florentine School, Italian, *Noli Me Tangere*, 1440-1441, Fresco, 180 x 146 cm, Convento di San Marco, Florence

77. Robert Campin (Master of Flémalle), c. 1378-1445, Northern Renaissance, Flemish, *Virgin and Child before a Firescreen*, c. 1440, Tempera on oak, 63.4 x 48.5 cm, National Gallery, London

Robert Campin of Tournai is also called the 'Master of Flémalle', because three paintings now in the Städelsches Kunstinstitut were wrongly supposed to have come from Flémalle. Together with van Eyck, he may be considered the founder of the Netherlandish painting of the Early Renaissance. The Virgin seems somehow clumsy, almost plebeian. The halo is replaced by the fire screen, which testifies of the homely detail and down-to-earth realism of the artist.

Rogier van der Weyden
(1399 Tournai, Flanders – 1464 Brussels)

He lived in Brussels where he was the city's official painter (from 1436), but his influence was felt throughout Europe. One sponsor was Philip the Good, an avid collector. Van der Weyden is the only Fleming who truly carried on van Eyck's great conception of art. He added to it a pathos of which there is no other example in his country except, though with less power and nobility, that of Hugo van der Goes towards the end of the century. He had a considerable influence on the art of Flanders and Germany. Hans Memling was his most renowned pupil. Van der Weyden was the last inheritor of the Giottesque tradition and the last of the painters whose work is thoroughly religious.

79

78. Rogier van der Weyden, 1399-1464, Northern Renaissance, Flemish, *St Luke Drawing the Virgin*, c. 1440, Oil on canvas, 102.5 x 108.5 cm, The State Hermitage Museum, St Petersburg

St Luke the Apostle, who is the accredited author of one of the four accepted versions of the New Testament Gospel, is also by tradition the first painter of the Virgin's portrait. Rogier van der Weyden kept up this tradition in his own picture of St Luke Drawing the Virgin. This meticulously detailed work, typical of the Flemish tradition, shows Mary seated under a canopy as she attempts to nurse her infant, and Luke in front of her, drawing her face. A panoramic view can be seen between the columns in the background. Nursing-Madonna images had been part of the Marian tradition and lore since the Middle Ages. "Mary's milk" had, indeed, been a source of veneration in the form of a miracle-working substance regarded as one among many holy relics during medieval times, and reverence for it lasted well into Renaissance times. The origins of such a tradition and symbolism go back several thousands of years into antiquity, when Creator Goddesses like Isis were celebrated as symbolic milk-givers in their roles as compassionate and nurturing Universal Mothers. The milky ribbon of stars called the Milky Way was believed to symbolise the Goddess, and Marian lore inherited that popular tradition.

79. Konrad Witz, c. 1400-1445, International Gothic, Swiss, *The Miraculous Draught of Fishes*, 1444, Oil on panel, 129 x 155 cm, Museum of Art and History, Geneva

80. Piero della Francesca, c. 1416-1492, Early Renaissance, Italian, *The Baptism of Christ*, 1445, Tempera on panel, 167 x 116 cm, National Gallery, London

80

The suspended dove symbolising the Holy Spirit is at the exact middle point of the circle implied in the upper part of the painting, while the navel of Jesus is the mid-point of the rectangle implied at the bottom portion of the painting. The upper mid-point alludes to the divinity of Jesus, while the lower mid-point relates to his humanity. The God-man is at geometric centre of the scene. The vertical balance is likewise between the heavenly angels on the left and the earthly community on the right. The latter includes a follower of the Baptist who is either getting dressed after his own baptism or preparing to be baptised. The group watching probably represents the sceptics or the undecided. Sansepolero, in northern Italy, was the hometown of the artist and the sponsor of most of the artist's mature works. In the tradition of such commissions, the sponsor appears in the painting. The town is pictured in the distance between Jesus and the left vertical third of the painting. Young plants in the foreground indicate new life, as the rebirth offered by baptism would symbolise thereafter for Christians. The Hebrew bible had predicted that the ones who prepared the way for the Lord would make the crooked straight, symbolised here as the river and roads in the landscape. All the roads and rivers lead to the feet of The Way, the name the seminal Christian community gave their religion as well as a descriptive title for their Messiah.

81

81. Domenico Veneziano, 1400-1461, Early Renaissance, Florentine School, Italian, *The Madonna with Child and Saints*, 1445, Tempera on wood, 209 x 216 cm, Galleria degli Uffizi, Florence

Painted for the high altar of the Uzzano in Santa Lucia dei Magnoli, this is perhaps Veneziano's greatest achievement. Veneziano, renowned for his use of perspective and colour, depicts the "sacra conversazione" within an harmonious architectural structure rendered more delicate by pastel shades of rose and green.

84

82. Petrus Christus, c.1410-1473, Northern Renaissance, Flemish, *Portrait of a Young Girl*, after 1446, Oil on panel, 29 x 22,5 cm, Gemäldegalerie, Alte Meister, Berlin

The most popular painting by Christus, this portrait is composed of simple volumes. The painter places the sitter in a defined setting, new to Flemish painting, which was traditionally depicted with a neutral, dark background (such as in van Eyck's and van der Weyden's portraits).

83. Francesco del Castagno, 1446-1497, Early Renaissance, Florentine School, Italian, *Last Supper* and above *Resurrection, Crucifixion and Entombment*, c. 1445-50, Fresco, 980 x 1025 cm, Convent of Sant'Apollonia, Florence

84. Rogier van der Weyden, 1399-1464, Northern Renaissance, Flemish, *Triptych: St. John Altarpiece* (right panel), c. 1446-53, Oil on oak panel, 77 x 48 cm (each panel), Gemäldegalerie, Alte Meister, Berlin

Van der Weyden gives a particularly strong effect of depth in the side panels of this Altarpiece, with the succession of rooms in the background.

85

86

JEAN FOUQUET
(1420 – 1481 Tours)

A painter and illuminator, Jean Fouquet is regarded as the most important French painter of the fifteenth century. Little is known about his life but it is quite sure that he executed, in Italy, the portrait of Pope Eugenius IV. Upon his return to France, he introduced Italian Renaissance elements into French painting. He was the court painter to Louis XI. Whether he worked on miniatures rendering the finest detail, or on larger scale in panel paintings, Fouquet's art had the same monumental character. His figures are modelled in broad planes defined by lines of magnificent purity.

85. Jean Fouquet, c. 1420-1481, Early Renaissance, French,
Virgin and Child Surrounded by Angels (right panel of Meulun's diptych), c. 14
Oil on panel, 91 x 81 cm, Royal Museum of Fine Arts, Antwerp

The particularity of this painting is due to its geometric composition, se convex pentagon often used by Fouquet. The volume given accentuate sculptural aspect of this Virgin whose face was inspired by Agnes Sore mistress of Charles VII). The diptych assembles the portrait of a Virgin with th of the patrons in prayer in front of his protector saint.

86. Stephan Lochner, c. 1410-1451, Northern Renaissance, German,
Madonna of the Rose Bush, c. 1448, Mixed technique on panel, 51 x 40 c
Wallraf-Richartz-Museum, Cologne

87. Jean Fouquet, c. 1420-1481, Early Renaissance, French,
Portrait of Charles VII of France, c. 1450-1455, Oil on oak panel, 86 x 71 cm,
Musée du Louvre, Paris

*The particularity of this painting is due to its squared shape, nearly full-scale,
exceptional at the time. The frontal representation is characteristic of the official
portraits of monarchs in the West. The two white curtains stand as symbols of
majesty. From the years 1420 to 1430 the upper-body intimate portrait was a new
fashion spread by Flemish masters. Here Fouquet carries out a synthesis between
the traditional full-length representation and the upper-body representation. He
enlarges the king's stature, exploiting the fashion of padded shoulders. This work
was painted in a precise political context: at the time, the victories of French
royalty were being celebrated. This portrait will have a great influence on Jean
Clouet and Holbein, who both travelled through the city of Bourges.*

88. Piero della Francesca, c. 1416-1492, Early Renaissance, Italian,
The Flagellation of Jesus, c. 1450, Oil and tempera on panel, 58.4 x 51.5 cm,
Galleria Nazionale delle Marche, Urbino

*Through the scientific use of perspective in a measured, symmetrical manner
and its symbolic contents, The Flagellation contributes to the humanistic
rendition of figures in painting and characterizes the painter's interests in
mathematics. The architecture is a predominant part of the scene, which is
divided by the column supporting the temple.*

Piero della Francesca
(1416 – 1492, Borgo San Sepulcro)

Forgotten for centuries after his death, Francesca has been regarded,
since his rediscovery in the early twentieth century, as one of the
supreme artists of the *Quattrocento*. Born in Borgo San Sepolcro
(now Sansepolcro) in Umbria he spent much of his life there. His
major work is a series of frescos on the *Legend of the True Cross*
in the choir of San Francesco at Arezzo (c. 1452-c. 1465).

While influenced at the beginning of his life by all the great
masters of the generation before, his work represents a synthesis
of all the discoveries these artists had made in the previous
twenty years. He created a style in which monumental, meditative
grandeur and almost mathematical lucidity are combined with
limpid beauty of colour and light. He was a slow and thoughtful
worker and often applied wet cloths to the plaster at night so
that - contrary to normal fresco practice – he could work for more
than one day on the same section. Piero's later career was spent
working at the humanist court of Federico da Montefeltro at
Urbino. Vasari said Piero was blind when he died, and failing
eyesight may have been his reason for giving up painting. He had
considerable influence, notably on Signorelli (in the weighty
solemnity of his figures) and Perugino (in the spatial clarity of his
compositions). Both are said to have been Piero's pupils.

89. Piero della Francesca, c. 1416-1492, Early Renaissance, Italian,
Adoration of the Holy Wood and the Meeting of Solomon and the Queen of Sheba, 1450-1465, Fresco, Choir of the Church of San Francesco, Arezzo

The cycle of frescos was commissioned by the richest family in Arrezo, the Bacci. The theme of the cycle is taken from the Golden Legend *by Jacobus de Voragine.*

90. Petrus Christus, c. 1410-1473, Northern Renaissance, Flemish,
The Lamentation, c. 1455, Oil on panel, 101 x 192 cm,
Musées Royaux des Beaux-Arts, Brussels

Fra Filippo Lippi
(1406 Florence – 1469 Spoleto)

A Carmelite monk, he lived in a monastery in Florence at the same time as Masolino and Masaccio were painting frescos in Florence. He was ordained a priest in Padua in 1434.

His works show the aesthetic interest of his time through sophisticated drawing and his ability to obtain transparent effects on opaque colours. After his death, his workshop members completed his unfinished frescos. Botticelli was one of his students, as was his son Filippino Lippi. The works of the two former Fra Lippi students link the Early and High Renaissance periods. Works include major fresco cycles for Santa Maria Novella in Florence and for Santa Maria sopra Minerva in Rome.

91

91. Fra Filippo Lippi, c. 1406-1469, Early Renaissance, Florentine School, Italian,
Virgin with the Child and Scenes from the Life of St Anne, c. 1452,
Tempera on wooden panel, Tondo, dia. 135 cm, Palazzo Pitti, Florence

Oral tradition, later encouraged by art such as this, names Anna and Joachim as Mary's parents, but there is no scriptural basis for the notion. In this masterpiece, often called The Bartolini Tondo, three highlights in the life of Anna are presented. The background scenes are dedicated to the Virgin's mother, St Anne (or Anna), and include the first meeting of Anne and her husband-to-be Joachim, and a scene of the subsequent birth of Mary. In the foreground, is the Madonna with her child. Like Persephone, the Greek goddess of natural cycle, she is holding a pomegranate, a symbol of rebirth, fertility and abundance in nature. The infant Jesus is also holding the fruit, and with his raised right hand, he is bringing its seed toward his mouth. The pensive expression of Mary in many paintings of her with the child Jesus is often interpreted as reflecting her prophetic awareness of the future sufferings that will befall her only son. But in this case the Virgin might be recalling her mother's life. The surrounding scenes might be intended to show her recollection of her mother. The artist's mastery of detail as in the transparency of Mary's veil and her fine features were inspirations for the later masterpieces of his most famous pupil, Botticelli.

92

94

93

92. Andrea Mantegna, 1431-1506, Early Renaissance, Florentine School, Italian, *Death of the Virgin*, c. 1461, Oil on panel, 54 x 42 cm, Museo Nacional del Prado, Madrid

93. Alesso Baldovinetti, c. 1425-1499, Early Renaissance, Florentine School, Italian, *Annunciation*, c. 1447, Tempera on panel, 167 x 137 cm, Galleria degli Uffizi, Florence

94. Fra Filippo Lippi, c. 1406-1469, Early Renaissance, Florentine School, *Madonna with the Child and Two Angels*, 1465, Tempera on wood, 95 x 62 cm, Galleria degi Uffizi, Florence

95. Benozzo Gozzoli, 1420-1497, Early Renaissance, Florentine School, Italian,
The Procession of the Magi, Procession of the Youngest King (detail), 1459-63,
Fresco, Palazzo Medici Riccardi, Florence

96. Rogier van der Weyden, 1399-1464, Northern Renaissance, Flemish,
Triptych: St. Columba Altarpiece (central panel), c. 1455, Tempera on wood,
138 x 153 cm, Alte Pinakothek, Munich

97

97. Cosimo di Domenico di Bonaventura Tura, c. 1431-1495,
Early Renaissance, Ferrarese School, Italian, *The Spring*, c. 1455-1460,
Oil with egg tempera, 116.2 x 71.1 cm, National Gallery, London

Favoured court artist of the Este family, Tura depicted a series of Muses for the commissioner's studiolo.

98. Carlo Crivelli, c. 1430/35-1495, Late Gothic Style, Venetian school, Italian,
Madonna of the Passion, c. 1460, Tempera on panel, 71 x 48 cm,
Museo di Castelvecchio, Verona

All of religious subjects, Crivelli's compositions remain within the late Gothic style and the constant use of a golden background is part of the painter's archaism. However, the depth given to the characters is a sign of modernity.

99. Alesso Baldovinetti, c. 1425-1499, Early Renaissance, Florentine School,
Italian, *Madonna and Child*, c. 1460, Tempera on panel, 104 x 76 cm,
Musée du Louvre, Paris

Alesso Baldovinetti was a Florentine painter as well as a mosaic- and stained-glass-maker. His paintings show the influence of Domenico Veneziano and Fra Angelico.

100. Piero della Francesca, c. 1416-1492, Early Renaissance, Italian, *Madonna of Senigallia*, 1460-75, Oil on panel, 61 x 53 cm, Palazzo Ducale, Urbino

101

102

101. Giovanni Bellini, c. 1430-1516, Early Renaissance, Venetian School, Italian, *Dead Christ Supported by the Madonna and St John (Pietà)*, c. 1460, Oil on panel, 60 x 107 cm, Pinacoteca di Brera, Milan

Bellini knows the Florentine pictorial researches (a lot of Florentine artists travelled to Venice at the time) and he introduced oil painting in Venice. Traditionally, the Virgin was holding the dead Christ on her knees. In this painting Bellini proposes a new iconography and a new-size landscape format. In the foreground, a stone pedestal evokes the tomb of Christ. The search for volume and geometry is characteristic of the artist's work.

102. Piero della Francesca, c. 1416-1492, Early Renaissance, Italian, *Resurrection*, 1463, Mural in fresco and tempera, 225 x 200 cm, Museo Civico, Sansepolcro

103. Andrea Mantegna, 1431-1506, Early Renaissance, Florentine School, Italian, *Agony in the Garden*, c. 1459, Oil on panel, Musée des Beaux-Arts de Tours, Tours

Mantegna took his inspiration from the drawing of his brother-in-law, Jacopo Bellini, in this painting.

104. Enguerrand Quarton, active 1444-1466, Early Renaissance, Provence School, French, *Pietà of Villeneuve-les-Avignon*, c. 1460, Oil on panel, 160 x 218 cm, Musée du Louvre, Paris

Masterpiece of the art from Provence, this painting, with its gilded background, still betrays the influence of Byzantine art. On the left, the donor is portrayed. He is represented as an intercessor between the divine group and the viewer.

103

104

Andrea Mantegna
(1431 Isola di Carturo – 1506 Mantova)

Mantegna; humanist, geometrist, archaeologist, of great scholastic and imaginative intelligence, dominated the whole of northern Italy by virtue of his imperious personality. Aiming at optical illusion, he mastered perspective. He trained in painting at the Padua School where Donatello and Paolo Uccello had previously attended. Even at a young age commissions for Andrea's work flooded in, for example the frescos of the Ovetari Chapel of Padua.

In a short space of time Mantegna found his niche as a modernist due to his highly original ideas and the use of perspective in his works. His marriage with Nicolosia Bellini, the sister of Giovanni, paved the way for his *entree* into Venice.

Mantegna reached an artistic maturity with his *Pala San Zeno*. He remained in Mantova and became the artist for one of the most prestigious courts in Italy – the Court of Gonzaga. Classical art was born.

Despite his links with Bellini and Leonardo da Vinci, Mantegna refused to adopt their innovative use of colour or leave behind his own technique of engraving.

105

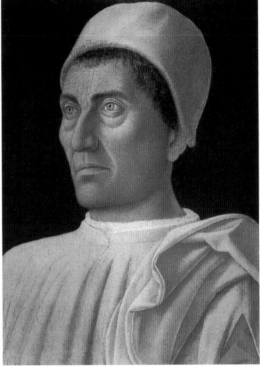

1

106

105. Domenico Veneziano, 1410-1461, Early Renaissance, Florentine School, Italian, *Portrait of a Young Woman*, c. 1465, Oil on panel, 51 x 35 cm, Gemäldegalerie, Alte Meister, Berlin

106. Dirk Bouts, c. 1410-1475, Northern Renaissance, Flemish, *The Last Supper*, c. 1467, Oil on panel, Altarpiece, 180 x 150 cm, Collégiale Saint-Pierre, Louvain

A major work by Bouts, The Last Supper was commissioned by the Confraternity of the Holy Sacrament in Louvain. The painter received the mission to conform to the advice of two theologians in the depiction of the scene. This is the first time that the consecration of bread is the moment chosen in the Last Supper's representation, rather than the prediction of the betrayal.

107. Andrea Mantegna, 1431-1506, Early Renaissance, Florentine School, Italian, *Portrait of Carlo de Medici*, 1467, Oil on panel, 40.6 x 29.5 cm, Galleria degli Uffizi, Florence

108. Hans Pleydenwurff, 1420-1472, Northern Renaissance, German, *Crucifixion of the Hof Altarpiece*, c. 1465, Mixed technique on pine panel, 177 x 112 cm, Sankt Peterskerk, Leuven

In the Crucifixion *Hans Pleydenwurff used motifs from a Deposition from Rogier van der Weyden's circle (Alte Pinakothek, Munich). Flemish painting also influenced the painter in the use of warm and rich colours.*

109

110

109. Andrea Mantegna, 1431-1506, Early Renaissance, Florentine School, Italian, *Camera Picta, Ducal Palace*, 1465-1474, Fresco, Palazzo Ducale, Mantova

Mantegna's originality comes to the foremost obviously in the central part of the ceiling, which breaks from the seriousness and formality of the rest of the room. It is perhaps Mantegna's most delightful and creative invention: the centre of the vault seems to open up, the first painting of the Renaissance to apply the notion of illusionism not just to an easel picture or wall but to a ceiling as well. This view upwards completes the trompe l'oeil vision Mantegna created in the Camera Picta, which is the first illusionistic room of the Renaissance; the ideal of the flat picture space as an extension of the real world is here given a spectacular expression, as a viewer in the middle of the room can see clouds overhead, fictive curtained walls, and classical architectural framework.

110. Piero della Francesca, c. 1416-1492, Early Renaissance, Italian, *Nativity*, 1470-75, Oil on panel, 124.4 x 122.6 cm, National Gallery, London

111. Dirk Bouts, c. 1415-1475, Northern Renaissance, Flemish, *The Ordeal by Fire*, 1470-1475, Oil on panel, Musées Royaux des Beaux-Arts, Brussels

Characteristic of the revival of a Gothic tendency in the fifteenth-century bourgeoisie, this painting, belonging to the genre of justice scenes, emphasises the figures' verticality and their lack of volume.

113

112

112. Francesco Botticini, c. 1446-1498, Early Renaissance, Florentine School, Italian, *Tobias and the Three Archangels*, c. 1470, Tempera on panel, 135 x 154 cm, Galleria degli Uffizi, Florence

113. Francesco del Cossa, 1436-1477, Early Renaissance, Ferrarese School, Italian, *The Triumph of Minerva: March, from the Room of the Months*, 1467-70, Fresco, Palazzo Schifanoia, Ferrara

114

115

114. **Michael Pacher**, c. 1430-1498, Northern Renaissance, Austrian,
St Wolfgang Altarpiece: Resurrection of Lazarus, 1471-1481,
Tempera on wood, 175 x 130 cm, Parish Church, St. Wolfgang

115. **Andrea del Verrocchio**, c. 1435-1488, Early Renaissance, Florentine
School, Italian, *The Baptism of Christ*, c. 1470, Oil on panel, 177 x 151 cm,
Galleria degli Uffizi, Florence

116. **Hugo van der Goes**, c. 1440-1482, Northern Renaissance, Flemish,
Diptych: The Fall of Man and the Lamentation (left panel),
c. 1470-1475, Tempera on wood, 32.3 x 21.9 cm, Kunsthistorisches
Museum, Vienna

*Contemporary of Piero della Francesca, van der Goes is resolute to depict
reality while using refined colours. His painting is more and more illusionist
here and betrays the artist's like for details and depiction of light.*

117. **Sandro Botticelli (Alessandro di Mariano Filipepi)**, 1445-1510, Early
Renaissance, Florentine School, Italian, *Adoration of the Kings*, c. 1470-1475,
Tempera on poplar, Tondo, dia. 130.8 cm, National Gallery, London

*This painting, in which the artist also depicted himself, shows the Magi but in
reality it is the Medici family, his patrons and rulers of Florence. The Magi
kneeling in front of Jesus Christ represents Cosimo the Elder, the founder of the
dynasty. Cosimo's son Piero can be seen from the back in red in the centre and
Lorenzo the Magnificent is the young man on his right, wearing a black and red
mantle.*

117

118

119

120

118. Hans Memling, 1433-1494, Northern Renaissance, Flemish,
   Last Judgment Triptych, 1467-1471, Oil on oak panel, 222 x 160 cm,
   Muzeum Pomorskie, Danzig

This triptych takes its inspiration from van der Weyden's Beaune Altarpiece.
A semi-circular line of bodies runs through the three panels, figuring on one
side the 'Reception of the Righteous into Heaven' and the 'Casting of the
Damned into Hell' on the opposite side.

119. Piero della Francesca, c. 1416-1492, Early Renaissance, Italian,
   Diptych: Portrait of Duke Frederico da Montefello and Battista
   Sforza (left panel), c. 1465, Oil and tempera on panel, 47 x 33 cm,
   Galleria degli Uffizi, Florence

120. Piero della Francesca, c. 1416-1492, Early Renaissance, Italian, *Diptych:*
   Portrait of Duke Frederico da Montefello and Battista Sforza (right panel),
   c. 1465, Oil and tempera on panel, 47 x 33 cm, Galleria degli Uffizi, Florence

As it was painted from the funeral mask of the chief warrior Montefeltro, the
face of the sitter remains hieratic. The profile portrait takes its inspiration from
the ancient medals and testifies to a certain will to preserve conventional
aspects: Frederico is blind in one eye and this representation enables not to
offend. Nevertheless, he is depicted with great realism (bent nose and wart
are shown). The elegance of the portrait rejoins the precepts of Alberti
(enounced in De Pictura). The recent discovering of oil painting enables
more realism and subtlety, especially in the illusionism one can see in the
background landscape.

Hans Memling
(1433 Seligenstadt, Germany – 1494 Bruges)

Little is known of Memling's life. It is surmised that he was a
German by descent but the definite fact of his life is that he
painted at Bruges, sharing with the van Eycks, who had also
worked in that city, the honour of being the leading artists of the
so-called 'School of Bruges'. He carried on their method of
painting, and added to it a quality of gentle sentiment. In his
case, as in theirs, Flemish art, founded upon local conditions and
embodying purely local ideals, reached its fullest expression.

121

122

121. Leonardo da Vinci, 1452-1519, Early Renaissance, Florentine School, Italian, *The Annunciation*, c. 1472, Oil and Tempera on panel, 98 x 217 cm, Galleria degli Uffizi, Florence

Leonardo da Vinci's The Annunciation, is one of the most popular versions of this subject. The angel, carrying white lilies, kneels to the Madonna, who is seated next to a building and has raised her left hand in a gesture of surprise. They both represent the ideal beauty and exuberance of youth. The Virgin's right hand is resting on the page of a book, symbolic of her knowledge as Mary-Sophia, the personification both of Wisdom and of the Logos, the Word of God. Below her hand, the shell that adorns the furniture represents the connection between Mary and the ancient Roman goddess of love, Venus.

122. Martin Schongauer, 1450-1491, Northern Renaissance, German, *Madonna at the Rose Bush*, 1473, Oil on panel, 200 x 115 cm, Eglise Saint-Martin, Colmar

Schongauer, painter from Alsace, is linked to the circle of painters influenced by Flemish and Burgundy artists. Executed for the Church of Saint Martin in Colmar, this painting displays one of the most beautiful illustrations of the Virgin in German art.

123. Antonello da Messina, 1430-1479, Early Renaissance, Southern Italian School, Italian, *Virgin Annunciate*, 1475, Oil on panel, 45 x 35 cm, Museo Nazionale, Palermo

The half-length representation of Mary and the absence of the Archangel Gabriel make an exceptional iconography out of this painting of the Annunciation.

124. Antonello da Messina, 1430-1479, Early Renaissance, Southern Italian School, Italian, *Portrait of a Man (Le Condottiere)*, 1475, Oil on panel, 36 x 30 cm, Musée du Louvre, Paris

This three-quarters view portrait on a dark background moves away from the profiles from the Early Renaissance. The face of the man is deeply individualised and betrays the influence of Flemish painters such as van Eyck or Campin.

125. **Antonio del Pollaiuolo**, 1432-1498, Renaissance, Florentine School, Italian, *Martyrdom of Saint Sebastian*, 1475, Oil on poplar, 291.5 x 202.6 cm, National Gallery, London

The pyramidal composition and the attention paid to the quality of the drawing are characteristic of the Florentine researches at the time.

Antonello da Messina
(1430 – 1479 Messina)

If little is known about his life, the name of Antonello da Messina corresponds to the arrival of a new technique in Italian painting; oils. He used them especially in his portraits where they were very popular in his day, such as *Portrait of a Man* (1475).

Now, if this appears to be not exactly true, still his work influenced Venetian painters. His work was a combination of Flemish technique and realism with typically Italian modelling of forms and clarity of spatial arrangement. Also, his practice of building form with colour, rather than line and shade, greatly influenced the subsequent development of Venetian painting.

126

128

127

126. **Leonardo da Vinci**, 1452-1519, Early Renaissance, Florentine School, Italian,
Madonna with a Flower (Madonna Benois), 1478, Oil on canvas,
49.5 x 33 cm, The State Hermitage Museum, St Petersburg.

127. **Antonello da Messina**, 1430-1479, Early Renaissance, Southern Italian
School, Italian, *San Cassiano Altar*, 1475-1476, Oil on panel, 115 x 65 cm
(central panel); 56 x 35 cm (left panel); 56.8 x 35.6 cm (right panel),
Kunsthistorisches Museum, Vienna

*This painting was a model for painters such as Bellini, with his San Giobbe
Altarpiece or Giorgione, the painter of the Castelfranco altar.*

128. **Nicolas Froment**, 1430-1485, Early Renaissance, French,
The Burning Bush, c. 1475, Tempera on panel, 410 x 305 cm,
Cathédrale St Sauveur, Aix-en-Provence

*Central panel of Froment's triptych commissioned by King René of Provence,
this is the most important work of the Provençal artist. The kneeling figures on
the wing portray the donor and his wife.*

129. **Martin Schongauer**, 1450-1491, Northern Renaissance, German,
The Holy Family, 1475-1480, Oil on panel, 26 x 17 cm,
Kunsthistorisches Museum, Vienna

129   130

131

130. Hans Memling, 1433-1494, Northern Renaissance, Flemish, *Madonna Enthroned with Child and Two Angels*, late 15th c., Oil on panel, 57 x 42 cm, Galleria degli Uffizi, Florence

Hans Memling painted his Madonna Enthroned with Child and Two Angels during the second half of the fifteenth century. The Virgin and her child are seated on a throne amid lavish surroundings. Golden rays emanate from the Queen of Heaven's head, and the two musical angels are eager to entertain her son. Above, an arch is adorned with cherubim who carry beautiful garlands of fruit and flowers, an allusion to abundance in nature, a gift which Mary, like female deities of the past, was believed to bestow on her followers.

131. Hugo van der Goes, c. 1440-1482, Northern Renaissance, Flemish, *Adoration of the Shepherds.* *(Central panel of the Portinari Altar)*, 1476-1478, Oil on wood, 250 x 310 cm, Galleria degli Uffizi, Florence

This big triptych, commissioned by the Florentine merchant, Tommaso Portinari, for the Church of S. Egidio in Florence, is van der Goes's masterpiece. It shows a great emotional intensity, rarely gained by other artists. The Child is isolated, in the core of a devotional circle as the Virgin meditates on his destiny. The sudden irruption of the shepherds contrasts with the solemnity of the other characters.

133. Hans Memling, 1433-1494, Northern Renaissance, Flemish,
Portrait of a Man at Prayer before a Landscape, c. 1480,
Oil on panel, 30 x 22 cm, Mauritshuis, The Hague

Memling's portraits show a lot of attention paid to the position of the head and hands. The man's devotion is made obvious here in the representation of his hands in prayer and the church in the distance. The tightly framed composition gives a strong sensation of intimacy to this portrait.

134. Sandro Botticelli (Alessandro di Mariano Filipepi), 1445-1510,
Early Renaissance, Florentine School, Italian, *Primavera*, c. 1478,
Tempera on panel, 203 x 314 cm, Galleria degli Uffizi, Florence

The painting, sometimes called Primavera, *but now and again also* Realm of Venus, *is Botticelli's most celebrated masterpiece. This work is one in a series of paintings depicting heathen myths and legends in the form of antique gods and heroes. Just as convincingly and naively, and with the same enthusiasm, Botticelli makes the beauty of the naked human body his task. In the large presentation of* Primavera *he does indeed describe an antique subject, stipulated by his clients and advisers, but he penetrates it with his mind, his imagination and his artistic sense. The composition is built up in nine, almost life-size figures in the foreground of an orange grove. The individual figures are borrowed from Poliziano's poem about the great tournament in the spring of 1475, the Giostra, in which Giuliano was declared the winner. The artistic appearance of* Primavera *which, apart from the dull old layer of varnish, is well preserved, deviates from most of Botticelli's paintings in so far as that the local colours are rather secondary. This is how the artist tried to bring out the full beauty of the figures' bodies, which, apart from Venus and Primavera, are more or less naked. He enhances this with the deep green background, covered with flowers and fruit. There, where local colours occur to a greater extent as, for example, in the short red robe of Mercury, the pale blue decoration of the god of wind or the blue dress and red cloak of Venus in the middle, the colours have been strongly tinted with gold ornaments and glaze.*

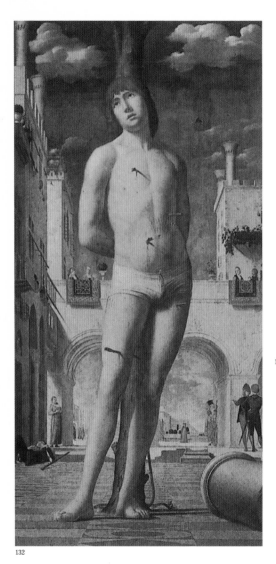

132

133

132. Antonello da Messina, 1430-1479, Early Renaissance, Southern Italian School, Italian, *St Sebastian*, c. 1476, panel transposed on canvas, 171 x 85 cm, Gemäldegalerie, Alte Meister, Dresden

Antonello da Messina had a fundamental influence on Venetian painting (especially on Bellini) because of his knowledge of oil painting (that he learnt from the Flemish artists). He also used a lot of this knowledge for his portraits. This painting was a pendant to St. Christopher. The perspective has a very low vanishing point and the frame is narrowed so that the saint is monumentalised.

84

Sandro Botticelli (Alessandro di Mariano Filipepi)
(1445 – 1510 Florence)

He was the son of a citizen in comfortable circumstances, and had been, in Vasari's words, "instructed in all such things as children are usually taught before they choose a calling." However, he refused to give his attention to reading, writing and accounts, continues Vasari, so that his father, despairing of his ever becoming a scholar, apprenticed him to the goldsmith Botticello: whence came the name by which the world remembers him. However, Sandro, a stubborn-featured youth with large, quietly searching eyes and a shock of yellow hair – he has left a portrait of himself on the right-hand side of his picture of the *Adoration of the Magi* – would also become a painter, and to that end was placed with the Carmelite monk Fra Filippo Lippi. But he was a realist, as the artists of his day had become, satisfied with the joy and skill of painting, and with the study of the beauty and character of the human subject instead of religious themes. Botticelli made rapid progress, loved his master, and later on extended his love to his master's son, Filippino Lippi, and taught him to paint, but the master's realism scarcely touched Lippi, for Botticelli was a dreamer and a poet.

Botticelli is a painter not of facts, but of ideas, and his pictures are not so much a representation of certain objects as a pattern of forms. Nor is his colouring rich and lifelike; it is subordinated to form, and often rather a tinting than actual colour. In fact, he was interested in the abstract possibilities of his art rather than in the concrete. For example, his compositions, as has just been said, are a pattern of forms; his figures do not actually occupy well-defined places in a well-defined area of space; they do not attract us by their suggestion of bulk, but as shapes of form, suggesting rather a flat pattern of decoration. Accordingly, the lines which enclose the figures are chosen with the primary intention of being decorative.

It has been said that Botticelli, "though one of the worst anatomists, was one of the greatest draughtsmen of the Renaissance." As an example of false anatomy we may notice the impossible way in which the Madonna's head is attached to the neck, and other instances of faulty articulation and incorrect form of limbs may be found in Botticelli's pictures. Yet he is recognised as one of the greatest draughtsmen: he gave to 'line' not only intrinsic beauty, but also significance. In mathematical language, he resolved the movement of the figure into its factors, its simplest forms of expression, and then combined these various forms into a pattern which, by its rhythmical and harmonious lines, produces an effect upon our imagination, corresponding to the sentiments of grave and tender poetry that filled the artist himself.

This power of making every line count in both significance and beauty distinguishes the great master- draughtsmen from the vast majority of artists who used line mainly as a necessary means of representing concrete objects.

135

136

135. Michael Pacher, c. 1430-1498, Northern Renaissance, Austrian,
Altarpiece of the Early Church Fathers, c. 1480, Oil on panel,
216 x 380 cm, Alte Pinakothek, Munich

*Gothic in the canopies, the characters' poses and the contorted hands, the
altar of the Austrian painter is also strongly influenced by Italian art in the use
of perspective, low viewpoint and figures close to the picture plane recalling
Mantegna's works.*

136. Ercole de'Roberti, 1450-1496, Early Renaissance, Ferrarese School, Italian,
Madonna with Child and Saints, 1480, Oil on panel, 323 x 240 cm,
Pinacoteca di Brera, Milan

*Ercole de'Roberti inherited the tradition of Tura and Cossa with their precise line
and metallic colours against elaborately fanciful ornamentation. But he
developed a very personal and expressive style in his works. In this Altarpiece,
which is his first documented work, his style is independent although it shows the
influence of his Ferrarese antecedents. The Altarpiece reveals a familiarity with
Venetian art and the work of Giovanni Bellini and Antonello da Messina in
particular.*

137. Leonardo da Vinci, 1452-1519, Early Renaissance, Florentine School,
Italian, *Adoration of the Magi*, c. 1481, Tempera, oil, varnish and white lead
on panel, 246 x 243 cm, Galleria degli Uffizi, Florence

*The Adoration of the Magi is an unrivalled work exclusively in brown cameos.
The drawing matters less than its special organisation. The central characters
(the Virgin and the Magi) draw a pyramidal shape. This kind of shape is unifying
the composition and will influence Raphael. Taking his inspiration in the
traditional representation of the Magi, Leonardo proposes a new iconography:
all the characters are depicted in action; each of them is individualised by a
particular facial expression or movement. The central position of the Virgin and
Child is enhanced by the gyratory movement surrounding them.*

7

138. Pietro Perugino, 1450-1523, High Renaissance, Florentine School, Italian,
Christ giving the Keys to St. Peter, 1481-1482, Oil on wood,
Vatican Museums, Rome

The fresco is from the cycle of the life of Christ in the Sistine Chapel. The principal group, showing Christ handing the keys to the kneeling St Peter, is surrounded by the other Apostles. The Christ giving the Keys to St. Peter shows the search for a classical rhythm. The artist begins to emancipate from the teaching of Piero della Francesca realising a frieze of characters placed on different grounds.

PIETRO PERUGINO
(1450 Città della Pieve – 1523 Perugia)

Perugino's art, like Fra Angelico's, had its roots in the old Byzantine tradition of painting. The latter had departed further and further from any representation of the human form, until it became merely a symbol of religious ideas. Perugino, working under the influence of his time, restored body and substance to the figures, but still made them, as of old, primarily the symbols of an ideal. It was not until the seventeenth century that artists began to paint landscape for its own sake.

However, the union of landscape and figures counts very much for Perugino, because one of the secrets of composition is the balancing of what artists call the full and empty spaces. A composition crowded with figures is apt to produce a sensation of stuffiness and fatigue; whereas the combination of a few figures with ample open spaces gives one a sense of exhilaration and repose. It is in the degree to which an artist stimulates our imagination through our physical experiences that he seizes and holds our interest. When Perugino left Perugia to complete his education in Florence he was a fellow-pupil of Leonardo da Vinci in the sculptor's *bottegha*. If he gained from the master something of the calm of sculpture, he certainly gained nothing of its force. It is as the painter of sentiment that he excelled; though this beautiful quality is confined mainly to his earlier works. For with popularity he became avaricious, turning out repetitions of his favourite themes until they became more and more affected in sentiment.

8

139

139. Sandro Botticelli (Alessandro di Mariano Filipepi), 1445-1510,
Early Renaissance, Florentine School, Italian,
The Birth of Venus, c. 1482, Tempera on canvas, 173 x 279 cm,
Galleria degli Uffizi, Florence

*The title announces the influence here of the Roman classics, as it selects
the Roman name, rather than the Greek name for the goddess of love –
Aphrodite. The geometric centre of the work is the gesture of modesty near
the left hand of Venus, the central figure, although the triangular
arrangement of the overall work leads our eye to accept her upper torso as
central. Her long tresses and flowing garments throughout make the overall
geometric arrangement soft and dynamic. The sides of an equilateral
triangle are formed by the bodies of the figures on either side of Venus; the
base of the triangle extends beyond the sides of the work, making the
painting seem larger than it is (Piet Mondrian will exploit that technique in
a minimalist way centuries later). The mature goddess has just been born
from the sea, blown ashore by Zephyr (The West Wind), and his abducted
nymph Chloris. The stylised waves of the sea bring the shell-boat forward
and counter-clockwise to The Hour waiting on the shore. The sea has
somehow already provided a ribbon for her hair. Her introspective
expression is typical of the central figures in the painter's work (See* Portrait
of a Man *(1417)). The Hour, symbolising Spring and rebirth, begins to
clothe the naked, new-born goddess with an elegant, high fashion robe
covered in flowers, similar to her own gown on which there are corn
flowers. Several spring flowers are sprinkled throughout the scene: orange
blossoms in the upper right; evergreen myrtle around The Hour's neck and
waist; a single blue anemone between The Hour's feet; over two dozen
pink roses accompany Zephyr and Chloris. Cattails in the lower left balance
the strong verticals of the orange trees. Each of the figures is outlined in thin
black lines, characteristic of the artist. Sometimes the artist doesn't follow
his outline, but doesn't cover it up either; as we see along the right arm of
Venus, the outline has become visible over the years.*

140

141

142

0. Sandro Botticelli (Alessandro di Mariano Filipepi), 1445-1510,
Early Renaissance, Florentine School, Italian,
Madonna of the Magnificat, c. 1483, Tempera on wood,
Tondo, dia. 118 cm, Galleria degli Uffizi, Florence

*The paintings of the Virgin by Botticelli dated between 1481 and 1485 may
embody the purest essence of the physical ideal, in relation to both the
Madonna and the baby Jesus, developed during the Renaissance. At the same
time, a deep sense of spirituality pervades the scene,* Madonna and Child with
Angels, *also known as the* Madonna of the Magnificat. *Mary is represented
seated, her child on her lap. The angels hold an elaborate crown above her
head, reminding the viewer that she is the Queen of Heaven, while mother and
child gaze in rapture at each other. The child has his hand on the page of a
book, pointing at the word "Magnificat", a reference to Mary's consent to bear
him, and her declaration to the archangel of the Annunciation that "my soul
magnifies the Lord" (in Latin, "Magnificat anima mea Dominum").*

1. Sandro Botticelli (Alessandro di Mariano Filipepi), 1445-1510, Early
Renaissance, Florentine School, Italian, *Pallas and the Centaure*, c. 1482,
Tempera on canvas, 205 x 147.5 cm, Galleria degli Uffizi, Florence

2. Andrea Mantegna, 1431-1506, Early Renaissance, Florentine School,
Italian, *Madonna and Child (Madonna of the Caves)*, 1485,
Oil on panel, 29 x 21.5 cm, Galleria degli Uffizi, Florence

3. Francesco Botticini, c. 1446-1498, Early Renaissance,
Florentine School, Italian, *Adoration of the Christ Child*, c. 1485,
Tempera on panel, Tondo, dia. 123 cm, Galleria degli Uffizi, Florence

143

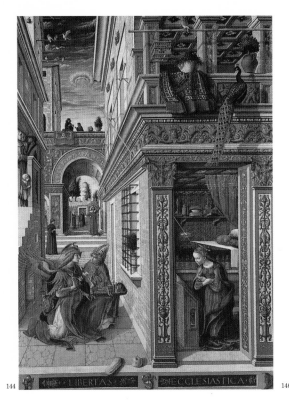

144. Carlo Crivelli, 1430-1495, Early Renaissance, Venetian School, Italian, *Annunciation with St Endimius*, 1486, Oil on canvas transferred to wood, 207 x 147 cm, National Gallery, London

145. Domenico Ghirlandaio, 1449-1494, Early Renaissance, Florentine School, Italian, *Adoration of the Magi*, 1488, Tempera on panel, Tondo, dia. 171 cm, Galleria degli Uffizi, Florence

This pyramidal composition with Mary at the top was influenced by Leonardo's uncompleted Adoration of the Magi *(1481, Uffizi)*

146. Piero di Cosimo, 1462-1521, Early Renaissance, Florentine School, Italian, *Portrait of Simonetta Vespucci*, c. 1485, Oil on panel, 57 x 42 cm, Musée Condé, Chantilly

Here is one of the artist's finest portraits. Simonetta Vespucci is depicted as Cleopatra with the asp around her neck. The snake, also being a symbol of immortality, reinforces the strange atmosphere of this work.

147. Fra Filippo Lippi, c. 1406-1469, Early Renaissance, Florentine School, Italian, *Madonna and the Child Enthroned with Saint John the Baptist, Victor, Bernard and Zenobius (Altarpiece of the Otto di Pratica)*, 1486, Tempera on panel, 355 x 255 cm, Galleria degli Uffizi, Florence

147

148

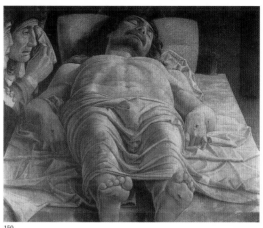

150

149

148. Sandro Botticelli (Alessandro di Mariano Filipepi), 1445-1510, Early Renaissance, Florentine School, Italian, *The Coronation of the Virgin*, c. 1490, Tempera on panel, 378 x 258 cm, Galleria degli Uffizi, Florence

149. Domenico Ghirlandaio, 1449-1494, Early Renaissance, Florentine School, Italian, *An Old Man with his Grandson*, 1488, Tempera on panel, 62 x 46 cm, Musée du Louvre, Paris

This is the first time that a character is portrayed with such realism showing clearly disfiguring details. This portrait conveys the deep affection between the man and the boy. The motif of the open window on a landscape in the background was borrowed from the Flemish Renaissance and brought to Italy in the mid-fifteenth century by artists such as Filippo Lippi.

150. Andrea Mantegna, 1431-1506, Early Renaissance, Florentine School, Italian, *The Lamentation over the Dead Christ*, c. 1490, Tempera on canvas, 68 x 81 cm, Pinacoteca di Brera, Milan

A nearly monochromatic vision of Jesus mourned by three figures was in Mantegna's collection at the time of his death; this Dead Christ includes Saint John, Mary, and Mary Magdalene. His inventory of 1506 referred to a work fitting this description, presumably the very same picture, and it ended up in Gonzaga collections later in the century. This is a searing image of Christ laid out on his funeral slab, an intense vision of Christ's suffering and death. The wounds in his hands are like torn paper, as is the spear gash in his side. Mantegna has played with the rules of perspective here, making the head large; it should be much smaller than the feet because the figure is strongly foreshortened. To make the work in proper perspective would have made the face of Christ too small to elicit strong empathy from the viewer. The monochromatic, golden-brown colouring helps to move this painting to another realm of passion and religious fervour. The viewers would sympathise with the sorrowful Mary, John, and Mary Magdalene who appear in truncated form on the left, pouring out their grief in open mourning.

151

151. Pietro Perugino, 1450-1523, High Renaissance, Florentine School, Italian, *St Sebastian*, c. 1490-1500, Oil on wood, 176x116 cm, Musée du Louvre, Paris

152

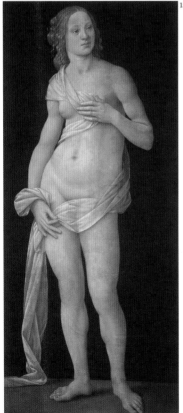

153

152. Leonardo da Vinci, 1452-1519, Renaissance, Florentine School, Italian,
The Last Supper, 1495-1498, Oil and tempera on stone, 460 x 880 cm,
Convent of Santa Maria delle Grazie, Refectori, Milan

The perfection of grouping achieved in The Last Supper *would of itself be sufficient to mark an epoch in the annals of painting. Its ease and rhythm are sublime. The figures, placed on two planes in perspective, are further arranged in groups of three, with the exception of Christ, who, isolated in the centre, dominates the action. If we turn to expression and gesture, we must again do homage to the master's extraordinary perception of dramatic effect. The Saviour has just uttered the fateful words: "One of you shall betray me," with sublime resignation. In a moment, as by an electric shock, he has excited the most diverse emotions among the disciples, according to the character of each. Sadly, Leonardo painted in oil and tempera on a dry wall, such a defective process that three-quarters of the work may be said to have been destroyed by the middle of the sixteenth century. The skill and the knowledge necessary in order not to destroy their balance, to vary the lines without detracting from their harmony, and finally to connect the various groups, were so tremendous that neither reasoning nor calculation could have solved a problem so intricate; but for a sort of divine inspiration, the most gifted artist would have failed.*

153. Lorenzo di Credi, c.1458-1537, High Renaissance, Florentine School, Italian,
Venus, c. 1493, Oil on canvas, 151 x 69 cm, Galleria degli Uffizi, Florence

154. Sandro Botticelli (Alessandro di Mariano Filipepi), 1445-1510, Early Renaissance, Florentine School, Italian, *Lamentation over the Dead Christ with Saints*, c. 1490, Tempera on panel, 140 x 207 cm, Alte Pinakothek, Munich

155. Giovanni Bellini, c. 1430-1516, Early Renaissance, Venetian School, Italian,
Sacred Allegory, c. 1490, Oil on panel, 73 x 119 cm, Galleria degli Uffizi, Florence

154

155

VITTORE CARPACCIO
(c. 1455 Venice – c. 1525 Capodistria)

Carpaccio was a Venetian painter strongly influenced by Gentile Bellini. The distinguishing characteristics of his work are his taste for fantasy and anecdote and his eye for minutely-observed crowd details. After completing the cycles of Scenes from the Lives of St Ursula, St George and St Jerome, his career declined and he remained forgotten until the nineteenth century. He is now seen as one of the outstanding Venetian painters of his generation.

157

156

HIERONYMUS BOSCH
(c.1450 – 1516 's-Hertogenbosch)

Born in the middle of the century, Bosch experienced the drama of the highly charged Renaissance and its wars of religion. Medieval traditions and values were crumbling, paving the way to thrust humankind into a new universe where faith lost some of its power and much of its magic. His favourite allegories were hell, heaven and lust. He believed that everyone had to choose between one of two options: heaven or hell. Bosch brilliantly exploited the symbolism of a wide range of fruit and plants to lend sexual overtones to his themes.

156. **Hieronymus Bosch,** c.1450-1516, Northern Renaissance, Dutch, *The Ship of Fools,* after 1491, Oil on panel, 58 x 33 cm, Musée du Louvre, Paris

157. **Vittore Carpaccio,** c.1465-c.1525, High Renaissance, Venetian School, Italian, *The Dream of St Ursula,* 1495, Tempera on canvas, 274 x 267 cm, Galleria dell'Accademia, Venice

158. **Hieronymus Bosch,** c.1450-1516, Northern Renaissance, Dutch, *Christ Mocked (The Crowning with Thorns),* 1490-1500, Oil on oak panel, 73.8 x 59 cm, National Gallery, London

159. Leonardo da Vinci, 1452-1519, Renaissance, Florentine School, Italian, *Lady with an Ermine (Portrait of Cecilia Gallerani),* 1483-1490, Oil on panel, 54 x 39 cm, Czartoryski Museum, Cracow

Favourite portrait of the Duke of Milan, the Lady with an Ermine *is part of a series of animated portraits painted by Leonardo in Milan: dynamism is given by the bust facing the left side of the panel and the head turned toward the right.*

160. Fra Bartolomeo, 1473-1517, High Renaissance, Florentine School, Italian, *Portrait of Girolamo Savonarola,* c. 1498, Oil on panel, 47 x 31 cm, Museo di San Marco, Florence

160

Leonardo da Vinci
(1452 Vinci – 1519 Le Clos-Lucé)

Leonardo's early life was spent in Florence, his maturity in Milan, and the last three years of his life in France. Leonardo's teacher was Verrocchio. First he was a goldsmith, then a painter and sculptor: as a painter, representative of the very scientific school of draughtsmanship; more famous as a sculptor, being the creator of the Colleoni statue at Venice, Leonardo was a man of striking physical attractiveness, great charm of manner and conversation, and mental accomplishment. He was well grounded in the sciences and mathematics of the day, as well as a gifted musician. His skill in draughtsmanship was extraordinary; shown by his numerous drawings as well as by his comparatively few paintings. His skill of hand is at the service of most minute observation and analytical research into the character and structure of form.

Leonardo is the first in date of the great men who had the desire to create in a picture a kind of mystic unity brought about by the fusion of matter and spirit. Now that the Primitives had concluded their experiments, ceaselessly pursued during two centuries, by the conquest of the methods of painting, he was able to pronounce the words which served as a password to all later artists worthy of the name: painting is a spiritual thing, *cosa mentale*.

He completed Florentine draughtsmanship in applying to modelling by light and shade, a sharp subtlety which his predecessors had used only to give greater precision to their contours. This marvellous draughtsmanship, this modelling and chiaroscuro he used not solely to paint the exterior appearance of the body but, as no one before him had done, to cast over it a reflection of the mystery of the inner life. In the *Mona Lisa* and his other masterpieces he even used landscape not merely as a more or less picturesque decoration, but as a sort of echo of that interior life and an element of a perfect harmony.

Relying on the still quite novel laws of perspective this doctor of scholastic wisdom, who was at the same time an initiator of modern thought, substituted for the discursive manner of the Primitives the principle of concentration which is the basis of classical art. The picture is no longer presented to us as an almost fortuitous aggregate of details and episodes. It is an organism in which all the elements, lines and colours, shadows and lights, compose a subtle tracery converging on a spiritual, a sensuous centre. It was not with the external significance of objects, but with their inward and spiritual significance, that Leonardo was occupied.

161

16th Century

The sixteenth century begins with the Reformation in 1517, when Martin Luther (1483-1546) issued his *Ninety-Five Theses* and John Calvin (1509-64) formally tried to reform the Catholic Church. These movements led to the establishment of Protestantism, which emphasised personal faith rather than doctrines of the church. The invention of moveable type by Gutenberg in the previous century helped to make access to the Bible and literacy an important feature of the Protestant Reformation. The Catholic Church, however, reacted with its own Catholic Counter-Reformation by convening the Council of Trent from 1545-63. The most prominent participants in the counter-Reformation were the Jesuits, a Catholic order founded by Ignatius of Loyola (1491-1556). The Jesuits also participated in the Age of Exploration as missionaries, establishing themselves throughout Asia, Africa, and the Americas. The Catholic Church also responded at this time with an extreme measure of policing the faith through the Holy Office of the Inquisition. Finally, the English Reformation was supported by King Henry VIII (1491-1547) who wanted a divorce from his wife Catherine of Aragon (1485-1536) because she had not produced a male child. Henry VIII then founded the Church of England, the new church that was formed in the wake of the split with the Catholic Church.

Galileo Galilei (1564-1642) began his experiments by inventing the pendulum and the thermometer in the sixteenth century. Galileo was also interested in astronomy, but it was Nicolaus Copernicus (1473-1543) who developed the heliocentric, or sun-centred, theory that the earth revolves around the sun.

The art of this century was mostly influenced by the apparition of Protestantism and the counter-Reformation as the need for clarity in the works of art meant the end of Mannerism.

The northern lands were embracing Protestantism and this changed the patronage system in art. Due to the wealth from increasing global trade, a new merchant class developed in northern Europe which commissioned more secular works of art for both church and private homes. Still-life paintings were popular, as were landscapes. Also, the formation of guilds and civic militias created a new market for the group portrait. In Italy, the Catholic Church was the primary patron of art, while in the north, individuals were the principal patrons, thereby creating a market force that determined subject matter. Artists could no longer depend on large church commissions for religious paintings the way they had prior to the Reformation. Conversely, much of Spanish and Italian art was still created through religious patronage. King Francis I of France (1494-1547) was generally considered a monarch who embodied the Renaissance. His courtly style and love of humanist knowledge was far reaching. Leonardo da Vinci (1452-1519) eventually wound up in his court in France, where he found generous patronage for his science and experiments and lived out the rest of his life near Amboise with the support of Francis I.

---

161. Raphael (Raffaello Sanzio), 1483-1520, High Renaissance, Florentine School, Italian, *The Virgin and Child with the Infant Saint John the Baptist (La Belle Jardinière)*, 1507-08, Oil on wood, 122 x 80 cm, Musée du Louvre, Paris

La Belle Jardinière, *or* The Virgin and Child with the Infant St John the Baptist, *completed in 1507, shows the trio surrounded by a pleasant rural environment. The similarity between the* Madonna of the Goldfinch *and this depiction of the Madonna is more than coincidental: it represents the ideal of female beauty according to Raphael. Perhaps the same model was used in both paintings.*

163

165

164

162. Sandro Botticelli (Alessandro di Mariano Filipepi), 1445-1510, Early Renaissance, Florentine School, Italian, *Mystic Nativity*, c. 1500, Oil on canvas, 108.6 x 74.9 cm, National Gallery, London

Inscribed in Greek at the top: "This picture, at the end of the year 1500, in the troubles of Italy, I Alessandro, in the half-time after the time, painted, according to the eleventh [chapter] of Saint John, in the second woe of the Apocalypse, during the release of the devil for three-and-a-half years; then he shall be bound in the twelfth [chapter] and we shall see [him buried] as in this picture." Botticelli's picture has been called the Mystic Nativity because of its mysterious symbolism.

163. Piero di Cosimo, 1462-1521, High Renaissance, Florentine School, Italian, *Immaculate Conception and Six Saints*, c. 1505, Oil on panel, 206 x 173 cm, Galleria degli Uffizi, Florence

164. Leonardo da Vinci, 1452-1519, High Renaissance, Florentine School, Italian, *The Virgin of the Rocks (The Virgin with the Infant Saint John adoring the Infant Christ accompanied by an Angel)*, 1483-86, Oil on panel, 199 x 122 cm, Musée du Louvre, Paris

The Virgin of the Rocks, also by Leonardo da Vinci, is probably the most well-known painting of the Virgin and Child within the Western world. Now located in the Louvre, this work is one of the best examples of the use of atmospheric perspective and the correct foreshortening of the human figure. The cavern and the group of figures are all seen as through a veil of shadowy mist. Leonardo believed that his destiny was to recreate the beauty of nature on his canvas. The figure of the Madonna occupies the apex of the pyramid-based composition of this painting – the most important location – due to her high ranking within contemporary Christian belief. She is accompanied by the infants Jesus and St John, and an angel. All four reflect the Renaissance ideal of the human form. Leonardo altogether eliminated the use of the halo effects to further humanise the group. The Virgin is depicted as the perfect woman, yet she also projects her tender Earth Mother qualities reminiscent of those seen in ancient renderings of the Great Goddess Isis.

165. Giovanni Bellini, c. 1426-1516, Early Renaissance, Venetian School, Italian, *The Doge Leonardo Loredan*, c. 1501-05, Oil on poplar, 61 x 45 cm, National Gallery, London

Bellini was an exquisite portrait painter. His Doge Leonardo Loredan, the elected ruler of Venice, is painted in a completely revolutionary way and had some beautiful effects. Rather than using gold-leaf to show the richness of the material of the Doge's robe, he painted the surface in a rough way, thus catching the light and rendering a metallic look.

166

166. Albrecht Dürer, 1471-1528, Northern Renaissance, German,
Self-portrait in a Fur-Collared Robe, 1500,
Oil on limewood panel, 67.1 x 48.9 cm, Alte Pinakothek, Munich

This flattering, Christ-like portrait is also innovative as the artist represented himself frontally. The painting bears the inscription: "Thus I, Albrecht Dürer from Nuremberg, painted myself with indelible colours at the age of 28 years."

167. Leonardo da Vinci, 1452-1519, Renaissance, Florentine School, Italian,
Mona Lisa (La Gioconda), c. 1503-06, Oil on poplar panel,
77 x 53 cm, Musée du Louvre, Paris

Everybody knows this portrait: oval face with broad, high forehead; dreamy eyes beneath drooping lids; a smile very sweet and a little sad, with a suggestion of conscious superiority. This small painting, one of only thirty extant works by Leonardo, ended up in the collection of the French King, Francis I, and was displayed in the castle of Fontainebleau until the reign of Louis XIV. It is the most famous portrait, one of the first easel paintings, the most often reproduced and satirised, and one of the most influential works of the Italian Renaissance, if not of all European art. The model was probably the wife of the Marquis Francesco del Giocondo, a Florentine merchant. The work is the perfection of Leonardo's pioneering technique of "sfumato," creating atmospheric scenery, or the layering of glazes in a way that blends one colour seamlessly to another. The work also demonstrates his mastery of anatomy, perspective, landscape and portrait painting. The disposition of the sitter, in three-quarter view and the background landscape is characteristic of Florentine painting at the time. But this picture is no longer presented to us as an almost fortuitous aggregate of details and episodes. It is an organism in which all the elements, lines and colours, shadows and light compose a subtle tracery converging on a spiritual, sensuous centre. On this small panel, Leonardo depicted an epitome of the universe, creation and created: woman, the eternal enigma, the eternal ideal of man and the sign of the perfect beauty to which he aspires, evoked by a magician in all its mystery and power. Mona Lisa represents a vast revelation of the eternal feminine.

Albrecht Dürer
(1471 – 1528 Nuremberg)

Dürer is the greatest of German artists and most representative of the German mind. He, like Leonardo, was a man of striking physical attractiveness, great charm of manner and conversation, and mental accomplishment, being well grounded in the sciences and mathematics of the day. His skill in draughtsmanship was extraordinary; Dürer is even more celebrated for his engravings on wood and copper than for his paintings. With both, the skill of his hand was at the service of the most minute observation and analytical research into the character and structure of form. Dürer, however, had not the feeling for abstract beauty and ideal grace that Leonardo possessed; but instead, a profound earnestness, a closer interest in humanity, and a more dramatic invention. Dürer was a great admirer of Luther; and in his own work is the equivalent of what was mighty in the Reformer. It is very serious and sincere; very human, and addressed the hearts and understanding of the masses. Nuremberg, his hometown, had become a great centre of printing and the chief distributor of books throughout Europe. Consequently, the art of engraving upon wood and copper, which may be called the pictorial branch of printing, was much encouraged. Of this opportunity Dürer took full advantage.

The Renaissance in Germany was more a moral and intellectual than an artistic movement, partly due to northern conditions. The feeling for ideal grace and beauty is fostered by the study of the human form, and this had been flourishing predominantly in southern Europe. But Albrecht Dürer had a genius too powerful to be conquered. He remained profoundly Germanic in his stormy penchant for drama, as was his contemporary Mathias Grünewald, a fantastic visionary and rebel against all Italian seductions. Dürer, in spite of all his tense energy, dominated conflicting passions by a sovereign and speculative intelligence comparable with that of Leonardo. He, too, was on the border of two worlds, that of the Gothic age and that of the modern age, and on the border of two arts, being an engraver and draughtsman rather than a painter.

167

168

Giovanni Bellini
(1430 – 1516 Venice)

Giovanni Bellini was the son of Jacopo Bellini, a Venetian painter who was settled in Padua at the time Giovanni and his elder brother, Gentile, were in their period of studentship. Here, they came under the influence of Mantegna, who was also bound to them by the ties of relationship, since he married their sister. To his brother-in-law, Bellini owed much of his knowledge of classical architecture and perspective, and his broad and sculptural treatment of draperies. Sculpture and the love of the antique played a large part in Giovanni's early impressions, and left their mark in the stately dignity of his later style. This developed slowly during his long life. Bellini died of old age, indeed in his eighty-eighth year, and was buried near his brother, Gentile, in the Church of Ss. Giovanni e Paulo. Outside, under the spacious vault of heaven, stands the Bartolommeo Colleoni, Verrocchio's monumental statue, which had been among the elevating influences of Bellini's life and art. After filling the whole of the north of Italy with his influence, he prepared the way for the giant colourists of the Venetian School, Giorgione, Titian, and Veronese.

169

168. **Giovanni Bellini**, c. 1430-1516, Early Renaissance, Venetian School, Italian, *Saint Zaccaria Altarpiece*, 1505, Oil on wood, transferred to canvas, 402 x 273 cm, Church of San Zaccaria, Venice

This altarpiece is often considered as the most perfect painting of sacra conversazione. *Bellini brings to life the traditional figure of the Virgin and saints. Here, the composition of the painting (an apse surrounding the Madonna and the saints) becomes the continuation of the altar.*

169. **Albrecht Dürer**, 1471-1528, Northern Renaissance, German, *Paumgartner Altar (Middle panel),* 1502-04, Oil on lime panel, 155 x 126 cm, Alte Pinakothek, Munich

The central panel is conceived in the traditional Gothic style but Dürer uses perspective with extreme rigour. It depicts a Nativity, set in an architectural ruin of a palatial building.

170. **Piero di Cosimo**, 1462-1521, High Renaissance, Florentine School, Italian, *Venus, Mars and Cupid*, c. 1500, Oil on panel, 72 x 182 cm, Stiftung Staatliche Museen, Gemäldegalerie, Berlin

171

172

171. Hieronymus Bosch, c. 1450-1516, Northern Renaissance,
Dutch, *The Haywain (triptych),* c. 1500,
Oil on panel, 135 x 100 cm, Museo Nacional del Prado, Madrid

*The central painting, now supposed to be an illustration of the
Flemish proverb, "The world is a haystack; everyone takes what he
can grab thereof," is dominated by a gigantic hay wagon which,
according to Jacques Combe, "evok[es] at the same time the late
Gothic motif of the procession of pageant, and the Renaissance
Triumph... drawn by semi-human, semi-animal monsters and
headed straight for hell, followed by a cavalcade of ecclesiastical
and lay dignitaries. From all sides of the wagon men scrabble over
one another to pull hay from the giant stack. The only heed they
take of their fellows is to thrust them out of their way or to raise
hands against them. One sticks a knife into the throat of the
unfortunate competitor whom he has pinned to the ground."*
*Many among the greedy mob wear ecclesiastical garb,
indicating Bosch's attitude that the holy as well as profane are
involved in this scavenging. A fat monk sits in a large chair and
lazily sips a drink while several nuns do service for him, packing
bundles of hay into the bag at his feet. One of his nuns turns to
the lure of sexual enticement, symbolised by the fool playing a
bagpipe, to whom she offers a handful of hay in hopes of
winning his favours.*

172. Hans Baldung Grien, c. 1484-1545, Northern Renaissance,
German, *The Knight, the Young Girl and Death,*
c. 1505, Oil on panel, 355 x 296 cm, Musée du Louvre, Paris

LUCA SIGNORELLI
(C. 1445 – 1523 CORTONA)

Signorelli was a painter from Cortona but was active in various cities of central Italy like Florence, Orvieto and Rome. Probably a pupil of Piero della Francesca, he added solidity to his figures and a unique use of light, as well as having an interest in the representation of actions like contemporary artists, the Pollaiuolo brothers.

In 1483, he was called to complete the cycle of frescos in the Sistine Chapel in Rome, which means he must have had a solid reputation at that time. He painted a magnificent series of six frescos illustrating the end of the world and *The Last Judgment* for the Orvieto Cathedral. There can be seen a wide variety of nudes displayed in multiple poses, which were surpassed at that time only by Michelangelo, who knew of them. By the end of his career, he had a large workshop in Cortona where he produced conservative paintings, including numerous altarpieces.

175

173. **Bartolomeo Veneto,** c. 1502-1555, High Renaissance, Venetian School, Italian, *Portrait of a Woman,* Oil on panel, 43.5 x 34.3 cm, Städelsches Kunstinstitut, Frankfurt

174. **Luca Signorelli,** c. 1445-1523, High Renaissance, Tuscan School, Italian, *Crucifixion,* c. 1500, Oil on canvas, 247 x 117.5 cm, Galleria degli Uffizi, Florence

175. **Bernardino Pinturicchio,** 1454-1513, Early Renaissance, Italian, *Annunciation,* 1501, Fresco, Santa Maria Maggiore, Spello

176

177

178

176. Lucas Cranach the Elder, 1472-1553, Northern Renaissance, German, *The Crucifixion*, 1503, Oil on pine panel, 138 x 99 cm, Alte Pinakothek, Munich

The Crucifixion *is a subject derived from an incident described only by St John. When Christ was hanging on the Cross, he saw John and Mary standing near, "He said to his mother, 'Woman, behold your son!' Then he said to the disciple, 'Behold, your mother!'" (John 19: 26f). The compositional scheme of the crucifixion, which was established some 500 years before Cranach, was symmetrical: Christ on the Cross in the centre, Mary to the right of him and John to the left, both turned to face the viewer. This arrangement began to strike Cranach's contemporaries as too stylised. Cranach moved the Cross from the centre, presented it side-on, and has the two looking up to Christ in such a way that the faces of all the figures are visible. The first hesitant attempt of this kind was made by Albrecht Dürer in a Crucifixion painted in Nuremberg in 1496 for the chapel of the Wittenberg castle. It is believed that Cranach adopted the device from that work.*

177. Hieronymus Bosch, c. 1450-1516, Northern Renaissance, Dutch, *The Garden of Earthly Delights (central panel of the triptych),* c. 1504, Oil on panel, 220 x 195 cm, Museo Nacional del Prado, Madrid

178. Albrecht Dürer, 1471-1528, Northern Renaissance, German, *Adoration of the Magi,* 1504, Oil on panel, 98 x 112 cm, Galleria degli Uffizi, Florence

179. Lucas Cranach the Elder, 1472-1553, Northern Renaissance, German, *Rest on the Flight into Egypt*, 1504, Tempera on panel, 69 x 51 cm, Stiftung Staatliche Museen, Gemäldegalerie, Berlin

The charming little scene is inscribed in a circle, at the centre of which is the offering of the strawberry. But this cosy little circle is not at all the centre of the painting. Above, on the left and below, it is surrounded by wild nature, and nature in its own way is involved in the concerns of the Holy Family. The clear sky greets them with the smile of the new day. The rising sun imparts a silvery hue to the clumps of grey moss on the branches of a mighty fir-tree which extends protectively towards a melancholy birch that waves its springy branches. The hills, repeating one another, draw the gaze in to the sunny distance, telling Joseph, "Egypt lies there." The earth is glad to offer Mary a soft carpet of grass sprinkled with flowers. The clear stream bending around the meadow becomes a boundary to protect the fugitives from their pursuers. Nobody before Cranach had painted nature so straightforwardly, as if directly from life. Nobody before him had been able to form such an intimate link between nature and scriptural figures. Nobody managed to animate every little detail so that all of them together breathe in unison. It was not pantheistic rationalisation that expressed itself here, but the primitive instinct aroused in Lucas's spirit through contact with his native land.

180. Michelangelo Buonarroti, 1475-1564, High Renaissance, Florence, Italian,
The Holy Family with the Young St. John the Baptist (The Doni Tondo), c. 1506, Oil on panel, dia. 120 cm,
Galleria degli Uffizi, Florence

The Holy Family with the Young St. John the Baptist, *also called the Doni Tondo, was painted by Michelangelo, a commission to celebrate the marriage of Agnolo Doni and Maddalena Strozzi. The fact that this work was not created for a church might explain Michelangelo's apparent freedom to place several young male nudes in the background, behind the little figure of St. John. The young, strong and elegantly poised figure of Mary, holding her infant up on her shoulder, is contrasted with the figure of Joseph, who is depicted – as was also customary during medieval times in order to de-emphasise his importance as a father – subject to the ravages of old age. The child, like the mother, is active and full of life. This is another work in which Mary and Jesus appear to be fully human.*

181. Master of the Saint Bartholomew Altar, active c. 1475-1510, Northern Renaissance, German, *St. Bartholomew Altarpiece*, 1505, Oil on panel, 129 x 161 cm (central panel), 129 x 74 cm (side panels), Alte Pinakothek, Munich

182. Raphael (Raffaello Sanzio), 1483-1520, High Renaissance, Florentine School, Italian, *The Madonna of the Goldfinch*, 1506, Oil on panel, 107 x 77.2 cm, Galleria degli Uffizi, Florence

The patron who commissioned the Madonna of the Goldfinch – a man called Lorenzo Nasi – was a wealthy merchant, and the painting commemorated his wedding to Sandra Canigiani. Raphael painted the figure of the Madonna in the centre, using the standard pyramidal design for the composition. In her left hand Mary holds a book, while her right arm encloses the child Jesus, whose small hands enfold the goldfinch. The infant St John endeavours to caress the bird. The figures are idealised, and both Mary and Jesus have barely visible haloes over their heads, rendered in perspective, in order not to disturb the realism of the style employed. A panoramic landscape opens up the background to a considerable depth.

183. Fra Bartolomeo, 1473-1517, High Renaissance, Florentine School, Italian, *Vision of St. Bernard*, c. 1505, Oil on panel, 220 x 213 cm, Galleria dell'Accademia, Florence

Key figure of the cinquecento, Bartolomeo sums up in his works the contradictions existing in Florence between Raphael's style and the early Mannerism.

183

184. Gerard David, 1460-1523, Northern Renaissance, Flemish, *The Virgin and Child with Saints and Donor,* 1505-10, Oil on oak panel, 105.8 x 144.4 cm, National Gallery, London

Gérard David was a pupil of Vien, who considered him the reformer of the French School. In this painting, the Virgin is surrounded by Saint Barbara, Mary Magdalene and Saint Catherine. The kneeling figure is Richard de Visch van der Capelle, the commissioner of the painting.

185. Giorgione (Giorgio Barbarelli da Castelfranco), 1477-1510, Early Renaissance, Venetian School, Italian, *The Tempest,* c. 1507, Oil on canvas, 82 x 73 cm, Galleria dell'Accademia, Venice

186

188

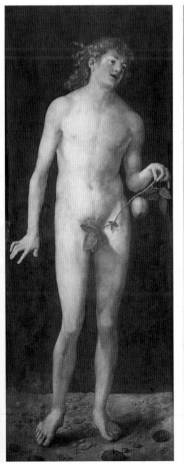

186. **Giorgione (Giorgio Barbarelli da Castelfranco),** 1477-1510, Early Renaissance, Venetian School, Italian, *The Pastoral Concert*, c. 1508, Oil on canvas, 109 x 137 cm, Musée du Louvre, Paris

187. **Albrecht Dürer,** 1471-1528, Northern Renaissance, German, *Adam and Eve*, 1507, Oil on panel, 209 x 81 cm and 209 x 83 cm, Museo Nacional del Prado, Madrid

The rules of proportion concerning the human body were a persistent theme in Dürer's oeuvre. His early efforts produced stiff postures, but he found how to keep the overall appearance beautiful and graceful. He hangs a plaque with an inscription and his unique logo signature on the tree, as he did in a similar signature statement on the wall next in his 1598 self-portrait. Eve's disposition seems coquettish, which would be appropriate for the traditional interpretation of the Genesis story. Adam's expression might reflect his confused interest.

188. **Giorgione (Giorgio Barbarelli da Castelfranco),** 1477-1510, Early Renaissance, Venetian School, Italian, *The Three Philosophers*, 1508-09, Oil on canvas, 123.5 x 144.5 cm, Kunsthistorisches Museum, Vienna

Characteristic in its style of Giorgione's use of light to create mood, The Three Philosophers illustrates the "figure in landscape" painting initiated by the artist.

189. Michelangelo Buonarroti, 1475-1564, High Renaissance,
Florence, Italian, *Delphic Sibyl,* 1508-12, Fresco, 350 x 380 cm,
Musei Vaticani, Sistine Chapel, Vatican

Art historian Germain Bazin compared the face of Michelangelo's Delphic
Sibyl *(1511) to the face of Carlo Crivelli's* Madonna della Candeletta *(1488),
and Raphael's* Madonna del Granduca *(1505). He demonstrated the
breakthrough importance of this detailed figure from the Sistine Chapel ceiling.
While the three works might be less than two decades apart, as Bazin points
out, "The clear-cut draughtsmanship of the fifteenth century seeks precision of
structure; whereas the sixteenth century painter smoothes out all the outlines
of his modelling by gentle transitions. Raphael sacrifices expression to
harmony, while Michelangelo achieves a synthesis of conflicting elements."
(Germain Bazin, History of Art from Prehistoric Times to the Present, Houghton
Mifflin, 1959, p. 243).*

Michelangelo Buonarroti
(1475 Caprese – 1564 Rome)

Michelangelo, like Leonardo, was a man of many talents; sculptor,
architect, painter and poet, he made the apotheosis of muscular
movement, which to him was the physical manifestation of
passion. He moulded his draughtsmanship, bent it, twisted it, and
stretched it to the extreme limits of possibility. There are not any
landscapes in Michelangelo's painting. All the emotions, all the
passions, all the thoughts of humanity were personified in his eyes
in the naked bodies of men and women. He rarely conceived his
human forms in attitudes of immobility or repose.

Michelangelo became a painter so that he could express in a
more malleable material what his titanesque soul felt, what his
sculptor's imagination saw, but what sculpture refused him.
Thus this admirable sculptor became the creator, at the Vatican,
of the most lyrical and epic decoration ever seen: the Sistine
Chapel. The profusion of his invention is spread over this vast
area of over 900 square metres. There are 343 principal figures
of prodigious variety of expression, many of colossal size, and in
addition a great number of subsidiary ones introduced for
decorative effect. The creator of this vast scheme was only thirty-
four when he began his work.

Michelangelo compels us to enlarge our conception of what is
beautiful. To the Greeks it was physical perfection; but
Michelangelo cared little for physical beauty, except in a few
instances, such as his painting of *Adam* on the Sistine ceiling,
and his sculptures of the Pietà. Though a master of anatomy and
of the laws of composition, he dared to disregard both if it were
necessary to express his concept: to exaggerate the muscles of his
figures, and even put them in positions the human body could
not naturally assume. In his later painting, *The Last Judgment* on
the end wall of the Sistine, he poured out his soul like a torrent.

Michelangelo was the first to make the human form express a
variety of emotions. In his hands emotion became an instrument
upon which he played, extracting themes and harmonies of
infinite variety. His figures carry our imagination far beyond the
personal meaning of the names attached to them.

190. Raphael (Raffaello Sanzio), 1483-1520, High Renaissance, Florentine
School, Italian, *The School of Athens,* 1509-10,
Fresco width at the base 770 cm, Stanza della Segnatura, Vatican

*Alleged pupil of Perugino, Raphael worked in Florence from 1504 to 1508,
until he was called to Rome by Julius II. The Pope encircled himself with artists
and wanted to raise Rome as the capital city of the Christian world: Bramante
constructed a basilica, Michelangelo was working on the ceiling of the Sistine
Chapel and Raphael worked on the decoration of the Vatican rooms until his
death in 1520.*

In The School of Athens, *Raphael used painted architecture to share out the
groups of characters in space and distribute the light. He used construction
motifs from the end the Roman Empire that also inspired Bramante in the
construction of St. Peter's Basilica. In the iconography, he included the idea of
the "Temple of Philosophy" launched by the Tuscan humanist, Marsile Ficin.
The light is depicted in a very realistic way, the colours are bright and the white
is dominant: in* The School of Athens, *this is the light that brings knowledge.
The composition is set around two central characters: Plato, holding the Time
in one hand and pointing to the sky with the other hand, and Aristotle, holding
the Ethic and a hand turned toward the earth. Raphael gives great importance
to the groups of characters, each group a pretext depicting expressive,
theatrical attitudes characteristic of Raphael's works.*

191

191. Lorenzo Lotto, 1480-1556, High Renaissance, Venetian School, Italian,
Portrait of a Youth Against a White Curtain, c. 1508,
Oil on panel, 42.3 x 35.5 cm, Kunsthistorisches Museum, Vienna

*One of Lotto's early paintings, it is still influenced by the artist's teacher,
Giovanni Bellini, especially in the use of light. Lotto painted this portrait with
a great realism, capturing the individual character of the sitter.*

Raphael (Raffaello Sanzio)
(1483 Urbino – 1520 Rome)

Raphael was the artist who most closely resembled Pheidias. The
Greeks said that the latter invented nothing; rather, he carried
every kind of art invented by his forerunners to such a pitch of
perfection that he achieved pure and perfect harmony. Those
words, "pure and perfect harmony," express, in fact, better than
any others what Raphael brought to Italian art. From Perugino,
he gathered all the weak grace and gentility of the Umbrian
School, he acquired strength and certainty in Florence, and he
created a style based on the fusion of Leonardo's and
Michelangelo's lessons under the light of his own noble spirit.

His compositions on the traditional theme of the Virgin
and Child seemed intensely novel to his contemporaries, and
only their time-honoured glory prevents us now from perceiving
their originality. He has an even more magnificent claim in the
composition and realisation of those frescos with which, from
1509, he adorned the Stanze and the Loggia at the Vatican. The
sublime, which Michelangelo attained by his ardour and
passion, Raphael attained by the sovereign balance of
intelligence and sensibility. One of his masterpieces, *The School
of Athens*, was created by genius: the multiple detail, the portrait
heads, the suppleness of gesture, the ease of composition, the
life circulating everywhere within the light are his most
admirable and identifiable traits.

Lorenzo Lotto
(1480 Venice – 1556 Loreto)

Lotto trained in the studio of Giovanni Bellini with Giorgione
and Titian. He worked in many cities apart from Venice, and
ended his life blind in a monastery. Known for his portraits, he
actually worked mainly as a religious painter. His work,
extremely erratic, shows a variety of influences from Italy as well
as northern Europe, but also an acute sense of observation and
freshness that is atypical of central Venetian tradition.

192. Lucas Cranach the Elder, 1472-1553, Northern Renaissance, German,
Venus and Cupid, 1509, Oil on canvas transferred from wood, 213 x 102 cm,
The State Hermitage Museum, St Petersburg

*This is the earliest depiction of Venus in northern Europe and Cranach's first
work on a theme taken from classical mythology.*

192

193

195

194

196

193. Hans Süss von Kulmbach, 1480-1522, Northern Renaissance, German,
The Calling of St. Peter, c. 1514-16,
Oil on panel, 130 x 100 cm, Galleria degli Uffizi, Florence.

194. Matthias Grünewald, c. 1475-1528, Northern Renaissance, German,
Isenheim Altarpiece, open: *Concert of Angels and Nativity,* 1515,
Oil on wood, 265 x 304 cm, Musée d'Unterlinden, Colmar

195. Raphael (Raffaello Sanzio), 1483-1520, High Renaissance,
Florentine School, Italian, *Sistine Madonna,* 1512-13,
Oil on canvas, 269 x 201 cm, Gemäldegalerie Alte Meister, Dresden

196. Matthias Grünewald, c. 1475-1528, Northern Renaissance, German,
Isenheim Altarpiece, closed: *Crucifixion,* 1515,
Oil on wood, 269 x 307 cm, Musée d'Unterlinden, Colmar

Matthias Grünewald
(c. 1475 Würzburg – 1528 Halle an der Saale)

Grünewald and Dürer were the most prominent artists of their era. Painter, draughtsman, hydraulic engineer and architect, he is considered the greatest colourist of the German Renaissance. But, unlike Dürer, he did not make prints and his works were not numerous: ten or so paintings (some of which are composed of several panels) and approximately thirty-five drawings. His masterpiece is the *Isenheim Altarpiece,* commissioned in 1515.

His works show a dedication to medieval principles, to which he brought expressions of emotion not typical of his contemporaries.

Realism is expressed in the mutilated body of Jesus, but the work is symbolic, thematically expressed in the words of John the Baptist displayed next to his figure, "He must increase; I must decrease." As in many Byzantine icons, the size of each person in the scene is relative to the person's importance, from Jesus down to the smallest, Mary Magdalene, who kneels at the base of the cross. The expressive hands of each subject point toward realism. However, the work might be the last of the famous medieval altarpieces to retain characteristic Gothic elements. In the foreground, the Agnus Dei pours its blood into the chalice of life-giving salvation.

The characters' dramatic expressions and the colours (black and red) arouse devotion; borrowings from Masaccio and Gossaert. Mary is shown as a co-redemptor: she seems as vivid as her son, and wears, like him, white robes. Saint Anthony, attacked by a monster and Saint Sebastian, pierced with arrows, stand on each side of the Crucifixion.

197

198

199

201

200

197. Joachim Patinir, c. 1480-1524, Northern Renaissance, Flemish,
The Baptism of Christ, c. 1515, Oil on oak, 59.7 x 76.3 cm,
Kunsthistorisches Museum, Vienna

Patinir is one of the greatest landscape painters. He sets the scene in this imaginary landscape. Two scenes are represented here: in the foreground, the baptism, and in the background, the Baptist preaches in a wood before a great congregation.

198. Titian (Vecellio Tiziano), 1490-1576, High Renaissance, Venetian School,
Italian, *Sacred and Profane Love,* c. 1514,
Oil on canvas, 118 x 279 cm, Galleria Borghese, Rome

Originally, this painting intended to depict earthly and heavenly loves. The title, giving a moralistic meaning to the figures, is the result of an eighteenth-century interpretation. The beauty and serenity coming out of this picture characterize the new researches of the painter at this time. The figure with the vase of jewels symbolises the ephemeral happiness on earth, whereas the one bearing the burning flame symbolises God's love and perpetual joy in paradise.

199. Quentin Massys, 1465-1530, Northern Renaissance, Flemish,
The Moneylender and His Wife, 1514,
Oil on panel, 71 x 68 cm, Musée du Louvre, Paris

The Moneylender and His Wife announces the development of genre painting in Flanders during the sixteenth century. The influence of van Eyck is noticeable in the representation of the painter himself in the convex mirror in the foreground.

200. Fra Bartolomeo, 1473-1517, High Renaissance, Florentine School, Italian,
Christ with the Four Evangelists, 1516,
Oil on panel, 282 x 204 cm, Palazzo Pitti, Florence

201. Raphael (Raffaello Sanzio), 1483-1520, High Renaissance, Florentine
School, Italian, *Madonna della Seggiola (Madonna of the Chair),* 1514-15,
Oil on panel, Tondo, dia. 71 cm, Palazzo Pitti, Florence

202. Bernhard Strigel, c. 1460-1528, Northern Renaissance, German,
Emperor Maximilian I with His Family, 1516,
Oil on panel, 72.8 x 60.4 cm, Kunsthistorisches Museum, Vienna

203. Andrea del Sarto, 1486-1530, High Renaissance, Florentine School,
Italian, *Portrait of a Young Man*, c. 1517,
Oil on linen, 72.4 x 57.2 cm, National Gallery, London

*One of the major artists of Florentine Classicism, del Sarto shows in his
portraits the first components of Mannerism.*

204. Titian (Vecellio Tiziano), 1490-1576, High Renaissance, Venetian School,
Italian, *Assumption of the Virgin*, 1516-18,
Oil on panel, 690 x 360 cm, Santa Maria Gloriosa dei Frari, Venice

*Classicism and naturalism are associated here, and emotions are depicted
with a dramatic intensity breaking with Venetian painting, revealing
Michelangelo's and Raphael's influence. The picture is composed of three
orders: the Apostles (embodiment of humankind), the Virgin (in the centre)
and above the Eternal Father.*

206

205. Andrea del Sarto, 1486-1530, High Renaissance, Florentine School, Italian, *Madonna of the Harpies,* 1517, Oil on panel, 208 x 178 cm, Galleria degli Uffizi, Florence

The work is oddly named, not for herself or her child, Jesus. Not even for St. Francis in his monkish robe on her right, or St. John the Evangelist, holding a book. Rather, it is named for the images of bird-like creatures representing demons shown on the pedestal on which the Virgin Mary stands, symbolising the her power and that of her son over evil: The Italian word for evil female demons appearing in the form of birds is harpie. As the most recent interpretation, this unusual presentation of Virgin is a depiction of the Book of Revelations. The Madonna of the Harpies bears witness to the elegant and solemn manner of artists of the early sixteenth century.

207. Bernaert van Orley, 1491/92-1542, Northern Renaissance, Flemish, *Joris van Zelle,* 1519, Oil on oak, 39 x 32 cm, Musées Royaux des Beaux-Arts, Brussels

206. Raphael (Raffaello Sanzio), 1483-1520, High Renaissance, Florentine School, Italian, *Portrait of Pope Leo X with Cardinals Guilio de 'Medici and Luigi de' Rossi,* 1518-19, Oil on panel, 155.2 x 118.6 cm, Galleria degli Uffizi, Florence

Leo X was elected Pope after Julius II and gathered around him many of Rome's leading writers, philosophers and artists. This portrait displays the painter's virtuosity in the rendering of texture in harmonious nuances of colour.

207

Andrea del Sarto
(1486 – 1530 Florence)

The epithet 'del sarto' (of the tailor) is derived from his father's profession. Apart from a visit to Fontainebleau in 1518-19 to work for Francis I, Andrea was based in Florence all his life. A pioneer of Mannerism and a leading fresco painter of the High Renaissance, Andrea selected subjects that were nearly always covered in bright solidly coloured robes without adornment. Major works include the John the Baptist series at the Chiostro dello Scalzo (1511-26) and his *Madonna of the Harpies* (1517). Andrea suffered from being the contemporary of such giants as Michelangelo and Raphael, but he undoubtedly ranks as one of the greatest masters of his time.

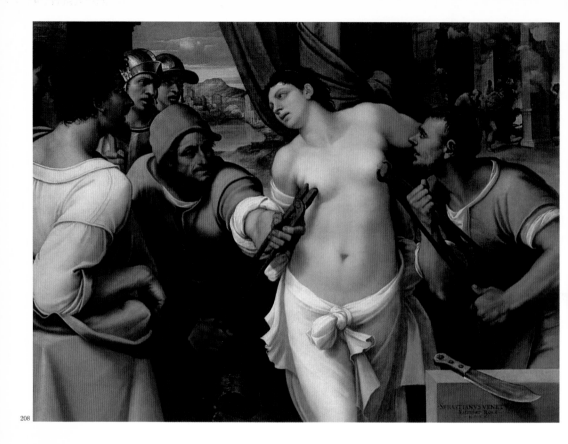

208

209

208. Sebastiano del Piombo, 1485-1547, High Renaissance, Venetian School, Italian, *The Martyrdom of St. Agatha,* 1520, Oil on panel, 127 x 178 cm, Palazzo Pitti, Florence

Michelangelo had a great influence on Sabastiano del Piombo's muscular figures and the masculine shape of his female character.

209. Niklaus Deutsch, 1484-1530, Northern Renaissance, German, *Pyramus and Thisbe,* c. 1520, Tempera on canvas, 152 x 161 cm, Kunstmuseum, Basle

Deutsch's paintings are related to the ones of Baldung Grien and Grünewald. This painting is among his later ones.

210. Correggio (Antonio Allegri), 1489-1534, High Renaissance, Parma School, Italian, *Vision of St John the Evangelist on Patmos,* 1520, Fresco, San Giovanni Evangelista, Parma

Contemporary with Raphael and Titian, Correggio was essentially influenced by Mantegna in his murals. He refused to submit this composition to pre-existing architectural norms and created his own extraordinary, illusionist architecture. The general composition is conceived around a fitting of concentric circles, creating dynamism. Correggio refers to Michelangelo in the representation of the nude and its muscle structure but the outline remains more blurred and integrates variations of light and shadow inspired by Leonardo. The innovative use of coloured shadows is especially notable.

211

212

Correggio (Antonio Allegri)
(c. 1489 – 1534 Correggio)

Correggio founded the Renaissance school in Parma, but little is known of his life. He was born in the little town of Correggio near Parma. There he was educated, but in his seventeenth year an outbreak of the plague drove his family to Mantova, where the young painter had an opportunity of studying the pictures of Mantegna and the collection of works of art accumulated originally by the Gonzaga family and later by Isabella d'Este. In 1514 he went back to Parma, where his talents found ample recognition; and for some years the story of his life is the record of his work, culminating in his wonderful re-creation of light and shade.

It was not, however, a record of undisturbed quiet, for the decoration which he made for the dome of the cathedral was severely criticised. Choosing the subject of the Resurrection, he projected upon the ceiling a great number of ascending figures, which, viewed from below, necessarily involved a multitude of legs, giving rise to the apt description that the painting resembled a "fry of frogs". It may have been the trouble which later ensued with the chapter of the cathedral, or depression caused by the death of his young wife, but at the age of thirty-six, indifferent to fame and fortune, he retired to the comparative obscurity of his birth place, where for four years he devoted himself to the painting of mythological subjects: scenes of fabled beings removed from the real world and set in a golden arcadia of dreams. His work prefigures mannerism and baroque style.

3

214

215

1. **Palma Vecchio,** 1480-1528, High Renaissance, Venetian School, Italian, *The Holy Family with Mary Magdalene and the Infant Saint John,* c. 1520, Oil on wood, 87 x 117 cm, Galleria degli Uffizi, Florence

2. **Correggio (Antonio Allegri),** 1489-1534, High Renaissance, Parma School, Italian, *Rest on the Flight to Egypt with Saint Francis,* c. 1517, Oil on canvas, 123.5 x 106.5 cm, Galleria degli Uffizi, Florence

3. **Hans Baldung Grien,** c. 1484-1545, Northern Renaissance, German, *Nativity,* 1520, Oil on panel, 105.5 x 70.4 cm, Alte Pinakothek, Munich

Hans Baldung signed with his monogram 'G' which stands for 'Grien', his nickname. He was probably dubbed with this name because of his liking for the colour green.

4. **Titian (Vecellio Tiziano),** 1490-1576, High Renaissance, Venetian School, Italian, *Man with a Glove,* c. 1525, Oil on canvas, 100 x 89 cm, Musée du Louvre, Paris

Titian invented a kind of expressive and natural portrait on a dark background that inspired pre-romantic painters from the end of the eighteenth century.

5. **Giovanni Francesco Caroto,** 1480-1555, High Renaissance, Veronese School, Italian, *Red-Headed Youth Holding a Drawing,* Oil on canvas, 37 x 29 cm, Museo di Castelvecchio, Verona

216

216. Parmigianino (Girolamo Francesco Mazzola), 1503-1540, Mannerism, Parma School, Italian, *Self-portrait in a Convex Mirror,* c. 1523-24, Oil on wood, Tondo, dia. 24.4 cm, Kunsthistorisches Museum, Vienna

Vasari celebrated in Vite de' più eccellenti architetti, pittori, et scultori Italiani Parmigianino's unusual special-effects, "Inquiring one day into the subtleties of art, he began to draw himself as he appeared in a barber's convex glass. He had a ball of wood made at a turner's and divided it in half, and on this he set himself to paint all that he saw in the glass, and because the mirror enlarged everything that was near and diminished what was distant, he painted the hand a little large."

217. Hans Holbein the Younger, 1497-1543, Northern Renaissance, German, *Portrait of Erasmus of Rotterdam Writing,* c. 1523, Oil on wood, 36.8 x 30.5 cm, Kunstmuseum, Öffentliche Kunstsammlung, Basle

Three portraits of Erasmus by Holbein are known. The painter encountered the humanist in Basle. When Holbein went to London, he was received there by a friend of Erasmus, Thomas Moore, who would later write about the painter, "Such a man, according to Erasmus, that since centuries, the sun has never seen more loyal and frank, more devoted and wiser."

218. Rosso Fiorentino, 1494-1540, Mannerism, Florentine School, Italian, *Moses Defending the Daughters of Jethro,* 1523, Oil on canvas, 160 x 117 cm, Galleria degli Uffizi, Florence

This is the most abstract of Rosso's compositions. The artist was inspired by Michelangelo's Battle of Cascina, which remained in the state of a cartoon.

219. Jacopo Pontormo, 1494-1557, Mannerism, Florentine School, Italian, *Deposition,* 1525-28, Oil on panel, 313 x 192 cm, Cappella Capponi, Santa Felicità, Florence

217

218

219

222

223

220. **Correggio (Antonio Allegri)**, 1489-1534, High Renaissance, Parma School,
    Italian, *Assumption of the Virgin*, 1526-30,
    Fresco, 1093 x 1195 cm, Duomo, Parma

    The artist received the order to paint frescos for Parma's cathedral in 1520.
    The domes indicate the artist's skills in depicting anatomy and perspective.

221. **Jan Gossaert (Mabuse)**, 1478-1532, Northern Renaissance, Flemish,
    Danaë, 1527, Oil on panel, 114.2 x 95.4 cm, Alte Pinakothek, Munich

    Danaë is one of Gossaert's later works and testifies to the artist's meticulous
    manner at the end of his career.

222. **Albrecht Altdorfer**, 1480-1538, Northern Renaissance, German,
    Suzanna in the Bath, 1526, Oil on panel, 74.8 x 61.2 cm,
    Alte Pinakothek, Munich

223. **Alejo Fernández**, 1475-1545, High Renaissance, Spanish,
    The Virgin of the Navigators, 1530-40, Oil on panel, Alcázar, Seville

224

226

227

224. Albrecht Dürer, 1471-1528, Northern Renaissance, German, *The Four Holy Men*, 1526, Oil on lindenwood panels, 215 x 76 cm, Alte Pinakothek, Munich

The artist gave this masterpiece, painted during the last years of his life, to his hometown of Nuremberg. In the work we see less of how the artist imagines four of the apostles might have looked, than we see which character traits in each subject the artist wanted to present. Saints John and Peter are depicted on the left and Mark with Paul on the right. Peter holds a large key, as a reminder that Jesus gave him the "keys of the kingdom". Peter and his proverbial keys are seen also in El Greco's The Burial of Count Orgaz (1586). The evangelist John seems to be pointing out something from scripture to the first head of the Church, as if books existed in that format in the times of these first century men. Paul holds a formidable volume, possibly one of his many epistles, in contrast to the little scroll held by Mark, the writer of the shortest gospel. Each pair seems to be caught in an informal moment. The use of colours is judicious here; the contrasts between complementary colours (red, green, blue, yellow) enhance the plasticity of the characters.

225. Sebastiano del Piombo, 1485-1547, High Renaissance, Venetian School, Italian, *Portrait of Pope Clement VII,* 1526, Oil on panel, Kunsthistorisches Museum, Vienna

In 1531, Pope Clement VII gave Sebastiano the position of "Piombo" (Italian for lead), keeping the papal seals that were made of lead.

226. Hans Baldung Grien, c. 1484-1545, Northern Renaissance, German, *Virgin and Child with Parrots,* c. 1527, Oil on panel, 91 x 63.2 cm, Germanisches Nationalmuseum, Nuremberg

227. Hans Holbein the Younger, 1497-1543, Northern Renaissance, German, *Portrait of Nikolaus Kratzer, Astronomer,* 1528, Tempera on oak, 83 x 67 cm, Musée du Louvre, Paris

228

231. Albrecht Altdorfer, 1480-1538, Northern Renaissance, German,
The Battle at the Issus (Alexander's Victory), 1529,
Oil on panel, 158.4 x 120.3 cm, Alte Pinakothek, Munich

Even though the majority of his works are based on religious themes, Altdorfer was one of the first artists of his time to paint landscapes as an independent genre. The Battle at the Issus is an incredible example of the use of colour in the artist's work. The landscape seen from above recalls the works of Patinir and the mountains' shapes those of Leonardo.

228. Hans Holbein the Younger, 1497-1543, Northern Renaissance, German,
Darmstadt Madonna, c. 1528, Oil on lindenwood, 146 x 102 cm,
Grossherzogliches Schloss, Damstad

229. Lucas van Leyden, 1494-1533, Northern Renaissance, Dutch,
The Engagement, 1527, Oil on panel, 30 x 32 cm,
Koninklijk Museum voor Schone Kunsten, Antwerp

230. Lorenzo Lotto, 1480-1556, High Renaissance, Venetian School, Italian,
Lucretia, 1530-32, Oil on canvas, 96.5 x 110.6 cm, National Gallery, London

The portrait proclaims the virtues of the character with the Latin inscription on the paper on the table, taken from the Roman historian, Livy: "After Lucretia's example, let no violated woman live."

229

232

234

233

232. Parmigianino (Girolamo Francesco Mazzola), 1503-1540, Mannerism, Parma School, Italian, *Turkish Slave,* 1530-31, Oil on wood, 67 x 53 cm, Galleria Nazionale, Parma

233. Jean Clouet, c. 1485-1541, Mannerism, French, *Francis I, King of France,* c. 1530, Oil on panel, 96 x 74 cm, Musée du Louvre, Paris

This portrait attributed to Jean Clouet reveals the influence of the School of Fontainebleau and of the realism of the Flemish school. The painter paid particular attention to the depiction of the costume and golden chain of the sitter, sumptuously dressed in Italian fashion.

234. Agnolo Bronzino, 1503-1572, Mannerism, Florentine School, Italian, *Portrait of a Young Man,* c. 1530, Oil on wood, 95.6 x 74.9 cm, The Metropolitan Museum of Art, New York

Bronzino was engaged in court portraiture. He introduces here witty motifs such as the grotesque head on the table, appreciated in literary circles.

235

236

235. Jan van Scorel, 1495-1562, Northern Renaissance, Dutch,
Mary Magdalene, c. 1530, Oil on panel, 67 x 76.5 cm,
Rijksmuseum, Amsterdam

*Influenced by Raphael and his travel to Italy, van Scorel makes his
composition dynamic by depicting the sitter slightly to the right of the middle
axis, her shoulder turned in the opposite direction to her head.*

236. Maerten Jacobsz van Heemskerck, 1498-1574,
Northern Renaissance, Dutch, *Family Portrait,* 1532,
Oil on panel, 118 x 140 cm, Staatliche Museen, Kassel

*This painting well represents the combination of Early Netherlandish painting
and Italian painting: the composition and plasticity given to the characters
derives from the Italian experience, whereas the abundance of details in the
foreground characterizes Netherlandish painting.*

237

238

237. Correggio (Antonio Allegri), c. 1490-1534,
High Renaissance, Parma School, Italian, *Jupiter and Io,* 1531,
Oil on canvas, 163.5 x 70 cm, Kuntshistorisches Museum, Vienna

*This is one of four works inspired by Ovid's Metamorphoses. These works
were commissioned by Ludovico de Gonzaga who wished to offer them to
Charles V for his consecration, but finally kept them for his studiolo. The
choice of the theme is rather a pretext to the representation of nudity. The
sensuality and voluptuous bodies, characterising Correggio's style, are pushed
to their extreme. At the same time, Titian was painting Venus of Urbino.
Therefore, the mythological painting evolves toward a more erotic and
monumental representation of the human form.*

238. Correggio (Antonio Allegri), c. 1489-1534, High Renaissance, Parma
School, Italian, *Abduction of Ganymede,* 1531,
Oil on canvas, 163 x 71 cm, Kunsthistorisches Museum, Vienna

239

Hans Holbein the Younger, 1497-1543,
Northern Renaissance, German, *The Ambassadors*
(Jean de Dinteville and Georges de Selve), 1533,
Oil on oak, 207 x 209.5 cm, National Gallery, London

*The perspective in The Ambassadors presents three different
viewpoints, passing virtually seamlessly from a distant point of
view to close-up and diagonal views. The pictorial reality
alone makes it possible for these mutually exclusive
perspectives to co-exist. The overall effect of the picture is
dominated by the imposing life-sized appearance of the two
men, whose posture and gaze confront the viewer en face.
The rich details of the still-life elements and the crucifix above
Jean de Dinteville in the upper left-hand corner need to be
viewed close up. The anamorphosis, on the other hand,
straightens out when the viewer relinquishes a head-on
position and stands next to the picture at an angle, to the right
of Georges de Selve as it were, his head at the level of the
crucifix. Thus, the viewer becomes, in a manner of speaking,
the third protagonist. The vantage point from which the
viewer regards the skull is in the extension of a diagonal axis
generated by the anamorphosis, to the right of the picture.*

Hans Holbein the Younger
(1497 Augsburg – 1543 London)

The genius of Holbein blossomed early. His native city of Augsburg was then at the
zenith of its greatness; on the highroad between Italy and the north, it was the richest
commercial city in Germany, and the frequent halting-place of the Emperor Maximilian.
His father, Hans Holbein the Elder, was himself a painter of merit, and took his son into
his studio. In 1515, when he was eighteen years old, he moved to Basle, the centre of
learning, whose boast was that every house in it contained at least one learned man. He
set out for London with a letter of introduction to Sir Thomas Moore, the King's
Chancellor, "Master Haunce," as the English called him, arriving towards the close of
1526. Here Holbein was welcomed, and made his home during this first visit to England.
He painted portraits of many of the leading men of the day, and executed drawings for a
picture of the family of his patron. He soon became a renowned Northern Renaissance
portrait painter of major contemporary figures. His work typically includes amazing
details showing natural reflections through glass or the intricate weave of elegant tapestry.

By 1537 Holbein had come to the notice of Henry VIII, and was established as court
painter, a position he held until his death.

240

Paris Bordone
(1500 Treviso – 1571 Venice)

Bordone was born in Treviso but he settled in Venice where he soon became Titian's pupil and was strongly influenced not only by him, but also by Giorgione.

His work was appreciated by the elite all across Europe thanks to his beautiful depictions of women, his giorgionesque pastoral scenes and mythologies, and the monumental architectural settings in which he excelled. Although his art is now eclipsed by that of other Venetian painters like Titian, Veronese or Tintoretto, Bordone was considered during his lifetime as an accomplished artist.

240. Paris Bordone, 1500-1571, High Renaissance, Venetian School, Italian, *The Fisherman Presenting the Ring to the Doge Gradenigo*, 1534, Oil on canvas, 370 x 300 cm, Galleria dell'Accademia, Venice

241. Giulio Romano, c. 1499-1546, Mannerism, *The Fall of the Giants* (detail), 1526-34, Fresco, Palazzo del Tè, Mantova

Romano's frescos in the Palazzo del Te testify to his classical learning and, later, had a great impact on Mannerist painters.

242. Michelangelo Buonarroti, 1475-1564, High Renaissance, Florence, Italian, *The Last Judgment*, 1536-41, Fresco, 12.2 x 13.7 m, Musei Vaticani Capella Sistina, Vatican

241

Started before the death of Clement VII, The Last Judgment *took until 1541 to complete, all of eight years.*

Overall, The Last Judgment *consists of twelve major groups. In the two uppermost lunettes, angels on one side are carrying a column, while others bring along a crucifix from the other end. Circled in angels and prophets to bear witness further down, Christ presides. Next, comes the group of the Elect. Still further down, we see the Elect rising toward heaven, with a group of angels blowing trumpets in the middle as the Damned on the right are being offloaded into hell. At the very bottom, the waking dead rise from their tombs while Charon's ark stands right of centre.*

Religious inspiration seems most wanting in the depiction of the wingless angels holding the instruments of Passion. Like some of Correggio's works, Michelangelo resorted to mass-scale foreshortenings: the figures are arranged with no rendering of depth, using ready-made, over-confident foreshortenings that make them look like two-dimensional cut-outs, cloned one after the other with no attempt at individualisation.

Towering in anger from above the clouds with his right arm raised as if to throw a curse, Christ looks thoroughly agitated, very far removed from the grandeur and majesty that Michelangelo awarded his Jehovah for the ceiling frescos. Next to Christ, the Virgin backs down by turning her head away. Around them, the Just and the Elect are troubled and worried for fear that this divine, merciless anger will strike them down too. St. Peter also appears insecure as he enters the scene, with an anxious, hesitant look on his face as he produces the keys, these now suddenly useless symbols of his authority. Slinging a frame from his shoulder, a terrified St. Lawrence looks furtively at Christ. Flayed skin in hand, the brilliantly executed St. Bartholomew holds up the skinning knife to Christ's view. Throughout the work, there is only anguish and terror, not a whit of serenity.

Once dear to Michelangelo, the realism that replaced lofty spiritual doctrine in The Last Judgment *transpires principally in the lower left scene depicting the resurrection of the dead. Looking strong and healthy except for a few skeletons, the dead rise up with more or less difficulty; some arch their backs to throw off the soil, others cross the divide one step at a time, still others throw their hands behind them for leverage to stand up.*

The most poignant and famous episode is that of Charon's ark, best approached through the enigmatic little scene in the lower middle. There we see a cavern befitting Cyclops, packed with demons watching for the Damned as their beastly appearances aggravate the horrors of hell, a theme ill-suited to painting.

To the right, the River Styx unfurls its rolling muddy waters as an overcrowded skiff ferries the Damned to their fate on the other bank. Upright at one end of the teetering vessel, Charon, with horned forehead and claw-tipped feet whom Dante describes as "the fiery-eyed demon whose oars strike the hesitant", raises his oar to press the grim masses onward.

243

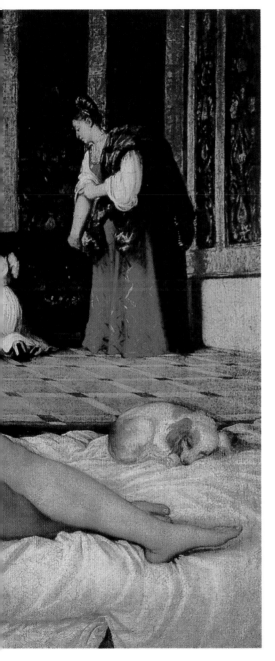

244

243. Titian (Vecellio Tiziano), 1490-1576,
High Renaissance, Venetian School, Italian, *Venus of Urbino*, 1538,
Oil on canvas, 119 x 165 cm, Galleria degli Uffizi, Florence

244. Parmigianino (Girolamo Francesco Mazzola), 1503-1540, Mannerism,
Parma School, Italian, *Madonna with Long Neck*, c. 1535,
Oil on wood, 216 x 132 cm, Galleria degli Uffizi, Florence

*A somewhat mysterious image of the Madonna and her son was created by the
Mannerist artist Parmigianino. This work features the large, centrally-located
figure of the Virgin. Her elongated, seated body holds the nude child Jesus on
her lap. A group of angels keeps her company, while the viewer is offered a
glimpse of a freestanding column surrounded by a considerable depth of open
space. A disproportionately small male figure is next to the column. The
Madonna has the look of an aristocratic lady of nobility or a queen, her
divinity overshadowed by her humanity.*

245

247

246

Francesco Primaticcio
(1504 Bologna – 1570 Paris)

Primaticcio's master was Guilio Romano, the most famous heir of Raphael. He started working with him in 1526 in Mantova then in 1532 was sent by his master to the court of France in the castle of Fontainebleau to work for Francis I. There he met another Italian painter, Rosso Fiorentino, who had arrived in 1530. The two Italians are known as the painters who brought High Renaissance art to France and their work is known as the Ecole de Fontainebleau. When Rosso died in 1540, Primaticcio became the master of the numerous artists working on the decoration of the castle.

Painter of the King, he was also an architect and a sculptor. He organised his workshop like those of his old masters Romano and Raphael, drawing and conceiving but leaving the work to his talented assistants. His most famous works in the castle are the gallery of Francis I and the ceiling of the ballroom.

Virtuoso and ambitious artist, Primaticcio developed a scholastic art mixed with sensual delight and epic heroism. He directed a world of gods and heroes. His gracious and seducing formulae, that were creative and poetic without precedent, created a primatician style that spread throughout Europe.

248

249

245. Hans Holbein the Younger, 1497-1543, Northern Renaissance, German,
Portrait of Anne of Cleves, Queen of England, 1539, Tempera on paper
mounted on canvas, 65 x 48 cm, Musée du Louvre, Paris

246. Francesco Primaticcio, 1504-1570, Mannerism, School of Fontainebleau,
Italian, *The Holy Family with St. Elisabeth and St. John the Baptist,* 1541-43,
Oil on slate, 43.5 x 31 cm, The State Hermitage Museum, St Petersburg

247. Hans Holbein the Younger, 1497-1543,
Northern Renaissance, German, *Portrait of Henry VIII,* c. 1539,
Tempera on panel, 89 x 75 cm, Galleria Nazionale d'Arte Antica, Rome

248. Jacopo Bassano, c. 1510-1592, High Renaissance, Venetian School, Italian,
The Adoration of the Shepherds, 1544-45,
Oil on canvas, 140 x 219 cm, National Gallery of Scotland, Edinburgh

*Son of Francesco Bassano the Elder, Jacopo adopted some of his father's style
as he created religious paintings.*

249. Marinus Claesz van Reymerswaele, 1493-1567, Northern Renaissance,
Flemish, *Money-Changer and his Wife,* 1539,
Oil on panel, 83 x 97 cm, Museo Nacional del Prado, Madrid

This painting is closely related to Quentin Massys' picture of the same subject.

250

Agnolo Bronzino
(Agnolo di Cosimo)
(1503 – 1572 Florence)

Florentine Mannerist painter Bronzino, (originally Agnolo di Cosimo), whose nickname may be derived from his dark complexion, was the pupil and adopted son of Pontormo. If he kept his master's manners for maniacal insistence on accurate drawing, he added a very personal use of colour, applied in a clear and compact fashion giving the aspect of varnish.

He excelled as a portraitist in the court of Duke Cosimo I de Medici, where he was a court painter for most of his career, but was less successful as a religious painter. Actually, he painted the type of religious work that gave a bad reputation to Mannerism. However, he was skilled in the nude as in *Allegory with Venus and Cupid*. His work influenced the evolution of European court portraiture for a century thanks to his cold and unemotional representation that conveyed an almost insolent assurance.

250. **Agnolo Bronzino,** 1503-1572, Mannerism, Florentine School, Italian,
An Allegory with Venus and Cupid, 1540-50,
Oil on wood, 146.5 x 116.8 cm, National Gallery, London

This picture was sent to the King of France in 1568, its erotic and erudite character suiting the taste of the ruler. This painting shows eroticism under the pretext of a moralising allegory.

251. **Michelangelo Buonarroti,** 1475-1564, High Renaissance, Florence, Italian,
Martyrdom of St. Peter, 1546-50, Fresco, 625 x 662 cm,
Cappella Paolina, Palazzi Pontifici, Vatican

252. **Michelangelo Buonarroti,** 1475-1564, High Renaissance, Florence, Italian,
Conversion of St. Paul, 1542-45, Fresco, 625 x 661 cm,
Cappella Paolina, Palazzi Pontifici, Vatican

253. **Agnolo Bronzino,** 1503-1572, Mannerism, Florentine School, Italian,
Portrait of Eleonora da Toledo with her Son Giovanni de' Medici, 1545,
Oil on panel, 115 x 96 cm, Galleria degli Uffizi, Florence

251

254

255

Lucas Cranach the Elder
(1472 Kronach – 1553 Weimar)

Lucas Cranach was one of the greatest artists of the Renaissance, as shown by the diversity of his artistic interests as well as his awareness of the social and political events of his time. He developed a number of painting techniques which were afterwards used by several generations of artists. His somewhat mannered style and splendid palette are easily recognised in numerous portraits of monarchs, cardinals, courtiers and their ladies, religious reformers, humanists and philosophers. He also painted altarpieces, mythological scenes and allegories, and he is well-known for his hunting scenes. As a gifted draughtsman, he executed numerous engravings on both religious and secular subjects, and as court painter, he was involved in tournaments and masked balls. As a result, he completed a great number of costume designs, armorials, furniture, and parade-ground arms. The high point of the German Renaissance is reflected in his achievements.

254. **Lucas Cranach the Elder,** 1472-1553, Northern Renaissance, German,
Fountain of Youth, 1546, Oil on lime panel, 122.5 x 186.5 cm,
Staatliche Museen, Berlin

The fountain, crowned by a statue of Venus and Cupid, is a sort of "font of love" accessible only to women. It is not enough to say that its waters restore lost youth – they affect a resurrection because the magical bath transforms old women whose vital energy is already exhausted. Venus's spring is the boundary between death and life. The women step onto the bank of life, as if into the next world, as happy captives of the goddess of love. This really is another world: the garden of love on the right bank and the ugly conglomeration of rocks on the left form a contrast as sharp as that between youth and old age.

55. **Titian (Vecellio Tiziano),** 1490-1576, High Renaissance, Venetian School,
Italian, *Pope Paul III and his Cousins Alessandro and Ottavio Farnese,*
c. 1546, Oil on canvas, 200 x 127, Museo Nazionale di Capodimonte, Naples

This triple portrait catches the nature of the sitters. The free movements of the characters and the restrained and emaciated face of Paul III contribute to the extraordinary qualities of this group.

256

257. Tintoretto (Jacopo Robusti), 1518-1594, Mannerism, Venetian School, Italian, *The Bathing Susanna*, 1560-62, Oil on canvas, 146.6 x 193.6 cm, Kunsthistorisches Museum, Vienna

Tintoretto managed to preserve the colours and light from Venetian tradition and even stated that he aspired to combine the colours of Titian and the drawing of Michelangelo. The painting describes the scene of the Old Testament of how Susanna is surprised at the bath by two intruders.

257

256. Pieter Brueghel the Elder, c. 1525-1569, Northern Renaissance, Flemish, *Netherlandish Proverbs,* 1559, Oil on oak panel, 117 x 163 cm, Stiftung Staatliche Museen, Gemäldegalerie, Berlin

258. Titian (Vecellio Tiziano), 1490-1576, High Renaissance, Venetian School, Italian, *Emperor Charles V at Mühlberg,* 1548, Oil on canvas, 332 x 279 cm, Museo Nacional del Prado, Madrid

Talented portraitist Titian became the accredited painter of Charles V, wh considered him the most prestigious portrait painter of the time. He later ha a great influence on Rubens in this field. The originality of this painting is i the scenery. Charles V is represented entirely and in action, in a triumphar and noble attitude, celebrating the victory of Charles V over the Protestan in 1547. Titian makes out of this subject a realist portrait, depicting th wilted face of the king in his old age.

259. Cecchino del Salviati (Francesco de' Rossi), 1510-1563, Mannerism, Florentine School, Italian, *Charity,* c. 1556, Oil on panel, 156 x 122 cm, Galleria degli Uffizi, Florence

260. Master of the Fontainebleau School, 1525-1575, Second School of Fontainebleau, French, *Diana Huntress,* c. 1555, Oil on canvas, 191 x 132 cm Musée du Louvre, Paris

The proportions of the sitter recall the Mannerism of the First School Fontainebleau founded by Rosso Fiorentino and Primaticcio. However, th landscape in the background characterizes the manner of the Second School Fontainebleau, announcing the French landscape painting of the seventeen century. This anonymous work is nonetheless very characteristic of the Secor School of Fontainebleau referring to both Flemish and Italian art.

154

259

260

Titian (Vecellio Tiziano)
(1490 Pieve di Cadore – 1576 Venice)

Titian was at once a genius and a favourite of fortune; he moved
through his long life of pomp and splendour serene and self-
contained. The details of his early life are not certain. He was of
an old family, born at Pieve in the mountain district of Cadore.
By the time that he was eleven years old he was sent to Venice,
where he became the pupil, first of Gentile Bellini, and later of
Gentile's brother, Giovanni. Then he worked with the great
artist Giorgione. He worked on major frescos in Venice and
Padua, as well as commissions in France for Francis I (1494-
1547), in Spain for Charles V (1500-58). His equestrian portrait
of Charles V (1549) symbolises a military victory over Protestant
princes in 1547. Titian then went to Rome for commissions by
Pope Paul III (1534-49), then in Spain to work exclusively for
Philip II (1527-98).

No artist's life was so completely and consistently superb; and
such, too, is the character of his work. He was great in portraiture,
in landscape, in the painting of religious and mythological subjects.
In any one of these departments others have rivalled him, but his
glory is that he attained an eminence in all; he was an artist of
universal gifts – an all-embracing genius; equable, serene, majestic.
Titian's beautiful reclining women, whether called Venus or any
other name, are among the most original of the creations of the
Venetian school and particularly of its great masters, to which he
and Giorgione belonged. His works differ greatly from the
Florentine nude, which is generally standing, resembling
sometimes, in the fine precision of its contours, the precious work
of a goldsmith and sometimes the great marble of a sculptor.

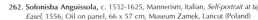

261

262

261. **Jacopo Bassano**, c. 1510-1592, Mannerism, Venetian School, Italian, *The Crucifixion*, 1562, Oil on panel, 315 x 177 cm, Museo Civico, Treviso

262. **Sofonisba Anguissola,** c. 1532-1625, Mannerism, Italian, *Self-portrait at the Easel*, 1556, Oil on panel, 66 x 57 cm, Museum Zamek, Lancut (Poland)

Anguissola (also spelt Anguisciola), inspired by the legend of St Luke as an depicted herself standing in front of her easel and painting the Madonna Child. Her round face is turned towards the invisible Mary and the viewer. painting on her easel (some art historians assume that the painting within painting actually existed) shows a seated Madonna leaning towards her ch who is standing next to her. The Virgin is tenderly kissing her beloved S Anguissola was using the popular theme of the kissing Madonna to convey message of the supreme and profound love that the Mother of the Church has her child and, by inference, for all her human children.

263. **Pieter Aertsen,** 1508-1575, Northern Renaissance, Dutch, *Peasants by the Hearth*, 1556, Oil on panel, 142.3 x 198 cm, Museum Mayer van den Bergh, Antwerp

Just as Brueghel, Aertsen is interested in a national and rustic realism.

263

Veronese (Caliari Paolo), 1528-1588, Mannerism, Venetian School, Italian, *The Wedding Feast at Cana,* c. 1562-63, Oil on canvas, 677 x 994 cm, Musée du Louvre, Paris

Born in Verona, a city open to the development of Mannerism, Veronese remains nevertheless independent in style. In contrast to Titian and his dramatic and realist paintings, Veronese's works represent the joyful contemplation of beauty. Influenced by Mantegna, he also takes his inspiration in the hue of colours from the Gothic period. His sejourn in Mantova led him to discover Michelangelo and Raphael and he also met Correggio. Wedding Feast at Cana – commissioned as part of the reconstruction of the Benedictine convent of San Giorgio Maggiore in Venice – decorated the refectory. At the time Veronese had already set his reputation in the city as he had already depicted the decorations of the church San Sebastiano and of the Doge Palace. The scene represents the first miracle of Christ but transposed here within a Venetian feast. Dramatised by the architecture, Veronese takes his inspiration in Palladio's contemporary constructions for the architecture and multiplies the vanishing points. The columns show the three architectural orders: Doric, Corinthian and Composite. The painter uses precious pigments, imported from the East. The richness of the colours is an important point in Venetian painting. This work, restored between 1990 and 1992 has found once again its original colours.

VERONESE (PAOLO CALIARI)
(1528 VERONA – 1588 VENICE)

Paolo Veronese was one of the great masters of the late Renaissance in Venice with Titian and Tintoretto, the three of them seen as a triumvirate. Originally named Paolo Caliari, he was called Veronese from his native city of Verona. He is known for his works of supreme colouring and for his illusionistic decorations in both fresco and oil. His large paintings of biblical feasts executed for the refectories of monasteries in Venice and Verona are especially celebrated (like *The Marriage of Cana*). He also painted many portraits, altarpieces and historical and mythological paintings. He headed a family workshop that remained active after his death. Although highly successful, he had little immediate influence. To the Flemish baroque master Peter Paul Rubens and to the eighteenth-century Venetian painters, especially Giovanni Battista Tiepolo, however, Veronese's handling of colour and perspective supplied an indispensable point of departure.

The quality of his paintings is of sober restraint. Veronese is simply what he was – a painter. The purpose of his pictures is immediately self-evident. Some people will say that this self-evidence is the proper scope of painting; that "art for art's sake" should be the sole object of the painter; that the representation of anything else but what is apparent to the eye is going outside the province of the art; and that the preference which so many people have for a picture which makes an appeal not only to the eye, but to the intellect or the poetic and dramatic sense, is a proof of vulgar taste which confuses painting with illustration. The best answer to this is that not solely laymen, but artists also in all periods – artists of such personality that they cannot be ignored – have tried to reinforce the grandeur of mere appearances with something that shall appeal to the mind and soul of men.

265

266

267

58

269

65. Jacopo Robusti Tintoretto, 1518-1594, Mannerism, Venetian School, Italian, Flemish, *The Miracle of St Mark Freeing the Slave*, c. 1565, Oil on canvas, 415 x 541 cm, Galleria dell'Accademia, Venice

66. Pieter Brueghel the Elder, c. 1525-1569, Northern Renaissance, Flemish, *The Tower of Babel*, 1563, Oil on oak panel, 114 x 155 cm, Kunsthistorisches Museum, Vienna

67. Pieter Brueghel the Elder, c. 1525-1569, Northern Renaissance, Flemish, *The Hunters in the Snow*, 1565, Oil on panel, 117 x 162 cm, Kunsthistorisches Museum, Vienna

68. Joachim Beuckelaer, c. 1530-1573, Mannerism, Flemish, *At the Market*, 1564, Oil on panel, 128 x 166 cm, Pushkin Museum, Moscow

69. Veronese (Paolo Caliari), 1528-1588, Mannerism, Venetian School, Italian, *The Mystical Marriage of Saint Catherine of Alexandria*, 1562, Oil on canvas, 130.5 x 130 cm, Musée Fabre, Montpellier

This painting well illustrates Venetian painting. Here, Veronese works as well on the colours as on the quality of drawing.

Jacopo Robusti Tintoretto
(1518 – 1594 Venice)

His father being a dyer of silk (tintore), Tintoretto was given this nickname in his youth, "The Little Dyer", "Il Tintoretto".
Tintoretto became the most important Italian Mannerist painter of the Venetian school. St. Mark, the patron saint of Venice, is thematic in two of his most important works. Most of his major works were on religious themes.

About his career, a story tells us that the Brothers of the Confraternity of San Rocco gave Tintoretto a commission for two pictures in their church, and then invited him to enter a competition with Veronese and others for the decoration of the ceiling in the hall of their school. When the day arrived, the other painters presented their sketches, but Tintoretto, being asked for his, removed a screen from the ceiling and showed it already painted. "We asked for sketches", they said. "That is the way", he replied, "I make my sketches." They still demurred, so he made them a present of the picture, and by the rules of their order they could not refuse a gift. In the end they promised him the painting of all the pictures they required, and during his lifetime he covered their walls with sixty large compositions.
Yet it is his phenomenal energy and the impetuous force of his work which are particularly characteristic of Tintoretto and earned for him the sobriquet among his contemporaries, *Il Furioso*. He painted so many pictures, and on so vast a scale, that some show the effects of over-haste and extravagance, which caused Annibale Carracci to say that, "while Tintoretto was the equal of Titian, he was often inferior to Tintoretto."

The main interest of his work is his love for foreshortening and it is said that to help him with the complex poses he favoured, Tintoretto used to make small wax models which he arranged on a stage and experimented on with spotlights for effects of light and shade and composition. This method of composing explains the frequent repetition in his works of the same figures seen from different angles.

270. **Tintoretto (Jacopo Robusti)**, 1518-1594, Mannerism, Venetian School, Italian, *Crucifixion* (detail), 1565, Oil on canvas, 536 x 1224 cm, Scuola di San Rocco, Venice

Tintoretto proposes here a new representation of the Crucifixion: *although Christ is on the Cross, life doesn't seem to stop. Three Roman soldiers are casting lots for Christ's clothes and other people are depicted working away at other tasks.*

Pieter Brueghel the Elder
(1525 near Breda – 1569 Brussels)

Pieter Brueghel was the first important member of a family of artists who were active for four generations. Firstly a drawer before becoming a painter later, he painted religious themes, such as Babel Tower, with very bright colours. Influenced by Hieronymus Bosch, he painted large, complex scenes of peasant life and scripture or spiritual allegories, often with crowds of subjects performing a variety of acts, yet his scenes are unified with an informal integrity and often with wit. In his work, he brought a new humanising spirit. Befriending the Humanists, Brueghel composed true philosophical landscapes in the heart of which man accepts passively his fate, caught in the track of time.

271

272

273

271. **Pieter Brueghel the Elder**, c. 1525-1569, Northern Renaissance, Flemish, *The Numbering at Bethlehem*, 1566, Oil on oak panel, 115.5 x 163.5 cm, Musées Royaux des Beaux-Arts, Brussels

272. **Pieter Brueghel the Elder**, c. 1525-1569, Northern Renaissance, Flemish, *Peasant Wedding*, 1568, Oil on panel, 114 x 164 cm, Kunsthistorisches Museum, Vienna

273. **Pieter Brueghel the Elder**, c. 1525-1569, Northern Renaissance, Flemish, *The Land of Cockayne*, 1567, Oil on panel, 52 x 78 cm, Alte Pinakothek, Munich

274

275

GIUSEPPE ARCIMBOLDO
(c. 1530 – 1593 Milan)

At his debut, Arcimboldo's contemporaries could not have imagined he would become what he is now famous for. His youthful works were normally made for cathedrals in Milan or Monza, but it is from 1562, when he was summoned to the Imperial court in Prague, that his style and subjects changed.

For the court he imagined original and grotesque fantasies made of flowers, fruit, animals and objects composed to form a human portrait. Some were satiric portraits, and others were allegorical personifications. If his work is now regarded as a curiosity of the sixteenth century, it actually finds its roots in the context of the end of the Renaissance. At that time, collectors and scientists started to pay more attention to nature, looking for natural curiosities to exhibit in their curio cabinets.

274. Veronese (Paolo Caliari), 1528-1588, Mannerism, Venetian School, Italian, *Feast in the House of Levi,* 1573, Oil on canvas, 555 x 1280 cm, Galleria dell'Accademia, Venice

Painted for the convent refectory, this work was initially called The Last Supper *and renamed* Feast in the House of Levi *after the Inquisition objected to Veronese's festive version.*

275. Niccolò dell' Abbate, 1510-1571, Mannerism, Italian, *The Rape of Proserpine,* 1552-70, Oil on canvas, 196 x 216 cm, Musée du Louvre, Paris

276. Giuseppe Arcimboldo, 1530-1593, Mannerism, Italian, *Summer,* 1573, Oil on canvas, 76 x 64 cm, Musée du Louvre, Paris

277. Alonzo Sánchez Coello, 1531-1588, Mannerism, Spanish, *The Infanta Isabella Clara Eugenia,* after 1570, Oil on canvas, 116 x 102 cm, Museo Nacional del Prado, Madrid

278. Giuseppe Arcimboldo, 1530-1593, Mannerism, Italian, *Spring,* 1573, Oil on canvas, 76 x 64 cm, Musée du Louvre, Paris

Arcimboldo produced his first series of the Seasons under the patronage of Maximilian II, at the Habsburg court in Vienna, creating portraits made of fruit, flowers, fish or other inanimate objects.

279. François Clouet, c.1505-1572, Mannerism, French, *A Lady in Her Bath,* c. 1571, Oil on panel, 92.1 x 81.3 cm, The National Gallery of Art, Washington, D.C.

A midwife nurses a baby, as the nude lady seems to reflect on what to write next with the instrument in her right hand. A mischievous child is about to grab a piece of fruit from the centrepiece on the board spread across the lady's bathtub. Domestic activity goes on elsewhere as the drapes are parted briefly for an intimate peek into a moment in the lady's life. The work includes several symbols of hope for the future; the open window, the nursing child, spring flowers, and the cheerful mid-wife. A balance and interplay of the many circles and ovals throughout the work is achieved by a few strong horizontal lines.

276

278

277

279

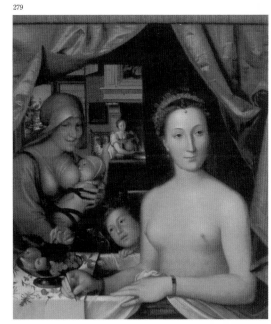

280

280. **Tintoretto (Jacopo Robusti),** 1518-1594, Mannerism, Venetian School,
Italian, *Christ in the House of Mary and Martha,* c. 1580,
Oil on canvas, 197.5 x 131 cm, Alte Pinakothek, Munich

281. **El Greco (Domenikos Theotokópoulos),** 1541-1614, Mannerism,
Native from Crete but considered a Spanish painter, *The Resurrection,* c. 1590,
Oil on canvas, 275 x 127 cm, Museo Nacional del Prado, Madrid

*This great interpretation of the subject was painted for the Colegio de Doña
María in Madrid and probably formed a pair with a painting of the Pentecost
of the same size.*

El Greco (Domenikos Theotokópoulos)
(1541 Crete – 1614 Toledo)

"The Greek" was an icon painter who immigrated to Venice.
There he began his blending of Byzantine influences with that
of the Italian High Renaissance masters. He studied under
Titian and was influenced by Tintoretto. Some years on, he
lived in Rome for about two years, then travelled to Madrid and
later found his permanent home in Toledo, where he died.
It was mainly in Spain where he focused on distinctively
Catholic subjects. The elongated bodies and unusual colour
arrangements became distinctive.

282. **El Greco (Domenikos Theotokópoulos),** 1541-1614, Mannerism, Native
from Crete but considered a Spanish painter, *Burial of Count Orgaz,* 1586-88,
Oil on canvas, 480 x 360 cm, Church of Santo Tomé, Toledo

*In the geometric centre of the painting, the dead benefactor's Guardian Angel
escorts the count's soul towards Mary as John the Baptist pleads on behalf of the
count to the Resurrected Jesus. Observing it all is St. Peter, who has the keys to
heaven loosely in hand indicating they are merely symbols. Somewhere in the
heavenly crowd of saints (upper right), probably easily located by his
contemporaries, is King Philip II of Spain. Below, the count's body is in the arms
of St. Augustine in bishop's vestment assisted by St. Stephen, the first martyr.
Stephen appropriately wears his deacon's vestment on which is a scene of his
own fatal stoning. The artist's torch-bearing son is shown in the lower left. His
birth date is seen on the handkerchief stuck in his pocket. The artist depicts
himself (directly above St. Stephen) as the only face looking directly at the
viewer. Over all, the heavenly half of the work is dynamic, but sombre; the
earthy half is static and introspective.*

283

284

285

283. Veronese (Paolo Caliari), 1528-1588, Mannerism, Venetian School, Italian,
The Adoration of the Magi, after 1571, Oil on canvas, 206 x 455 cm,
Gemäldegalerie, Alte Meister, Dresden

284. Annibale Carracci, 1560-1609, Baroque, Italian,
The Fishing, c. 1585-88, Oil on canvas, 136 x 255 cm, Musée du Louvre, Paris

285. Federico Barocci(o), 1526-1612, Mannerism, Italian, *The Flight of Aeneas from
Troy (2nd version),* 1598, Oil on canvas, 184 x 258 cm, Galleria Borghese, Rome

*The greatest painter between Correggio and Caravaggio, Barocci has also been
influenced by Raphael. The flight from Troy is his only known classical subject.*

286. Michelangelo Merisi da Caravaggio, 1571-1610, Baroque, Italian,
Bacchus, c. 1596, Oil on canvas, 95 x 85 cm, Galleria degli Uffizi, Florence

This is the first time in the history of painting that the theme of Bacchus is used as a pretext to gather objects such as fruit or a glass of wine. This is an early work of Caravaggio but it already shows the elements of the artist's style such as the tenebrism (tenebroso) of the dark background, the androgynous face of the lute player or the still-life in the foreground.

287

288

Michelangelo Merisi da Caravaggio
(1571 Caravaggio – 1610 Port'Ercole)

After staying in Milan for his apprenticeship, Michelangelo da Caravaggio arrived in Rome in 1592. There he started to paint with both realism and psychological analysis of the sitters. Caravaggio was as temperamental in his painting as in his wild life. As he also responded to prestigious Church commissions, his dramatic style and his realism were seen as unacceptable. Chiaroscuro had existed well before he came on the scene, but it was Caravaggio who made the technique definitive, darkening the shadows and transfixing the subject in a blinding shaft of light. His influence was immense, firstly through those who were more or less directly his disciples. Famous during his lifetime, Caravaggio had a great influence upon Baroque art. The Genoese and Neapolitan Schools derived lessons from him, and the great movement of Spanish painting in the seventeenth century was connected with these schools. In the following generations the best endowed painters oscillated between the lessons of Caravaggio and the Carracci.

290. **Michelangelo Merisi da Caravaggio,** 1571-1610, Baroque, Italian, *Boy with a Basket of Fruit,* c. 1595, Oil on canvas, 70 x 67 cm, Galleria Borghese, Rome

The subject of the painting is definitely the basket of fruit. The sitter and the basket of fruit receive the diagonal cellar light characteristic of the artist's style.

291. **Michelangelo Merisi da Caravaggio,** 1571-1610, Baroque, Italian, *The Fortune-Teller,* c. 1594, Oil on canvas, 99 x 131 cm, Musée du Louvre, Paris

In the first period of his career, Caravaggio often depicted humble characters, anti-heroic, in non-historical paintings. The artist focused on the sensuality of the characters in this new representation of the theme.

292. **El Greco (Domenikos Theotokópoulos),** 1541-1614, Mannerism, Native from Crete but considered a Spanish painter, *Portrait of a Cardinal, Probably Cardinal Don Fernando Niño de Guevara,* 1600, Oil on canvas, 170.8 x 108 cm, The Metropolitan Museum of Art, New York

El Greco's portraits retain the psychological insight of the sitter. This painting is one of the most startling portrayals of the cleric.

293

17th Century

The start of the seventeenth century in Europe is marked by the Thirty Years' War (1618-48). The Holy Roman Empire and the Ottoman Empire, as well as France, Spain, Sweden, Denmark, the Netherlands, Germany, Austria, and Poland were all engaged in the conflict. Although there were many local reasons for the war, the primary one was the disagreement between the Catholics and the Protestants. The war ended with the Treaty of Westphalia in 1648, which essentially provided religious choice in much of Europe and also gave rise to new nation states. By the seventeenth century most geographical exploration had taken place and the expanding mercantilism led to refinements in trading practices, such as holding money on account, as instituted by the Bank of Amsterdam in 1609. Cartography, ship building, and the expansion of the slave trade all led to increased prosperity in European markets, thereby expanding the incomes of a new wealthy class who patronised the arts and sought luxury goods through conspicuous consumption.

The seventeenth century is widely known under the umbrella term of the Baroque, although there were local and national specifics to the art of the Baroque period. Italian Baroque was still heavily patronised by the Catholic Church, as were Spanish and Flemish Baroque works. Yet the Northern Baroque, leaning heavily towards a new Protestant wealthy class, favoured secular scenes and group portraits based on guild memberships or companies of citizen militias, which protected the north from Spanish rule in the period of separatist revolt in the Netherlands.

In Italy, the Baroque period was characterized by the Catholic Church's Counter-Reformation movement and the edicts of the Council of Trent (1545-63) in which the Church insisted on the use of images in religious teaching. The Jesuit Order was highly influential in Baroque art, due to the canonisation of St. Ignatius of Loyola in 1622 and the popularity of his important text, the *Spiritual Exercises*. Theatricality, sensuousness, passionate faithfulness, motion, and a dramatic impact on the viewer were all principles of Catholic Baroque art. The Church had lost a great deal of power during the Reformation and was ardently trying to regain the masses by welcoming the faithful with building campaigns designed to expand the Church's body, often quite literally by expanding the nave plans to accommodate more people, such as at St. Peter's in Rome and the Jesuit mother church of *Il Jesu*.

The Dutch Republic, established after the United Provinces of the Netherlands were officially formed following the Treaty of Westphalia, was predominantly protestant, if not largely Calvinist.

Therefore, while the Netherlands was incredibly economically successful, there was a puritanical prohibition on art in churches. Consequently, there were far fewer religious commissions than in France, Italy, or Spain in the Baroque period. Dutch genre scenes were far more common.

In France, the Age of Absolutism created a powerful environment in which the French Classicism formed under the patronage of Louis XIV (r. 1661-1715). The park and buildings of Versailles displayed his preference for rationalism and control. The French classical style was established by the founding of the Royal Academy of Painting and Sculpture in 1648.

Scientifically, the period is important because of Galileo's telescope invention in 1609, which helped Johannes Kepler establish his laws of planetary motion from 1609-1619. Meanwhile, René Descartes' *Discourse on Method* was published in 1637 while Blaise Pascal was founding statistics and probability studies. After the Royal Society was founded in London in 1662, Sir Isaac Newton's laws of motion and gravitation were elaborated in 1687.

---

293. **Michelangelo Merisi da Caravaggio**, 1571-1610, Baroque, Italian,
The Death of the Virgin, 1601-1605/06, Oil on canvas, 369 x 245 cm,
Musée du Louvre, Paris

This painting, much admired by Rubens, was rejected by its commissioner because of its lack of conformism; the Madonna was suspected to be modelled on a prostitute, her legs were exposed, and her swollen body was too realistic.

Peter Paul Rubens
(1577 Siegen –1640 Antwerp)

The eclectic art of which the Carracci family dreamed was realised by Rubens with the ease of genius. However, the problem was much more complicated for a man of the north, who wished to add to it a fusion of the Flemish and Latin spirits, of which the rather pedantic attempts of Romanism had illustrated the difficulties. He achieved it without losing anything of his overflowing personality, his questing imagination, and the enchanting discoveries of the greatest colourist known to painting.

Rubens, the greatest master of Baroque painting's exuberance, took from the Italian Renaissance what could be of use to him, and then built upon it a style of his own. It is distinguished by a wonderful mastery of the human form and an amazing wealth of splendidly lighted colour. He was a man of much intellectual poise and was accustomed to court life, travelling from court to court, with pomp, as a trusted envoy.

Rubens was one of those rare mortals who do real honour to humanity. He was handsome, good and generous, and he loved virtue. His laborious life was well ordered. The creator of so many delightful pagan feasts went each morning to mass before proceeding to his studio. He was the most illustrious type of happy and perfectly balanced genius, and combined in his personage passion and science, ardour and reflection. Rubens expressed drama as well as joy, since nothing human was foreign to him, and he could command at will the pathos of colour and expression which he required in his religious masterpieces. It might be said that he was as prolific in the representation of the joy and exuberance of life as Michelangelo was in the representation of passionate emotions.

294. Guido Reni, 1575-1642, Classicism, Italian, *David with the Head of Goliath*, c. 1605, Oil on canvas, 237 x 137 cm, Musée du Louvre, Paris

295. Peter Paul Rubens, 1577-1640, Baroque, Flemish, *Descent from the Cross*, 1610-11, Oil on canvas, 460 x 340 cm (central panel), 460 x 150 cm (wings), O.-L. Vrouwekathedraal, Antwerp

297

296. Adam Elsheimer, 1578-1610, Mannerism/Baroque, German,
Flight into Egypt, 1609, Oil on copper, 31 x 41 cm, Alte Pinakothek, Munich

Famous for his night scenes, Elsheimer shows a great sensitivity to the effect
of light. This miniature-like painting shows a new type of landscape
romantic and encircling the characters with chiaroscuro effects.

297. El Greco (Domenikos Theotokópoulos), 1541-1614, Mannerism,
Native from Crete but considered a Spanish painter, *View of Toledo,* c. 1610,
Oil on canvas, 121.3 x 108.6 cm, The Metropolitan Museum of Art, New York

298. Frans Pourbus The Younger, 1569-1622, Baroque, Dutch, *Louis XIII as a*
Child, 1611, Oil on canvas, 165 x 100 cm, Galleria degli Uffizi, Florence

299. Cristofano Allori, 1577-1621, High Renaissance, Florentine School, Italian,
Judith with the Head of Holofernes, c. 1613,
Oil on canvas, 120.4 x 100.3 cm, Palazzo Pitti, Florence

One of the most famous paintings in the eighteenth and nineteenth centuries
in Italy, Judith with the Head of Holofernes is increased in its dramatic effect
through the intensified contrasts between the dark face of Holofernes and the
depiction of Judith with warm and light colours.

300. Diego Velázquez, 1599-1660, Baroque, Spanish, *Christ in the House of*
Mary and Marthe, 1618, Oil on canvas, 60 x 103.5 cm,
National Gallery, London

299

301

303

302

Guido Reni
(1575 – 1642 Bologna)

Guido Reni was a painter, a draughtsman and an etcher. He joined the naturalistic Carracci School when he was twenty, after having studied under Denis Calvaert. Deeply influenced by Greco-Roman art and Raphael, whom he greatly admired, by Parmigianino and by Veronese, his work was celebrated for its compositional and figural grace. He depicted the light, the perfection of the body, and shining colours. He was greatly noted and distinguished during the pontificate of Paul V.

304

305

306

01. Guido Reni, 1575-1642, Classicism, Italian, *The Massacre of the Innocents,*
c. 1611, Oil on canvas, 268 x 170 cm, Pinacoteca Nazionale, Bologna

*Guido Reni's early works betray the influence of the Caravaggesque manner
and Baroque painting, but Raphael and the antique remained the main
inspiration for his classical style.*

02. Bernardo Strozzi, 1581-1644, Baroque, Italian, *The Cook,* c. 1620,
Oil on canvas, 177 x 241 cm, Galleria di Palazzo, Genoa

03. El Greco (Domenikos Theotokópoulos), 1541-1614, Mannerism,
Native from Crete but considered a Spanish painter, *El Espolio
(Christ Stripped of his Garments),* c. 1608, Oil on canvas, 285 x 173 cm,
Sacristy of the Cathedral of Toledo, Toledo

*The powerful effect of the painting is due to its size, bigger than nature, on the
strictly centralised composition as well as on the forceful use of colour,
recalling Venetian painting and, particularly, the works of Titian.*

04. Giovanni Lanfranco, 1582-1647, Baroque, Italian, *Annunciation,* c. 1616,
Oil on canvas, 296 x 183 cm, San Carlo Catinari, Rome

05. Giovanni Francesco Barbieri Guercino, 1591-1666, Baroque, Bolognese
School, Italian, *William of Aquitaine Receives the Crown of St. Bishop Felix,*
1620, Oil on canvas, 345 x 231 cm, Pinacoteca Nazionale, Bologna

06. Peter Paul Rubens, 1577-1640, Baroque, Flemish, *The Rape of the
Daughters of Leucippus,* 1617-18, Oil on canvas, 222 x 209 cm,
Alte Pinakothek, Munich

307

308

307. Pieter Lastman, 1583-1633, Baroque, Dutch, *Odysseus and Nausicaa,* 1619, Oil on panel, 91.5 x 117.2 cm, Alte Pinakothek, Munich

308. Peter Paul Rubens, 1577-1640, Baroque, Flemish, *The Landing of Marie de' Médici at Marseille,* c. 1623, Oil on canvas, 394 x 295 cm, Musée du Louvre, Paris

This large painting is one of sixteen in a cycle on the life of Queen Marie de'Medic (1573-1642). The series, the most important in his prolific life, was completed in fou years for the Palais du Luxembourg in Paris. The historical event being dramaticall presented actually took place a month or so after the October wedding of Marie t Henry IV. In the scene, the queen's ship is in the Marseilles harbour shortly after he marriage. Both heaven and earth welcome her. The city welcomes her in the personag of allegorical figures from the legendary history of the city. Fama, the goddess fron whom the word 'fame' comes, hovers above and with her double bugle announces th arrival of the Queen. Representing all of the earth, the god Neptune and thre Rubenesque sirens and tritons add even more beauty and festivity to the event. In 161(ten years after the Queen's landing, she would take charge of Paris, just one day befor the King's death.

309 310

311

09. Domenico Fetti, 1589-1623, Baroque, Venetian School, Italian, *Melancholy,* c. 1620, Oil on canvas, 171 x 128 cm, Musée du Louvre, Paris

10. Anthonis van Dyck, 1599-1641, Baroque, Flemish, *Crowning with Thorns,* c. 1620, Oil on canvas, 223 x 196 cm, Museo Nacional del Prado, Madrid

The composition, based on Titian's works, is also influenced by Rubens and the Baroque style.

11. Anthonis van Dyck, 1599-1641, Baroque, Flemish, *Self-Portrait,* c. 1622, Oil on canvas, 117 x 94 cm, The State Hermitage Museum, St. Petersburg

Van Dyck's mature art reached its apogee in the Hermitage Self-Portrait painted possibly in Rome in 1622 or 1623, the finest of the artist's known self-depictions. Here van Dyck paints himself in the bloom of youth, as a slender, elegantly dressed gallant, nonchalantly leaning against the pedestal of a broken column and fixing the observer with a dreamy, slightly enigmatic look.

Graceful posture, his aristocratically slender, long-fingered, lithe hands, and the magnificence of his black silk costume all vividly bear out the impression that van Dyck was said to have made in Rome on his fellow artists, who nicknamed him 'il pittore cavalieresco' (the gentleman-artist) for his taste for the high society way of life.

The idea of man's innate nobility and of his spiritual and intellectual supremacy in the world, expressed in the Hermitage Self-Portrait, finds its closest analogy in Italian Renaissance art. Researchers have suggested that the artist's posture in the portrait, his proud bearing, the free turn of the figure and the intricate silhouette of his costume, with its luxuriant puffed sleeves, were inspired by Raphael's Portrait of a Young Man, *of which van Dyck made a sketch on a page of his* Italian Sketchbook. *The style of the portrait – a three-quarter-length figure leaning against the pedestal of a column – follows a Venetian prototype, more specifically that of Titian. Several pages of the* Italian Sketchbook *are devoted to copies of Titian's portraits.*

In his portraits of artists, scholars, patrons, and collectors, van Dyck always strove to stress the spiritual inspiration and eliteness of a human nature close to his ideal of the beautiful individual (Lucas van Uffelen, The Metropolitan Museum of Art, New York).

313

314

315

Johann Liss, 1597-1631, Baroque, German, *Sacrifice of Abraham*, c. 1624, Oil on canvas, 88 x 70 cm,
Galleria degli Uffizi, Florence

Frans Hals, c. 1582-1666, Baroque, Dutch,
The Laughing Cavalier, 1624, Oil on canvas, 83 x 67 cm,
The Wallace Collection, London

Orazio Gentileschi, 1563-1639, Baroque, Italian,
The Lute Player, c. 1626, Oil on canvas, 144 x 130 cm,
The National Gallery of Art, Washington, D.C.

315. Anthonis van Dyck, 1599-1641, Baroque, Flemish, *Marchesa
Elena Grimaldi, Wife of Marchese Nicola Cattaneo,* c. 1623,
Oil on canvas, 242.9 x 138.5 cm,
The National Gallery of Art, Washington, D.C.

181

316

317

FRANS HALS
(C. 1582 ANTWERP – 1666 HAARLEM)

Hals must have had fine qualities of mind; howelse could he have seen things so simply and completely, and rendered them with such force and expression, inventing for the purpose a method of his own? His method was distinguished by placing his subject in clear light and by working largely in flat tones, to get at the essential facts of a subject, and to set them down rapidly and precisely, so that all may understand them and be impressed. He was, however, so shiftless that in his old age he was dependent upon the city government for support. That he received it, however, and that his creditors were lenient with him, seems to show that his contemporaries recognised greatness behind his intemperance and improvidence; and, when in his eighty-second year he died, he was buried beneath the choir of the Church of St. Bavon in Haarlem.

For a long time after his death, Hals was thought little of, even in Holland, where artists forsook the traditions of their own school and went in search of other mentors – to wit, those of the Italian "grand style". It was not until well into the nineteenth century that artists returning to the truth of nature, discovered that Hals had been one of the greatest seers of the truth and one of its most virile interpreters. Today he is honoured for these qualities, and of all the much-admired Dutch pictures of the seventeenth century, his are the most characteristic of the Dutch race and of the art which it produced.

320

321. Frans Hals, c. 1582-1666, Baroque, Dutch, *Gypsy Girl,* c. 1626, Oil on panel, 58 x 52 cm, Musée du Louvre, Paris

318. Judith Leyster, 1609-60, Baroque, Dutch, *Carousing Couple,* 1630, Oil on panel, 68 x 57 cm, Musée du Louvre, Paris

Judith Leyster is one of the very few women to have been accepted as a member of the Haarlem Guild of Painters. Although a contemporary historian described her as a leading light in art, she remained unknown for a long time, and her works were either believed lost or were attributed to Frans Hals.

319. Diego Velázquez, 1599-1660, Baroque, Spanish, *The Feast of Bacchus* or *The Drunkards,* 1629, Oil on canvas, 165 x 227 cm, Museo Nacional del Prado, Madrid

320. Hendrick Jansz ter Brugghen, 1588-1629, Baroque, Dutch, *Duet,* 1628, Oil on canvas, 106 x 82 cm, Musée du Louvre, Paris

The title of this painting was given by the donator but doesn't match with what should rather be considered as the portrait of a courtesan.

321

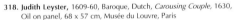

322. **Francisco de Zurbarán,** 1598-1664, Baroque, Spanish, *St Agatha,* c. 1634, Oil on canvas, 129 x 61 cm, Musée Fabre, Montpellier

St. Agatha, a third-century virgin martyred by the Roman emperor Decius, was also painted later by Tiepolo (1756) and Cassatt (1891). St. Agatha is the patron saint of bell makers and is also invoked against the outbreak of fire. This portrait is from the beginning of the peak years of the artist's output, at the start of his role as city painter in Seville. This masterpiece demonstrates the Spanish artist's ability to capture warm, realistic expressions and intense, ascetic sobriety, a quality he shared with his contemporary and fellow countryman, Velázquez. Zurbarán also focused on the rendering of sculptural volumes, particularly noticeable in the depiction of the draperies.

323. **Simon Vouet,** 1590-1649, Baroque, French, *Time Overcome by Hope and Beauty,* 1627, Oil on canvas, 107 x 142 cm, Museo Nacional del Prado, Madrid

324. **Simon Vouet,** 1590-1649, Baroque, French, *Allegory of Wealth,* 1627, Oil on canvas, 107 x 142 cm, Musée du Louvre, Paris

SIMON VOUET
(1590 – 1649 PARIS)

Vouet was exceedingly precocious. At fourteen he already enjoyed such a reputation as a portrait painter that he was invited to visit England in order to paint the portrait of a lady of quality. He was honoured also in Constantinople by Louis XIII in 1628, and for twenty years held sovereign sway over the arts. It is obvious that he was a little carried away by his enormous talent, but his clear colour and sense of decoration layed a part in the evolution of French painting. He had more influence than Poussin on Le Sueur, Le Brun and Mignard and through them on the great work of Louis XIV's reign; the decoration of Versailles. From him derives Boucher, and hence a substantial part of eighteenth-century art.

325

Diego Velázquez
(1599 Sevilla – 1660 Madrid)

Diego Velázquez was an individualistic artist of the contemporary Baroque period. At age twenty-four, Velázquez made his first trip to Madrid with his teacher, Francisco Pacheco. Quickly, he qualified as a master painter. King Philip IV noticed his genius and appointed him court painter in 1627. Shortly afterward the artist befriended Rubens in Madrid. He developed a more realistic approach to religious art in which figures are naturalistic portraits rather than depicted in an idealistic style. The use of chiaroscuro is reminiscent of Caravaggio's works. Velázquez made at least two trips to Rome to buy Renaissance and neoclassical art for the King. In Rome, he joined the Academy of St. Luke in 1650 and was knighted into the order of Santiago in 1658. His large commissioned work, *Surrender of Breda* (c. 1634), shows the defeat of the Dutch at the hands of the Spanish, and glorified the military triumph of Philip's reign. The artist painted *Pope Innocent X* (1650) during his second trip to Rome, most likely recalling similar works by Raphael and Titian. This portrait is considered one of the greatest masterpieces of portraiture in the history of art, so realistic that the Pope himself would have said, "troppo vero". He mastered the art of portraiture because he looked beyond external trappings into the human mystery beneath his subjects, as evidenced in his remarkable series of dwarfs, who were present in many royal courts at that time. He depicted their humanity instead of doing caricatures. His later works were more spontaneous, but still disciplined. The culmination of his career is his masterwork, *Las Meninas* (1656). It is indeed one of the most complex essays in portraiture. Velázquez is acknowledged to be the most important Spanish painter of his century. He influenced major painters such as Goya and Manet.

325. **Diego Velázquez**, 1599-1660,
Baroque, Spanish,
The Surrender of Breda, c. 1634,
Oil on canvas, 307 x 367 cm,
Museo Nacional del Prado, Madrid

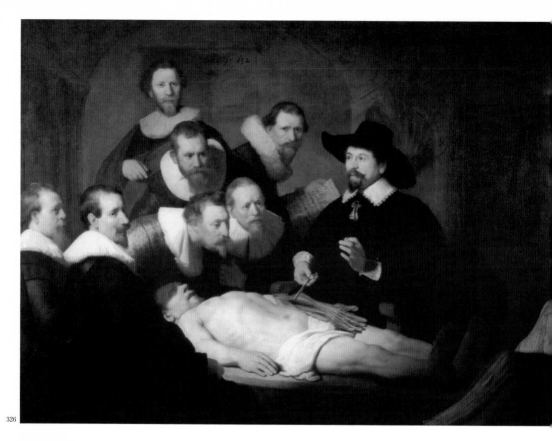

326

327

326. Harmensz van Rijn Rembrandt,
1606-1669, Baroque, Dutch,
*The Anatomy Lesson of
Dr. Tulp,* 1632,
Oil on canvas, 169.5 x 216.5 cm,
Royal Cabinet of Paintings
Mauritshuis, The Hague

327. Willem Claesz Heda, 1594-1680,
Baroque, Dutch, *Breakfast Table wi*
Blackberry Pie, 1631,
Oil on panel, 54 x 82 cm,
Gemäldegalerie, Alte Meister, Dresde

Heda is, with Pieter Claesz, the me
important representative of breakfa
piece painting in the Netherlands.

186

328

329

328. Nicolas Poussin, 1594-1665, Classicism, French,
The Abduction of the Sabine Women, 1633-34,
Oil on canvas, 154.6 x 209.9 cm,
The Metropolitan Museum of Art, New York

*Poussin was undoubtedly a highly significant master
of the historical genre. He shaped its aesthetics
which, regrettably, subsequently became regarded as
a set of hard-and-fast rules (a trap which the Russian
followers of the founder of Classicism also fell into).
We know that Poussin attributed prime significance
to the actual choice of matter for depiction, giving
preference to subjects which provided food for
profound thought. Creatively reworking the aesthetic
legacy of the Ancients, he introduced into the realm
of painting the concept of the "modus" (mood of
depiction), which established the functional unity of
three components: the idea, the structure of the
depiction, and its perception by the viewer.
Composition assumed a predominant significance in
his artistic system.*

329. Adriaen Brouwer, 1605-1638, Baroque, Flemish,
The Operation, 1631, Oil on panel, 31.4 x 39.6 cm,
Alte Pinakothek, Munich

330

330. Pietro da Cortona (Pietro Berrettini), 1596-1669, Baroque, Italian,
Allegory of Divine Providence and Barberini Power, 1633-39,
Fresco, Palazzo Barberini, Rome

This fresco is one of the key works in the development of Baroque painting. It is a triumph of illusionism: the centre of the ceiling appears open to the sky and the figures seen from below (sotto insù) appear to come down into the room as well as soar out of it.

331. Georges de La Tour, 1593-1652, Baroque, French, *The Card-Sharp with the Ace of Diamonds,* 1635, Oil on canvas, 106 x 146 cm,
Musée du Louvre, Paris

Georges de La Tour's workshop was in Lorraine, where the troops of King Louis XIII were wreaking massive destruction. But Lorraine is also a region from which numerous travels to Italy were taking place. Whether La Tour went to Italy or not is still a mystery but the painter was influenced by Caravaggio's style.

331

GEORGES DE LA TOUR
(1593 VIC SUR VILLE –1652 LUNÉVILLE)

Georges de La Tour was well known in his own time but then forgotten until the twentieth century. His painting depicted genre and religious subjects, seen often in candlelight, such as his interior scenes. The influence of Caravaggio is evident in his painting, especially in the use of chiaroscuro. Simplification of form and rigour of composition in his work underlined the ideas of the Counter-Reformation.

333

Anthonis van Dyck
(1599 Antwerp –1641 London)

Van Dyck was accustomed early to Rubens' sumptuous lifestyle; and, when he visited Italy with letters of introduction from his master, lived in the palaces of his patrons, himself adopting such an elegant ostentation that he was spoken of as 'the Cavalier Painter'. After his return to Antwerp his patrons belonged to the rich and noble class, and his own style of living was modelled on theirs; so that, when in 1632 he received the appointment of court painter to Charles I of England, he maintained an almost princely establishment, and his house at Blackfriars was a resort of fashion. The last two years of his life were spent travelling on the Continent with his young wife, the daughter of Lord Gowry. His health, however, had been broken by the excesses of work, and he returned to London to die. He was buried at St. Paul's Cathedral.

Van Dyck tried to amalgamate the influences of Italy (Titian, Veronese, Bellini) and Flanders and he succeeded in some paintings, which have a touching grace, notably in his *Madonnas and Holy Families*, his *Crucifixions* and *Depositions from the Cross*, and also in some of his mythological compositions. In his younger days he painted many altarpieces full of sensitive religious feeling and enthusiasm. However, his main glory was as a portraitist, the most elegant and aristocratic ever known. The great *Portrait of Charles I* in the Louvre is a work unique for its sovereign elegance. In his portraits, he invented a style of elegance and refinement which became a model for the artists of the seventeenth and eighteenth centuries, corresponding as it did to the genteel luxury of the court life of the period. He is also considered one of the greatest colourists in the history of art.

332. **Anthonis van Dyck,** 1599-1641, Baroque, Flemish, *Charles I: King of England at the Hunt,* 1635, Oil on canvas, 266 x 207 cm, Musée du Louvre, Paris

333. **Peter Paul Rubens,** 1577-1640, Baroque, Flemish, *Bathsheba at the Fountain,* 1635, Oil on oak panel, 175 x 126 cm, Gemäldegalerie, Alte Meister, Dresden

334. **Jan van Goyen,** 1596-1656, Baroque, Dutch, *River Landscape,* 1636, Oil on panel, 39.5 x 60 cm, Alte Pinakothek, Munich

334

335

335. Peter Paul Rubens, 1577-1640, Baroque, Flemish, *The Garden of Love,*
c. 1633, Oil on canvas, 198 x 283 cm, Museo Nacional del Prado, Madrid

336. Frans Hals, c. 1582-1666, Baroque, Dutch, *Company of Captain Reinier
Reael,* also known as the *'Meagre Company',* 1637,
Oil on canvas, 209 x 429 cm, Rijksmuseum, Amsterdam

337. Sébastien Bourdon, 1616-1671, Atticism, French, *The Death of Dido,* 1637-40,
Oil on canvas, 158.5 x 136.5 cm, The State Hermitage Museum, St. Petersburg

*This painting is comparable to one on the same theme by Simon Vouet for the
lyrical style in which both are depicted. Also, Bourdon enhanced the dramatic
effects using arabesques and rejecting strong colours, as he remained under the
influence of Venetian painting.*

336

338

338. Nicolas Poussin, 1594-1665, Classicism, French, *'Et in Arcadia Ego'*, 1638-39, Oil on canvas, 85 x 121 cm, Musée du Louvre, Paris

339. Francesco Albani, 1578-1660, Classicism, Italian, *The Rape of Europa*, 1639, Oil on canvas, 76.3 x 97 cm, Galleria degli Uffizi, Florence

Nicolas Poussin
(1594 Villers – 1665 Rome)

Although Nicolas Poussin was only four years younger than Vouet, his influence made itself felt in France much later. He was not precocious like Vouet, but may be numbered amongst those great men who have need of reflection and meditation, whose inspiration comes only with maturity.

None of his early works has been preserved. His career begins, historically speaking, in 1624 with his arrival in Rome at the age of thirty. He came to Italy in quest of Raphael, whose genius he had discerned from the engravings of Marc-Antoine while still in Paris. The master of the Farnesine and of the Vatican Stanze and Loggia did not disappoint him. However, Titian was a profound surprise to him, and from that time onwards his constant preoccupation was to reconcile the spirit of these two great men. At times he seemed to prefer a method hovering between these magnetic poles, and vacillated between the linear element derived from Raphael and the warm and coloured atmosphere which he admired in Titian. This clear-sighted and impassioned study which Poussin devoted to Raphael and Titian appears perfectly natural today, but this was not so in 1624, when foreign artists in Rome had no eyes except for the Academic art derived from the Bolognese or from the brutal naturalism of the disciples of Caravaggio. Poussin equally detested both, and with his robust, philosophical frankness, condemned both unsparingly. The finest aspect of Poussin's genius is to have put into his masterpieces more thought than it was ever given to any other painter to express, and to have found for that poetic and philosophical thought an original and plastic interpretation.

Poussin is one of the greatest landscape painters. His sketches are comparable only to those of Lorrain, and are perhaps yet finer, while some recall Turner's most dazzling watercolours. Poussin is inferior to Titian in richness of colour as well as fullness and purity of form; but his poet philosopher's genius added a lofty spirituality and an indefinable touch of the heroic to the symphony of man and nature. Poussin, who from the age of thirty spent most of his life in Rome, remains the most French of the great painters, and always kept in view that wise and noble balance between reason and feeling, which was the ideal of the Ancients and has been that of artists and writers alike in France.

341. Laurent de La Hyre, 1606-1656, Atticism, French, *Mercury Takes Bacchus to be Brought Up by Nymphs,* 1638, Oil on canvas, 112.5 x 135 cm, The State Hermitage Museum, St. Petersburg

Although La Hyre had never been to Italy, he took his inspiration from Raphael as well as from painters from the School of Fontainebleau.

. **José de Ribera,** 1591-1652, Baroque, Spanish, *Martyrdom of St Philip,* 1639, Oil on canvas, 234 x 234 cm, Museo Nacional del Prado, Madrid

341

Claude Lorrain (Claude Gellée)
(1604 Chamagne –1682 Rome)

Claude Gellée, called Claude Lorrain was neither a great man nor a lofty spirit like Poussin. His genius cannot, however, be denied and he was, like Poussin, a profoundly original inventor within the limitations of a classical ideal. He too spent most of his life in Rome though the art he created was not specifically Italian, but French. For more than two centuries afterwards everyone in France who felt called upon to depict the beauties of nature would think of Lorrain and study his works, whether it be Joseph Vernet in the eighteenth century or Corot in the nineteenth. Outside France it was the same; Lorrain was nowhere more admired than in England. There is an element of mystery in the vocation of this humble and almost illiterate peasant whose knowledge of French and Italian was equally poor, and who used to inscribe on his drawings notes in a strange broken Franco-Italian. This mystery is in some way symbolic of that with which he imbued his pictures, *le mystère dans la lumière*. This admirable landscapist drew from within himself the greatest number of extraordinary pictures, in which all is beauty, poetry and truth. He sometimes made from nature drawings so beautiful that several have been attributed to Poussin, but in his paintings his imagination dominates, growing in magnitude as he realised his genius. He understood by listening to Poussin and watching him paint that a sort of intellectual background would be an invaluable addition to his own imagination, visions, dreams and reveries.

343

342

342. Harmensz van Rijn Rembrandt, 1606-1669, Baroque, Dutch, *Self-Portrait at the Age of Thrity-Four,* 1639-40, Oil on canvas, 102 x 80 cm, National Gallery, London

Inspired by the Portrait of Castiglione by Raphael (1514-16), Rembrand instituted a dialogue with the great Italian masters. The artist, overwhelmed b commissions, had not travelled in Italy but he knew Italian painting throug other artists, who imported pieces to the Dutch provinces. Amsterdam crossroad of exchanges, received Raphael's Portrait of Castiglione in a sale a Alfonso Alvarez's shop, an art broker working for Cardinal Richelieu Rembrandt also took his inspiration from Dürer's Self-Portraits for the guardra and the arm leaning in the foreground. His work remains original for th anachronistic costume setting (not being of the period) and therefor preventing us knowing his social rank.

343. Claude Lorrain (Gellée), c. 1604-1682, Classicism, French, *Embarkation o St Paula Romana at Ostia,* 1639, Oil on canvas, 211 x 145 cm, Museo Nacional del Prado, Madrid

Francisco de Zurbarán
(1598 Fuente de Cantos –1664 Madrid)

Contemporary and friend of Velázquez, Zurbarán distinguished himself in his religious paintings. There, his works reveal great force and mysticism. The emblematic artist of the Counter-Reformation, he was first influenced by Caravaggio and acquired an austere and dark style before getting closer to the Italian Mannerists. Later, his compositions moved away from Velázquez's realism and became lighter. He was commissioned by Franciscan and Carthusian monasteries to produce religious works, including several versions on the theme of Mary's Immaculate Conception. He also painted still-lifes, and mythological themes.

344. Antoine Le Nain, c. 1600-1648, Baroque, French, *Blacksmith at His Forge,* c. 1640, Oil on canvas, 69 x 57 cm, Musée du Louvre, Paris

None of the three brothers Le Nain, Louis, Antoine and Mathieu, signed their works with their first name. All three were foundation members of the Academie Royale, but only Antoine had a certificate and was therefore exhibiting for his brothers.

345. Francisco de Zurbarán, 1598-1664, Baroque, Spanish, *Saint Francis in Meditation,* 1639, Oil on canvas, 152 x 99 cm, National Gallery, London

346. Jan Verspronck, 1606-1662, Baroque, Dutch, *Portrait of a Girl Dressed in Blue,* 1641, Oil on canvas, 82 x 66.5 cm, Rijksmuseum, Amsterdam

Verspronck was one of the best representations of Haarlem's school of portraiture.

345

344

346

347

348

347. Jan Davidsz de Heem, 1606-1684,
Baroque, Dutch, *Still-Life with Dessert,*
c. 1640, Oil on canvas, 149 x 203 cm,
Musée du Louvre, Paris

348. Louis Le Nain, c. 1598-1648,
Baroque, French, *The Cart* or *Return
from Haymaking,* 1641, Oil on wood,
56 x 72 cm, Musée du Louvre, Paris

*Usually said to have been painted b
Louis Le Nain, the attribution of th
painting to one of the three brothers
still uncertain. The depiction of simp
life with delicate nuances of colour
characteristic of their style.*

349

349. Louis Le Nain, c. 1598-1648, Baroque, French, *Family of Country People,* 1640, Oil on canvas, 113 x 159 cm, Musée du Louvre, Paris

The golden brown tone of the work helps create a simple and quiet moment, except for the crackling of the fire in the back and the playing of the musical instrument by the central figure. The artist has revealed the closeness of the family by drawing the viewer into their intimate circle. The circular bowl on the circular table and the circle of people around them echo the chain of six or more circles from the lower right corner, from the basket, its shadow, the ladle, its shadow, and lid, more shadows, and to the pot. In the lower right, the ladle, the child's legs and the legs of the seated lady on the right draw our attention to the group. The legs of the other seated lady do likewise from the left. The gaze of the family dog also draws our attention into the painting. It is in the lower left corner, the area where pets in group portraits are so often placed. The painter preserves the peasants' dignity, yet this is a realist painting. This aspect is emphasised by the fact that this genre scene is the size of a history painting.

Le Nain Brothers
(Antoine c.1600-1648, Louis c.1598-1648 and Mathieu c.1607-1677 (born in Laon, died in Paris))

For a long time it appeared impossible to discriminate amongst the three Le Nain brothers' individual works, which have survived under their common signature. Antoine Le Nain, who studied at Laon under a 'foreign painter' (probably from Flanders), painted in a manner and with a colouring more or less derived from Flemish models; little panels where people are assembled in modest interiors, but of the town rather than of the country. His style was still slightly archaic, but it is already possible to discern in him that love of humble truth. It was from his style the inspiration for the most original works bearing the signature derived: those of Louis, the man of genius and the breaker of new ground. It was he who produced the gatherings of peasants, which are painted with such freedom, and filled with such dignity, sobriety and humanity. Contrast these with the very different treatments of similar subjects by contemporary Spanish and Italian followers of Caravaggio on one hand, and the Flemish and Dutch on the other. Mathieu, the youngest of the brothers, survived the others by almost thirty years. His works generally possess less depth, but he painted family gatherings in which he showed himself almost as good a judge of human physiognomy and expression as his brother Louis.

352

352. José de Ribera, 1591-1652, Baroque, Spanish, *Boy With a Club Foot,* 1642, Oil on canvas, 164 x 94 cm, Musée du Louvre, Paris

This portrait is often called simply Clubfoot. *The charming smile of the boy is disarming and makes his request for alms (stated in Latin) on the paper he holds all the more touching. The artist also appeals to the viewer's sensitivity elsewhere, as in his earlier* The Martyrdom of St. Bartholomew *(1639-40). Influenced by Caravaggio, José de Ribera used that master's chiaroscuro technique aggressively. The technique was appropriate as he sought out his models from the unfortunate poor or handicapped. He was sometimes criticised in his day for exploiting these unfortunate people.*

350. Georges de La Tour, 1593-1652, Baroque, French, *Magdalene of the Night Light,* 1642-44, Oil on canvas, 128 x 94 cm, Musée du Louvre, Paris

Several of the artist's masterpieces show his fascination with candlelight and shadows, or what later came to be known as 'night' paintings. This theme has been depicted three times by Georges de La Tour. The Louvre painting has the most rigorous structure. Seen here also is his skill in still-life painting as well as in portraiture. The painter showed a great virtuosity in the depiction of light and objects: note the magnifying effect of the glass produced by the oil in the lamp. The viewer can bring what he knows and believes about Mary Magdalene to the moment. She is portrayed in an introspective mood. So often in medieval art the human skull is symbolic of death and the inevitable fate of each human. Here that powerful symbol is coupled with a cross as a reminder that God incarnate chooses not to escape death.

351. Georges de La Tour, 1593-1652, Baroque, French, *Young Christ with St. Joseph in the Carpenter's Shop,* c. 1642, Oil on canvas, 137 x 101 cm, Musée du Louvre, Paris

353

353. Eustache Le Sueur, 1616-1655, Atticism, French, *The Muses: Clio, Euterpe and Thalia,* c. 1643, Oil on wood, 130 x 130 cm, Musée du Louvre, Paris

Atticist painter (a movement gathering Le Sueur, La Hyre and Bourdon and set in reaction against Vouet and Vignon aesthetics) Le Sueur worked on the precision of his drawing. His works reflect the influence of Poussin, Raphael and Carracci. In this work the artist gave homage to Italian Mannerist painting. Made with rich and elegant colours, it decorated the room of the Muses (Clio, muse of History, Euterpe, muse of Music, and Thalia, muse of Comedy) in the Mansion of Lambert de Thorigny, built by Le Vau.

354

354. Harmen Steenwyck, 1612-after 1656, Baroque, Dutch, *An Allegory of the Vanities of Human Life*, 1645, Oil on oak, 39.2 x 50.7 cm, National Gallery, London

Steenwyck's allegorical paintings are simple and intimate. Gold and grey are the dominant colours and bring this painting closer to Claesz's and Heda's works in the years 1620-30. They are typical of the refined manner existing in Leyde.

355. Nicolas Poussin, 1594-1665, Classicism, French, *Landscape with the Funeral of Phocion*, 1648, Oil on canvas, 114 x 115 cm, National Museum of Wales, Cardiff

356. Harmensz van Rijn Rembrandt, 1606-1669, Baroque, Dutch, *The Company of Frans Banning Cocq and Willem van Ruytenburch,* also known as the *'Night Watch'*, 1642, Oil on canvas, 363 x 437 cm, Rijksmuseum, Amsterdam

The theme is the one of the defence of the city by the bourgeois militia. The painting dates from the period of maturity in the artist's career. Rembrandt chose to represent the most intense moment of the scene, introducing drama and action in the work. He represented the departure of the captain towards the gates of the city. Each group is in movement and the light is spread in order to unify space.

355

HARMEN STEENWYCK
(1612 Delft – 1655 Leyde)

Harmen Steenwyck was the leading expert of the 'Leiden vanitas painters'. Their pictorial arrangements of books, writing materials, rare and precious objects, instruments, pipes and, above all, a skull are readily interpreted as symbols of transience and the vanity of all earthly endeavours. They are known as 'vanitas still-lifes'. One of his few extant works is the masterpiece, *The Vanities of Human Life* (1645), a visual sermon on Calvinist interpretations of passages from the Book of Ecclesiastes.

356

Rembrandt (Rembrandt Harmensz van Rijn)
(1606 Leyde – 1669 Amsterdam)

Rembrandt is completely mysterious in his spirit, his character, his life, his work and his method of painting. What we can divine of his essential nature comes through his painting and the trivial or tragic incidents of his unfortunate life; his penchant for ostentatious living forced him to declare bankruptcy. His misfortunes are not entirely explicable, and his oeuvre reflects disturbing notions and contradictory impulses emerging from the depths of his being, like the light and shade of his pictures. In spite of this, nothing perhaps in the history of art gives a more profound impression of unity than his paintings, composed though they are of such different elements, full of complex significations. One feels as if his intellect, that genial, great, free mind, bold and ignorant of all servitude and which led him to the loftiest meditations and the most sublime reveries, derived from the same source as his emotions. From this comes the tragic element he imprinted on everything he painted, irrespective of subject; there was inequality in his work as well as the sublime, which may be seen as the inevitable consequence of such a tumultuous existence.

It seems as though this singular, strange, attractive and almost enigmatic personality was slow in developing, or at least in attaining its complete expansion. Rembrandt showed talent and an original vision of the world early, as evidenced in his youthful etchings and his first self-portraits of about 1630. In painting, however, he did not immediately find the method he needed to express the still incomprehensible things he had to say, that audacious, broad and personal method which we admire in the masterpieces of his maturity and old age. In spite of its subtlety, it was adjudged brutal in his day and certainly contributed to alienate his public.

From the time of his beginnings and of his successes, however, lighting played a major part in his conception of painting and he made it the principal instrument of his investigations into the arcana of interior life. It already revealed to him the poetry of human physiognomy when he painted *The Philosopher in Meditation* or the *Holy Family*, so deliciously absorbed in its modest intimacy, or, for example, in *The Angel Raphael leaving Tobias*. Soon he asked for something more. The *Night Watch* marks at once the apotheosis of his reputation. He had a universal curiosity and he lived, meditated, dreamed and painted thrown back on himself. He thought of the great Venetians, borrowing their subjects and making of them an art out of the inner life of profound emotion. Mythological and religious subjects were treated as he treated his portraits. For all that he took from reality and even from the works of others, he transmuted it instantly into his own substance.

357. Bartolomé Esteban Perez Murillo, 1618-1682, Baroque, Spanish, *Our Lady of the Immaculate Conception,* c. 1645-50, Oil on canvas, 235 x 196 cm, The State Hermitage Museum, St. Petersburg

358. Diego Velázquez, 1599-1660, Baroque, Spanish, *The Toilet of Venus (The Rokeby Venus),* 1647-51, Oil on canvas, 122.5 x 177 cm, National Gallery, London

359. Jacob Jordaens, 1593-1678, Baroque, Dutch, *Jesus Driving the Merchants from the Temple,* 1645-50, Oil on canvas, 288 x 436 cm, Musée du Louvre, Paris

This exceptionally lively scene testifies to the artist's ease with Baroque art. Although the scene is filled with characters and animals, it follows a strict compositional arrangement with the architecture in the background and the light bringing dynamism to the foreground.

JACOB JORDAENS
(1593 – 1678 ANTWERP)

Jordaens was the pupil and son-in-law of Adam van Noort. Because he often assisted Rubens, his huge influence is very apparent. Jordaens also used the warmth of colour and the truth of nature, and mastered chiaroscuro, but he is inferior in his choice of forms. His work is characterized by great stylistic versatility. He also employed his pencil in biblical, mythological, historical and allegorical subjects, and is well-known as a portrait painter. He was also a tapestry designer and an etcher.

359

360

361

360. Paulus Potter, 1625-1654, Baroque, Dutch, *Three Cows in a Pasture,* 1648, Oil on canvas, 23.2 x 29.5 cm, Musée Fabre, Montpellier

This painting, which belonged to Talleyrand, is one of Potter's masterworks, illustrating both Italian and Dutch influences.

361. Paulus Potter, 1625-1654, Baroque, Dutch, *Young Bull,* 1647, Oil on canvas, 236 x 339 cm, Mauritshuis, The Hague

362. Frans Snyders, 1579-1657, Baroque, Flemish, *Wild Boar Hunt,* 1649, Oil on canvas, 214 x 311, Galleria degli Uffizi, Florence

363. Evaristo Baschenis, 1617-1677, Baroque, Italian, *Still-life with Musical Instruments,* c. 1650, Oil on canvas, 115 x 160 cm, Accademia Carrara, Bergamo

Most of Baschenis' works depict arrangements of musical instruments, reflecting the European reverence of stringed-instrument makers in the sixteenth and seventeenth centuries.

362

363

Paulus Potter
(1625 Enkhuizen – 1654 Amsterdam)

Dutch painter and etcher, Paulus overshadowed his father, Pieter Potter, who signed his works 'P. Potter' whereas Paulus signed typically with his full name, 'Paulus Potter'. Influenced by Claes Moeyaert, he painted historic subjects such as *Abraham returning from Canaan* (1642). However, he is mostly known for his detailed images of cattle, horses and other farm animals in landscapes that depict a naturalistic vision of Dutch rural scenes. He always searched for a way to integrate his figures into landscape, suggesting space by the positioning of the figures. Animals appear mostly in small groups silhouetted against the sky, or in greater numbers with peasant figures and rustic buildings.

364. Jan van de Cappelle, 1626-1679, Baroque, Dutch, *A Shipping Scene with a Dutch Yacht,* 1650, Oil on oak panel, 85 x 115 cm, National Gallery, London

Van de Cappelle often painted seascapes, inventing patterns of clouds, bringing dynamism and drama to the composition.

365. David Teniers the Younger, 1610-1690, Baroque, Dutch, *Archduke Leopold William in his Gallery at Brussels,* c.1651, Oil on canvas, 123 x 163 cm, Kunsthistorisches Museum, Vienna

366

367

366. Diego Velázquez, 1599-1660, Baroque, Spanish, *Las Meninas,* 1656,
Oil on canvas, 318 x 276 cm, Museo Nacional del Prado, Madrid

It is sometimes titled, The Family of Philip IV, *or* The Maids of Honour. *While
the adorably dressed five-year-old Infanta Margherita is the central focus of the
work, the painter (a self-portrait) is studying the couple, who are located
outside the painting in the viewer's place, but reflected in the mirror at the rear
of the studio. Velázquez was appointed court painter to the King. At the time
of this work he had already been Lord Chamberlain for four years. Members
of the royal household seem to be present to attend to the Infanta more than
to the royal couple. Also in attendance is a dwarf, one of the favourite subjects
of the painter, as in his* Portrait of a Dwarf at Court *(c. 1644). In the mirror, one
can see the reflection of King Philippe IV and of the Queen Marie Anne of
Austria. Also present are a nun, a man (possibly a monk or priest), and a man
waiting outside the studio, who might be eager to have the King get back to
more important matters.*

368

367. Pieter de Hooch, 1629-1684, Baroque, Dutch, *The Courtyard of a House in
Delft,* 1658, Oil on canvas, 74 x 60 cm, National Gallery, London

The Courtyard of a House in Delft *shows all the originality of the artist and the
hidden meaning often displayed in Dutch genre painting. The stone tablet over
the doorway, originally over the entrance of the Hieronymusdale Cloister in
Delft, reads, "This is in Saint Jerome's vale, if you wish to repair to patience and
meekness. For we must first descend if we wish to be raised."*

368. Harmensz van Rijn Rembrandt, 1606-1669, Baroque, Dutch, *Bathsheba
bathing with King David's Letter,* 1654, Oil on canvas, 142 x 142 cm,
Musée du Louvre, Paris

*With Bathsheba, Rembrandt establishes a dialogue with the Venetians and,
especially with Veronese, seen in the feminine canon, the peace and the balance
of the composition. Besides, this work was made with a free technique influenced
by Titian, avoiding the constriction of precise drawing. The tint, gold and ochre,
applied with thick touches of painting is characteristic of the late works of
Rembrandt. The painter interprets the theme in a special way, bringing to the fore
the internalisation of feelings more than the anecdotal aspect of the story.*

369.

369. **Jacob van Ruisdael,** 1628-1682, Baroque, Dutch, *Two Watermills and an Open Sluice near Singraven,* c. 1650-52, Oil on canvas, 87.3 x 111.5 cm, National Gallery, London

370.

370. **Jacob van Ruisdael,** 1628-1682, Baroque, Dutch, *The Jewish Cemetery at Ouderkerk,* 1653-1655, Oil on canvas, 84 x 95 cm, Gemäldegalerie, Alte Meister, Dresden

Jacob van Ruisdael
(1628 Haarlem – 1682 Amsterdam)

Ruisdael received his early training from his father, the painter and picture framer Isaack van Ruisdael and his uncle Salomon van Ruysdael (sic). He moved to Amsterdam around 1656, where he lived for the rest of his life, and where he became one of the most important Dutch landscape artists of his day. Trees became the main subject of his paintings and he imbues them with personality. His pencil is meticulous and impasto adds depth and character to the foliage and trunks. While dark clouds hovered over many of his scenes, his most sombre meditation on mortality is *The Jewish Cemetery at Ouderkerk* (1670). His paintings inspired many artists such as Gainsborough, Constable and the Barbizon School. He also produced several fine etchings.

371. **Jacob van Ruisdael,** 1628-1682, Baroque, Dutch, *Landscape during a Storm,* 1649, Oil on canvas, 25.5 x 21.5 cm, Musée Fabre, Montpellier

373

374

375

72. **Bartolomé Esteban Perez Murillo,** 1618-1682, Baroque, Spanish, *Madonna and Child,* c. 1655, Oil on canvas, 155 x 105 cm, Palazzo Pitti, Florence

73. **Pier Francesco Mola,** 1612-1666, Baroque, Italian, *Self-portrait,* 1650-66, Pastel on paper, 34.7 x 24.9 cm, Galleria degli Uffizi, Florence

Dominant figure of the neo-Venetian manner in Rome, Mola combines the aesthetics of Bolognese school with the colours of the Venetian painters.

74. **Philippe de Champaigne,** 1602-1674, Classicism, French, *Cardinal Richelieu,* 1650, Oil on canvas, 222 x 155 cm, Musée du Louvre, Paris

In such a portrait, bigger than nature, Philippe de Champaigne shows his will to get as close as possible to the physical reality of the sitter.

75. **Emmanuel de Witte,** 1616-1691, Baroque, Dutch, *Interior of the Nieuwe Kerk (New Church), Delft with the Tomb of William I of Orange, so-called William the Silent,* 1656, Oil on canvas, 97 x 85 cm, Musée des Beaux-Arts, Lille

Once he settled in Amsterdam, de Witte concentrated on architectural paintings, primarily church interiors, both real and imaginary.

376. Aelbert Cuyp, 1620-1691, Baroque, Dutch, *View of the Valkhof at Nijmegen,* c. 1655-65, Oil on panel, 48.9 x 73.7 cm, Indianapolis Museum of Art, Indianapolis

377. Bartolomé Esteban Perez Murillo, 1618-1682, Baroque, Spanish, *Boy with a Dog,* 1655-60, Oil on canvas, 70 x 60 cm, The State Hermitage Museum, St. Petersburg

Brown noted that Murillo's genre paintings have a concealed meaning (J. Brown, "Murillo, pintor de temas eroticos. Una faceta inadvertida de su obra", Goya, 1982, Nos. 169-171, p. 35-43). He compared them with the bambocciata genre paintings executed by the Italian, Dutch and Flemish artists living in Rome in the mid-seventeenth century; such themes were very popular among the same allegories in his works. Although Brown did not mention Boy with a Dog and Girl with Fruit and Flowers, thanks to his analysis their hidden symbolism can be easily revealed; the girl smiling shyly holds a basket with fruit, a symbol of maturity while the laughing boy shows the dog a basket that contains a jar, an object associated with women in the iconography of seventeenth-century art.

BARTOLOMÉ ESTEBAN PEREZ MURILLO
(1618 – 1682 SEVILLE)

Painter and draughtsman, Murillo began his art studies under Juan del Castillo, with some influence from Zurbarán. He painted in Seville, especially religious themes such as the Immaculate Conception, illustrating the doctrines of the Counter-Reformation. He was also one of the greatest portrait painters of his time. However his fame was established by painting genre scenes of beggar children. He founded the Seville Academy with Valdés Leal and Francisco Herrera the Younger, and became its first president. He excelled in the painting of clouds, flowers, water and drapery, and in the use of colour. His painting served as an example to such artists as Gainsborough, Reynolds and Greuze.

378

378. Charles Le Brun, 1619-1690, Classicism, French, *Chancellor Séguier at the Entry of Louis XIV into Paris in 1660,* 1655-61, Oil on canvas, 295 x 357 cm, Musée du Louvre, Paris

Pierre Séguier, French Chancellor, was Le Brun's first important patron. Le Brun made this monumental portrait when he came back from a trip to Italy. This official portrait displays the pomp and dignity of the chancellor showing all the talent of Le Brun in depicting scenery.

CHARLES LE BRUN
(1619 – 1690 Paris)

Son of a sculptor, Le Brun was protected in his youth by Chancellor Séguier. A prodigy, he studied with grand masters including Simon Vouet (1590-1649) and became the court painter of Louis XIII. He also studied later with the widely praised Nicolas Poussin, and both had early success as accomplished painters. He spent four years in Italy with Poussin, whose classical influence took him away from Vouet's Baroque. Back in France, Vouet advanced to be the King's favourite painter and a pioneer in French Neoclassicism, virtually founded by Poussin. In 1648, Le Brun together with Colbert, founded the Academy of Painting and Sculpture and the Academy of France in Rome. He worked several years to realise the decoration of *Château de Versailles,* especially *Escaliers des Ambassadeurs* (1674-1678), *Galerie des Glaces* and *Salons de la Guerre et de la Paix* (1684-1687). He was also in charge of *Manufacture des Gobelins* and royal collections. At his end of his life, he mainly painted religious themes.

379

379. Nicolas Poussin, 1594-1665, Classicism, French,
The Holy Family in Egypt, 1655-57, Oil on canvas, 105 x 145 cm,
The State Hermitage Museum, St. Petersburg

The late masterpiece The Holy Family in Egypt *is frequently underestimated, chiefly because its rhythmic structure is reduced to a somewhat abstracted combination of local colours. In point of fact it is a genuine masterpiece of integrity and compositional unity; and pure painterly taste can afford to make sacrifices for the sake of a visual value of a higher order. Calm and majesty — that is the overall atmosphere of the scene that Poussin depicted. Mary and Joseph have taken refuge in the shadow of a temple to slake their thirst and hunger. Their movements are retardedly smooth. The same slowness is seen in the gestures of the women standing nearby and of the boy who has gotten down on his knees. The silhouettes of these figures seem to have come down off some ancient fresco. The prime significance of the Holy Family is indicated by the placement of the group in the centre and also by the dominant vertical element, the distant temple and obelisk, which combine with the horizontally extended procession (in the same distant plane) to produce something like a system of geometrical axes. There is not a single line here that is not reconciled with the others. Their rhythm is entirely devoted to harmony. The philosophical message of the "Egyptian Virgin" (Poussin's own expression) is indicated with a clarity which makes detailed commentary superfluous. In essence, what is presented is one of the key moments in the spiritual development of mankind: old superstitions are passing away into the depths of time, while advancing to the front stage of history are the Christian heroes who are destined to change the world.*

380

380. Johannes Vermeer van Delft, 1632-1675, Baroque, Dutch, *The Procuress,*
1656, Oil on canvas, 143 x 130 cm, Gemäldegalerie, Alte Meister, Dresden

381

383

382

381. **Gabriel Metsu**, 1629-1667, Baroque, Dutch, *A Man and a Woman Seated by a Virginal*, c. 1665, Oil on canvas, 38.4 x 32.2 cm, National Gallery, London

382. **Gerard ter Borch the Younger,** 1617-1681, Baroque, Dutch, *Dancing Couple*, 1660, Oil on canvas, 76 x 68 cm, Polesden Lacey, Dorking

383. **Johannes Vermeer van Delft,** 1632-1675, Baroque, Dutch, *Girl Reading a Letter at an Open Window*, c. 1658, Oil on canvas, 83 x 65 cm, Gemäldegalerie, Alte Meister, Dresden

This painting shows the painter's range of colour tended to get clearer at this time in his career and the white background takes more and more space. The materials depicted are treated in a very subtle way in an illusionist aspect (note the precious texture of the sumptuous carpet in the foreground). A curtain deepens and closes the composition like a jewel box. The window, the source of light, and the reflection of the sitter in the glass recall that the epoch is marked by scientific research on optic radiance.

384. Johannes Vermeer van Delft, 1632-1675, Baroque, Dutch, *The Milkmaid*, c. 1659, Oil on canvas, 46 x 41 cm, Rijksmuseum, Amsterdam

Vermeer grants a plastic reality to each object depicted, and amplifies this with thickenings. The daub catches the light, which is introduced in a natural way thanks to the open window, a recurrent theme in the painter's works. The composition is minimal and stable, made around horizontals and verticals and the angle of the room keeps it steady. The sitter, concentrating on her action confers nobility to the task she does. The geometry of the character, her slow gestures and the subtle nuances of colours characterize the work of the painter.

389. **Willem Kalf,** 1619-1693, Baroque, Dutch, *Still Life with Chinese Porcelain Jar,* 1662, Oil on canvas, 64 x 53 cm, Gemäldegalerie, Alte Meister, Berlin

Philippe de Champaigne
(1602 Brussels – 1674 Paris)

Philippe's link to Rubens is through his teacher, Jacques Fouquières, who was an assistant to that important Flemish painter of the Baroque. After first painting landscapes, Philippe went to Paris in 1621 where he met Poussin. His decoration of churches won the attention of King Louis XIII (1601-43), as well as Cardinal Richelieu (1595-1642), the powerful statesman who built France into a great power. The artist's portrait of the Cardinal (1635) is among his masterworks, showing the influences of van Dyck in his full-length portrait style. He in turn introduced Flemish forms to French art. After several personal difficulties and after his daughter, a nun, overcame a serious illness, he painted his most devotional work, *Ex Voto 1662* or *Abbess Catherine – Agnes Arnauld and Sister Catherine de Saint-Susanne.*

385. **Johann Heinrich Schönfeld,** 1609-1684, Baroque, German, *The Oath of Hannibal,* c. 1660, Oil on canvas, 98 x 184.5 cm, Germanisches National-Museum, Nuremberg

386. **Philippe de Champaigne,** 1602-1674, Classicism, French, *Ex-Voto 1662,* Oil on canvas, 165 x 229 cm, Musée du Louvre, Paris

The inscription in the background tells the story that inspired this painting: the younger daughter of the painter suffered from paralysis, but she miraculously recovered after nine days of prayers.

387. **Gerrit Dou,** 1613-1675, Baroque, Dutch, *The Dropsical Lady,* c. 1663, Oil on panel, 87 x 67 cm, Musée du Louvre, Paris

388. **Gerrit Dou,** 1613-1675, Baroque, Dutch, *The Mousetrap,* 1645-50, Oil on panel, 47 x 36 cm, Musée Fabre, Montpellier

391

392

90. Jan Steen, 1626-1679, Baroque, Dutch, *As the Old Sing, so Twitter the Young,* 1663-65, Oil on canvas, 94.5 x 81 cm, Musée Fabre, Montpellier

Steen is a painter of lively, popular and comic scenes. His illustration of proverbs, such as this painting, recalls the tradition of Brueghel.

91. Adriaen van Ostade, 1610-1685, Baroque, Dutch, *Interior with Peasants,* 1663, Oil on panel, 34 x 40 cm, The Wallace Collection, London

92. Jan Steen, 1626-1679, Baroque, Dutch, *Beware of Luxury,* 1663, Oil on canvas, 105 x 145 cm, Kunsthistorisches Museum, Vienna

Jan Steen depicted his historical scenes on the grounds of genre painting. In seventeenth-century Holland, brothel scenes were common and often depicted without ambiguity or moral judgment.

393

394

393. Bartolomé Esteban Perez Murillo, 1618-1882, Baroque, Spanish,
Rest on the Flight into Egypt, c. 1665, Oil on canvas, 136.5 x 179.5 cm,
The State Hermitage Museum, St. Petersburg

The subject of the Rest on the Flight into Egypt *is related to the Flight into Egypt,*
primary literary source of the New Testament (Matthew 2: 13-51). The Gospels, howe
tell only about the flight of the Holy Family. The scenes of the rest on the flight are ba
on apocryphal literature. The Seville painters who treated this subject took their guida
from Francisco Pacheco's book, Art of Painting, *in which he tells in detail how the Vi*
and Joseph had to hurry and could not take with them enough food and clothes, and
difficult their journey was in the wilderness.

394. Johannes Vermeer van Delft, 1632-1675, Baroque, Dutch,
Girl With a Pearl Earring, c. 1665-66, Oil on canvas, 44.5 x 39 cm,
Royal Cabinet of Paintings Mauritshuis, The Hague

395. Johannes Vermeer van Delft, 1632-1675, Baroque, Dutch, *The Artist's Studio,*
c. 1665, Oil on canvas, 120 x 100 cm, Kunsthistorisches Museum, Vienna

The plaster death mask on the table to the artist's left in the painting seems to be an omin
sign for the painting's future. Between the viewer and the mask is a chair inviting the vie
to enter and become involved in the painting. It also invites the viewer to look at the pain
from every angle. The lively line of the tiles on the floor directs the eye to the model, w
the presence of several horizontal lines (from the ceiling beams to the bottom edges of
easel and stool) create a secure air of tranquillity. This work is representative of Verme
interest in interior scenes and quiet atmospheres. The drapes on the left seem to be pu
back by the viewer so as to peek in on the artist at work. Vermeer's signature is on the lo
left corner of the map tapestry, as if forming a line between the artist and model, perh
implying a personal relationship between the model and the artist. The wall map is a pictu
in-the-picture as it too has pictures-in-the-picture, giving the picture depth of meaning as
as visual perspective. The model's headpiece, book, and slide bugle point to her represen
Clio, *the muse of history. In a continuation of Dutch painting from the fifteenth century,*
depth is created by sweet slanting light from the window on the left.

395

Johannes Vermeer van Delft
(1632 – 1675 Delft)

Vermeer is perhaps the heroic type of placid, for in none of his pictures is there the least breath of disquietude. We have the impression that he laid the strokes on slowly, but with faultless certainty, and that he was as interested in a reflection in a bottle, or a curtain on a wall, in the stuff of a carpet or a dress, as in the faces of his men and women. No apparent virtuosity, no prowess of the brush, no superfluities; all leads simply to perfection and to the maximum effect expressible through simple precision. His exactness of composition, of draughtsmanship, and of colouration in its clear and rather cold range under a silvery light, is a rare and original creation. Unlike his predecessors, he used a camera obscura to help in his meticulous rendering of perspective. He revolutionised how paint was made and used. His technique of applying paint anticipated some of the methods of the impressionists over two centuries later.

396

396. Claude Lorrain (Gellée), c. 1604-1682, Classicism, French,
*Landscape with Psyche outside the Palace of Cupid ('The Enchanted
Castle')*, 1664, Oil on canvas, 87.1 x 151.3 cm, National Gallery, London

397

398

97. Claude Lorrain (Gellée), c. 1604-1682, Classicism, French, *Landscape with Jacob, Rachel and Leah at the Well (Morning),* 1666, Oil on canvas, 113 x 157 cm, The State Hermitage Museum, St. Petersburg

399

Landscape with Jacob, Rachel and Leah at the Well (Morning) is one of Lorrain's most fascinating lyrical pieces. He recreated the beauty of the nascent day with the same thrill of love, the same fervour of feeling that filled his hero's heart at young Rachel's first appearance. In the group of people, however, this feeling is only hinted at; its full force is brought out by the emotional impact of the landscape as a whole. The dominance of the lyrical mood is due to the artist's complete identification of the subject and object in the process of creating art. Nature is animated and endowed, as it were, with a soul capable of experiencing the subtlest gradations of feeling. Using his favourite device of contre jour painting, he suggests a flow of light in the direction of the spectator, and this gives the impression of the day dawning. The faintly outlined crowns of trees, enveloped in the morning mist, are echoed by the shapes of the clouds lightly gilded by the rising sun. The pictorial structure of the painting is based on finely nuanced colours with prevailing silvery tones. The colouring, clear and soft, harmonises with the emotions aroused by the picture.

98. Claude Lorrain (Gellée), c. 1604-1682, Classicism, French, *The Expulsion of Hagar,* 1668, Oil on canvas, 106.4 x 140 cm, Alte Pinakothek, Munich

At his maturity, the artist painted with a more monumental style, severe compositions and subjects often taken from the Old Testament.

99. Willem van de Velde the Younger, 1633-1707, Baroque, Dutch, *The Cannon Shot,* c. 1670, Oil on canvas, 78.5 x 67 cm, Rijksmuseum, Amsterdam

A painter from Haarlem, one of the two most prestigious Dutch schools of painting, van de Velde belonged to a family of engravers; an important activity for painters as it enabled them to broadcast and promote their works. He painted numerous panoramic views, depicting simple daily life from Haarlem. His works contrast with those of Seghers who intended to give a more dramatic representation to his landscapes.

400

401

400. Harmensz van Rijn Rembrandt, 1606-1669, Baroque, Dutch, *Portrait of Two Figures from the Old Testament,* also known as *'The Jewish Bride',* 1667, Oil on canvas, 121.5 x 166.5 cm, Rijksmuseum, Amsterdam

401. Frans van Mieris, 1635-1681, Baroque, Dutch, *Carousing Couple,* undated Oil on panel, Private collection

403

404

402. Harmensz van Rijn Rembrandt, 1606-1669, Baroque, Dutch,
The Return of the Prodigal Son, 1668, Oil on canvas, 262 x 205 cm,
The State Hermitage Museum, St. Petersburg

*The story of the prodigal son is told here in an expressive and laconic way,
about six years before the painter's death: the strict verticals of the solemn
and majestic figures stand as the dominant aspect of the painting. The
father's clothes and the line of his face find an extension in his son's face,
underlining the union between the two men and granting a certain
monumentality to the grouping. The figures seem to come out of the
shadow to reach a blaze of colour. The manner is characteristic of
Rembrandt's later works.*

403. Pierre Mignard, 1612-1695, Classicism, French, *Girl Blowing Soap
Bubbles,* 1674, Oil on canvas, 130 x 96 cm, Château de Versailles

*Pierre Mignard studied under Vouet after he trained with Boucher. This
classical composition displays an allegorical figure of homo bulla,
illustrating the ephemeral life, where human existence is comparable to a
soap bubble.*

404. Gerard ter Borch The Younger, 1617-1681, Baroque, Dutch, *A Concert,*
c. 1675, Oil on panel, 58.1 x 47.3 cm, Cincinnati Art Museum, Cincinnati

406

407

405. Baciccio (Giovanni Battista Gaulli), 1639-1709, High Baroque, Italian, *Adoration of the Name of Jesus,* 1674-79, Fresco, Sant'Ignazio, Rome

Masterpiece of High Baroque illusionism, this theatrical fresco is the result of the prestigious commission for decorating the interior of the Jesuit church of Il Gesù in Rome.

406. Andrea Pozzo, 1642-1709, High Baroque, Italian, *Allegory of the Missionary Work of the Jesuits,* 1685-94, Fresco, Sant' Ignazio, Rome

407. Frans Snyders, 1579-1657, Baroque, Flemish, *A Game Stall,* c. 1675, Oil on canvas, 177 x 274 cm, York City Art Gallery, York

408

409

408. Claudio Coello, 1642-1693,
Baroque, Spanish, *Charles II
Adoring the St Sacrament,*
1685-90, Oil on canvas,
El Escorial (sacristy), Madrid

*The last important master of
the Madrid School of the
seventeenth century, Coello
painted here his masterpiece.
The painter is influenced by
Baroque dynamic compositions
and by the refined colours of the
Venetians.*

409. Gaspar van Wittel, c.1653-1736,
Baroque, Dutch, *The Villa Medici
in Rome,* 1685, Tempera on
parchment, 29 x 41 cm,
Palazzo Pitti, Florence

410

411

410. Jacques Stella, 1596-1657,
Baroque, French, *Christ Served by Angels*, before 1693,
Oil on canvas, 111 x 158 cm,
Galleria degli Uffizi, Florence

411. Meindert Hobbema, 1638-1709,
Baroque, Dutch, *The Avenue at Middleharnis*, 1689,
Oil on canvas, 103.5 x 141 cm,
National Gallery, London

This is one of the later Vedute *(a painting depicting a panoramic view of a place) painted by Hobbema. Having been a pupil of Ruisdael, his landscapes were influenced by the master's manner but tended to be more simplified, all the accessory details being removed while the expanse of sky was emphasised.*

412. Nicolas de Largillière,
1656-1746, Rococo, French,
*The Provost and Municipal
Magistrates of Paris Discussing
the Celebration of Louis XIV's
Dinner at the Hotel de Ville after
his Recovery in 1687*, 1689,
Oil on canvas, 68 x 101 cm,
The State Hermitage Museum,
St. Petersburg

413

18ᵗʰ CENTURY

'The Enlightenment' marks the eighteenth century as a period heavily invested in ideas. Salon culture developed through the taste and social initiative of women during the Rococo period in the courts of France, Austria and Germany. These women were known as *femmes savantes*, or learned women. In addition to art, the salons propagated Enlightenment ideas that rejected superstition and favoured provable theories based on scientific methods. Empiricism flourished, coming out of the seventeenth century achievements in science, most notably those of Britons Sir Isaac Newton (1642-1727) and John Locke (1632-1704). Their insistence on tangible data and empirical proof changed the course of ideas.

In France, the *philosophes* helped to spread rational ideas based on reason into the areas of church and state. They believed that through the progress of ideas, there existed a possibility for the perfection of mankind. Gathering and ordering knowledge was part of the Enlightenment project. Accordingly, Denis Diderot (1713-1784) edited the first encyclopaedia (thirty-five volumes, 1751-1780) in an attempt to systematically record all existing knowledge. Diderot also became the first art critic by publishing his commentaries on the official French Salon exhibitions of the Royal Academy of Painting and Sculpture. Voltaire (1674-1778) wrote against the despotic rule of kings and the hegemony of the church. Later, revolutionary thinkers would recall his seminal ideas. Natural history and zoology were catalogued by the Comte de Buffon (1707-1778), while in Sweden, Carolus Linnaeus (1707-1778) created a comprehensive classification of plants.

Worldwide, the eighteenth century marks the start of the 'modern' period in which a self-conscious awareness of the present in relation to past begets a preoccupation with newness, or being current. Americans in the colonies were also noted for their commitment to Enlightenment ideas, most notably Benjamin Franklin and Thomas Jefferson. Scientific inventions flourished as much as social inventions, and the Industrial Revolution began in England in the 1740s. It was spurred on by research into steam power, electricity, the discovery of oxygen, and mechanical advances in technology, including the first use of iron for a bridge in 1776.

A renewed interest in classical antiquity was fuelled by the discovery and excavation of Herculaneum (1738) and Pompeii (1748), as well as the growing trend of aristocrats to make a 'Grand Tour' of travel through Europe, but Italy in particular.

The American (1775-1783) and French (1789-1792) Revolutions also helped to create an appeal for a new style: Neoclassicism. The neoclassical style is characterized by moral content, strong, clear compositions, and often appeals to patriotic virtue. Napoleon Bonaparte (1769-1821) filled the power gap in the revolutionary chaos by ascending to power and crowning himself emperor of France in 1804. He too, embraced the neoclassical style as it created a symbolic system to bolster his authority, and he particularly favoured connections to the Roman Empire in his expansionist phase of military conquest.

13. **Jean-Baptiste Chardin**, 1699-1779, Rococo, French,
Saying Grace (Le Benedicité), 1744, Oil on Canvas, 49.5 x 38.4 cm,
The State Hermitage Museum, St Petersburg

Chardin chooses here a theme often depicted by the Dutch masters of the seventeenth century. In contrast with the thick layer of painting he was using in his former works, Chardin uses here a smoother touch.

414

416

414. Rachel Ruysch, 1664-1750, Baroque, Dutch, *Flower Still-Life*, After 1700, Oil on canvas, 75.5 x 60.7 cm, The Toledo Museum of Art, Toledo

415. Jean Raoux, 1677-1734, Rococo, French, *Taste (From the Five Senses series)*, c. 1715-34, Oil on canvas, 56.5 x 72 cm, Pushkin Museum of Fine Arts, Moscow

416. Sebastiano Ricci, 1659-1734, Rococo, Italian, *Allegory of Tuscany*, 1706, Oil on canvas, 90 x 70.5 cm, Galleria degli Uffizi, Florence

417. Antoine Watteau, 1684-1721, Rococo, French, *An Embarrassing Proposal*, c. 1716, Oil on canvas, 65 x 85 cm, The State Hermitage Museum, St Petersburg

415

417

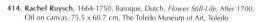
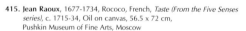

418

418. Nicolas de Largillière, 1656-1746, Rococo, French, *Portrait of a Lady,*
c. 1710, Oil on canvas, 80 x 64 cm, Pushkin Museum of Fine Arts, Moscow

419

420

419. Antoine Watteau, 1684-1721, Rococo, French,
A Love Festival, 1717, Oil on canvas, 61 x 75 cm,
Gemäldegalerie, Alte Meister, Dresden

420. Canaletto (Giovanni Antonio Canal), 1697-1768, Rococo,
Italian, *Venice: Campo S. Vidal and Santa Maria della Carità
(The Stonemason's Yard)*, 1727-28,
Oil on panel, 123.8 x 162.9 cm, National Gallery, London

The bold composition, the densely applied paint and the ca
execution of the figures are characteristic of Canaletto's wor
the mid to late 1720s. This unusual view across the Grand C
shows the campanile *(bell-tower) of Santa Maria della Carita*
collapsed after the painting was made and was never rebuilt.

421

422

21. **Jean-Marc Nattier**, 1685-1766, Rococo, French,
  The Battle of Lesnaya, 1717, Oil on canvas, 90 x 112 cm,
  Pushkin Museum of Fine Arts, Moscow

22. **Jean-Baptiste Oudry**, 1686-1755, Baroque, French,
  Still Life with Fruit, 1721, Oil on Canvas, 74 x 92 cm,
  The State Hermitage Museum, St Petersburg

423

23. Hyacinthe Rigaud, 1659-1743, Rococo, French, *Louis XIV,* 1701, Oil on canvas, 277 x 194 cm, Musée du Louvre, Paris

Ordered to be given to the King of Spain, this portrait was such a success at the French court that it remained in the country. It represented 'the power, pomp and circumstance' of the absolutist ruler.

24. Antoine Watteau, 1684-1721, Rococo, French, *Gilles,* 1717-19, Oil on canvas, 185 x 150 cm, Musée du Louvre, Paris

This painting, either called Gilles *or* Pierrot *still has an undefined subject. The sitter taking over the foreground is exceptionally monumental for a work by Watteau. In the background are the four traditional characters from the Commedia dell'arte, accompanying Pierrot but contrasting in their attitude.*

425. Antoine Watteau, 1684-1721, Rococo, French, *The Pilgrimage to the Island of Cythera,* 1718, Oil on canvas, 129 x 194 cm, Schloss Charlottenburg, Berlin

This painting caused Watteau to be dubbed with the official title of peintre de fêtes galantes. *The scene is set on the Isle of Cythera, the island of love itself; a statue of Aphrodite stands at the edge of the woods and cupids accompany their new acquaintances, hovering above the cavaliers and their female companions. There is no emotional crescendo despite the assumption implied by the artist's choice of subject. The story of Watteau's* The Pilgrimage to the Island of Cythera *is also noteworthy. The minutes of the Royal Academy of Painting and Sculpture of 30 June, 1712, stated that the painter would be given a subject by the Academy's director. Then these words were crossed out and replaced by the following statement: "The subject for his acceptance work has been left to his discretion." Watteau's choice of subject matter was undoubtedly determined by his own ideas and by his opposition not only to the official hierarchy of genres, but also to the practice of the times whereby distinguished patrons imposed their own choice of subject on painters. Watteau's* The Pilgrimage to the Island of Cythera *was probably another example of his own imaginary "theatre". In such paintings, the landscape is bathed in a soft golden hue reminiscent of Venetian painting. The gradual change of this tone, which becomes increasingly light and translucent in the distance, brilliantly conveys the atmosphere and demonstrates the golden, warm range of tones used by the artist in his prime.*

426

428

427

426. Noël Nicolas Coypel, 1690-1734, Rococo, French, *The Birth of Venus*, 1732, Oil on canvas, 81 x 65 cm, The State Hermitage Museum, St Petersbu

427. Jean-Baptiste Chardin, 1699-1779, Rococo, French, *Child with Top*, c. 1738, Oil on canvas, 68 x 76 cm, Musée du Louvre, Paris

428. Giovanni-Battista Tiepolo, 1696-1770, Rococo, Italian, *Sarah and the Archangel*, 1726-28, Fresco, Height c. 400 cm, Palazzo Arcivescovile, Udin

429. Jean-Baptiste Chardin, 1699-1779, Rococo, French, *The Ray*, 1725-26, Oil on canvas, 114 x 146 cm, Musée du Louvre, Paris

Nearly all the artist's works are small, thirty centimetres square or even les They were made to be affordable for middle-class customers or sponsors. Th work was the still-life with which Chardin was accepted at the Royal Academ of Painting and Sculpture. The artist selected common objects for the commo person. Chardin painted ordinary scenes with respect for both the har working middle class and their objects. Kitchen scenes were a favourite, th one dominated by a ray, a flat fish that has no bones but noted for its broa wing-like pectoral fins.

430. Giovanni-Battista Tiepolo, 1696-1770, Rococo, Italian, *The Finding of Moses*, 1730, Oil on canvas, 202 x 342 cm, National Gallery of Scotland, Edinburgh

The dramatic impact of the painting is heightened by its impressive size (th painting was originally even larger but a section has been cut, probably in th nineteenth century), the colouring and the theatrical character.

29

Jean-Baptiste Siméon Chardin
(1699 – 1779 Paris)

Chardin in 1728 gained admittance to the Academy with two large canvases which were merely still-lifes: *The Ray* and *The Buffet*. Their technical merit is immediately striking: in these pieces, handled with extraordinary tact and felicity, are all the riches and subtlety of oil painting. But there also appears, even this early, the sense of intimacy and poetry of humble things which gives Chardin a place apart from even the best still-life and genre painters. Chardin is purely French; he is far nearer to the feeling of meditative quiet which animates the rustic scenes of Louis Le Nain a century earlier than to the spirit of light and superficial brilliance surrounding him, even in the so-called realism of his time. He did not, like his predecessors, seek his models among the peasantry; he painted the petty bourgeoisie of Paris. But manners have been softened; the petty bourgeoisie were far removed from Le Nain's austere peasants. The housewives of Chardin are simply but neatly dressed and the same cleanliness is visible in the houses where they dwell. Everywhere a sort of refinement and good-fellowship constitute the charm of these little pictures of domestic life, unique in their way and superior, both in feeling and subject, to the masterpieces of some of the Dutch masters.

30

431

432

431. Giovanni Paolo Pannini, 1691-1765, Rococo, Italian, *The River Arno with Ponte Santa Trinita,* 1742, Oil on canvas, 62 x 90 cm, Szépmüvészeti Múzeum, Budapest

432. Giovanni Battista Piazzetta, 1683-1754, Rococo, Italian, *Susanna and the Elders,* 1740, Oil on canvas, 100 x 135 cm, Galleria degli Uffizi, Florence

433. Canaletto (Giovanni Antonio Canal), 1697-1768, Rococo, Italian, *The Bucintoro at the Molo on Ascension Day,* 1732, Oil on canvas, 182 x 259 cm, Aldo Crespi Collection, Milan

433

434

436

435

434. François Boucher, 1703-1770, Rococo, French, *An Afternoon Meal*, 1739, Oil on canvas, 81 x 65 cm, Musée du Louvre, Pa

435. William Hogarth, 1697-1764, Rococo, English, *A Rake's Pro Tavern Scene*, c. 1735, Oil on canvas, 62.2 x 75 cm, Courtesy of the Trustees of Sir John Soane's Museum, London

This work is also called The Orgy. *It is scene III of the series the exploits of a rake, a debouched or corrupt man. The loca the scene is a brothel that was popular in London at the Novelists describing the period have described how enter young ladies, shockingly without stockings, would dance while a mirror (the silver plate on the left in the painting) and car display themselves provocatively. But that is merely one of visual references in the scene of the story this art is illus Viewers can see Hogarth's engraving of the work at the Metro Museum of Art in New York City.*

436. Jean-Baptiste Pater, 1695-1736, Rococo, French, *Scene in a first half of the 18th century, Oil on canvas, 149 x 84 cm, The State Hermitage Museum, St Petersburg

437

438

439

437. Jean-Baptiste Chardin, 1699-1779, Rococo, French, *The Governess,* 1739,
Oil on canvas, 46.7 x 37.5 cm, National Gallery of Canada, Ottawa

438. Pietro Longhi, 1702-1785, Rococo, Italian, *The Introduction,* 1740,
Oil on canvas, 66 x 55 cm, Musée du Louvre, Paris

439. Jean-Marc Nattier, 1685-1766, Rococo, French, *The Duchesse d'Orléans,
as Hebe,* 1744, Oil on canvas, 144 x 110 cm,
Musée du Louvre, Paris

*Noticed by Louis XIV, Nattier specialised in Court portraiture and realised a
series of allegorical portraits marked with the soft modelling of the faces.*

William Hogarth
(1697 – 1764 London)

Hogarth's case is a strange one. The famous series of paintings, *The
Harlot's Progress, The Rake's Progress,* and *Marriage à la Mode,* are
pictorial moralities of a kind which seems completely outside the
domain of art; for Hogarth's considerations of morality counted
infinitely more than those of art and beauty. He is known to have
said that he created "painted comedy" and considered it as a work
"of public utility". His morality was founded on good, sturdy,
practical truths and was not stirred by any breath of heroism, but he
imbued it all with such verve, such powerful vitality, he paraded and
set in motion such a gallery of types, of characters whose blatant
truthfulness hits us in the eye, that all criticism is silenced and
reservations of the fastidious melt away.

This auto-didactic personage, disdainful of all culture, this
Englishman who desired to be nothing more, was not without
influence on the most cultured, refined, intelligent, learned and
cosmopolitan of the great English painters, the instigator and first
president of the Royal Academy, a great amateur and collector and
perfect gentleman, and author of remarkable writings on art.

247

441

Canaletto
(Giovanni Antonio Canal)
(1697 – 1768 Venice)

Canaletto began his career as a theatrical scene painter, like his father, in the Baroque tradition. Influenced by Giovanni Panini, he is specialised in vedute (views) of Venice, his birth place. Strong contrast between light and shadow is typical of this artist. Furthermore, if some of those views are purely topographical, others include festivals or ceremonial subjects. He also published, thanks to John Smith, his agent, a series of etchings of Cappricci. His main purchasers were British aristocracy because his views reminded them of their Grand Tour. In his paintings geometrical perspective and colours are structuring. Canaletto spent ten years in England. John Smith sold Canaletto's works to George III, creating the major part of the Royal Canaletto Collection. His greatest works influenced landscape painting in the nineteenth century.

442

François Boucher
(1703 – 1770 Paris)

Boucher is typical of the artist, whose ambitions are clearly defined and exactly proportioned to his capacity: he desired to please his contemporaries, to decorate walls and ceilings for them, and, in his better moments, realised perfectly what he set out to do. Thus it is he who best sums up the taste of the century. He played, *mutatis mutandis*, and with all the differences implied by the very names of the two sovereigns, Louis XIV – le roi soleil and Louis XV – le bien aimé, a role similar to that of Le Brun. He had decorative genius and the gift of composition; facile, elegant, and always perfectly balanced. He bore the weight of an immense output, illustrating a book, or finishing off a fan as aptly as he rumpled the draperies of complaisant goddesses or peopled sky and wave with rosy and golden nudes. As a decorator he had gifts in no way inferior to those of his fascinating contemporary Tiepolo; he could also paint excellent portraits, or render intimate scenes with brilliance and deftness.

440. Canaletto (Giovanni Antonio Canal), 1697-1768, Rococo, Italian, *Venice: The Feast Day of St Roch*, c. 1735, Oil on canvas, 147 x 199 cm, National Gallery, London

441. Bernardo Bellotto, 1720-1780, Rococo, Italian, *Square with the Kreuz Kirche in Dresden*, 1751, Oil on canvas, 197 x 187 cm, The State Hermitage Museum, St Petersburg

442. François Boucher, 1703-1770, Rococo, French, *Diana Resting after her Bath*, 1742, Oil on canvas, 57 x 73 cm, Musée du Louvre, Paris

This painting shows the interest that Boucher took in the representation of women in nature. Both are matching in a subtle combination of colours. The sensuality of the women is enhanced by the light coming from the left of the painting and the modelling of their bodies. Here Diana is accompanied by her traditional symbols: the moon crescent, the bow and quiver.

443

444

443. **William Hogarth**, 1697-1764, Rococo, English, *The Shrimp Girl*, 1740-50, Oil on canvas, 64 x 53 cm, National Gallery, London

444. **François Boucher**, 1703-1770, Rococo, French, *The Toilet of Venus*, 1751, Oil on canvas, 108.3 x 85.1 cm, The Metropolitan Museum of Art, New York

Commissioned by Mme de Pompadour, mistress of Louis XV, for her Château de Bellevue, this work shows Boucher's contribution to Rococo painting and to the repertoire of mythology.

445. **William Hogarth**, 1697-1764, Rococo, English, *The Painter and his Pug*, 1745, Oil on canvas, 90 x 70 cm, Tate Gallery, London

446

447

448

46. Giovanni-Battista Tiepolo, 1696-1770, Rococo, Italian, *The Banquet of Cleopatra*, 1746, Fresco, 650 x 300 cm, Pallazzo Labia, Venice

47. Jean-Etienne Liotard, 1702-1789, Baroque, Swiss, *The Chocolate-Girl*, 1744-45, Pastel on paper, 82.5 x 52.5 cm, Gemäldegalerie, Alte Meister, Dresden

48. Pietro Longhi, 1701-1785, Rococo, Italian, *The Rhinoceros*, 1751, Oil on canvas, 62 x 50 cm, Ca' Rezzonico, Venice

Coming from exotic territories, the rhinoceros was displayed in popular shows. Longhi depicts this Venetian scene during the period of carnival and pays great attention to the depiction of the characters and the atmosphere of excitement.

449

451

450

Thomas Gainsborough
(1727 Sudbury, Suffolk – 1788 London)

Thomas Gainsborough, four years younger than Reynolds rivalled him in fame. He had nothing of the theorist, the teacher, the leader of a school, and he never thought of combining in his art skilful borrowings from the greatest artists of various foreign schools. Unlike Reynolds he never left England and, after several years of apprenticeship in London, spent the greater part of his life successively at Sudbury, Ipswich and Bath. Gainsborough is not an impeccable draughtsman, his compositions are not skilfully balanced like those of Reynolds, and his figures often seem disposed haphazardly on the canvas. But he has charm. He is a poet, and a poet by instinct, quivering with sensitivity, capricious and fantastic but always natural. Although he painted some good portraits of men he is, par excellence, the painter of women and children. A profound admirer of van Dyck – he took him for a model – this admiration does not detract from his originality, which has a unique quality of seductiveness. On van Dyck's themes, such as that of the boy clad in costly satin, a woman's face, long and delicate in its aristocratic grace, he composed entirely new variations.

449. Paul Troger, 1698-1762, Rococo, Austrian, *St Sebastian and the Women*, 1746, Oil on canvas, 60 x 37 cm, Österreichische Galerie, Vienna

450. Gaspare Traversi, c. 1722-1770, Rococo, Italian, *The Music Lesson*, c. 1750, Oil on canvas, 152 X 204.6 cm, Nelson-Atkins Museum of Art, Kansas City

451. Thomas Gainsborough, 1727-1788, Rococo, English, *Mr and Mrs Andrews*, c. 1750, Oil on canvas, 70 x 119 cm, National Gallery, London

This portrait is the masterpiece of Gainsborough's early years. The landscape, the gun and the dog evoke Robert Andrews' estate and suggest the idea of an important landlord. His wife sits on an elaborate wooden bench; the painting of her lap is actually unfinished. The outdoor scene and informal postures o the couple follow the fashionable convention of the conversation piece.

452. Canaletto (Giovanni Antonio Canal), 1697-1768, Rococo, Italian, *Dresden, View from the Right Bank of the Elbe*, 1747, Oil on canvas, 133 x 237 cm, Gemäldegalerie, Alte Meister, Dresden

453

454

453. François Boucher, 1703-1770, Rococo, French
Reclining Girl, 1752, Oil on canvas, 59 x 73 cm
Alte Pinakothek, Munich

*At the peak of Madame de Pompadour's influence
on her commissioned artists, and as mistress of
Louis XV, she called on Boucher to paint works for
her personal quarters. Like the coquettish nude
painted for her, this young girl brings to mind
scented silk, sensual touches, and other pleasures
of the flesh. She looks away, maybe into her own
life, ignoring but not resisting a voyeur's gaze. The
bedding in the upper right helps push the wall into
the background, as do the hues of brown used for
both the wall and bedding. The rose and white in
the sheets extend the soft flesh tones of the relaxed
but pensive girl. Every curve in the work is soft and
flowing, as lines are only implied. Smoke circles
from the incense burner in the lower left is carried
off in the direction of the girl's daydream. The
artist's more classic and familiar work is The Toilet
of Venus (1751).*

454. Gaspare Traversi, c. 1722-1770, Rococo, Italian
The Drawing Lesson, c. 1750, Oil on canvas,
161.7 x 204 cm, Nelson-Atkins Museum of Art,
Kansas City

456

Giovanni Paolo Pannini, 1691-1765, Baroque, Italian, *Roma Antica*, 1758, Oil on canvas, 231 x 303 cm, Musée du Louvre, Paris

Giovanni Paolo Pannini, 1691-1765, Baroque, Italian, *Picture Gallery with Views of Modern Rome*, 1759, Oil on canvas, 231 x 303 cm, Musée du Louvre, Paris

457

Giovanni Battista Tiepolo, 1696-1770, Rococo, Italian, *The Ceiling of the Kaisersaal: The Marriage of The Emperor Frederick Barbarosa and Beatrice of Burgundy*, 1750-53, Fresco, 400 x 500 cm, Residence of the prince-bishop of Würzburg, Kaisersaal, Schloss Würzburg

Asked to provide a work that would fill the space where a window once was, Tiepolo produced a dramatic recollection of the marriage of Beatrice of Burgundy and Frederick Barbarossa. Although the event took place 500 years earlier, the artist placed it in a contemporary setting. An elaborate guilt-stucco drape is drawn back by a carved putto. The steps of the bishop's platform seem to progress from the architecture of the wall. As an acknowledgment of the historical context of the event, and to give it the dignity it demanded, elements from classical periods (the architecture in the background) are atypically included. After achieving these works at the peak of mastering his technique, Tiepolo was invited to Madrid where he experienced the end of the influence of Rococo in himself. He also got caught up there in the energy of the Neoclassical as followed by the German painter Anton Raphael Mengs (1728-79).

Giovanni Battista Tiepolo
(1696 Venice – 1770 Madrid)

Giovanni Battista (Giambattista) Tiepolo was the last of the great Venetian decorators and the purest master of the Italian Rococo. He was a prodigy, a pupil of Gregorio Lazzarini, but already by age twenty-one he was established as a painter in Venice. He was an Italian artist of large-scale frescos, such as for the Residence in Würzburg and the Palacio Real in Madrid, both of which he did with his sons, Giovanni Dominico and Lorenzo, when he was in his fifties. In 1755, after his return from Würzburg, he was elected the first President of the Venetian Academy, before leaving for Spain where he died.

458

459

458. Carle Vanloo, 1705-1765, Neoclassicism, French,
Reading from a Spanish Book, 1754, Oil on canvas, 164 x 128 cm,
The State Hermitage Museum, St Petersburg

459. Allan Ramsey, 1713-1784, Rococo, Scottish, *The Artist's Wife: Margaret
Lindsay of Evelick*, 1758, Oil on canvas, 74.3 x 61.9 cm,
National Gallery of Scotland, Edinburgh

460. Carle Vanloo, 1705-1765, Neoclassicism, French, *The Concert*, 1754,
Oil on canvas, 164 x 129 cm, The State Hermitage Museum, St Petersburg

461. Joseph Vernet, 1714-1789, Neoclassicism, French, *The City and Harbour of
Toulon*, 1756, Oil on canvas, 165 x 263 cm, Musée du Louvre, Paris

*Influenced by the light and atmosphere of Claude Lorrain, Vernet then became
a leading expert of a type of idealised and sentimental landscape, along with
Hubert Robert. This tableau is part of a series commissioned by Louis XV
showing the most important and strategic French harbours.*

462. Joseph Vernet, 1714-1789, Neoclassicism, French, *Morning*, 1760,
Oil on canvas, 65.5 x 98.5 cm, The Art Institute of Chicago, Chicago

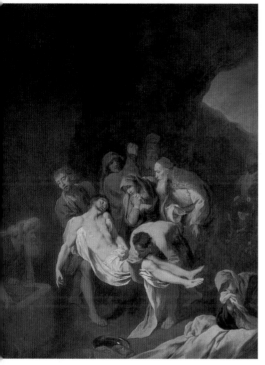

465

466

Louis Tocque, 1696-1772, Rococo, French, *Portrait of Empress Elizabeth Petrovna*, 1758, Oil on canvas, 262 x 204 cm, The State Hermitage Museum, St Petersburg

Christian Wilhelm Ernst Dietrich, 1712-1774, Rococo, German, *The Entombment*, 1759, Oil on panel, 35 x 28 cm, The State Hermitage Museum, St Petersburg

Jean-Honoré Fragonard, 1732-1806, Rococo, French, *Blind-Man's Bluff*, c. 1760, Oil on canvas, 114 x 90 cm, Toledo Museum of Art, Toledo

Joshua Reynolds, 1723-1792, Rococo, English, *The Countess Spencer with her Daughter Georgiana*, 1760, Oil on canvas, 122 x 115 cm, Collection of Earl Spencer, Althorp

467

468

467. **Thomas Gainsborough**, 1727-1788, Rococo, English, *Miss Ann Ford,* 1760
Oil on canvas, 192 x 135 cm, Cincinnati Museum of Art, Cincinnati

468. **George Romney**, 1734-1802, Rococo, English, *The Leigh Family,* 1767-6
Oil on canvas, 185.5 x 202 cm, National Gallery of Victoria, Melbourne

469. **Thomas Gainsborough**, 1727-1788, Rococo, English, *Mary, Countess
Howe,* 1760, Oil on canvas, 244 x 152.4 cm, Kenwood House, London

470. **Johann Conrad Seekatz**, 1719-1768, Rococo, German,
The Repudiation of Hagar, 1760-65, Oil on canvas, 37.5 x 50.5 cm,
The State Hermitage Museum, St Petersburg

471. **Joseph Marie Vien**, 1716-1809, Neoclassicism, French,
The Seller of Loves, 1763, Oil on canvas, 98 x 122 cm,
Musée National du Château, Fontainebleau

470

471

472

473

472. Angelica Kauffmann, 1741-1807, Neoclassicism, Swiss, *David Garrick*, 1764, Oil on canvas, 84 x 69 cm, Burghley House, Lincolnshire

473. Jean-Honoré Fragonard, 1732-1806, Rococo, French, *Inspiration*, c. 1769 Oil on canvas, 80 x 64 cm, Musée du Louvre, Paris

474. Alexander Roslin, 1718-1798, Rococo, Swedish, *Woman with a Veil: Marie Suzanne Roslin*, 1768, Oil on canvas, 65 x 54 cm, Nationalmuseum, Stockholm

477

475. Jean-Baptiste Greuze, 1725-1805, Rococo, French,
L'Accordée de village, 1761, Oil on canvas, 92 x 117 cm, Musée du Louvre, Paris

L'Accordée de village *depicts a scene in which a father is talking with his future son-in-law, witnessed by a notary, the crying mother and the siblings of the future bride.*

476. Jean-Baptiste Greuze, 1725-1805, Rococo, French,
Portrait of Countess Ekaterina Shuvalova, c. 1770, Oil on canvas, 60 x 50 cm,
The State Hermitage Museum, St Petersburg

476

477. Joseph Wright, 1734-1797, Romanticism, English, *An Experiment on a Bird in the Air Pump*, 1768, Oil on canvas, 183 x 244 cm, National Gallery, London

Influenced by Caravaggio's realism and mystery of light, Wright was interested in the contrasts between light and shadow, as was a contemporary, Anton Raphael Mengs. Wright was specifically fascinated by the effects of candlelight, as seen in El Greco's Boy Lighting a Candle *(1573). In this work, the candle is seen as a ghostly image from the other side of the beaker in which there is a skull and cloudy liquid. Wright was also interested in drawing attention to current discoveries or advances in science. In this masterpiece of classical realism, the phenomena of vacuum, which we take for granted today, is being demonstrated. Each witness to the air pump experiment has a distinct reaction, shown mainly by facial expressions. Unfortunately, a cockatoo will suffocate if the cruel experiment sucks too much air out of his glass container. The moon is a reference to the Lunar Society, a group of people interested in discussing science. The work might be showing the family of a member in one such group, as there is indeed a full moon.*

JEAN-BAPTISTE GREUZE
(1725 TOURNUS – 1805 PARIS)

Greuze is without question one of the most important painters of the French school of the eighteenth century. He possessed a unique asset: he created his own style – sentimental and melodramatic genre scenes. Very early in his career his work was praised by the critics, such as Diderot who talked about "morality in paint". While *L'Accordée de village*, where every detail is like an actor playing a part, seems borrowed from some *comédie-larmoyante* or contemporary melodrama, much of Greuze's later work consisted of titillating pictures of young girls, which contain thinly veiled sexual allusions under their surface appearance of mawkish innocence. The end of the century saw the end of his career as his reception piece was not accepted by the academy in 1769 and a new glorified style was appearing carried out by Jacques-Louis David: Neoclassicism.

478

479

478. George Stubbs, 1724-1806, Romanticism, E
Mares and Foals in a River Landscape, 1763-
Oil on canvas, 99 x 159 cm, Tate Gallery, Lo

479. Jacob Philipp Hackert, 1737-1807, Neoclas
German, *The Destruction of the Turkish Fleet*
Chesme Harbour, 1771, Oil on panel, 162 x 2
The State Hermitage Museum, St Petersburg

480. Benjamin West, 1738-1820, Neoclassicism,
American, *The Death of General Wolfe*, 1770
Oil on canvas, 152 x 214 cm, National Galle
Canada, Ottawa

In 1771, West upset the art world with t
because it placed contemporary figures in a
composition. His work was generally critic
considered derivative, but it made a breakthr
moved art to greater realism. He showed the c
the victorious British Army general, James Wol
battlefield, after the capture of Quebec, Car
the French in 1759. Grieving officers ar
American Indians surround him. His victo
British supremacy in Canada. It was this pai
won West the appointment as painter to the
such he applied especially his self-taught skill
painting.

481. Francesco Guardi, 1712-1793, Rococo, Ital
An Architectural Caprice, c. 1770,
Oil on canvas, 54 x 36 cm, National Gallery,

480

481

Benjamin West
(1738 Springfield, Pennsylvania – 1820 London)

In 1760, West was the first American to study art in Italy. During his three years there he was influenced by Titian and Raphael, as well as the contemporary art he saw there during the advent of the Neoclassical movement. He won the attention and praise of George III, who appointed him to be a charter member of the Royal Academy. He became president of the Royal Academy in 1792. He restored and reshaped Neoclassicism in historical paintings in France over a decade before David. Yet, he also earned the title, 'Father of American Painting', not due to his paintings, but because he taught influential American painters John Singleton Copley, Charles Peale, Gilbert Stuart, and John Trumbull, as well as talented men not best known as painters, including Robert Fulton and Samuel F.B. Morse. Although he never returned to the United States, he remained true to its heritage by rejecting the offer of knighthood. He is buried in St. Paul's Cathedral.

482

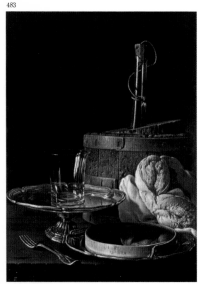

483

Jean Honoré Fragonard
(1732 Grasse – 1806 Paris)

Fragonard closes, with a burst of fireworks, the curve of the eighteenth century opened by Watteau with his fairy poems of love and melancholy. Watteau was ethereal and profound; Fragonard was merely light. He amuses us while amusing himself; he is never moved. He painted mainly fetes-galantes in Rococo style. Pupil of François Boucher, Fragonard also studied under Chardin. Always remembering Boucher's advice, he depicted romantic gardens, with their fountains, grottos, temples and terraces where one can also recognise the influence of Tiepolo. With King Louis XV as a patron he turned himself towards the depiction of the pleasure-loving and licentious court, scenes of love and voluptuousness.

482. Luis Eugenio Meléndez, 1716-1780, Rococo, Spanish, *Still-Life with Melon and Pears*, c. 1770, Oil on canvas, 64 x 85 cm, Museum of Fine Arts, Boston

483. Luis Eugenio Meléndez, 1716-1780, Rococo, Spanish, *Still-Life with a Box of Sweets and Bread Twists*, c. 1770, Oil on canvas, 49 x 37 cm, Museo Nacional del Prado, Madrid

484. Jean-Honoré Fragonard, 1732-1806, Rococo, French,
The Swing, 1767, Oil on canvas, 81 x 64.2 cm, The Wallace Collection, London

The Neoclassicism of the revolutionaries did not impress this genre painter. Rather, he produced fêtes galantes (this term appears with Watteau) for patrons, such as the Rococo series of four scenes depicting the Progress of Love (1770) intended for the boudoir of Madame du Barry's Pavilion de Louveciennes of which The Swing is the most popular. Both the man's voyeurism and the lady's exhibitionism are justified by the seemingly innocent situation. The man 'happens' to fall at the base of a statue of cupid. He thereby 'happens' to align himself conveniently to 'accidentally' see up the young lady's petticoats. The lady's dainty left shoe is kicked into the air, again quite by accident, of course. From the shadows, a servant dutifully continues to pull ropes so as to swing the teasing lady as a playful putto plays approvingly. Fragonard's free strokes and clear palette served his gallant and fickle subjects.

485

486

Joshua Reynolds
(1723 Plympton – 1792 London)

Reynolds was a British portrait painter who dominated English artistic life in the second half of the eighteenth century. Influenced by the Italian Renaissance during a trip in Italy to Rome, Florence and Venice and later by Italian Bolognese Baroque and northern painters like Rubens and van Dyck, he attempted to lead British painting towards continental Grand Style. In his writings, he evolved a doctrine of imitation, a fact with which he has sometimes been reproached, but wrongly so, since he succeeded in making his borrowings his own and giving to a composite creation a homogeneous, personal and national character. In 1768 he helped found the Royal Academy, was elected first president and knighted by King George III. Reynolds' discourses, delivered at the Royal Academy between 1769 and 1791, are considered the most important art criticism of that time. In them he outlined the essence of grandeur in art and suggested the means of achieving it was through rigorous academic training and study of the old masters of art.

488

489

Benjamin West, 1738-1820, Rococo, American, *Penn's Treaty with the Indians*, 1771-72, Oil on canvas, 191.8 x 273.7 cm, The Pennsylvania Academy of the Fine Arts, Philadelphia

John Singleton Copley, 1738-1815, Realism, American, *Watson and the Shark*, 1778, Oil on canvas, 182.1 x 229.7 cm, The National Gallery of Art, Washington, D.C.

Joshua Reynolds, 1723-1792, Rococo, English, *Self-portrait*, 1775, Oil on canvas, 71.5 x 58 cm, Galleria degli Uffizi, Florence

Anton Raphael Mengs, 1728-1779, Neoclassicism, German, *Self-portrait*, c. 1775, Oil on panel, 97 x 72.6 cm, Galleria degli Uffizi, Florence

Joshua Reynolds, 1723-1792, Rococo, English, *Miss Bowles (and her Dog)*, 1775, Oil on canvas, 91 x 71 cm, The Wallace Collection, London

The rosy-cheeked girl embraces her dog as if caught during a playful time together. There is a mutual affection and trust between the girl and her slightly reluctant pet, yet the formality of the pose is retained as in typical commissioned works of the period. Seen here is a simple and unpretentious example of how Reynolds, with his contemporary rival Gainsborough, followed the formal philosophies of fellow countrymen, playwright Samuel Johnson and philosopher David Hume. The artists especially respected Hume's directive that painting must respect the principles of nature as well as art. Their works ennobled their patrons and captured the sophisticated tone of the British affluent. Reynolds was very successful in retaining Old World elegance while often, such as in this work, capturing charming moments.

490

491

492

493

494

490. Johann Heinrich Fuseli, 1741-1825, Romanticism, Swiss, *Titania and Bottom,* 1780-90, Oil on canvas, 217 x 275 cm, Tate Gallery, London

491. Charles-François de La Croix, 1700-1782, Romanticism, French, *Harbour with a Fortress,* 1781, Oil on canvas, 73 x 98 cm, The State Hermitage Museum, St Petersburg

492. Hubert Robert, 1733-1808, Romanticism, French, *Architectural Landscape with a Canal,* 1783, Oil on canvas, 129 x 182.5 cm, The State Hermitage Museum, St Petersburg

493. Francesco Guardi, 1712-1793, Rococo, Italian, *Departure of Bucentaure towards the Lido of Venice, on Ascension Day,* 1775-1780, Oil on canvas, 66 x 101 cm, Musée du Louvre, Paris

Around 1770, Francesco Guardi painted a series of twelve 'views' of historical events related to the coronation of the Doge Alvise Mocenigo. All of them work as pretext for an unusual description of some of Venice's monuments with a great sense of space and repartition of light and colourful details.

494. Johann Heinrich Fuseli, 1741-1825, Romanticism, Swiss, *The Nightmare,* 1781, Oil on canvas, 101.6 x 127 cm, The Detroit Institute of Arts, Detroit

495

497

496

Angelica Kauffmann
(1741 Chur – 1807 Rome)

Angelica Kauffmann was a Swiss painter, although she was also
a great musician. Her early works were influenced by the French
Rococo whereas her later were more influenced by the
Neoclassical, especially when she visited Italy. She was a prolific
painter of portraits, and her portraits of female sitters are certainly
her finest works.

495. Thomas Gainsborough, 1727-1788, Rococo, English, *Mr and Mrs
William Hallett ('The Morning Walk')*, 1785,
Oil on canvas, 236 x 179 cm, National Gallery, London

496. Angelica Kauffmann, 1741-1807, Neoclassicism, Swiss, *Allegory of
Poetry and Painting*, 1782, Oil on canvas, Tondo, dia. 61 cm,
Private collection, London

497. Thomas Gainsborough, 1727-1788, Rococo, English, *Mrs. Richard
Brinsley Sheridan*, 1785, Oil on canvas, 220 x 154 cm,
The National Gallery of Art, Washington, D.C.

498

JOHN SINGLETON COPLEY
(1738 BOSTON — 1815 LONDON)

Copley was an American painter of portraits and historical subjects who, in 1775, studied under Benjamin West in London. Copley perfected the American Colonial style. Famous for his American portraits, he also used one of the great themes of nineteenth-century Romantic art, the struggle of man against nature, in *Watson and the Shark*. He was elected to the Royal Academy in 1779.

John Singleton Copley, 1738-1815, Realism, American, *The Death of Major Peirson, 6 January 1781*, 1783, Oil on canvas, 251.5 x 365.8 cm, Tate Gallery, London

After being invaded by the French in 1781 the governor of St. Helier (the capital of Jersey) surrendered. However, twenty-four year old British Major Peirson rejected the surrender. Instead, the major led a successful counter-attack, but he was killed shortly before the battle. For dramatic effect, Copley combined the moment of British victory with the death of the young commander as if it happened during the battle. In the painting, Peirson can be seen under the Union Flag. Several portraits of officers are in the painting, as is an image of Peirson's black servant. The servant is seen avenging his master's death. Peirson became a national hero, probably due, in no small part, to the popularity of this painting and the artist's convenient manipulation of history. Copley contributed to create the genre of historical painting in England, and the power of art to influence the perception of history is here demonstrated clearly.

Angelica Kauffmann, 1741-1807, Neoclassicism, Swiss, *Self-portrait*, 1780-85, Oil on canvas, 76.5 x 63 cm, The State Hermitage Museum, St Petersburg

499

501

500. **Francesco Guardi**, 1712-1793, Roco
Italian, *Ladies' Concert at the Philhar
Hall*, c. 1782, Oil on canvas,
67.7 x 90.5 cm, Alte Pinakothek, Mu

501. **Jacques-Louis David**, 1748-1825,
Neoclassicism, French,
The Death of Socrates, 1787,
Oil on canvas, 129.5 x 196.2 cm,
The Metropolitan Museum of Art, Ne

The Death of Socrates *exalts moral
rejoining in this aspect the recit*
the painting's style and compositic
printmaker and publisher John Boyde
to Sir Joshua Reynolds that it w
greatest effort of art since the Sistine
and the Stanze of Raphael [...]. Th
would have done honour to Athens
time of Pericles".

503

503. **Jacques-Louis David**, 1748-1825, Neoclassicism, French, *Oath of the Horatii*, 1784, Oil on canvas, 330 x 425 cm, Musée du Louvre, Paris

David recalled an important event in Roman history in which the fate of the city of Alba Longa was determined by a battle between two rival families: the Horatii from Rome and the Curiatii from Alba. One of the Curiatii's sisters was married to one of the Horatii and one of the Horatii's sisters was betrothed to one of the Curiatii. As their families resign themselves to the inevitable violence, the Horatii brothers embrace each other, strike a formal oath-taking pose in a public place and pledge loyalty to Rome. Eager to take up their swords, the brothers point their common spear beyond the approaching battle and towards the source of light and hope. David pays particular attention to the depiction of human passions, from the vigour and heroism of the Horatii brothers to the grief of the women. But, by emphasising the civic values through antic themes, The Oath of the Horatii bears the banner of Neoclassical art, which defends the priority of reason over emotion. David's painting is theatrical and highlights a precise moment at the pinnacle of the drama.

Jacques-Louis David
(1748 Paris – 1825 Brussels)

Celebrated nowadays as the Imperial Court Painter, David started his apprenticeship with Boucher and then with Joseph-Marie Vien, who was a famous painter renowned for his antique style. In 1774, David won the prix de Rome where he confirmed his passion for antique art. Back in Paris in 1784, he painted his *Oath of the Horatii*, a perfect example of his Neoclassical style: a return to classical painting, to the line, but with something more rigid in the choice of the subjects, influenced by Roman behaviour, love of country and individual heroism. That is why he became the official painter of the French Revolution and its Roman ideals. His *Death of Marat*, showing Marat as a secular Christ, is a denunciation of Counter-Revolution crime. However, David stayed the official painter of the Empire, executing the monumental *Coronation of Napoleon* after 1804, the finest official picture in the world, breathing life into a huge ceremonial composition, leaving the Greeks and Romans in order to paint the doings of his contemporaries.

After the fall of the Empire, he left France for Belgium at the Restoration and finished his career there, still inspired by Antiquity but in a less didactic way.

Master of a whole generation of Academic painters like Gros, Ingres or Girodet, he thus had a great influence on the first half of nineteenth-century Academic painting.

502. **Christian-Bernard Rode**, 1725-1797, *Allegory of Spring*, 1785, Oil on canvas, 218 x 109 cm, The State Hermitage Museum, St Petersburg

504

Elisabeth Vigée-Lebrun
(Marie-Louise Elisabeth Vigée-Le Brun)
(1755 – 1842 Paris)

Elisabeth Vigée-Lebrun was her father's student but she benefited from more advice from Gabriel Francois Doyen, Jean-Baptiste Greuze and Joseph Vernet. In 1776 she married the famous painter and art dealer Jean-Baptiste-Pierre Le Brun. Before becoming a member of the Royal Academy of Painting and Sculpture in 1783, she became in 1779 the official court painter of Queen Marie-Antoinette. She made more than twenty-five portraits of her. At the beginning of the French Revolution she left France and lived in Austria and in Italy, where she was made a member of Academia di San Luca, and in Russia, where she was elected at Academy of Fine Arts of St. Petersburg. She travelled also in the Netherlands, England and Switzerland before going back to Paris. Her memoirs depict a very interesting, intimate and lively vision of her times as a woman artist working in a period dominated by the royal academies. She is seen as one of the most fluent portraitists of her era and as one of the most successful female artist of all time.

507

508

04. Johann Heinrich Wilhelm Tischbein, 1751-1829, Romanticism, German, *Goethe in the Roman Campagna*, 1786, Oil on canvas, 164 x 206 cm, Städelsches Kunstinstitut, Frankfurt

05. Nicolai Abildgaard, 1743-1809, Romanticism, Danish, *The Spirit of Culmin Appears to his Mother*, c. 1794, Oil on canvas, 62 x 78 cm, Nationalmuseum, Stockholm

06. Thomas Gainsborough, 1727-1788, Rococo, English, *Mrs Sarah Siddons*, 1785, Oil on canvas, 126 x 99.5 cm, National Gallery, London

07. Elisabeth Vigée-Lebrun, 1755-1842, Neoclassicism, French, *Self-portrait*, 1790, Oil on canvas, 100 x 81 cm, Galleria degli Uffizi, Florence

Elisabeth Vigée-Lebrun was very famous across Europe for the smooth and flattering style of her portraits.

08. Jacques-Louis David, 1748-1825, Neoclassicism, French, *The Death of Marat*, 1793, Oil on canvas, 162 x 128 cm, Musées royaux des Beaux-Arts, Brussels

David was the greatest proponent of Neoclassicism in France during the Napoleonic era. As a member of the National Convention (1792) he supported the Revolution and the execution of Louis XVI. The most famous of his major contemporary historical paintings is the one created the following year, the same year as the assassination of his friend Jean Paul Marat (1744-93), by the young royalist Charlotte Corday. The man sat at The Convention, and was a fervent spokesman of "sans-culotte". Striving to show the victim as a political martyr of the Revolution, the artist positions the dead victim so as to recall representations of the crucified Jesus, as in Bronzino's Deposition of Christ (1549). The light from the left, which extracts the body from the dark background, gives a dramatic intensity, not unlike Caravaggio's manner, and a religious density. The weapon is seen on the floor in contrast to the nearby writing quills, one of Marat's weapons for fighting for the Revolution. His body still clutches both a quill and his final letter, as if to show he is not giving up on his causes even in death.

509

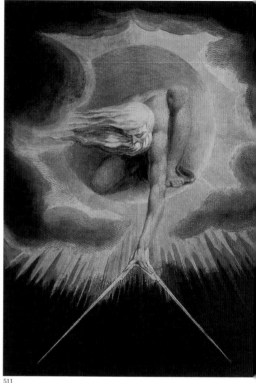

511

510

513

514

509. **Elisabeth Vigée-Lebrun**, 1755-1842, Neoclassicism, French, *Portrait of Stanislas Auguste Poniatowski*, c. 1789-96, Oil on canvas, 101.5 x 86.5 cm, Kiev Museum of Western Art, Kiev

510. **William Blake**, 1757-1827, Romanticism, English, *Pity*, 1795, Watercolour heightened with ink on paper, 42 x 54 cm, Tate Gallery, London

511. **William Blake**, 1757-1827, Romanticism, English, *The Ancient of Days*, 1794, Etching in relief with watercolour, 23.3 x 16.8 cm, British Museum, London

512. **Gilbert Stuart**, 1755-1828, Rococo, American, *Josef de Jaudenes y Nebot*, 1794, Oil on canvas, 128 x 101 cm, The Metropolitan Museum of Art, New York

513. **Thomas Lawrence**, 1769-1830, Rococo, English, *Portrait of Master Ainslie*, 1794, Oil on canvas, 91.5 x 71.4 cm, Fundación Lázaro Galdiano, Madrid

514. **Henry Raeburn**, 1756-1823, Romanticism, Scottish, *Reverend Robert Walker Skating on Duddingston Loch*, 1795, Oil on canvas, 76.2 x 63.5 cm, National Gallery of Scotland, Edinburgh

This serene skater is thought to be the Reverend Robert Walker, minister of the Canongate Kirk and a member of the Edinburgh Skating Society. This small piece, showing a figure in action, is quite unlike other known portraits by Raeburn.

516

515. Jacob Philipp Hackert, 1737-1807, Rococo, German, *View of the Ruins of the Antique Theatre of Pompei*, 1793, Gouache on cardboard, 58.7 x 85 cm, Goethe-Nationalmuseum, Weimar

516. Pierre Henri Valenciennes, 1750-1819, Neoclassicism, French, *Storm by the Banks of a Lake*, Late 18t century, Oil on canvas, 39.8 x 52 cm, Musée du Louvre, Paris

517. Francesco de Goya y Lucientes, 1746-1828, Romanticism, Spanish, *El Aquelarre (The Witches' Sabbath)*, 1797-98, Oil on canvas, 44 x 31 cm, Fundación Lázaro Galdiano, Madrid

518

519

518. Hubert Robert, 1733-1808, Rococo, French,
Design for the Grande Galerie in the Louvre, 1796,
Oil on canvas, 115 x 145 cm, Musée du Louvre, Paris

519. Hubert Robert, 1733-1808, Rococo, French, *Imaginary
View of the Grande Galerie in the Louvre in Ruins*, 1796,
Oil on canvas, 115 x 145 cm, Musée du Louvre, Paris

520. Anne-Louis Girodet, 1767-1824, Neoclassicism, French,
Mademoiselle Lange as Danaë, 1799, Oil on canvas,
60.3 x 48.6 cm, Minneapolis Insitue of Arts, Minneapolis

521

19th Century

Romanticism dominated the start of the nineteen century. While the broader movement of Romanticism across disciplines is described by scholars as occurring from 1750-1850, in art history, the Romantic movement is narrowly defined from 1800-1840 and bridges Neoclassicism and Realism. Romanticism is a very heterogeneous style, based on ideas rather than formal characteristics. It is primarily concerned with the individual and promotes emotion and feeling, rather than rationalism. Romanticism revived medieval ideas and introduced the sublime in landscape.

The sublime was articulated by Edmund Burke (1729-1797) in 1757 in his philosophical text, *A Philosophical Enquiry into the Origins of Our Ideas of the Sublime and Beautiful*. Feelings of awe invoked by the landscape or terror associated with the power of nature over man were prominent themes. Romantic works tended towards the macabre, the fantastic or the nightmarish, which was often evoked through colour or dramatic action to elicit strong emotion. Landscape painting flourished at this time as it invoked moods compatible with the prevailing sentiments of the time.

Revivals of earlier styles, most notably those of the Middle Ages, contributed to the pluralism of the romantic style, especially in architecture. This was largely due to a new interest in cultural heritage, which in France, for example, was the result of the vandalism to its monuments just after the Revolution. Similarly, the vast empires held by European powers brought exotic styles back from far colonies. Orientalist painters and architects modelled their buildings and paintings on fantasies of the Middle East and North Africa. Cast iron technology led to ever increasing modular constructions with large panes of glass to let light inside some of the more industrially designed buildings.

Photography was invented in 1839 with the advent of two different processes. One in France, patented by Louis J.M. Daguerre (1789-1851) and another in England by Henry Fox Talbot (1800-1877). Daguerre's process was innovative chemically, but created only one unique work each time. Whereas Fox Talbot's process allowed for a negative to print more than one copy of the same image. Photography significantly challenged painting on the basis of realism, and great debates ensued about the artistic merits of photography due to its status as technology. Significantly, towards the end of the century, painting began to look at vision itself in the movements known as Impressionism and Post-impressionism. The act of seeing and perceiving with the human eye became the subject of painting, while photography usurped the tradition of portraiture. Freed from miming nature, painters began to observe light phenomena and later, to use colour expressively, rather than naturalistically. The seeds of abstraction were sewn.

Karl Marx (1818-1883) wrote the *Communist Manifesto* while living in London in 1848 in which he outlined a new theory and definition of the working class and labour markets in relation to society. He theorised that the advent of a wealthier new middle class, with all the goods and services provided by the Industrial Revolution's excess capital and leisure time, would alienate the poorer lower-class workers from the products they produced. He posited that this would lead to social unrest, and in fact in 1848 workers rebelled in France. Many painters in the Realist style championed the working class in unrealistic ways, due to the fact that few painters belonged to the working or labour class. While Realism was concerned with an idealised rural landscape, later Impressionism would take up urban subjects and paint everyday life in the city and suburbs.

21. **Jacques-Louis David,** 1748-1825, Neoclassicism, French,
   Napoleon Crossing the Alps, 1800,
   Oil on canvas, 271 x 232 cm, Schloss Charlottenburg, Berlin

After having met Napoleon in a reception organised by the Directoire, David developed a real enthusiasm for Napoleon. In this work, he depicts Bonaparte, younger than in nature, and over-dimensioned, dominating the small army.

522

Francisco de Goya y Lucientes
(1746 Fuendetodos –1828 Bordeaux)

Goya is perhaps the most approachable of painters. His art, like his life, is an open book. He concealed nothing from his contemporaries, and offered his art to them with the same frankness. The entrance to his world is not barricaded with technical difficulties. He proved that if a man has the capacity to live and multiply his experiences, to fight and work, he can produce great art without classical decorum and traditional respectability. He was born in 1746, in Fuendetodos, a small mountain village of a hundred inhabitants. As a child he worked in the fields with his two brothers and his sister until his talent for drawing put an end to his misery. At fourteen, supported by a wealthy patron, he went to Saragossa to study with a court painter and later, when he was nineteen, on to Madrid.

Up to his thirty-seventh year, if we leave out of account the tapestry cartoons of unheralded decorative quality and five small pictures, Goya painted nothing of any significance, but once in control of his refractory powers, he produced masterpieces with the speed of Rubens. His court appointment was followed by a decade of incessant activity – years of painting and scandal, with intervals of bad health.

Goya's etchings demonstrate a draughtsmanship of the first rank. In paint, like Velázquez, he is more or less dependent on the model, but not in the detached fashion of the expert in still-life. If a woman was ugly, he made her a despicable horror; if she was alluring, he dramatised her charm. He preferred to finish his portraits at one sitting and was a tyrant with his models. Like Velázquez, he concentrated on faces, but he drew his heads cunningly, and constructed them out of tones of transparent greys. Monstrous forms inhabit his black-and-white world: these are his most profoundly deliberated productions. His fantastic figures, as he called them, fill us with a sense of ignoble joy, aggravate our devilish instincts and delight us with the uncharitable ecstasies of destruction. His genius attained its highest point in his etchings on the horrors of war. When placed beside the work of Goya, other pictures of war pale into sentimental studies of cruelty. He avoided the scattered action of the battlefield, and confined himself to isolated scenes of butchery. Nowhere else did he display such mastery of form and movement, such dramatic gestures and appalling effects of light and darkness. In all directions Goya renewed and innovated.

22. Francisco de Goya y Lucientes, 1746-1828, Romanticism, Spanish,
Family of Charles IV, 1800-1801, Oil on canvas, 280 x 336 cm,
Museo Nacional del Prado, Madrid

524

As principal painter to Charles IV, Goya's main task was to provide numerous portraits of the king and his family. Goya's large painting of The Family of Charles IV of 1800, places life-sized members of the royal family in an ostentatious display of costume and jewellery. Queen Maria Luisa is centre stage with her two youngest children. She wears a sleeveless dress to show off her arms, of which she was so proud that she forbade the use of gloves in court. Although the costumes sparkle, the king's and queen's expressions are so dull that they provoked the French novelist, Théophile Gautier, to compare them to "the corner baker and his wife after they have won the lottery". On the left of the painting, in blue, stands the heir to the throne, the future despot Ferdinand VII. Beside him are his brother, the Infante Don Carlos María Isidro, and a woman who turns towards the queen and may be Ferdinand's future wife. It is thought that her features were not included because, at the time of the painting, the engagement was not official. Peeking between the couple is Doña Maria Josefa, the king's sister, who died shortly after the completion of the painting. To the right of the king are other close relatives: his brother, the Infante Antonio Pascal; his eldest daughter, the Infanta Doña Carlota Joaquina; and, holding a child, another daughter, the Infanta Doña Maria Luisa Josefina and her husband, Don Luis de Borbón. Once again, Goya includes himself in the painting, in the shadows on the left, at work on a canvas. Without expression, he stares out of the painting as if looking at the group in a mirror. The royal family is depicted without any attempt at flattering their features, and with their decadence and pretensions clearly exposed, it is somewhat surprising that they did not object.

23. Francisco de Goya y Lucientes, 1746-1828, Romanticism, Spanish,
The Clothed Maja, 1800-03, Oil on canvas, 95 x 190 cm,
Museo Nacional del Prado, Madrid

24. Jean-Auguste-Dominique Ingres, 1780-1867, Neoclassicism, French,
Mademoiselle Caroline Rivière, 1806, Oil on canvas, 100 x 70 cm,
Musée du Louvre, Paris

Curves and counter-curves organise the composition. For the attitude of the sitter, Ingres took his inspiration from Raphael's paintings and for the depiction of the fur from Parmiganino.

525

526

525. Pierre-Paul Prud'hon, 1758-1823, Neoclassicism, French, *The Empress Joséphine,* 1805, Oil on canvas, 244 x 179 cm, Musée du Louvre, Paris

His nickname was the "French Correggio". Prud'hon represents Josephine o Beauharnais in a poetic landscape emulating the admired English "plein-ai portraits.

526. Elisabeth Vigée-Lebrun, 1755-1842, Neoclassicism, French, *Mme de Stael as Corinne,* 1808, Oil on canvas, 140 x 118 cm, Musée d'Art et d'Histoire, Geneva

527. Gottlieb Schick, 1776-1812, Neoclassicism, German, *Wilhelmine von Cotta,* 1802, Oil on canvas, 133 x 140.5 cm, Staatsgalerie, Stuttgart

528. Jacques-Louis David, 1748-1825, Neoclassicism, French, *Madame Récamier,* 1800, Oil on canvas, 174 x 244 cm, Musée du Louvre, Paris

529. François Gérard, 1770-1837, Neoclassicism, French, *Portrait of Katarzyna Starzenska,* c. 1803, Oil on canvas, 215 x 130.5 cm, Picture Gallery, Lvov

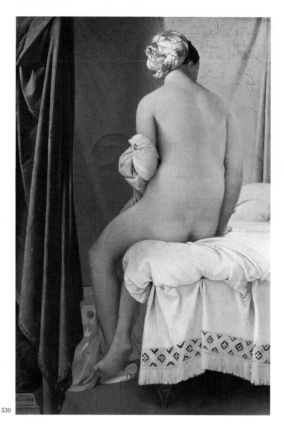

530

530. Jean-Auguste-Dominique Ingres, 1780-1867, Neoclassicism, French,
Valpinçon Bather, 1808, Oil on canvas, 146 x 97 cm,
Musée du Louvre, Paris

*The discovery of exotic and oriental art by the nineteenth-century artists
impacted on Ingres' depiction of women. The female nude appears throughout
the artist's body of work. His fascination with long, immaculate backs of young
women appears in several of his popular works, including this earlier work and
his* Grande Odalisque *(1814). Also very late in life he carried out his theme yet
again in his work* The Turkish Bath *(1863) in which there are twenty such
women, but the dominant one in the foreground is displaying her beautiful
back. Ingres said he was taking Poussin as an example as the master often
depicted the same subjects several times, until he reached perfection. But
Ingres was influenced also by Tuscan mannerists such as Bronzino, and from
Raphael. In all three works, a lady wears a turban and nothing else. In this early
work, the drapery is pulled to the side to allow the voyeur an unobstructed
view, but at a respectful distance.*

531. Anne-Louis Girodet, 1767-1824, Romanticism, French, *The Burial of Atala,*
1808, Oil on canvas, 207 x 267 cm, Musée du Louvre, Paris

*Pupil of David, Girodet took his inspiration from Chateaubriand's book, published
in 1801. In it, Atala, in love with Chactas, who came from the enemy tribe,
remembers her oath of virginity. In order not to succumb to temptation, she kills
herself. The scene is represented in the tradition of the "burial of Christ". But here,
passion, love, and death are mixed up. The cave opens itself on a wild and
romantic landscape. The cross in the background echoes to the cross set up by the
shovel and the mattock in the foreground and recalls the reason of Atala's
sacrifice. This work, displayed at the Salon in 1808 in Paris, aroused much
attention, and even Josephine asked for a replica.*

JEAN–AUGUSTE–DOMINIQUE INGRES
(1780 MONTAUBAN – 1867 PARIS)

Ingres at first seemed destined to continue brilliantly the work
of his master David both in portrait and historical painting. He
won the *Prix de Rome* in 1801. Ingres, however, soon
emancipated himself. He was only twenty-five when he painted
the Rivière portraits. These show an original talent and a taste
for composition not without some mannerism, but the
mannerism is full of charm, and the refinement of undulating
lines is as far removed as possible from the simple and slightly
rough realism which is the strength of David's portraits. His
contemporary rivals were not deceived. They attacked his
"archaic" and "singular" taste and dubbed him "Gothic" and
"Chinese". During the Salon of 1824 however, back from Italy,
Ingres was promoted to leader of the Academic style in
opposition to the new romanticism led by Delacroix.

In 1834, he was appointed director of the French School in
Rome, where he stayed for seven years. Then after his return he
was again acclaimed as master of traditional values and finished
his days in his home town in southern France. The biggest
contradiction in Ingres' career is his title of *Guardian of the
Classical Rules and Precepts*, although we still perceive
eccentricity in some of the most beautiful of his works. A
pedant, seeing the back of *La Grande Odalisque* and various
exaggerations of form in *The Turkish Bath* would point to this
incomparable draughtsman's faults. But are these not the means
by which a great and extremely sensitive artist interprets his
passion for the beautiful female form? When he wanted to
group a large number of people in a monumental work such as
L'Apothéose d'Homère, Ingres never attained the ease, the
suppleness, the life, or the unity which we admire in the
magnificent decorative compositions of Delacroix. On the other
hand, he had an impeccable sureness, original taste, a fertile and
appropriate invention in the pictures where only two or three
figures appear, and even more in those where he illustrates,
standing or reclining, a single effigy of the female figure, which
was the enchantment and sweet torment of his whole life.

531

2. Joseph Mallord Turner, 1775-1851, Romanticism, English,
Snow Storm: Hannibal and his Army Crossing the Alps, c. 1811,
Oil on canvas, 146 x 237.5 cm, Tate Gallery, London

*This painting is an example of how Turner used the artistic effect of the
'Sublime' (Theory of art put forward by Edmund Burke in those words:
Whatever is in any sort terrible or is conversant about terrible objects or
operates in a manner analogous to terror, is a source of the Sublime). This effect
is meant to produce a strong emotion, and is an important element of
Romanticism.*

533. Caspar David Friedrich, 1774-1840, Romanticism, German, *Monk by the
Sea,* c. 1808, Oil on canvas, 110 x 172 cm, Alte Nationalgalerie, Berlin

*Friedrich painted his masterpieces after a career as a theatrical scenery painter.
The artist was not presenting nature realistically. Rather he was focused on the
awesome quality of nature and the humbling influence nature's grandeur has on
one's interior life. He especially liked the coastline, where he could witness
major forces of nature interacting. The human subjects in his works are always
tiny relative to the largeness and the majesty of nature. In this work the figure of
the monk occupies only 1/800th or so of the work area. The vastness of the sea
and sky is captured. The viewer discovers little if anything about the character
of the monk, standing as the only vertical line of the composition.*

Caspar David Friedrich
(1774 Geifswald – 1840 Dresden)

Like Gainsborough, Friedrich is mostly known for his
landscapes. They depict trees, hills, and misty mornings based
on his strong observation of nature. Mountains symbolise an
immovable faith while the trees are an allegory of hope.
Therefore, his landscapes reflect his spiritual relationship with
nature and his religious aspirations. His *Monk by the Sea*
expresses his recurring theme of the insignificance of the
individual in relation to the vastness of nature. Painter as
draughtsman or printmaker, he was one of the greatest German
leaders of Romanticism.

533

536

4. Antoine-Jean Gros, 1771-1835, Romanticism, French,
Napoléon at the Battlefield of Eylau, 1807, Oil on canvas, 521 x 784 cm,
Musée du Louvre, Paris

*Gros respected the instructions given for the representation of Napoleon on the
battle field of Eylau after the bloodbath. But he depicted the scene with an
exceptional realism, new in the genre of historical painting.*

5. Jacques-Louis David, 1748-1825, Neoclassicism, French, *Consecration of
the Emperor Napoleon I and Coronation of the Empress Josephine,*
1806-1807, Oil on canvas, 621 x 979 cm, Musée du Louvre, Paris

*There were to be three other paintings by David in a series showing highlights in
the life of Napoleon (1769-1821), who called the artist the country's "first painter".
However, the artist was unable to produce the envisioned other works. The
majestic vertical columns and exceptionally tall candles of the grand Notre Dame
cathedral in Paris, redecorated in a Neoclassical style for the event, buttress the
grandeur of the coronation. By raising the crown as high as he can, Napoleon is
challenging the authority of even the Church, symbolised by the processional
crucifix held high by the Pope, Pie VII. Cardinals and bishops witness the event
with quiet resignation. The whole imperial court is represented: each character
can be identified. Thanks to its size, David intended to give to this contemporising
fact an historical importance. A prominent pietà, the altar, and even the tabernacle
are set aside so Napoleon, then the coronation, are the centre of attention. The
problem of presenting a crowd on tiers, as is often seen in Byzantine and Gothic
works, is partly solved here by use of the balconies. There is an unexpected
objectivity of the artist, as a loyal follower of the Emperor, by his nearly journalistic
or non-emotional reporting of the event combined with the overall neo-Baroque
attention to elaborate detail. Appropriately, this is one of the artist's very large
works, if not the largest, being nearly twice as large as his The Rape of the Sabine
Women (1799), which is also displayed at the Musée du Louvre, Paris.*

536. Francisco de Goya y Lucientes, 1746-1828, Romanticism, Spanish,
Third of May, 1808, 1814, Oil on canvas, 266 x 345 cm,
Museo Nacional del Prado, Madrid

The Third of May 1808 *recalls the executions of more than forty men and
women, on the hill of Principe Pio. The focal point of the painting is a man who
gasps and spreads his arms in horror at his fate. His gesture suggests that he
faces death with both defiance and despair. Isolated from the shadowy figures
around him, the severe light of a lantern set on the ground before his
executioners highlights his white shirt and yellow trousers. His innocence is
implied by the brightness of his clothes, while his gesture and wounded right
palm remind us of Christ crucified. Beside him, his companions give varying
reactions to their hopeless situation: a Franciscan priest hangs his head in
prayer while another victim tightens his fists in futile resistance. To the left, a
man shields his eyes from the sight of the carnage and the gruesome pile of
dead. The head of the figure in the foreground is riddled with bullets; his arms
hug the ground, outstretched like those of the central figure, while his blood
pours onto the barren earth. Time is frozen, but the outcome is clear. Within
seconds the group will have fallen and been replaced by another that shuffles
up the hill to face the firing squad. The merciless soldiers appear anonymous,
their backs forming an impenetrable wall and their actions uniform as they
prepare to fire, their feet set firmly apart to resist the rifles' recoil.*

537

538

537. Pierre-Narcisse Guérin, 1774-1833, Neoclassicism, French,
Aurora and Cephalus, 1811-1814, Oil on canvas, 257 x 178 cm,
The Pushkin Museum of Fine Arts, Moscow

538. Georg Friedrich Kersting, 1785-1847, Romanticism, German,
Caspar David Friedrich in his Studio, 1811,
Oil on canvas, 51 x 40 cm, Alte Nationalegalerie, Berlin

539. Philipp Otto Runge, 1777-1810, Neoclassicism, German, *Morning
(first version),* 1808-09, Oil on canvas, 109 x 85.5 cm, Kunsthalle, Hamb

540. Théodore Géricault, 1791-1824, Romanticism, French,
An Officer of the Imperial Horse Guards Charging, 1812,
Oil on canvas, 349 x 266 cm, Musée du Louvre, Paris

*In 1812, the French Empire staggered. Géricault catches this aspect in this
realistic portrait that, rather than exalting the virtues of the war, criticise
Géricault rejected the classical linearity and contravenes the neo-class
glacis as he painted with a thick touch. Just one character is depicted. Géric
went to the essential, and gave up the superfluous with every aneco
element he added. The sitter, bending toward the viewer, transgresses
academic representation of cavaliers who concentrate on action.*

Joseph Mallord William Turner
(1775 – 1851 London)

At fifteen, Turner was already exhibiting *View of Lambeth*. He soon acquired the reputation of an immensely clever watercolourist. A disciple of Girtin and Cozens, he showed in his choice and presentation of theme a picturesque imagination which seemed to mark him out for a brilliant career as an illustrator. He travelled, first in his native land and then on several occasions in France, the Rhine Valley, Switzerland and Italy. He soon began to look beyond illustration. However, even in works in which we are tempted to see only picturesque imagination, there appears his dominant and guiding ideal of lyric landscape. His choice of a single master from the past is an eloquent witness for he studied profoundly such canvases of Claude as he could find in England, copying and imitating them with a marvellous degree of perfection. His cult for the great painter never failed. He desired his *Sun Rising through Vapour* and *Dido Building Carthage* to be placed in the National Gallery side by side with two of Claude's masterpieces. And, there, we may still see them and judge how legitimate was this proud and splendid homage.

It was only in 1819 that Turner went to Italy, to go again in 1829 and 1840. Certainly Turner experienced emotions and found subjects for reverie which he later translated in terms of his own genius into symphonies of light and colour. Ardour is tempered with melancholy, as shadow strives with light. Melancholy, even as it appears in the enigmatic and profound creation of Albrecht Dürer, finds no home in Turner's protean fairyland – what place could it have in a cosmic dream? Humanity does not appear there, except perhaps as stage characters at whom we hardly glance. Turner's pictures fascinate us and yet we think of nothing precise, nothing human, only unforgettable colours and phantoms that lay hold on our imaginations. Humanity really only inspires him when linked with the idea of death – a strange death, more a lyrical dissolution – like the finale of an opera.

542

541. Joseph Mallord Turner, 1775-
1851, Romanticism, English, *Dido
Building Carthage,* or *The Rise of
the Carthaginian Empire,* 1815,
Oil on canvas, 155.5 x 232 cm,
National Gallery, London

542. Joseph-Anton Koch, 1868-1939,
Neoclassicism, Austrian, *Swiss
Landscape (Berner Oberland),* 1817,
Oil on canvas, 101 x 134 cm,
Tiroler Landesmuseum
Ferdinandeum, Innsbruck

**543. Jean-Auguste-Dominique
Ingres,** 1780-1867,
Neoclassicism, French,
La Grande Odalisque, 1814,
Oil on canvas, 91 x 162 cm,
Musée du Louvre, Paris

*The oriental setting is a pretext for
Ingres to show his virtuosity in the
depiction of materials, nacre, and
silks. The proportions of the model
are wrong, the body is elongated
and the face flattened. Ingres got his
inspiration from Italian mannerism
and, for the arabesques, from the
School of Fontainebleau.*

543

544

545

544. Washington Allston, 1779-1843,
Romanticism, American,
Elijah in the Desert, 1818,
Oil on canvas, 125.1 x 184.8 cm,
Museum of Fine Arts, Boston

*Samuel Taylor Coleridge said about the artist:
"Washington Allston is a man of highland rare
genius, whether I contemplate him in the
character of a Poet, a Painter or a Philosophic
Analyst." Allston is known as the 'American
Titian'.*

545. Caspar David Friedrich, 1774-1840,
Romanticism, German,
Two Men Looking at the Moon, 1819,
Oil on canvas, 35 x 44 cm,
Gemäldegalerie Neue Meister, Dresden

546

547

546. Théodore Géricault, 1791-1824, Romanticism, French, *Raft of the Medusa,*
c. 1818, Oil on canvas, 491 x 716 cm, Musée du Louvre, Paris

*The work is significant in art history mainly as an example of political
controversy and protest. The makeshift raft supports the realistic theme of
the horrific event. The geometric centre of the large work is the dark area
above the base of the mast, where some of the most despairing survivors are.
Here Géricault applied his meticulous study of anatomy. The dead or
resigned men are collapsed along the bottom third of the work. In the right
half of the work a pyramid of bodies builds up to its most hopeful point,
where shirts are waved as if the tiny ship on the horizon could see their
efforts. The ship in the distance represents the Argus, the ship which rescued
the survivors. The naked and draped bodies weaken the anecdotal aspect of
the story, to reach a timeless and also a romantic value. Géricault was
influenced by the sculptural work of Michelangelo, and by the dramatic
effects of chiaroscuro.*

547. John Crome, 1768-1821, Romanticism, English, *The Poringland Oak,*
c. 1818-20, Oil on canvas, 125 x 100 cm, Tate Gallery, London

*The oak was the pinnacle of tree portraiture for British artists. It was associated
with the sturdy character of the British people, and ships constructed from it
defended their liberty. Crome's picture was exhibited in 1824 as* A Study from
Nature.

548. John Constable, 1776-1837, Romanticism,
English, *Dedham Mill,* 1820,
Oil on canvas, 70 x 90.5 cm,
David Thomson Collection, London

549

550   551

552

553

49. **David Wilkie,** 1785-1841, Genre Painter, Scottish, *Reading the Will,* 1820,
Oil on canvas, 76 x 115 cm, Neue Pinakothek, Munich

50. **Ferdinand Victor Eugène Delacroix,** 1798-1863, Romanticism, French,
Scenes from the Massacre at Chios, 1824, Oil on canvas, 419 x 354 cm,
Musée du Louvre, Paris

The non-finito of the sky and light effects of the Scenes from the Massacre at Chios were
characteristic of Delacroix's works. The scene has been inspired by the Turkish
Atrocities during the Greek War of Independence. It was Géricault who inspired the
lifeless figures in the foreground.

51. **Francisco de Goya y Lucientes,** 1746-1828, Romanticism, Spanish, *Saturn*
Devouring One of his Children ('Black painting'), 1820-1823,
Oil on canvas, 143.5 x 81.4 cm, Museo Nacional del Prado, Madrid

52. **Ferdinand Victor Eugène Delacroix,** 1798-1863, Romanticism, French,
The Barque of Dante, 1822, Oil on canvas, 189 x 241 cm, Musée du Louvre, Paris

It is the first time that this theme is represented. The dark and dramatic composition as
well as the references to Rubens and Michelangelo contribute to lead painting toward
the new orientation of Romanticism.

53. **Théodore Géricault,** 1791-1824, Romanticism, French, *The Madwoman, or The*
Obsession of Envy, c. 1822, Oil on canvas, 72 x 58 cm, Musée des Beaux-Arts, Lyon

This work is part of a set of five paintings ordered by Esquiro, a reformer of an asylum,
who pleaded in favour of the recognition of monomaniacs as normal people. Géricault
reaches the psychological depth of his sitter that he dresses conventionally in order to
claim her social recognition.

554

555

554. Caspar David Friedrich, 1774-1840, Romanticism, German, *The Sea of Ice,*
1823-1824, Oil on canvas, 96.7 x 126.9 cm, Kunsthalle, Hamburg

Numerous sketches prove that Friedrich studied ice drifts on the River Elbe in 1821. In th
work, he depicts the ice field with extreme precision, referring to both the expedition to th
North Pole around 1820 by the English explorer Edward William Parry and the cold politic
climate in Germany in the same period.

557

5. Carl Gustav Carus, 1789-1869, Romanticism, German,
Woman on a Balcony, 1824, Oil on canvas, 42 x 33 cm,
Gemäldegalerie Neue Meister, Dresden

6. Jean-Baptiste Camille Corot, 1796-1875, Realism, School of
Barbizon, French, *The Colosseum: View from the Farnese
Gardens,* 1826, Oil on paper mounted on canvas,
30 x 49 cm, Musée du Louvre, Paris

*Corot went to Italy in 1825. There he painted very fine landscapes
inspired by classical and realist art and bathed in Mediterranean light.*

7. John Constable, 1776-1837, Romanticism, English, *Salisbury
Cathedral from the Bishop's Grounds,* 1823, Oil on canvas,
88 x 112 cm, Victoria and Albert Museum, London

*In 1811, Constable was invited to stay at Salisbury, where he was
introduced to the bishop's nephew, the Reverend John Fisher
(who subsequently became Archdeacon of the cathedral). He
and Constable enjoyed a lifelong friendship, and consequently
Salisbury and its cathedral became one of the artist's most
important subjects. This version, a south-west view, was
commissioned by Fisher's uncle for his London house. The
bishop and his wife are introduced on the left, where they are
seen apparently admiring the church. The commission gave
Constable a great deal of trouble, for although he had sketched
and drawn the cathedral before, he then had no patron to satisfy
and could gloss over the kind of architectural detail that the
Bishop would expect to see. As he confided to John Fisher: "It
was the most difficult subject in landscape I ever had upon my
easel. I have not flinched at the work, of the windows, buttresses,
etc, etc, but I have as usual made my escape in the evanescence
of the chiaroscuro." Unfortunately, the bishop was not as satisfied
with the chiaroscuro as the artist was; he disliked the "dark
cloud" in the painting, saying, according to his nephew: "[If]
Constable would but leave out his black clouds! Clouds are only
black when it is going to rain. In fine weather the sky is blue." At
first Constable agreed to repaint it, but preferred in the end to
paint another, more acceptable version with the aid of Johnny
Dunthorne.*

John Constable
(1776 East Bergholt – 1837 Hampstead)

John Constable was the first English landscape painter to take no lessons
from the Dutch. He is rather indebted to the landscapes of Rubens, but
his real model was Gainsborough, whose landscapes, with great trees
planted in well-balanced masses on land sloping upwards towards the
frame, have a rhythm often found in Rubens. Constable's originality does
not lie in his choice of subjects, which frequently repeated themes beloved
by Gainsborough.

Nevertheless, Constable seems to belong to a new century; he ushered
in a new era. The difference in his approach results both from technique
and feeling. Excepting the French, Constable was the first landscape
painter to consider as a primary and essential task the sketch made direct
from nature at a single sitting; an idea which contains in essence the
destinies of modern landscape, and perhaps of most modern painting. It
is this momentary impression of all things which will be the soul of the
future work. Working at leisure upon the large canvas, an artist's aim is to
enrich and complete the sketch while retaining its pristine freshness. These
are the two processes to which Constable devoted himself, while
discovering the exuberant abundance of life in the simplest of country
places. He had the palette of a creative colourist and a technique of vivid
hatchings heralding that of the French impressionists. He audaciously and
frankly introduced green into painting, the green of lush meadows, the
green of summer foliage, all the greens which, until then, painters had
refused to see except through bluish, yellow, or more often brown
spectacles.

Of the great landscape painters who occupied so important a place in
nineteenth-century art, Corot was probably the only one to escape the
influence of Constable. All the others are more or less direct descendants
of the master of East Bergholt.

558

559

558. Ferdinand Victor Eugène Delacroix, 1798-1863, Romanticism, French,
Liberty leading the People (28 July, 1830), 1830,
Oil on canvas, 260 x 325 cm, Musée du Louvre, Paris

559. Friedrich Overbeck, 1789-1869, Nazarene, German, *Italia and Germania,*
1828, Oil on canvas, 95 x 105 cm, Gemäldegalerie, Neue Meister, Dresden

Friedrich Overbeck was one of the founders of the Lukasbund (T
Brotherhood of St. Luke), from which the Nazarenes were later to emerge.
1810, Overbeck went to Rome settling at the former San Isidoro cloister, whe
he followed their ideals and lived as a quasi monk in seclusion. Other artis
including Peter Cornelius and Wilhelm Schadow, soon joined him. The
motivation was to relate art to the Church and state and they were interested
the effect of art on the public.

560. Ferdinand Victor Eugène Delacroix, 1798-1863, Romanticism, French,
Death of Sardanapalus, 1827, Oil on canvas, 392 x 496 cm,
Musée du Louvre, Paris

This painting was inspired by Byron's Sardanapale. *Its dynamic and colourf*
composition, its arabesques, and its fierceness mixed with sensuality led t
classical painters to consider this work subversive.

Ferdinand Victor Eugène Delacroix
(1798 Charenton–Saint–Maurice – 1863 Paris)

Delacroix was one of the greatest colourists of the nineteenth century, in the sense of one who thinks and feels and expresses himself by means of colours and sees them, in his mind's eye as a composition, before he begins to resolve the whole into its parts, and work out the separate details of form.

He nutured himself upon the works of the colourists in the Louvre, especially upon Rubens. Indirectly it came out of the heart of the Romantic movement which had spread over Europe. Delacroix was inspired by the writers Goethe, Scott, Byron, and Victor Hugo. His own romantic nature flamed up through contact with theirs; he was possessed with their souls and became the first of the Romantic painters. He took many of his subjects from the poets of his preference, not to translate into literal illustrations, but to make them express in his own language of painting the most agitated emotions of the human heart.

On the other hand it is generally in the relationship of several figures, in other words in drama, that Delacroix finds the natural and striking expression of his ideas. His work is an immense and multiform poem, at once lyrical and dramatic, on passions – the violent and murderous passions which fascinate, dominate, and rend humanity. In the elaboration and execution of the pages of this poem, Delacroix does not forego any of his faculties as a man and an artist of vast intelligence standing on a level with the thoughts of the greatest in history, legend and poetry. Rather, he makes use of a feverish imagination always controlled by lucid reasoning and cool willpower. His expressive and life-like drawing, strong and subtle colour, sometimes composing a bitter harmony, sometimes overcast by that "sulphurous" note already observed by contemporaries, produce an atmosphere of storm, supplication, and anguish. Passion, movement and drama must not be supposed to engender disorder. With Delacroix as with Rubens, there hovers over the saddest representations, over tumults, horrors and massacre, a kind of serenity which is the sign of art itself and the mark of a mind master of its subject.

561

562

561. John Constable, 1776-1837, Romanticism, English,
The Opening of Waterloo Bridge (Whitehall Stairs, 18ᵗʰ June, 1817), 1832,
Oil on canvas, 130.8 x 218 cm, Tate Gallery, London

*Waterloo Bridge is unique within Constable's output, both for the length o
time he took to complete it, and for the fact that it is an urban subject on the
same grand scale as his Stour Valley "six-footers". Constable's anxieties were
revealed in a famous incident at the Royal Academy's "varnishing days" — the
period allotted for any final modifications to the pictures before the exhibition
opened. The Waterloo Bridge was hung alongside Turner's Helvoetsluys, a
muted sea-piece that was eclipsed by the strong reds of its neighbour. Turner
responded, according to Leslie, by "putting a round daub of red lead,
somewhat bigger than a shilling, on his grey sea", which made the colours o
the Waterloo Bridge seem pale by comparison.*

562. Carl Blechen, 1798-1840, Romanticism, Swiss, *The Gardens of the Villa
d'Este,* 1830, Oil on canvas, 126 x 93 cm, Alte Nationalgalerie, Berlin

563. Adrian Ludwig Richter, 1803-1884, Romanticism, German, *Ave Maria,*
1834, Oil on canvas, 85 x 104 cm, Museum der bildenden Künste, Leipzig

564. Ferdinand Victor Eugène Delacroix, 1798-1863, Romanticism, French,
Algerian Women in their Chamber, 1834, Oil on canvas, 180 x 229 cm,
Musée du Louvre, Paris

563

564

566

567

565

565. **Karl Briullov,** 1799-1852, Romanticism, Russian, *The Last Day of Pompeii,*
1830-1833, Oil on canvas, 456 x 651 cm, The State Russian Museum, St. Petersburg

*The ultimate manifestation of the infatuation with classical themes was Karl Briullov's
masterpiece, The Last Day of Pompeii. Painted between 1830 and 1833, while he was
living in Italy, it caused a stir throughout Europe. Gogol described it as "a feast for the
eyes". It was also admired by Earl Edward George Bulwer-Lytton, who visited Italy in
1833 and whose almost identically entitled book was published in 1834. The painting
earned Briullov all sorts of honours, including the prestigious Grand Prix at the Paris
Salon, and was instrumental in establishing his reputation as the greatest Russian
painter of his day.*

566. **Carl Spitzweg,** 1808-1885, Romanticism, German, *English Tourists in the Roman
Campagna,* 1835, Oil on canvas, 40 x 50 cm, Alte Nationalgalerie, Berlin

567. **Carl Anton Joseph Rottmann,** 1797-1850, Romanticism, German, *Sicyon and
Corinth,* c. 1836-1838, Oil on canvas, 85.2 x 102 cm, Neue Pinakothek, Munich

568. Adrian Ludwig Richter, 1803-1884, Romanticism, German,
Crossing the Elbe at Aussig, 1837, Oil on canvas, 116.5 x 156.5 cm,
Gemäldegalerie, Neue Meister, Dresden

569. Théodore Rousseau, 1812-1867, Realism, School of Barbizon, French,
The Avenue of Chestnut Trees, 1841, Oil on canvas, 79 x 144 cm,
Musée du Louvre, Paris

569

570

570. **Joseph Mallord Turner,** 1775-1851, Romanticism, English, *The Fighting "Temeraire",* 1839, Oil on canvas, 91 x 122 cm, National Gallery, London

It was a standing order of the Royal Navy that everything salvable and reusable from a ship should be taken off her before she was moved from her customary anchorage for destruction. As a result, when the "Temeraire" was towed upriver in 1838, all her masts had already been removed; had Turner been able to see the man-of-war under tow, he would only have witnessed the hull being transported. By replacing all her masts and sails, the painter was therefore restoring the ship to her original glory, as she had appeared in her heyday some thirty years earlier. And by representing her in such comparatively light tones, he made her look unearthly, like a ghost ship. Naturally that ethereal delicacy is greatly intensified by the contrasting dark tones of the tug. Moreover, to make the "Temeraire" look as majestic as possible – as though she has now risen above the earthly fray – Turner also raised her very high in the water. Consequently, she appears to glide above the Thames, rather than in it, a lofty sight indeed. When this painting was displayed at the Royal Academy in 1839 Turner was criticised for transposing the foremast and funnel of the tug: instead of locating the stack midway between the paddles and thus immediately above the engine, he positioned it at the very prow of the vessel, with the foremast taking its place above the engine. Yet it is easy to see why he effected this transposition: by situating the funnel at the very prow of the tug, he stood it in the vanguard of all the wind-powered shipping in the picture. Clearly he did so in order to symbolise the 'prophetic idea of smoke, soot, iron and steam, coming to the fore in all naval matters', as one of his more astute contemporaries commented. Turner has most appropriately matched his time of day to dramatic meaning; just as the "Temeraire" approaches its end, so the day nears its end, with a moonrise reminding us of the proximity of night. In the case of the doomed vessel, that night will be an extremely long one, indeed.

571. **Joseph Mallord Turner,** 1775-1851, Romanticism, English, *The Burning of the Houses of Lords and Commons, 16 October, 1834,* c. 1835, Oil on canvas, 91 x 122 cm, Museum of Art, Philadelphia

571

572

573

572. Alexander Ivanov, 1806-1858, Neoclassicism, Russian,
Christ's First Appearance to the People, 1837-1857, Oil on
canvas, 540 x 750 cm, The State Tretyakov Gallery, Moscow

A contemporary of Briullov, Alexander Ivanov was indisputab.
the most influential religious painter of his day. After making h.
mark with pictures such as Apollo, Hyacinth and Zephyr and Th.
Appearance of Christ to Mary Magdalene *(1836), he embarke.*
on The Appearance of Christ to the People, *a huge canvas tha*
was to occupy much of his energy for the next twenty years, fro.
1837 to the year before he died. Nevertheless, despite all tho.
years of effort, Ivanov was never happy with the painting an.
never regarded it as finished. Indeed, it has an undeniab.
laboured quality, and many of his preparatory studies -
landscapes, nature studies, nudes and portraits, including a he.
of John the Baptist that is masterpiece in its own right — have
vitality that is absent from the painting itself.

573. Carl Spitzweg, 1808-1885, Romanticism, German,
The Poor Poet, 1839, Oil on canvas, 36.2 x 44.6 cm,
Neue Pinakothek, Munich

Spitzweg often depicted caricatures of contemporary socie.
with some realist effects borrowed to Dutch painting of th.
seventeenth century.

74. **Joseph Mallord Turner,** 1775-1851, Romanticism, English,
Rain, Steam and Speed, before 1844, Oil on canvas, 91 x 121.8 cm,
National Gallery, London

Turner here celebrated both the coming of steam locomotion on land, and
British technological triumph over water. When this painting was first exhibited
at the Royal Academy in 1844 the anonymous critic of Fraser's Magazine
warned its readers to hasten to see the work lest the locomotive "[should] dash
out of the picture, and be away up Charing Cross through the wall opposite".
The warning seems prudent, given the suggested velocity of the engine. Today
that implied movement derives only from the pronounced perspective of the
train, railway line and bridge emerging from a distant haze of rain. However,
when the paint was still fresh, the sense of speed was augmented by three puffs
of steam emanating from the locomotive, whiffs that had already been "left
behind by the engine". Sadly, time has rendered them far less visible. Turner
joked about speed here, for in front of the train is a hare which has been
startled by the approaching machine and is possibly outpacing it. Because of
the pictorial proximity of the animal to a ploughman at work in a field beyond
the bridge, it seems certain that the artist intended the conjunction of fast hare
and slow plough to remind his audience of a popular song 'Speed the Plough',
with which he was familiar. In addition to the 'Speed' of the title and the 'Rain'
falling across the entire picture, we can also perceive the 'Steam', for Turner
has removed the front of the locomotive in order to reveal the inner workings
of its boiler. Nothing else would explain the brilliant fiery mass at the front of
the engine, for it is too formless to be an outside light. Turner may well have
derived this image from explanatory cut-away diagrams of the type that were
frequently to be seen in the Victorian popular press. By means of it we are
witnessing yet another realization of his desire to make visible the underlying
"causes" of things.

575. **Joseph Mallord Turner,** 1775-1851, Romanticism, English, *Snow Storm –
Steam-Boat off a Harbour's Mouth,* 1842, Oil on canvas, 91.4 x 121.9 cm,
Tate Gallery, London

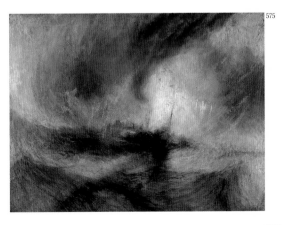

576

577

576. Gustave Courbet, 1819-1877, Realism, School of Barbizon, French,
The Stone Breakers, 1849, Oil on canvas, 165 x 257 cm,
Formerly Gemäldegalerie in Dresden. Believed to have been destroyed in
World War II, Dresden

577. Thomas Cole, 1801-1848, Hudson River School, American,
The Last of the Mohicans, 1848, Oil on canvas, 64.5 x 89 cm,
Wadsworth Atheneum, Hartford

*Cole is considered the most remarkable painter of the Hudson River School.
The painters of the group essentially worked along the Catskill Mountains of
New York and the White Mountains of New Hampshire where few Europeans
had never gone.*

578. George Caleb Bingham, 1811-1879, Realism, American,
Fur Traders Descending the Missouri, 1845, Oil on canvas, 73.7 x 92.7 cm,
The Metropolitan Museum of Art, New York

*Bingham started as a portrait painter. But this work, one of his later works, is
masterpiece of genre painting.*

579

79. Thomas Couture, 1815-1879, Neoclassicism, French, *The Romans of the Decadence,* 1847, Oil on canvas, 466 x 775 cm, Musée d'Orsay, Paris

580. Rosa Bonheur, 1822-1899, Realism, French, *Ploughing in the Nivernais,* 1848-49, Oil on canvas, 134 x 260 cm, Musée d'Orsay, Paris

580

581

582

583

581. **Adolf Friedrich Erdmann Menzel,** 1815-1905, Realism, German,
Livingroom with Menzel's Sister, 1847, Oil on cardboard, 46 x 32 cm,
Bayerische Staatsgemäldesammlungen, Munich

582. **Adolf Friedrich Erdmann Menzel,** 1815-1905, Realism, German,
The Balcony Room, 1845, Oil on cardboard, 58 x 47 cm,
Alte Nationalgalerie, Berlin

583. **Théodore Chassériau,** 1819-1856, Neoclassicism, French, *The Two Sister*,
1843, Oil on canvas, 180 x 135 cm, Musée du Louvre, Paris

*Chassériau was one of Ingres' students. This influence of the master
discernable through the fine use of colours and elegant dresses and shawls.*

584

. Pavel Fedotov, 1815-1852, Realism, Russian,
The Major's Courtship, 1848, Oil on canvas, 58.3 x 75.3 cm,
The State Tretyakov Gallery, Moscow

By the middle of the nineteenth century, Russian writers and painters were also beginning to focus attention on other sectors of society that had, until then, scarcely figured in art. Landowners, civil servants, the military and the clergy all became possible subjects for artistic comment. As a reaction against the repressive and bureaucratic regime of Nicholas I, the behaviour of the ruling class was frequently depicted in a satirical light. One of the most astute social commentators was Pavel Fedotov. Fedotov's contemporaries would have immediately recognised the social status of the dramatis personae in his best-known picture — The Major's Courtship, painted in 1848. Marriageable young ladies, like the one whose hand the languid major is seeking, could be seen promenading on Saint Petersburg's Nevsky Prospekt and in the city's parks. All the figures, down to the servants in the background, are portrayed with an unerring eye for detail. Fedotov's art pillories social evils (in this case the way women were treated as marketable chattels), mostly with humour though occasionally with bitterness. In 1844, at the age of twenty-nine, Fedotov abandoned a military career in favour of painting. Eight years later he died in a mental institution, his mental state unbalanced by poverty and frustration.

585

. Jean-Léon Gérôme, 1824-1904, Academism, French,
The Cock Fight, 1846, Oil on canvas, 143 x 204 cm,
Musée d'Orsay, Paris

586

587

Dante Gabriel Rossetti
(1828 London –1882 Birchington)

Rossetti's father, an Italian patriot who had sought refuge in London where he became professor of Italian at King's College, was a distinguished Dante scholar. Dante Gabriel was poet as well as painter.

Rossetti was extraordinarily precocious, and very early he became acquainted with Scott and Shakespeare, but the chief influence of his childhood was the worship of Dante; he knew the poems by heart. He could not find the help he wanted in the systematic methods of the Royal Academy, and he was impatient to paint the pictures that thronged his brain. Consequently he never acquired a complete command of drawing. Perhaps he was not encouraged to try for such mastery, because of his fondness for subjects from Dante and his instinctive feeling that they must be represented with the almost childlike simplicity of feeling.

At the age of twenty-one Rossetti founded, together with Hunt, John Millais, three young sculptors, and Rossetti's younger brother, a society with the title of the Pre-Raphaelite Brotherhood, who were in the habit of affixing to their signatures the letters, P. R. B. The object of the Brotherhood was revolt against existing views and conditions of art; in its original intention not unlike the revolt of Courbet; a plea for Realism. He was ridiculing the dry formalism of the Classicists.

Additionally, while he persevered in painting, he was continually experimenting in poetry. In 1850 he met Miss Elizabeth Siddal, who was introduced to him as a model. She satisfied at once his conception of a perfectly balanced soul and body, of soul beauty shining through the beauty of form, which was his ideal of woman. She also became his ideal of Beatrice, and as such he painted her many times. He loved her, but for some reason marriage was postponed for ten years, and then after scarcely two years of marriage she died. But the memory of her abided with him, and almost all his subsequent painting was a representation, in one character or another, of her.

Suffering from the loss of his wife, and being the victim of insomnia, he became a prey to the most morbid sensibility. Only at intervals, encouraged by his friends, who clung to him, could he work. He spent his last year as an invalid recluse, and died in 1882.

586. **Dante Gabriel Rossetti,** 1828-1882, Pre-Raphaelite, British,
Girlhood of Mary Virgin, 1849, Oil on canvas, 86 x 66 cm, Tate Gallery, Lon

*A scene from Mary's childhood is the subject of a variation on the theme pa
in 1849 by Dante Gabriel Rossetti and titled* Girlhood of Mary Virgin. *Inspir
the artists of the Renaissance, this member of the Pre-Raphaelite Brothe
shows Mary working at her needlepoint with her doting mother, St Anne (or A
An angel, lilies, a stack of books and a dove comprise the traditional symbols
by the artist to allude to the perfect purity and the holy wisdom of Mary.*

587. **Jean-Auguste-Dominique Ingres,** 1780-1867, Neoclassicism, French,
Mme Moitessier, 1856, Oil on canvas, 120 x 92 cm,
National Gallery, London

*It took twelve years for Ingres to achieve this portrait. The mirror reflects
profile of the sitter. This association of face and profile in the same painting
inspire Picasso.*

88. Gustave Courbet, 1819-1877, Realism,
School of Barbizon, French, *A Burial at Ornans,* 1850,
Oil on canvas, 311.5 x 668 cm, Musée d'Orsay, Paris

*The artist's effort to paint realistic scenes is exemplified in this
unsentimental scene of a burial in the village of his birth.
Realism is especially effective in that the figures in the work are
life-sized. Courbet asked each inhabitant of Ornans to pose in
his workshop for this painting. The variety of expressions reflects
grief, yet a certain individuality is given to each. Several of the
women look away, too sad to watch the final tribute to one they
rather obviously loved. The processional cross seems to align
with the crucified Jesus on the distant hillside as if making the
past tragedy present among the sorrowful townspeople. The
bleak landscape reflects the sadness of the mourners. The main
cause of scandal for this painting was the burial scene showing
ordinary country life elevated to high historical painting level,
because of its large size. Courbet considers the little gentries as
important and dignified as historical heroes. The critics hissed.
After this work was rejected by the Jury at the Salon, Courbet
created a place called "Pavillon du Réalisme" where he
presented an exhibition of forty works. The catalogue for this
exhibition included a manifesto of Realism.*

89. John Martin, 1789-1854, Romanticism, English, *The Great
Day of His Wrath,* 1851, Oil on canvas, 196 x 303 cm,
Tate Gallery, London

GUSTAVE COURBET
(1819 ORNANS – 1877 LA TOUR DE PEILZ)

Ornans, Courbet's birthplace, is near the beautiful valley of the Doubs River, and
it was here as a boy, and later as a man, that he absorbed the love of landscape.
He was by nature a revolutionary, a man born to oppose existing order and to
assert his independence; he had that quality of bluster and brutality which makes
the revolutionary count in art as well as in politics. In both directions his spirit
of revolt manifested itself.

He went to Paris to study art, yet he did not attach himself to the studio of
any of the prominent masters. Already in his country home he had had a little
instruction in painting, and preferred to study the masterpieces of the Louvre. At
first his pictures were not sufficiently distinctive to arouse any opposition, and
were admitted to the Salon. Then followed the *Funeral at Ornans,* which the
critics violently assailed: "A masquerade funeral, six metres long, in which there
is more to laugh at than to weep over."

Indeed, the real offence of Courbet's pictures was that they represented live
flesh and blood. They depicted men and women as they really are and realistically
doing the business in which they are engaged. His figures were not men and
women deprived of personality and idealised into a type, posed in positions that
will decorate the canvas. He advocated painting things as they are, and
proclaimed that *la vérité vraie* must be the aim of the artist. So at the Universal
Exposition of 1855 he withdrew his pictures from the exhibition grounds and set
them in a wooden booth, just outside the entrance. Over the booth he posted a
sign with large lettering. It read, simply: "Courbet – Realist."

Like every revolutionary, he was an extremist. He ignored the fact that to every
artist the truth of nature appears under a different guise according to his way of
seeing and experiencing. Instead, he adhered to the notion that art is only a
copying of nature and not a matter also of selection and arrangement.

In his contempt for prettiness Courbet often chose subjects which may fairly
be called ugly. But that he also had a sense of beauty may be seen in his
landscapes. That sense, mingled with his capacity for deep emotion, appears in
his marines – these last being his most impressive work. Moreover, in all his
works, whether attractive or not to the observer, he proved himself a powerful
painter, painting in a broad, free manner, with a fine feeling for colour, and with
a firmness of pigment that made all his representations very real and stirring.

590

590. **Jean-François Millet,** 1814-1875, Realism, School of Barbizon, French,
The Sower, 1850, Oil on canvas, 101.6 x 82.6 cm, Museum of Fine Arts, Boston

591. **John Everett Millais,** 1829-1896, Pre-Raphaelite, British, *Mariana,* 1851,
Oil on canvas, 59.7 x 49.5 cm, Makins collection

592. **Ford Madox Brown,** 1821-1893, Pre-Raphaelite, English,
The Last of England, 1852-1855, Oil on canvas, 82 x 74 cm,
Birmingham Museum and Art Gallery, Birmingham

Jean-François Millet
(1814 Gruchy –1875 Barbizon)

Millet was the son of a small farmer, which explains the fact that when he painted rural life, it was not as if he were a city gentleman visiting the country, but as if he belonged to that class. His early life was very close to nature. He grew up with the air of the hills and of the sea in his nostrils, both conducive to sturdiness of character and to the development of imagination, if a boy chances to have any. He knew nothing of art or artists, but he had the desire to represent what he saw, and in the periods between work on the poor farm he would copy the engravings from the family Bible, or take a piece of charcoal and draw upon a white wall.

An uncle, who was a priest, had taught him as a boy, so that in his manhood he read Shakespeare and Virgil in the original texts. Therefore, although he was of the peasant life, he was greater than it, and brought to the interpretation of its most intimate facts a breadth of view and depth of sympathy which made his pictures much more than studies of peasants. The determination of the farmer in *The Sower* suggests he is not a man to be reckoned with. After the sowing is complete, one could imagine him leading thousands of peasants to Paris; perhaps it is the empowerment of peasants by the skilled hands of artists like Millet that led to this painting's confiscation prior to the revolution.

Millet, with no direct thought of being poetical (or political), sought only to portray the truth as he saw and felt it. He has represented dull, homely facts with such an insight into the relation they bear on the lives of the people engaged in them, that he has created an atmosphere of imagination around the facts.

591

592

593

593. Ivan Aivazovsky, 1817-1900, Romanticism,
Russian, *The Ninth Wave,* 1850,
Oil on canvas, 221 x 332 cm,
The State Russian Museum, St. Petersburg

One of Aivazovsky's most famous works, The Ninth
Wave, *owes its title to the superstition among Russian
sailors that in any sequence of waves, the ninth is the
most violent. Like many of his paintings, it bears the
imprint of Romanticism: the sea and sky convey the
power and grandeur of nature, while in the
foreground, the survivors of a shipwreck embody
human hopes and fears. Although the sea is the
dominant theme in the majority of the 6,000 paintings
that Aivazovsky produced, he also painted views of
the coast and countryside, both in Russia (especially
in the Ukraine and Crimea) and during travels abroad.*

594. John Everett Millais, 1829-1896, Pre-Raphaelite,
British, *Ophelia,* 1851, Oil on canvas, 76 x 112 cm,
Tate Gallery, London

The beautiful Ophelia from Shakespeare's Hamlet
*floats in the stream with eyes heavenward and hands
open in resignation to her tragic state of insanity. Her
gesture is like that of the prayerful posture Catholic
clergy give from their altar of sacrifice. Flower petals
have delicately fallen onto her as if nature was
welcoming her into its ongoing cycle of life and
death. They also recall Hamlet's words, "sweets to the
sweet: farewell!" By blending into its rustic textures
and liquid flow, her gown anticipates the woman's
union with nature: "Let her i' the earth, and from her
fair and unpolluted flesh may violets spring."*

594

595

595. William Holman Hunt, 1827-1910, Pre-Raphaelite, British,
The Awakening Conscience, 1853, Oil on canvas, 76 x 55 cm,
Tate Gallery, London

*The Pre-Raphaelite Brotherhood involved several British artists t
existed for only five years between 1880 and 1900. However, Hunt
a charter member continued his life-long commitment to their cau
He continued to be judgmental about what the Brotherhood consider
immoral sexual activity. In this work, inspired by Charles Dicke
David Copperfield, the artist shows a man and a woman, who might
his mistress. The man plays the piano and sings a song intended
seduce her, but the sheet music, apparently hers rather than his choic
is for "Oft in the Stilly Night," a song about a girl recalling I
childhood innocence. The woman is about to stand up perhaps as s
remembers the words to the song that awakens her conscience. Like t
song sheet on the piano, the music sheets in the lower left corner a
also about lost innocence. It is an adaptation of a poem by Tennys
(1809-92), familiar in the popular culture at the time. The mirror on t
far wall reveals that the woman is looking out, apparently towards t
future, where there are white roses symbolising the purity to which t
kept woman can return. The cat, like the man, is playing with its pre
But the bird (like the woman) seems to have a chance to escape.*

596. Adolf Friedrich Erdmann Menzel, 1815-1905, Realism, German,
The Flute Concert of Frederick II at Sanssouci, c. 1851,
Oil on canvas, 142 x 205 cm, Alte Nationalgalerie, Berlin

597. Gustave Courbet, 1819-1877, Realism, School of Barbizon, French
The Wheat Sifters, 1854, Oil on canvas, 131 x 167 cm,
Musée des Beaux-Arts, Nantes

598. Gustave Courbet, 1819-1877, Realism, School of Barbizon, French
Bonjour Monsieur Courbet! (detail), 1854,
Oil on canvas, 129 x 149 cm, Musée Fabre, Montpellier

596

597

599

599. Gustave Courbet, 1819-1877, Realism, School of Barbizon, French,
The Artist's Studio, 1855, Oil on canvas, 361 x 598 cm, Musée d'Orsay, Paris

Courbet noted: "Painting is an essentially concrete art and can only consist of the representation of real and existing objects." When he was asked to include angels in a painting for a church, he answered: "Show me an angel and I will paint one." Courbet represented Baudelaire and the painter Prod'hon on the right side of the painting.

600. William Powell Frith, 1819-1909, Victorian Art, English,
Derby Day, 1856-1858, Oil on canvas, 101 x 223 cm, Tate Gallery, London

Extremely popular during his lifetime, Frith's art, like Victorian art in general was re-evaluated after World War II. This work presents a satirical panorama modern Victorian life. It was first exhibited at the Royal Academy in 1858.

600

601. Jean-François Millet, 1814-1875, Realism, School of Barbizon, French,
The Angelus, c. 1858, Oil on canvas, 55.5 x 66 cm, Musée d'Orsay, Paris

*There is a religious, or at least a sincerely sentimental, tone to Millet's view of
labourers ploughing, sowing, or harvesting. This painting, the most popular of
his views of that simple life, shows a couple pausing from their toil to pray. The
title informs the viewer that the couple is praying the prayer known as the
Angelus (Latin for "angel"), the traditional Catholic prayer to the Virgin Mary
that is said at six o'clock in the morning, noon and again at six o'clock in the
evening. The word refers to the archangel Gabriel, who invited the Virgin
during the Annunciation to be the mother of Jesus (Luke 1:26). An earlier work
by Millet, The Sower, is nearly as popular. It likewise shows a slice of the
simple but dignified life of farming. Millet brought a dignity to the images of
peasants, whereas artists such as Brueghel the Elder often made them appear
as standard personifications of human destiny.*

602. Gustave Courbet, 1819-1877, Realism, School of Barbizon, French,
Young Ladies on the Banks of the Seine, 1856, Oil on canvas, 174 x 206 cm,
Musée du Petit Palais, Paris

*After 1855, Courbet limited his palette and simplified his compositions,
depicting his sitters with great realism, and without idealisation. Fustigated by
the critics, this painting was accused of depicting vulgar and shameless women.*

603

60

604

603. Francesco Hayez, 1791-1882, Romanticism, Italian, *The Kiss,* 1859, Oil on canvas, 112 x 88 cm, Pinacoteca di Brera, Milan

Emblematic of Italian Romanticism, this painting also works as a political allegory of the union between Italy and France.

604. German Hilaire Edgar Degas, 1834-1917, Impressionism, French, *The Bellelli Family,* 1858-1867, Oil on canvas, 200 x 250 cm, Musée d'Orsay, Paris

605. Edouard Manet, 1832-1883, Impressionism, French, *The Absinthe Drinker,* 1858-59, Oil on canvas, 180.5 x 105.6 cm, Ny Carlsberg Glyptotek, Copenhagen

607

608

06. **Moritz von Schwind,** 1804-1871, Romanticism, Austrian, *On the Travels,* c. 1860, Oil on canvas, 22 x 37 cm, Schack-Galerie, Munich

07. **Carl Spitzweg,** 1808-1885, Romanticism, German, *The Farewell,* 1855, Oil on canvas, 54 x 32 cm, Schack-Galerie, Munich

08. **Moritz von Schwind,** 1804-1871, Romanticism, Austrian, *Honeymoon,* 1867, Oil on wood, 52 x 41 cm, Schack-Galerie, Munich

609

James Abbott McNeill Whistler
(1834 Lowell –1903 London)

Whistler suddenly shot to fame like a meteor at a crucial moment in the history of art, a field in which he was a pioneer. Like the impressionists, with whom he sided, he wanted to impose his own ideas. Whistler's work can be divided into four periods. The first may be called a period of research in which he was influenced by the Realism of Gustave Courbet and by Japanese art.

Whistler then discovered his own originality in the Nocturnes and the Cremorne Gardens series, thereby coming into conflict with the academics who wanted a work of art to tell a story. When he painted the portrait of his mother, Whistler entitled it *Arrangement in Grey and Black* and this is symbolic of his aesthetic theories. When painting the *Cremorne Pleasure Gardens* it was not to depict identifiable figures, as did Renoir in his work on similar themes, but to capture an atmosphere. He loved the mists that hovered over the banks of the Thames, the pale light, and the factory chimneys which at night turned into magical minarets. Night redrew landscapes, effacing the details. This was the period in which he became an adventurer in art; his work, which verged on abstraction, shocked his contemporaries.

The third period is dominated by the full-length portraits that brought him his fame. He was able to imbue this traditional genre with his profound originality. He tried to capture part of the souls of his models and placed the characters in their natural habitats. This gave his models a strange presence so that they seem about to walk out of the picture to physically encounter the viewer. By extracting the poetic substance from individuals he created portraits described as "mediums" by his contemporaries, and which were the inspiration for Oscar Wilde's *The Picture of Dorian Gray*.

Towards the end of his life, the artist began painting landscapes and portraits in the classical tradition, strongly influenced by Velázquez. Whistler proved to be extremely rigorous in ensuring his paintings coincided with his theories. He never hesitated in crossing swords with the most famous art theoreticians of his day. His personality, his outbursts, and his elegance were a perfect focus for curiosity and admiration. He was a close friend of Stéphane Mallarmé, and admired by Marcel Proust, who rendered homage to him in *A La Recherche du Temps Perdu*. He was also a provocative dandy, a prickly socialite, a demanding artist, and a daring innovator.

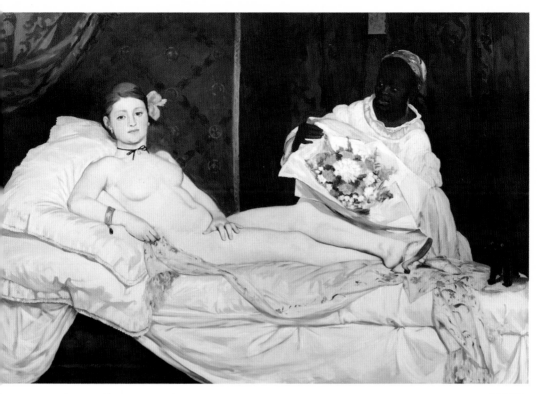

09. **Jean-Auguste-Dominique Ingres,** 1780-1867, Neoclassicism, French, *The Turkish Bath*, 1862, Oil on canvas, Tondo, dia. 108 cm, Musée du Louvre, Paris

10. **Édouard Manet,** 1832-1883, Impressionism, French, *Olympia*, 1863, Oil on canvas, 130 x 190 cm, Musée d'Orsay, Paris

11. **Wjatscheslaw Grigorjewitsch Schwarz,** 1838-1869, Realism, Russian, *Ivan the Terrible Meditating at the Deathbed of his Son Ivan*, 1861, Oil on canvas, 71 x 89 cm, The State Tretyakov Gallery, Moscow

12. **James Abbot McNeill Whistler,** 1834-1903, Post-impressionism, American, *Symphony in White, No. 2: The Little White Girl*, 1864, Oil on canvas, 76.5 x 51.1 cm, Tate Gallery, London

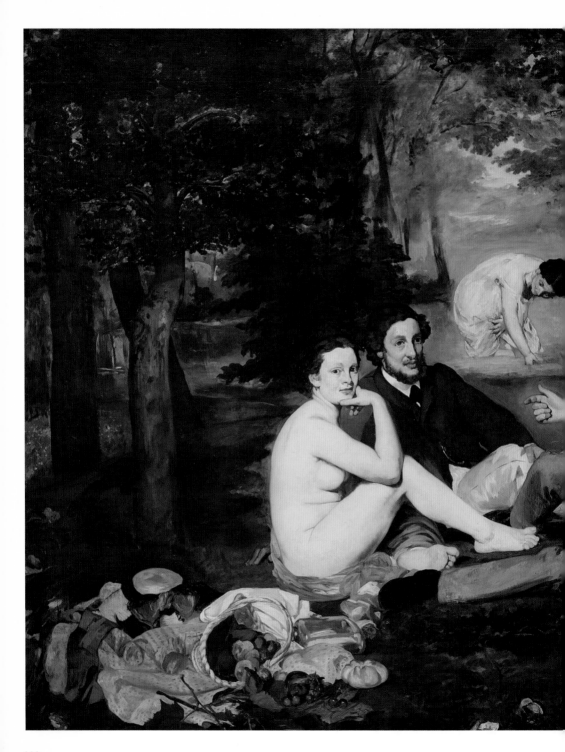

Édouard Manet
(1832 Paris –1883)

Manet is one of the most famous artists from the second half of the nineteenth century linked to the impressionists, although he was not really one of them. He had great influence on French painting partly because of the choice he made for his subjects from everyday life, the use of pure colours, and his fast and free technique. He made, in his own work, the transition between Courbet's Realism and the work of the impressionists.

Born a high bourgeois, he chose to become a painter after failing the entry to the Marine School. He studied with Thomas Couture, an Academic painter, but it was thanks to the numerous travels he made around Europe from 1852 that he started to find out what would become his own style.

His first paintings were mostly portraits and genre scenes, inspired by his love for Spanish masters like Velázquez and Goya. In 1863 he presented his masterpiece *Luncheon on the Grass* at the Salon des Refusés. His work started a fight between the defenders of Academic art and the young "refusés" artists. Manet became the leader of this new generation of artists.

From 1864, the official Salon accepted his paintings, still provoking loud protests over works such as *Olympia* in 1865. In 1866, the writer Zolá wrote an article defending Manet's work. At that time, Manet was friends with all the future great impressionist masters: Edgar Degas, Claude Monet, Auguste Renoir, Alfred Sisley, Camille Pissarro and Paul Cézanne, and he influenced their work, even though he cannot strictly be counted as one of them. In 1874 indeed, he refused to present his paintings in the First Impressionist Exhibition. His last appearance in the official Salon was in 1882 with *A Bar at the Folies-Bergère*, one of his most famous works. Suffering from gangrene during the year 1883, he painted flower still-lifes until he became too weak to work. He died leaving behind a great number of drawings and paintings.

---

613. Édouard Manet, 1832-1883, Impressionism, French, *Luncheon on the Grass*, 1863, Oil on canvas, 208 x 264 cm, Musée d'Orsay, Paris

In 1863, Manet shocked viewers at the Salon des Refusés with his large painting Le Déjeuner sur l'herbe in which he includes both naked women and dressed male students. He at first had in mind to present a work like Titian's Pastoral Symphony (1508). In his previous paintings naked women typically did not look directly at the viewer. In this painting, the expression of the lady is natural, relaxed, and without embarrassment. Manet said that light was the chief actor in the work. The basket of fruit on the blue dress in the foreground takes as much importance as the characters and shows Manet's skills at depicting still-lifes. Reproductions and parodies of the unforgettable work in many media have been presented over the past 150 years. But two decades after this painting was created, Manet no longer needed to shock in order to win attention. See his masterpiece, A Bar at the Folies-Bergère. Louise Gardner comments, "Manet raises the veils of allusion and reverie and bluntly confronts the public with reality, demonstrating, incidentally, the incompatibility of myth and realism."

613

614

614. Dante Gabriel Rossetti, 1828-1882, Pre-Raphaelite, British, *Beata Beatrix,* c. 1864-70, Oil on canvas, 86.4 x 66 cm, Tate Gallery, London

Rossetti was one of the founders of the Pre-Raphaelite movement that reacted against Victorian artists and wanted to get back to the simplicity of painting before Raphael. This painting, inspired by the Vita Nuova by Dante, present the characteristics of Pre-Raphaelite techniques such as the large spots of light and the meticulous attention paid to the symbolic details.

615. Honoré Daumier, 1808-1879, Realism, French, *The Washer Woman,* c. 1860-63, Oil on panel, 49 x 33.5 cm, Musée d'Orsay, Paris

616. Camille Pissarro, 1830-1903, Impressionism, French, *The Marne at Chennevières,* 1864, Oil on canvas, 91.5 x 145.5 cm, National Gallery of Scotland, Edinburgh

617. Alexandre Cabanel, 1825-1905, Academism, French, *The Birth of Venus,* c. 1863, Oil on canvas, 130 x 225 cm, Musée d'Orsay, Paris

6

7

618

619

620

618. **Charles-François Daubigny,** 1817-1878, Realism, School of Ba
French, *On the Banks of the Oise,* c. 1860-65,
Oil on canvas, 32.5 x 60 cm, Private collection

619. **James Tissot,** 1836-1902, Victorian art, French, *Portrait of Mlle*
called *Woman in Red Vest,* 1864, Oil on canvas, 124 x 99.5 cm
Musée d'Orsay, Paris

In 1864, Tissot turned with great success to scenes of contempo
usually involving fashionable women.

620. **Carl Spitzweg,** 1808-1885, Romanticism, German, *A Hypochond*
c. 1865, Oil on canvas, 53 x 31 cm, Shack-Galerie, Munich

621. **Germain Hilaire Edgar Degas,** 1834-1917, Impressionism, Fre
Race Horses before the Stands, c.1866, Essence on paper mount
canvas, 46 x 61 cm, Musée d'Orsay, Paris

622. **Jean-Baptiste Camille Corot,** 1796-1875, Realism, School of B
French, *Souvenir of Mortefontaine,* c. 1864, Oil on canvas, 65 x
Musée du Louvre, Paris

623

JEAN-BAPTISTE CAMILLE COROT
(1796 –1875 PARIS)

Corot's parents were court dressmakers in the days of the first Napoleon. Living in comfortable circumstances, their son never wanted for money. His father had apprenticed him to a linen-draper, but after eight years consented to his son's desire to become a painter.

When Corot paid his first visit to Italy, he was so attracted by the moving life on the streets of Rome and Naples that he transferred it to his sketch-book. Because his subjects would not remain still long enough to be treated methodically, he learned to draw, with a few strokes, the general effect of a moving picture and with such success that after a time he could rapidly suggest the appearance of even so intricate a scene as a ballet. This acquired skill became very useful, as when he sought to represent the tremble of foliage in the morning or evening air. It taught him also, by degrees, the value of generalisation, that is, of not representing details so much as of discovering the salient qualities of objects, and of uniting them into a whole that suggested rather than definitively described.

The first inspiration of his work was Italy and the Italian landscape; next the landscape of France began to appeal to his imagination. In his little house in Ville d'Avray, near Paris, he spent his time filling his soul with visions of nature, which, when he returned to Paris, were transferred to canvas. Corot interpreted his moods concerning nature, rather than strictly depicting nature itself. He was not a great descriptive, epic poet, alive to the mighty forces that underlie the vastness of his subject, but a sweet, lyric singer of a few choice moments.

623. **Jean-Baptiste Camille Corot,** 1796-1875, Realism, School of Barbizon, French, *Agostina*, 1866, Oil on canvas, 132.4 x 97.6 cm, The National Gallery of Art, Washington, D.C.

Degas said of Corot because of his generosity and noble character: "He is angel who smokes a pipe".

624. **Anselm Feuerbach,** 1829-1880, Neoclassicism, German, *Paolo and Francesca*, 1864, Oil on canvas, 136.5 x 99.5 cm, Shack-Galerie, Munich

625. **Peter Cornelius,** 1783-1867, Realism, School of Barbizon, German, *The Recognition of Joseph by his Brothers*, 1866, Fresco, 236 x 290 cm, Alte Nationalgalerie, Berlin

626

26. Johan Barthold Jongkind, 1819-1891, Impressionism, Dutch, *The Maas at Maassluis,* 1866, Oil on canvas, 33 x 47 cm, Musée des Beaux-Arts, Le Havre

27. Henri Fantin-Latour, 1836-1904, Realism, French, *Still-Life with Flowers and Fruit,* 1866, Oil on canvas, 73 x 60 cm, The Metropolitan Museum of Art, New York

627

HENRI FANTIN-LATOUR
(1836 GRENOBLE – 1904 BURÉ)

For Henri Fantin-Latour, still-life painting was almost a curse. He was continually beset by collectors who wanted nothing else from his otherwise immense artistic talent. Consequently, he is known almost exclusively for his delicate still-lifes in which he excelled, although his extraordinary figure depictions and portrait groups also should have stood test of time.

Many of the best examples of Fantin-Latour's floral paintings and still-lifes can be found in English galleries and museums. When viewed close up, they reveal details and objects which lend a starkly realistic impression. They combine drawing with intricate brushwork and lovely harmonies of colour. In this way his still-lifes, like his portraits, have a truthful quality and great pictorial depth.

629

8. Claude Monet, 1840-1926, Impressionism, French, *Women in the Garden,* 1867, Oil on canvas, 255 x 205 cm, Musée d'Orsay, Paris

9. Alfred Sisley, 1839-1899, Impressionism, French, *Avenue of Chestnut Trees at La Celle-Saint-Cloud,* 1867, Oil on canvas, 95.5 x 122.2 cm, Southampton City Art Gallery, Southampton

The earliest influence on Sisley's impressionistic painting was Camille Corot. Later he befriended Monet, Renoir and Bazille. Yet, he developed a distinctive style of shimmering landscapes with thinly painted surfaces and small flecks of colour laid side by side. For over twenty or more productive years his style didn't change aside from gradually using a slightly free brushstroke and bolder colours. All of Sisley's paintings are of small landscapes; most are scenes from the countryside near his home that he painted while out of doors, which few painters did at that time.

0. Frédéric Bazille, 1841-1870, Impressionism, French, *Family Reunion,* 1867, Oil on canvas, 152 x 230 cm, Musée d'Orsay, Paris

630

631

631. **Eugène Boudin,** 1824-1898, Impressionism, French,
The Beach at Trouville, 1871, Oil on canvas, 19 x 46 cm,
The Pushkin Museum of Fine Arts, Moscow

632

632. **Honoré Daumier,** 1808-1879, Realism, French, *Don Quixote
and Sancho Pansa,* c. 1868, Oil on canvas, 52 x 32 cm,
Neue Pinakothek, Munich

633. **James Abbot McNeill Whistler,** 1834-1903, Post-impressionism,
American, *Nocturne: Blue and Gold – Old Battersea Bridge,* 1872-75,
Oil on canvas, 68.3 x 51.2 cm, Tate Gallery, London

634

635

634. James Abbot McNeill Whistler, 1834-1903, Post-impressionism, American, *Arrangement in Grey and Black Nr.1* or *Portrait of the Artist's Mother,* 1871, Oil on canvas, 144.3 x 162.5 cm, Musée d'Orsay, Paris

Whistler's most famous work is widely, but incorrectly called Whistler's Mother. The artist insisted that the focus in the painting should be the work's arrangement of shapes and the colours. The severity of the masses is assuaged by the two gathering points of intimate expression: the hands and the face. The prevailing gravity, deliberately chosen, and the accent of tenderness contribute largely to the emotion aroused in the spectator's imagination. The expression of the face is the centre and climax of a corresponding expression that pervades the whole canvas, the result of the balance of the full and empty spaces and the colour scheme of black and grey. Whistler reduced his content to its more essential expressive forms, placing his subjects in full length before neutral backgrounds, not unlike works by John Singer Sargent.

635. Henri Fantin-Latour, 1836-1904, Realism, French, *A Studio in the Batignolles,* 1870, Oil on canvas, 204 x 273.5 cm, Musée d'Orsay, Paris

636. **Germain Hilaire Edgar Degas,** 1834-1917,
     Impressionism, French, *Dance Foyer at the Opera,* 1872,
     Oil on canvas, 32 x 46 cm, Musée d'Orsay, Paris

637. **Alfred Sisley,** 1839-1899, Impressionism, French,
     The Bridge at Villeneuve-la-Garenne, 1872, Oil on canvas, 49.5 x 65.5 cm,
     The Metropolitan Museum of Art, New York

Germain Hilaire Edgar Degas
(1834 –1917 Paris)

Degas was closest to Renoir in the impressionist's circle, for both favoured the animated Parisian life of their day as a motif in their paintings. Degas did not attend Gleyre's studio; most likely he first met the future impressionists at the Café Guerbois.

He started his apprenticeship in 1853 at the studio of Louis-Ernest Barrias and, beginning in 1854, studied under Louis Lamothe, who revered Ingres above all others, and transmitted his adoration for this master to Edgar Degas. Starting in 1854 Degas travelled frequently to Italy: first to Naples, where he made the acquaintance of his numerous cousins, and then to Rome and Florence, where he copied tirelessly from the Old Masters. His drawings and sketches already revealed very clear preferences: Raphael, Leonardo da Vinci, Michelangelo, and Mantegna, but also Benozzo Gozzoli, Ghirlandaio, Titian, Fra Angelico, Uccello, and Botticelli.

During the 1860s and 1870s he became a painter of racecourses, horses and jockeys. His fabulous painter's memory retained the particularities of movement of horses wherever he saw them. After his first rather complex compositions depicting racecourses, Degas learned the art of translating the nobility and elegance of horses, their nervous movements, and the formal beauty of their musculature.

Around the middle of the 1860s Degas made yet another discovery. In 1866 he painted his first composition with ballet as a subject, *Mademoiselle Fiocre dans le ballet de la Source* (*Mademoiselle Fiocre in the Ballet 'The Spring'*) (New York, Brooklyn Museum). Degas had always been a devotee of the theatre, but from now on it would become more and more the focus of his art. Degas' first painting devoted solely to the ballet was *Le Foyer de la danse à l'Opéra de la rue Le Peletier* (*The Dancing Anteroom at the Opera on Rue Le Peletier*) (Paris, Musée d'Orsay). In a carefully constructed composition, with groups of figures balancing one another to the left and the right, each ballet dancer is involved in her own activity, each one is moving in a separate manner from the others. Extended observation and an immense number of sketches were essential to executing such a task. This is why Degas moved from the theatre on to the rehearsal halls, where the dancers practised and took their lessons. This was how Degas arrived at the second sphere of that immediate, everyday life that was to interest him. The ballet would remain his passion until the end of his days.

637

Alfred Sisley
(1839 Paris –1899 Moret–sur–Loing)

Alfred Sisley was born in Paris on 30 October 1839 to English parents. He spent five years in England from 1857 to 1861, and in the country of Shakespeare he felt himself to be English for the first time. He studied English literature, but was even more interested in England's great master painters. It was most likely in this way – through exposure to the free brushwork of Turner, and Constable's landscapes, which resembled preparatory studies – that Sisley sensed he had a vocation for the genre.

In October 1862 fate brought him to Charles Gleyre's free studio, where Claude Monet, Auguste Renoir, and Frédéric Bazille had come to study. It was Sisley who had encouraged his friends to give up their apprenticeship at Gleyre's studio and go out to paint from nature. He was outraged, far more so than his friends, at Gleyre's arrogant attitude towards landscapes.

From the beginning, landscape for Sisley was not just an essential pictorial genre; it was the one and only genre in which he was to work his entire life. After leaving Gleyre, Sisley often painted together with Monet, Renoir, and Bazille in the environs of Paris.

From 1870 the first characteristics of the style that later became Impressionism began to appear in Sisley's painting. From this point forward the colour scheme in Sisley's paintings becomes distinctly lighter. This new technique creates an impression of vibrating water, of brightly coloured shimmering on its surface, and of a crisp clarity in the atmosphere. Light, in Sisley's paintings, was born.

Over the course of the four years he lived in Louveciennes, Sisley painted numerous landscapes of the banks of the Seine. He discovered Argenteuil and the little town of Villeneuve-la-Garenne, which in his work would remain the very image of silence and tranquillity; a world that civilisation and industry had not yet disfigured. He was not, in contrast to Pissarro, searching for prosaic accuracy. His landscapes were always coloured by his emotional attitude towards them. As with Monet, Sisley's bridges are set in the countryside in a completely natural way. A serene blue sky is reflected in the barely stirring surface of the river. In harmony with this, some small, light-coloured houses and the coolness of the greenery create the impression of sunlight.

After the First Impressionism Exhibition Sisley spent several months in England. On his return, Sisley moved from Louveciennes to Marly-le Roi. Around this period Sisley truly became a painter of water. It cast a spell over him, forcing him to scrutinise its changing surface and to study its nuances of colour, as Monet did with meadows at Giverny.

638

639

640. Ilya Repin, 1844-1930, Realism, Russian,
Barge Haulers on the Volga, 1872-73, Oil on canvas, 131.5 x 281 cm,
The State Russian Museum, St. Petersburg

638. Camille Pissarro, 1830-1903, Impressionism, French,
The Crossroads, Pontoise, 1872, Oil on canvas, 54.9 x 94 cm,
The Carnegie Museum of Art, Pittsburg

639. Arnold Böcklin, 1827-1901, Symbolism, Swiss, *Centaur Fight,* 1873,
Tempera on canvas, 105 x 195 cm, Kunstmuseum, Basle

*Repin's reputation was founded on his Barge Haulers, the artist's thoughts on
life in the Russian countryside after the reforms of the 1860s, and on the lot of
peasants who had to leave the land to take on seasonal work. However, this
early canvas, in spite of the fact that it was based on preparatory work in open
air, still shows a certain contradiction between the artist's desire to remain true
to life and his rationalistic approach to the composition of the picture which
consequently acquired a somewhat spectacular quality. In the Chuguyev and
Moscow years, the peasant theme at first, a simple expression of the artist's
social orientation, became an integral part of his realism.*

Arnold Böcklin
(1827 Basle –1901 San Domenico)

The son of a Swiss merchant, Böcklin was born in Basle, "one of the most prosaic towns in Europe". At nineteen he entered the art school at
Düsseldorf, but was advised by his master to proceed to Brussels and Paris and, later, to Rome where he copied the Old Masters. In this way he
learned the art of painting, which, in Germany, had been neglected for some time. There the subject of the painting was held to be of more
importance than the method of representing it. Though he returned for a time to Germany and after 1886, lived in Zurich until his death, the
country which affected Böcklin's life most deeply, where he lived during the period in which his particular genius unfolded, was Italy. It was from
the Roman Campagna, sad and grand, where the Anio plunges down in cataracts, that he drew the inspiration for his landscapes.

He was, in fact, a Greek in his healthy love of nature and his instinct for giving visible expression to her voices; a modern in his feeling for
the moods of nature; and in his union of the two, unique. Moreover, he was a great colourist. "At the very time," writes Muther, "when Richard
Wagner lured the colours of sound from music, with a glow of light such as no master had kindled before, Böcklin's symphonies of colour
streamed forth like a crashing orchestra. Many of his pictures have such an ensnaring brilliancy that the eye is never weary of feasting upon their
floating splendour. Indeed, later generations have honoured him as one of the greatest colour-poets of the century."

641

642

643

644

41. Claude Monet, 1840-1926, Impressionism, French, *Impression: Sunrise*, 1873,
Oil on canvas, 48 x 63 cm, Musée Marmottan, Paris

While surely not one of Monet's masterpieces, this work is one of the most important because of its influence on the evolution of art. Ironically, the critic, Louis Leroy, of the exhibition in which this work was first shown, referred to the group of artists in the show as "impressionists". However, in context, the critic was referring to what he thought was the sloppy and "unfinished" work of the group; he wanted the term to be derogatory. As the title indicates, this is not a realistic depiction of nature but "the impression" the artist had of it. Monet gets away from the academic rules, rejects the preliminary drawing and uses a loose brushstroke that suggests rather than delineates, and that represents the variations of light upon each element of the scene. The sun is the only warm touch in the painting, its light reflecting itself in the blue-grey sky and water, and it brings the composition to life.

645

42. Winslow Homer, 1836-1910, Realism, American, *Breezing Up (A Fair Wind)*,
1873-1876, Oil on canvas, 61 x 97 cm, The National Gallery of Art, Washington, D.C.

43. Germain Hilaire Edgar Degas, 1834-1917, Impressionism, French,
The Rehearsal of the Ballet on Stage, c. 1874, Oil colours freely mixed with turpentine, with traces of watercolour and pastel over pen-and-ink drawing on cream-coloured woven paper, laid down on bristol board and mounted on canvas, 54.3 x 73 cm, The Metropolitan Museum of Art, New York

44. Alfred Sisley, 1839-1899, Impressionism, French, *Flood at Port-Marly*, 1876,
Oil on canvas, 60 x 81 cm, Musée d'Orsay, Paris

Sisley's landscapes devoted to the Port-Marly flood are a crowning achievement. The painter played with space and perspective, in the end finding the only possible solution: the pink house is frozen in a world where the sky merges with the earth, where the reflection barely ripples, and the clouds glide slowly by. Sisley was the only impressionist whose landscapes do not limit themselves to nature's changing beauty but extend to other realms, sometimes of dreams, sometimes of philosophical reflection.

45. Berthe Morisot, 1841-1895, Impressionism, French, *The Cradle*, 1872,
Oil on canvas, 56 x 46 cm, Musée d'Orsay, Paris

646

647

648

646. Gustave Moreau, 1826-1898, Symbolism, French, *Apparition (Salome),* 1876-98, Oil on canvas, 142 x 103 cm, Musée Gustave Moreau, Paris

647. Thomas Eakins, 1844-1916, Realism, American, *The Gross Clinic,* 1875, Oil on canvas, 244 x 198 cm, Jefferson University, Philadelphia

As a pioneer in multiple-exposure photography with a single camera, Eak
knew how to capture and freeze a dramatic moment. His collaboration w
pioneering photographer Edward Muybridge (1830-1904) in studying hum
action impressed academics in France, influenced Degas, and prepared the w
for motion pictures. He was also a mathematician and taught human anatom
However, Eakins became a leader with Winslow Homer of the emerg
American School of realism. His paintings reflected his scientific knowledge
both photography and surgery. He witnessed, and later captured on canv
operations performed by the renowned doctors Gross and Agnew. A la
painting is titled The Agnew Clinic. (1889). In business suits and with to
objectivity, the surgeons focus on the patient as Dr. Gross gives the lecture. C
the left, a woman presumed to be an assisting nurse seems to need to rest. T
viewer is made to feel closer and more intimate to the operation than even t
note-taking observers in the gallery. Presenting surgery realistically was upsett
for Eakins' contemporaries who considered his works to be "anatomy lesson
rather than fine art to be viewed. Some art historians contrast this work with
unnatural formality of Rembrandt's The Anatomy Lesson of Dr. Tulp (1632).

648. Jean-Baptiste Camille Corot, 1796-1875, Realism, School of Barbizon, French, *Woman in Blue,* 1874, Oil on canvas, 80 x 50.5 cm, Musée du Louvre, Paris

650

651

49. Pierre-Auguste Renoir, 1841-1919, Impressionism, French,
Portrait of the Actress Jeanne Samary, 1877, Oil on canvas, 56 x 46 cm,
The Pushkin Museum of Fine Arts, Moscow

"I look at the portrait of Jeanne Samary as I would look at the portrait of my dead sister," Jean Renoir said. Separate strokes of colour — blue, brown and green — are scattered around the sitter's head. They have no visual meaning, do not evoke ideas of drapes or wallpaper, but without them there would not be the shining halo that encircles the head with its chestnut-gold hair. The pink light dissolves contours and is restrained only by the bright patch of the blue dress. There is practically no chiaroscuro here, yet the roundness of Jeanne's arms and shoulders is tangible. The uneven, disorderly texture of the work prompted Louis Leroy, the man who gave Impressionism its name, to remark that one could eat the painting with a spoon.

50. Pierre-Auguste Renoir, 1841-1919, Impressionism, French, *The Swing,*
1876, Oil on canvas, 92 x 73 cm, Musée d'Orsay, Paris

"Why shouldn't art be pretty?" Renoir mosed, "There are enough unpleasant things in the world."

51. Gustave Caillebotte, 1848-1894, Impressionism, French, *Young Man at his Window,* 1876, Oil on canvas, 116.3 x 80.9 cm, Private collection

652

653

2. Germain Hilaire Edgar Degas, 1834-1917, Impressionism, French,
In a Café (The Absinthe Drinker), 1875-1876, Oil on canvas, 92 x 68 cm,
Musée d'Orsay, Paris

In 1876 Degas painted Dans *or* L'Absinthe un Café *(In the Café/Absinthe). At that time most artists had already abandoned the Café Guerbois and reunited at La Nouvelle Athènes in the Place Pigalle. Degas had lived in this neighborhood for a large portion of his life: in Rue Blanche, Rue Fontaine, and Rue Saint-Georges. He could now be seen regularly in the evenings, on the terrace of La Nouvelle Athènes, with Edouard Manet, Emile Zolá, and various impressionists and critics. For his new painting he asked his friend the engraver Marcellin Desboutin, just back from Florence, and the pretty actress Ellen Andrée to pose for him. Ellen Andrée would later pose at the same location, on the terrace of La Nouvelle Athènes, for Edouard Manet's* La Prune *(The Plum), and also for Renoir's* Le Déjeuner sur les Canotiers *(The Rower's Lunch) on the island of Croissy.*

Degas depicted her as a prostitute of the Parisian streets with a lost look, sitting absolutely still before a glass of absinthe, absorbed in thought. At her side, a pipe clenched between his teeth and hat pushed back onto his neck, one of the café regulars is seated. He seems to be looking into the distance, not aware of the woman seated just beside him. Squeezed into a corner behind little empty tables, they are almost touching one other, but each is in their own world. Again, Degas succeeded in setting down on the canvas something almost impossible to capture: the bitter solitude of a human being in the merriest, liveliest city in the world. Here, as well, there is nearly an absence of colour. Only some delicate pinkish and bluish accents work to enhance the range of greys. This attracted attention, and astonished many in the bright, colour-filled world of the impressionists. Degas was indeed a "strange artist". In many respects his positions were identical with those of the impressionists but, at the same time, so many things set him apart from his painting allies.

653. Claude Monet, 1840-1926, Impressionism, French, *The Saint-Lazare Station,* 1877, Oil on canvas, 75 x 104 cm, Musée d'Orsay, Paris

654. Pierre-Auguste Renoir, 1841-1919, Impressionism, French, *The Moulin de la Galette,* 1876, Oil on canvas, 131 x 175 cm, Musée d'Orsay, Paris

654

655

656

655. Gustave Caillebotte, 1848-1894, Impressionism, French,
Paris Street, Rainy Day, 1877, Oil on canvas, 212.2 x 276.2 cm,
The Art Institute of Chicago, Chicago

*The five hundred or more paintings of Caillebotte were not given m
attention during his lifetime. For years, he was considered primaril
generous patron of impressionists, but not as a painter in his own ri
Later, his style was seen to be more realistic than those of his frie
Degas, Monet and Renoir. In 1874, he helped to organise the F
Impressionist Exhibition. However, he did not include his own work –
would show in later impressionist exhibitions. In this typical work
captures the feeling of a new Parisian boulevard in an area of
Batignolles quarter on a rainy day. The realism with which Cailleb
depicts the scene is later praised by the writer Emile Zola: " Paris Str
Rainy Day displays strollers and, in particular, a man and a woman
foreground, of a beautiful realism. When his talent will have softene
little, Caillebotte will certainly be the most audacious of the group."*

6. Paul Cézanne, 1839-1906,
Post-impressionism, French, *Fruit*, 1879-80,
Oil on canvas, 45 x 55.3 cm,
The State Hermitage Museum, St. Petersburg

Cézanne painted two groups of still-lifes composed of the same objects: a milk jug, a decanter, a painted bowl, and fruit. The first group is dated, by Venturi, to the years 1873-1877 in Pontoise or Paris. The Hermitage canvas belongs to the second group featuring the same objects but with leaf-patterned wallpaper in the background. Venturi dates this group to 1879-1882. Around 1880, two tendencies were happily combined in Cézanne's work – an inclination to massive, baroque forms and a striving for orderly constructivism. The artist was then evolving his favourite colour range of warm oranges and cool grey-blues, and his brushstroke was becoming extremely flexible, capable of conveying a sense of heavy density or almost weightless transparency.

7. Mary Cassatt, 1844-1926, Impressionism, American, *Little Girl in a Blue Armchair*, 1878, Oil on canvas, 89.5 x 129.8 cm, The National Gallery of Art, Washington, D.C.

Noticed by Degas, Mary Cassatt joined the impressionists in the 1870s. Her works, influenced by Japanese prints, show domestic and intimate scenes where feminine emotions often prevail.

Mary Stevenson Cassatt
(1844 Pittsburgh – 1926 Château de Beaufresne)

Mary was born in Pittsburgh. Her father was a banker of liberal educational ideas and the entire family appears to have been sympathetic to French culture. Mary was no more than five or six years old when she first saw Paris, and she was still in her teens when she decided to become a painter. She went to Italy, on to Antwerp, then to Rome, and finally returned to Paris where in 1874, she permanently settled.

In 1872, Cassatt sent her first work to the Salon, others followed in the succeeding years until 1875, when a portrait of her sister was rejected. She divined that the jury had not been satisfied with the background, so she re-painted it several times until, in the next Salon, the same portrait was accepted. At this moment Degas asked her to exhibit with him and his friends, the Impressionist Group, then rising into view, and she accepted with joy. She admired Manet, Courbet and Degas, and hated conventional art.

Cassatt's biographer stressed the intellectuality and sentiment apparent in her work, as well as the emotion and distinction with which she has painted her favourite models: babies and their mothers. He then speaks of her predominant interest in draughtsmanship and her gift for linear pattern, a gift greatly strengthened by her study of Japanese art and her emulation of its style in the colour prints she made. While her style may partake of the style of others, her draughtsmanship, her composition, her light, and her colour are, indeed, her own. There are qualities of tenderness in her work which could have been put there, perhaps, only by a woman. The qualities which make her work of lasting value are those put there by an outstanding painter.

658

660

659

658. Paul Cézanne, 1839-1906, Post-impressionism, French, *Self-portrait*, 1879-
1885, Oil on canvas, 45 x 37 cm, The Pushkin Museum of Fine Arts, Mosco

*In the Moscow Self-Portrait, advancing and receding tones are kept under str
rational control by the artist. Cézanne's way of working on form is reminisc
of the methods of an architect building a cupola or erecting a vault, o
Cézanne's material consists of a wide chromatic range of paints, from cold
warm. The nearer to the periphery, the thicker their layer, the more intens
their dark, cold hues; nearer to the centre, warmer yellowish tones gradua
changing to yellow, orange, and pink, begin to show through. These dabs
paint are not perceived here as colour reflections shifting over the surface of
object; they are transformed into certain spatial microplanes used by Cézan
to indicate the extension of form from the surface of the canvas into the dep
of the picture.*

659. Gustave Moreau, 1826-1898, Symbolism, French, *Galatea,* 1880,
Oil on panel, 85 x 67 cm, Musée d'Orsay, Paris

660. William Bouguereau, 1825-1905, Academism, French, *The Birth of Venu
1879, Oil on canvas, 303 x 216 cm, Musée d'Orsay, Paris

661. Pierre-Auguste Renoir, 1841-1919, Impressionism, French,
Luncheon of the Boating Party, c.1880, Oil on canvas, 129.5 x 172.7 cm,
The Phillips Collection, Washington, D. C.

662. Arnold Böcklin, 1827-1901, Symbolism, Swiss, *Island of the Dead,* 1880,
Oil on wood, 73.7 x 121.9 cm, The Metropolitan Museum of Art, New Yo

*Together with Hodler, Böcklin is the most important Swiss painter of
nineteenth century. This painting is the first of five versions on the same ther
His increasing success led him to paint several versions of a subject to respo
to subsequent commissions. The composition projects an effect of sole
grandeur and tranquil isolation, reinforced by the contrast between
monumental permanence of the island and the frailty and insignificance of
boat. The isolated boat approaches the in hospitable island, symbolising
immensity of nature's elements.*

661

662

663

664

663. Wasily Surikov, 1848-1916, Realism, Russian, *The Morning of the Execution of the Streltsy,* 1878-81, Oil on canvas, 218 x 379 cm, The State Tretyakov Gallery, Moscow

Interesting in this context are the comments on the Streltsy made by Surikov's biographer, which the artist read and approved without changing a word: "The picture turned out powerful, frightening, and above all, truly historical. Looking at it you feel how harrowing the situation is for all concerned. You feel an agonizing pity for these hundreds of people condemned to death, but you understand Peter too, as he sits there with clenched teeth, gripping the reins in his fist, and boldly looks into the faces of men he considers sworn enemies of his great cause. As in history itself, you can side with either party, depending on your sympathies and antipathies, but you know that in the final analysis nobody is right in history and nobody wrong, there is only the horror of collisions such as this, that are never resolved but with the shedding of a sea of blood." In three pictures he painted in the 1880s, The Morning of the Execution of the Streltsy, Menshikov at Beriozovo and The Boyarynia Morozove, Surikov depicts seventeenth- and early eighteenth-century history as a tragic chapter of strife in the life of the Russian people.

664. Ilya Repin, 1844-1930, Realism, Russian, *Portrait of Anton Rubinstein,* 1881, Oil on canvas, 80 x 62 cm, The State Tretyakov Gallery, Moscow

Inspired by Rembrandt's portraits, Repin painted many of his celebrated compatriots, including Tolstoy and Mendeleyev. Tolstoy said about the artist: "Repin depicts our national way of life much better than any other artist."

65. Ilya Repin, 1844-1930, Realism, Russian, *Religious Procession in Kursk Province*, 1880-83, Oil on canvas, 175 x 280 cm, The State Tretyakov Gallery, Moscow

The artist was intensively seeking an image of his Russia – a Russia which lived in the expectation of divine benevolence. The story told in the work is of a time of drought, and a crowd of people is moving across the parched earth. They are carrying a miracle-working icon to a nearby church or monastery, carrying it in such a way as to observe at least the outward form of ritual procession. It is not a homogeneous gathering – the viewer immediately detects a great variety of social types and characters. Depicted here is not just a stream of people but the flow of life itself – a life bereft of joy, full of profound contradictions, social hostility and inequality, but a life which never stops living for a moment. By placing rough peasant clothes on colourful holiday caftans next to a range of city attire, Repin precisely illustrates the differences in class and wealth between those participating in the procession. The behaviour of the people, their attitudes to what was happening around them, suggests equally vividly another "hierarchy" within the crowd, from the sanctimonious piety of the gentry to the impetuous absorption of the hunchback.

Ilya Repin
(1844 Chuguyev – 1930 Kuokkala)

Ilya Repin was the most gifted of the group known in Russia as "The Itinerants". When only twelve years old, he joined Ivan Bounakov's studio to learn the icon-painter's craft. Religious representations always remained of great importance for him. From 1864 to 1873 Repin studied at the Academy of the Arts in Saint Petersburg under Kramskoï.

Repin also studied in Paris for two years, where he was strongly influenced by outdoor painting without, becoming an Impressionist, a style that he judged too distant from reality. Taken with French pictorial culture, he worked to understand its role in the evolution of contemporary art. Most of Repin's powerful work deals with the social dilemmas of Russian life in the nineteenth century. He established his reputation in 1873 with the celebrated picture *Barge Haulers on the Volga*, symbol of the oppressed Russian people pulling their chains. This struggle against the autocracy inspired many works. He also painted Russia's official history in such works as *Ivan the Terrible Meditating at the Deathbed of his Son Ivan*. Seen as one of the masters of realist painting, he devoted himself to portraying the lives of his contemporaries: the most renowned Russian writers, artists, and intellectuals; peasants at work; the faithful in procession; and revolutionaries on the barricades. He understood the pains of the people perfectly, as well as the needs and the joys of ordinary lives. Kramskoï said on this subject: "Repin has a gift for showing the peasant as he is. I know many painters who show the *moujik*, and they do it well, but none can do so with as much talent as Repin."

Repin's works, which depart from the academic constraints of their predecessors, are both delicate and powerful. He achieved a superior mastery of skill, and found new accents to transcribe the many-coloured and brilliant vibrations he sensed in the ordinary world around him.

Pierre-Cécile Puvis de Chavannes
(1824 Lyon –1898 Paris)

Puvis de Chavannes came from an aristocratic family. His father was an engineer of bridges and roads in Lyon and, after receiving a classical and mathematical education, Puvis de Chavannes proceeded to the Polytechnic in Paris to adopt his father's profession. It was not until he was thirty-five that some vacant panels in his brother's new house drew his attention to mural decoration. He made an enlarged copy of one of his drawings and sent it to the Salon. Its acceptance encouraged him to go on in the same vein and that was the beginning of his public career as a mural painter.

Puvis's skill for colour is manifested particularly in the landscape parts. He selected for the sky a tone of blue that has more light in it than the greens of the earth, and varied the tones of the latter by almost imperceptible gradations of light and less light tones. In this management of values and knowledge of forms and construction, he is the equal of the best landscape painters. While his landscapes give an impression of space and seem filled with air that surrounds the figures, they also give the impression of being flat to the wall until by a process of severely logical experiments he was able to depict not form, but its essence and abstract suggestion. The result is that his decorations do not impress upon us the idea of paint; they seem rather to have grown upon the wall like a delicate efflorescence.

666. Pierre-Cécile Puvis de Chavannes, 1824-1898, Symbolism, French, *The Poor Fisherman*, 1881, Oil on canvas, 155.5 x 192.5 cm, Musée d'Orsay, Paris

667. Édouard Manet, 1832-1883, Impressionism, French, *A Bar at the Folies-Bergère*, 1882, Oil on canvas, 96 x 130 cm, Courtauld Institute of Art, London

Manet was in the inner circle of impressionists with his friends Monet and Renoir. While he did not set out to present symbolism, he observed and shared his impressions of what he saw. The artist loved to frequent this location, popular with other artists. He incorporated electric lights that were becoming popular in such public places. The overhead lights seemed to eliminate shadows, as a symbol of modernity and urban life. The geometric centre of the work is the barmaid's bodice, drawing attention to how her right and left sides are nearly identical and centred in the work, showing her resigned conformity to her work.

However, to her left there at first seems to be a mirrored reflection. However, the mirror is not reflecting the present moment as the women' posture and the alignment do not square properly with the "reflection". He reflective moment is frozen, as is the movement of the acrobatic entertainer o a trapeze in the upper left corner. The strong horizontal line of the balcon from the left does not align properly with the right side, again showing that the reflection breaks the barrier between present and another time, as well a between classes of people.

668. Henri Fantin-Latour, 1836-1904, Realism, French, *Flowers in an Earthenware Vase*, 1883, Oil on canvas, 22.5 x 29 cm, The State Hermitage Museum, St. Petersburg

667

668

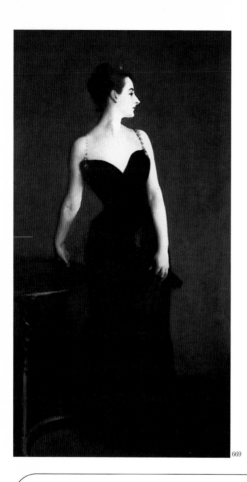

669

John Singer Sargent
(1856 Florence –1925 London)

Sargent was born in Florence, in 1856, the son of cultivated parents. When Sargent entered the school of Carolus-Duran he attained much more than the average pupils. His father was a retired Massachusetts gentleman, having practised medicine in Philadelphia. Sargent's home life was penetrated with refinement, and outside it were the beautiful influences of Florence, combining the charms of sky and hills with the wonders of art in the galleries and the opportunities of an intellectual and artistic society. Accordingly, when Sargent arrived in Paris, he was not only a skilful draughtsman and painter as a result of his study of the Italian masters, but he also had a refined and cultivated taste, which perhaps had an even greater influence upon his career. Later in Spain, it was chiefly upon the lessons learned from Velázquez that he found his own brilliant method.

Sargent belongs to America, but is claimed by others as a citizen of the world, or a cosmopolitan. Sargent, with the exception of a few months at distant intervals, spent his life abroad. The artistic influences which affected him were those of Europe. Yet his Americanism may be detected in his extraordinary facility to absorb impressions, in the individuality he evolved, and in the subtlety and reserve of his methods – qualities that are characteristic of the best American art.

669. John Singer Sargent, 1856-1925,
Post-impressionism, American, *Madame X
(Madame Pierre Gautreau)*, 1883-1884,
Oil on canvas, 208.6 x 109.9 cm,
The Metropolitan Museum of Art, New York

*The American painter John Singer Sargent visited th[e]
States on short trips during the thirty years he lived
Paris, as he retained his American parents' loyalty
their native land. The stereotypically American love
glamour more than class is seen here as the portr[ait]
captures a pose rather than a candid moment. He se[es]
appearance more than character. Madame Gautre[au]
is presented in what was a risqué gown, shocking[ly]
low-cut for the times. For this and his other unorthod[ox]
portraits, he was criticised for being improper. Historia[n]
German Bazin referred to him as "a painter
superficial fashionable portraits in a facile and dazzli[ng]
technique that went far to disguise their empty ideality[.]*

670. Wilhelm Leibl, 1844-1900, Realism, German,
Three Women In Church, 1882,
Oil on panel, 113 x 77 cm, Kunsthalle, Hamburg

GEORGES SEURAT
(1859 PARIS – 1891 PARIS)

Georges Seurat studied at the Ecole des Beaux-Arts between 1878 and 1879. At that time, scientist-writers such as Chevreul, Rood or Sutter wrote treatises about colour and optical perception. Those theories largely influenced Neo-impressionism of which Seurat is one of the pioneers with Paul Signac, Henri-Edmond Cross, Maximilien Luce, and Pissarro. Neo-impressionist painters were interested in colours and their interplay, and would make extensive use of complementary colours in their paintings. But, whereas impressionism was more instinctive, Seurat is well-known for his technique of pointillism and divisionism – the controlled, precise juxtaposition of different coloured painted dots on the canvas. His thoughts and techniques were most respected by Cubists and Neo-constructivists who would follow him.

671. Arnold Böcklin, 1827-1901, Symbolism, Swiss, *Playing in the Waves*, 1883, Oil on canvas, 180 x 238 cm, Neue Pinakothek, Munich

672. Georges Seurat, 1859-1891, Neo-impressionism, French, *Sunday Afternoon on 'La Grande Jatte'*, 1884-86, Oil on canvas, 207.5 x 308 cm, The Art Institute of Chicago, Chicago

After two years of work on this painting and after thrity-eight preliminary oils and twenty-three sketches, the thrity-year old artist amazed the art world by showing his masterpiece at the last Impressionist Exhibition (1886). Different classes of people (see the trio in the lower left corner) mix to enjoy the island on the River Seine. Between the capuchin monkey, a favourite pet of the upper class at the time, and the mutt of the reclined worker, a pampered toy dog leaps into play. In the work a peaceful moment in time is frozen for the leaping dog, the skipping girl, the rowing crews, smoke from a pipe and a cigar, smoke blowing in opposite directions from two different boats, and for six butterflies in flight. Yet, the viewer can notice by the shadows that the sun progresses from midday at the top of the lawn, to evening in the foreground. Moreover, shorter subjects cast long shadows and vice versa. The tall trombonist casts nearly no shadow. There seems to be no object from which the shadow is cast to the left of the lady with the red umbrella. The entire work is done using pointillism or divisionism, whereby a desired colour is broken down into its colour elements. Then tiny dots of those elemental colours were applied to the surface so that when seen at the right distance the dots are virtually "mixed by the eye". Perfecting this technique and this work are Seurat's major contributions to neo-Impressionism.

673. Georges Seurat, 1859-1891, Neo-impressionism, French, *Bathers at Asnières*, 1884, Oil on canvas, 201 x 300 cm, National Gallery, London

Pierre-Auguste Renoir
(1841 Limoges – 1919 Cagnes-sur-Mer)

Pierre-Auguste Renoir was born in Limoges on 25 February 1841. In 1854, the boy's parents took him from school and found a place for him in the Lévy brothers' workshop, where he was to learn to paint porcelain. Renoir's younger brother Edmond had this to say about the move: "From what he drew in charcoal on the walls, they concluded that he had the ability for an artist's profession. That was how our parents came to put him to learn the trade of porcelain painter." One of the Lévys' workers, Emile Laporte, painted in oils in his spare time. He suggested Renoir makes use of his canvases and paints. This offer resulted in the appearance of the first painting by the future impressionist. In 1862 Renoir passed the examinations and entered the Ecole des Beaux-Arts and, simultaneously, one of the independent studios, where instruction was given by Charles Gleyre, a professor at the Ecole des Beaux-Arts. The second, perhaps even the first, great event of this period in Renoir's life was his meeting, in Gleyre's studio, with those who were to become his best friends for the rest of his days and who shared his ideas about art. Much later, when he was already a mature artist, Renoir had the opportunity to see works by Rembrandt in Holland, Velázquez, Goya and El Greco in Spain, and Raphael in Italy. However, Renoir lived and breathed ideas of a new kind of art. He always found his inspirations in the Louvre. "For me, in the Gleyre era, the Louvre was Delacroix," he confessed to Jean.

For Renoir, the First Impressionist Exhibition was the moment his vision of art and the artist was affirmed. This period in Renoir's life was marked by one further significant event. In 1873 he moved to Montmartre, to the house at 35 Rue Saint-Georges, where he lived until 1884. Renoir remained loyal to Montmartre for the rest of his life. Here he found his "plein-air" subjects, his models and even his family. It was in the 1870s that Renoir acquired the friends who would stay with him for the remainder of his days. One of them was the art-dealer Paul Durand-Ruel, who began to buy his paintings in 1872. In summer, Renoir continued to paint a great deal outdoors together with Monet. He would travel out to Argenteuil, where Monet rented a house for his family. Edouard Manet sometimes worked with them too.

In 1877, at the Third Impressionist Exhibition, Renoir presented a panorama of over twenty paintings. They included landscapes created in Paris, on the Seine, outside the city and in Claude Monet's garden; studies of women's heads and bouquets of flowers; portraits of Sisley, the actress Jeanne Samary, the writer Alphonse Daudet and the politician Spuller; and also *The Swing* and *The Ball at the Moulin de la Galette*.

Finally, in the 1880s Renoir hit a "winning streak". He was commissioned by rich financiers, the owner of the Grands Magasins du Louvre and Senator Goujon. His paintings were exhibited in London and Brussels, as well as at the Seventh International Exhibition held at Georges Petit's in Paris in 1886. In a letter to Durand-Ruel, then in New York, Renoir wrote: "The Petit exhibition has opened and is not doing badly, so they say. After all, it's so hard to judge about yourself. I think I have managed to take a step forward towards public respect. A small step, but even that is something."

674. Pierre-Auguste Renoir, 1841-1919, Impressionism, French, *Dance in the City,* 1883, Oil on canvas, 180 x 90 cm, Musée d'Orsay, Paris

*In 1883 Renoir's friend and dealer Paul Durand-Ruel commissioned three decorative panels on the theme of dance from him. He displayed two of them that same year at Renoir's first one-man exhibition which was held in his gallery (*Dance in the City *was entitled* Dance in Paris*), and the third,* Dance *in Winter, in Brussels in 1886. Renoir's models, as always, were people close to him. The man's face cannot be seen, but it was probably the artist's friend Paul Lhote who posed for this figure. His partner is the main, and in point of fact the only, concrete figure in the work: a proud head on a long neck, powerful shoulders, and an enchanting profile with a short nose. Her name was Marie-Clementine. She had been a dressmaker in Montmartre before becoming an acrobat. Then, after injuring her leg, she began posing for artists. Later, she made a name for herself as the painter Susanne Valadon and became the mother of the Montmartre landscape painter Maurice Utrillo.*

Edward Coley Burne-Jones
(1833 Birmingham – 1898 London)

Burne-Jones' oeuvre can be understood as an attempt to create in paint a world of perfect beauty, as far removed from the Birmingham of his youth as possible. At that time Birmingham was a byword for the dire effects of unregulated capitalism – a booming, industrial conglomeration of unimaginable ugliness and squalor.

The two great French symbolist painters, Gustave Moreau and Pierre Puvis de Chavannes, immediately recognised Burne-Jones as an artistic fellow traveller. But, it is very unlikely that Burne-Jones would have accepted or even, perhaps, have understood the label of 'symbolist'. Yet he seems to have been one of the most representative figures of the symbolist movement and of that pervasive mood termed "fin-de-siecle".

Burne-Jones is usually labelled as a Pre-Raphaelite. In fact he was never a member of the Brotherhood formed in 1848. Burne-Jones' brand of Pre-Raphaelitism derives not from Hunt and Millais but from Dante Gabriel Rossetti.

Burne-Jones' work in the late 1850s is, moreover, closely based on Rossetti's style. His feminine ideal is also taken from that of Rossetti, with abundant hair, prominent chins, columnar necks and androgynous bodies hidden by copious medieval gowns. The prominent chins remain a striking feature of both artists' depictions of women. From the 1860s their ideal types diverge. As Rossetti's women balloon into ever more fleshy opulence, Burne-Jones' women become more virginal and ethereal to the point where, in some of the last pictures, the women look anorexic.

In the early 1870s Burne-Jones painted several mythical or legendary pictures in which he seems to have been trying to exorcise the traumas of his celebrated affair with Mary Zambaco.

No living British painter between Constable and Bacon enjoyed the kind of international acclaim that Burne-Jones was accorded in the early 1890s. This great reputation began to slip in the latter half of the decade, however, and it plummeted after 1900 with the triumph of Modernism.

With hindsight we can see this flatness and the turning away from narrative as characteristic of early Modernism and the first hesitant steps towards Abstraction. It is not as odd at it seems that Kandinsky cited Rossetti and Burne-Jones as forerunners of Abstraction in his book, "Concerning the Spiritual in Art".

675

Edward Coley Burne-Jones, 1833-1898, Pre-Raphaelite, British,
King Cophetua and the Beggar-Maid, 1884, Oil on canvas, 293 x 136 cm,
Tate Gallery, London

When Burne-Jones' mural-sized canvas of King Cophetua and the Beggar-maid was exhibited in the shadow of the newly constructed Eiffel Tower at the Paris Exposition Universelle in 1889, it caused a sensation scarcely less extraordinary than the tower itself. Burne-Jones was awarded not only a gold medal at the exhibition but also the cross of the Légion d'Honneur. Burne-Jones did not want King Cophetua's armour to look like that of any particular period, so he studied armour until he felt that he understood the principles of armour-making well enough to design his own. The result is quite extraordinary — a strange, organic, proto-art nouveau, body hugging armour that looks as though it was made of plastic or leather rather than of metal. Burne-Jones also agonised over the elegant designer rags worn by the beggar-maid, wanting them to look "sufficiently beggarly" but at the same time perfectly beautiful. In a letter of 1883, he wrote that he hoped that this had been achieved so that "she shall look as if she deserved to have it made of cloth of gold and set with pearls. I hope the king kept the old one and looked at it now and then". The beggar-maid stares forward fixedly. Her stance and her absence of facial expression convey a vague sense of unease and dread. This princess of hearts, a simple girl destined to be the wife of a king, could be bulimic. Her bruised eyes and her unhealthy pallor are the fin-de-siècle equivalent of "heroin chic".

676

676. Ivan Shishkin, 1831-1898, Realism, Russian, *Woods*, 1887,
Oil on canvas, 125 x 193 cm, Museum of Russian Art, Kiev

677. Hans von Marées, 1837-1887, Symbolism, German, *The Hesperides,*
central panel of *The Hesperides triptych*, 1885-1887, Oil and tempera on
wooden panel, 341 x 482 cm, Neue Pinakothek, Munich

678. Ilya Repin, 1844-1930, Realism, Russian, *Ivan the Terrible and His Son Ivan
on 15 November 1581*, 1885, Oil on canvas, 199.5 x 224 cm,
The State Tretyakov Gallery, Moscow

The artist started work on this painting only when the execution of the
members of the People's Will Revolutionary Group – those responsible for the
assassination of Tsar Alexander II in 1881 – was still fresh in his mind. "A trail
of blood ran through that year," Repin later recalled. "Terrible scenes were in
everybody's mind… It was natural to look for a way out of this painful and
tragic situation in history. I began on an impulse and the picture progressed in
fits and starts. My emotions were overburdened with the horrors of
contemporary life."

677

Odilon Redon
(1840 Bordeaux – 1916 Paris)

Redon started drawing as a young child, and at the age of ten he was awarded a drawing prize at school. At age fifteen, he began to study drawing but, upon the insistence of his father, switched to architecture. Any career in architecture ended when he failed to pass the entrance exams at the Ecole des Beaux-Arts in Paris but eventually he studied there under Jean-Léon Gerôme. Back home in his native Bordeaux, he took up sculpture, and Rodolphe Bresdin instructed him in etching and lithography. However, joining the army in 1870 to serve in the Franco-Prussian War interrupted his artistic career. At the end of the war he moved to Paris, working almost exclusively in charcoal and lithography. It would not be until 1878 before his work gained any recognition with *Guardian Spirit of the Waters*, and he published his first album of lithographs titled *Dans le Rêve* in 1879. In the 1890s, he began to use pastel and oils, which dominated his works for the rest of his life. In 1899, he exhibited with the Nabis at Durand-Ruel's. In 1903 he was awarded the Legion of Honour. His popularity increased when a catalogue of etchings and lithographs was published by André Mellerio in 1913 and that same year, he was given the largest single representation at the New York Armory Show.

680

79. James Ensor, 1860-1949, Symbolism/Expressionism, Belgian,
Entry of Christ into Brussels, 1887-1888, Oil on canvas, 256 x 378 cm,
Getty Museum, Los Angeles

Jesus (slightly up and left from the midpoint of the work) is only one of dozens of interesting figures in this contemporary setting. It seems only a few faces are of masks, while most are of the faces of the 'evil-self' within each person. Commentators usually refer to the scene as a contemporary 'Second Coming' or 'Last Judgment', but it might in fact be more of a Palm Sunday event. These three possibilities are symbolically and theologically related, but in any event, the artist is expressing his identification (before his own artistic success) with Jesus who also was persecuted by his critics. For the Palm Sunday interpretation, consider the carnival, or Mardi Gras, reception such as by the marching band in the centre of the work and the "Viva Jesus" sign on the right.

80. Odilon Redon, 1840-1916, Symbolism, French, *Lady with Wildflowers*,
1890-1900, Pastel and charcoal on paper, 52 x 37.5 cm,
The State Hermitage Museum, St. Petersburg

81. Pierre-Cécile Puvis de Chavannes, 1824-1898, Symbolism, French,
Woman on the Beach, 1887, Oil on paper pasted on canvas, 75.3 x 74.5 cm,
The State Hermitage Museum, St. Petersburg

681

Berthe Morisot
(1841 Bourges –1895 Paris)

Amongst the women painters in modern history, Berthe Morisot achieved a distinction equalled only by that of Mary Cassatt. Her gifts did not at once receive public recognition, but in recent years they have won more and more appreciation. She was an interesting person. Degas once said of her that she painted pictures as she made bonnets – a suggestion of the femininely instinctive and impulsive action of her talent. One source of her strength, however, was the thoroughness of her training. Her father, an official at Bourges, saw that his daughter's tastes were genuine, and made it easy for her to develop her faculties. She and her sister Edma were sent for instruction to Paris. Edma Morisot abandoned painting when she married, but Berthe continued to work with the brush, exhibiting at the Salon. It was while she was making copies from old masters in the Louvre that she first came to know Edouard Manet. Later, Berthe became intimate with the great impressionist, modifying her style in the light of his example and developing the broad, vivid qualities for which her works are loved today. In 1874 she married Eugene Manet. Degas, Renoir, Pissarro, and Monet frequented her house. She continued to paint, signing her pictures with the name by which she is still remembered in artistic annals. Her rank as an artist was obscured by her position as a woman of the world.

She was not, it is true, a creative artist. It may even be said that she would not have made the progress that is shown in her best works, would not have given them their special character, if Manet had not been there to help her to form her style. Yet upon the groundwork that she owed to her contact with Manet she superimposed qualities of her own. There is a delicate fragrance about her art, a certain feminine subtlety and charm, through which she proved herself an individualised painter.

Mikhaïl Vrubel
(1856 Omsk –1910 St Petersburg)

One of the first symbolist painters in Russia, and one of the most intriguing, was Mikhaïl Vrubel. Many of his paintings have a surreal, dreamlike quality. Some of the most remarkable, such as The Bogatyr (1898), Pan (1899) and The Swan Princess (1900), are of mythological figures. And many of them feature either the elaborate patterns characteristic of Art Nouveau or mosaic-like patches of colour akin to those found in the paintings of Gustav Klimt.

In 1890 Vrubel was commissioned to illustrate a special edition of the works of Mikhaïl Lermontov, to mark the fiftieth anniversary of the poet's death.

In terms of style, Vrubel's portraits, like Nesterov's, vary enormously in the 1890s. They range from the sober and conventional, for example, the portrait of *Konstantin Artsybushev* that he painted in 1897, to highly decorative works such as Girl Against a Persian Carpet, which is both a sensitive portrait of a child and an inspired exploration of pattern and colour.

Tormented by mental illness, Vrubel spent most of the last nine years of his life in hospital, where he continued to work until, in 1906, he lost his sight.

685

32. Berthe Morisot, 1841-1895, Impressionism, French, *Paule Gobillard Painting,* 1886, Oil on canvas, 85 x 94 cm, Musée Marmottan, Paris

33. Valentin Serov, 1865-1911, Impressionism, Russian, *Girl with Peaches (Portrait of Vera Mamontowa),* 1887, Oil on canvas, 91 x 85 cm, The State Tretyakov Gallery, Moscow

34. Paul Gauguin, 1848-1903, Post-impressionism, French, *The Vision after the Sermon (Jacob Wrestling with the Angel),* 1888, Oil on canvas, 73 x 92 cm, National Gallery of Scotland, Edinburgh

35. Mikhaïl Vrubel, 1856-1910, Symbolism, Russian, *Young Girl against a Persian Carpet,* 1886, Oil on canvas, 104 x 68 cm, Museum of Russian Art, Kiev

686

336. **Wasily Surikov,** 1848-1916, Realism, Russian,
Boyarina Morozova, 1887, Oil on canvas, 304 x 587.5 cm,
The State Tretyakov Gallery, Moscow

371

687

689

688

687. Paul Cézanne, 1839-1906, Post-impressionism, French,
Pierrot and Harlequin (Mardi Gras), 1888, Oil on canvas, 102 x 81 cm,
The Pushkin Museum of Fine Arts, Moscow

This picture is painted in dense strokes, and outlines are clearly visible. T
melancholic expression on the faces of the models, the nature of t
movement, and the specific arrangement of the figures, give the painting
mood of disquiet, almost tragedy, quite out of keeping with the theme o
carnival. Harsh contrasts are also used in the young men's costumes – the loo
coat worn by Pierrot and the closely fitting ensemble of Harlequin – wh
differ sharply both in their forms and colour.

688. Paul Sérusier, 1864-1927, Nabism, French, *Talisman,* 1888,
Oil on wood, 27 x 21 cm, Musée d'Orsay, Paris

Sérusier met Gauguin in Pont-Aven and painted a simplified landscape und
his guidance. It became the Talisman. This painting became the foundatio
element of the Nabis group (meaning 'prophet' in Hebrew).

689. Georges Seurat, 1859-1891, Neo-Impressionism, French,
Le Chahut (can-can), c. 1889, Oil on canvas, 172 x 140 cm,
Rijksmuseum Kröller-Müller, Otterlo

690. **Vincent van Gogh,** 1853-1890, Post-impressionism, Dutch, *Sunflowers,* 1888, Oil on canvas, 92.1 x 73 cm, National Gallery, London

Four works depicting sunflowers were painted by van Gogh but he considered only two of them good enough to sign. This is his first try of "light-colour on light-colour". Through the variations of brush strokes and the thickness of the paint, van Gogh brings the limited nuances of colours to life. The hatching of the background contrasts with the flat surface of the vase. The colours are crushed on the flowers, for a vibrant aspect.

691. **Vincent van Gogh,** 1853-1890, Post-impressionism, Dutch, *Café Terrasse by Night,* 1888, Oil on canvas, 81 x 65 cm, Rijksmuseum Kröller-Müller, Otterlo

In a letter from van Gogh to his brother Théo, on 8 September, 1888: "Finally, for the pleasure of the landlord, of the postman I have depicted, of the visitors, night prowlers and for my own pleasure, I have stayed up three nights in a row, sleeping during the day. It often seemed to me that the night is livelier and richer in colour than the day."

VINCENT VAN GOGH
(1853 ZUNDERT –1890 AUVERS-SUR-OISE)

Vincent van Gogh's life and work are so intertwined that it is hardly possible to observe one without thinking of the other. Van Gogh has indeed become the incarnation of the suffering, misunderstood martyr of modern art, the emblem of the artist as an outsider. An article, published in 1890, gave details about van Gogh's illness. The author of the article saw the painter as "a terrible and demented genius, often sublime, sometimes grotesque, always at the brink of the pathological."

Very little is known about Vincent's childhood. At the age of eleven he had to leave "the human nest", as he called it himself, for various boarding schools. The first portrait shows us van Gogh as an earnest nineteen year old. At that time he had already been at work for three years in The Hague and, later, in London in the gallery Goupil & Co. In 1874 his love for Ursula Loyer ended in disaster and a year later he was transferred to Paris, against his will. After a particularly heated argument during Christmas holidays in 1881, his father, a pastor, ordered Vincent to leave. With this final break, he abandoned his family name and signed his canvases simply "Vincent". He left for Paris and never returned to Holland. In Paris he came to know Paul Gauguin, whose paintings he greatly admired.

The self-portrait was the main subject of Vincent's work from 1886c88. In February 1888 Vincent left Paris for Arles and tried to persuade Gauguin to join him. The months of waiting for Gauguin were the most productive time in van Gogh's life. He wanted to show his friend as many pictures as possible and decorate the Yellow House. But Gauguin did not share his views on art and finally returned to Paris.

On 7 January, 1889, fourteen days after his famous self-mutilation, Vincent left the hospital where he was convalescing. Although he hoped to recover from and to forget his madness, but he actually came back twice more in the same year. During his last stay in hospital, Vincent painted landscapes in which he recreated the world of his childhood.

It is said that Vincent van Gogh shot himself in the side in a field but decided to return to the inn and went to bed. The landlord informed Dr Gachet and his brother Theo, who described the last moments of his life which ended on 29 July, 1890: "I wanted to die. While I was sitting next to him promising that we would try to heal him. [...], he answered, '*La tristesse durera toujours* (The sadness will last forever).'"

692

694

692. Vincent van Gogh, 1853-1890, Post-impressionism, Dutch, *Starry Night,* 1888, Oil on canvas, 72.5 x 92 cm, Musée d'Orsay, Paris

Van Gogh painted another Starry Night the same year but it was lost after bei in Bremen's Kunsthalle. Van Gogh painted Starry Night while in an asylum Saint-Remy in 1889.

693. Paul Gauguin, 1848-1903, Post-impressionism, French, *The White Horse,* 1889, Oil on canvas, 140 x 91.5 cm, Musée d'Orsay, Paris

694. Ivan Shishkin, 1831-1898, Realism, Russian, *Morning in a Wood,* 1889, Oil on canvas, 139 x 213 cm, Tretjakow Galerie, Moscow

Morning in a Pine Forest, *unforgettable for its bears, and Counte Mordvinova's Forest at Peterhof are among the hundreds of paintings Shishkin that capture the magic of the forest and the character of the tree Indeed, Morning in a Wood describes the awakening of the forest, the s coming up, the fog slowly lifting; the foreground is in focus whereas t trees that are further away have fuzzy contours. The sliding light of the s which chases the mist away little by little bestows great poetry on th magnificent piece of work. The lyricism of this wakening forest is like t signature of Shishkin's immense maturity with respect to nature.*

693

PAUL GAUGUIN
(1848 PARIS – 1903 ATUONA, MARQUESAS ISLANDS)

Paul Gauguin was first a sailor, then a successful stockbroker in Paris. In 1874 he began to paint at weekends as a Sunday painter. Nine years later, after a stock-market crash, he felt confident of his ability to earn a living for his family by painting and he resigned his position and took up the painter's brush full time. Following the lead of Cézanne, Gauguin painted still-lifes from the very beginning of his artistic career. He even owned a still-life by Cézanne, which is shown in Gauguin's painting *Portrait of Marie Lagadu.* The year 1891 was crucial for Gauguin. In that year he left France for Tahiti, where he stayed till 1893. This stay in Tahiti determined his future life and career, for in 1895, after a sojourn in France, he returned there for good.

In Tahiti, Gauguin discovered primitive art, with its flat forms and violent colours, belonging to an untamed nature. With absolute sincerity, he transferred them onto his canvas. His paintings from then on reflected this style: a radical simplification of drawing; brilliant, pure, bright colours; an ornamental type composition; and a deliberate flatness of planes. Gauguin termed this style "synthetic symbolism".

697

695. Vincent van Gogh, 1853-1890, Post-impressionism, Dutch,
Self-Portrait with Bandaged Ear, 1889, Oil on canvas, 60 x 49 cm,
Courtauld Institute of Art, London

Notice the right ear has bandages in this portrait, whereas van Gogh injured his left ear, therefore the portrait must have been made in front of a mirror. In a letter preceding this Self-Portrait (dating from January 1889, as he came out of hospital), van Gogh wrote to Théo: "I have bought a good mirror on purpose, to work on my own portraits as I am lacking a model, because, if I manage to depict the colours of my own head, challenging enough in itself, I would be able to portrait other men and women."

696. Giovanni Fattori, 1825-1908, Realist, Macchiaioli, Italian,
Portrait of the Stepdaughter, 1889, Oil on canvas, 70 x 55 cm,
Galleria d'Arte Moderna, Florence

697. Paul Gauguin, 1848-1903, Post-impressionism, French, *The Yellow Christ,*
1889, Oil on canvas, 92 x 73 cm, Albright-Knox Art Gallery, Buffalo

Colours are the means of Gauguin's expression. He used them pure, in flat layers on the canvas and nuanced in function of perspective. In this sense he is considered a precursor of the Fauves.
The Yellow Christ's background shows a landscape from Brittany. Gauguin settled in Brittany, in Pont-Aven, between 1886 and 1890. In this virgin land, empty of any modern element, the artist discovered the churches and their primitive statues. In The Yellow Christ he took his inspiration from a wooden Christ, found in a chapel, and he also refers to medieval and Byzantine iconography. This work also betrays a Japanese aspect. At the end of the nineteenth century, Japanese artists began to exhibit in Paris. The eccentric setting and the figures, shown from the back, cut the importance given to the costumes (the women surrounding Christ wear traditional costumes from Brittany). The technique of large, flat brush strokes, and the flattened perspective are different aspects that echo Japanese artworks that, Utamaro Hokusaï would have brought to France.

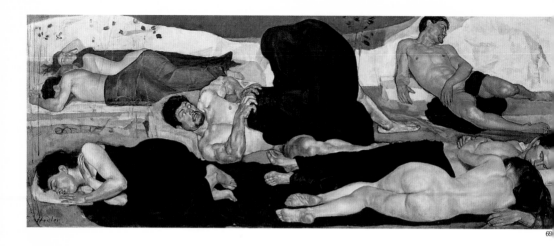

698

699

698. Ferdinand Hodler, 1853-1918, Art Nouveau,
Swiss, *Night*, 1889-1890, Oil on canvas,
116 x 229 cm, Kunstmuseum, Berne

699. Hans Thoma, 1839-1924, Baroque, German,
Landscape, 1890, Oil on canvas, 113 x 88.8 cm
Neue Pinakothek, Munich

700

701

700. John Singer Sargent, 1856-1925, Post-impressionism, American, *Paul Helleu Sketching with his Wife,* 1889, Oil on canvas, 66 x 81.5 cm, The Brooklyn Museum of Art, New York

701. Giovanni Fattori, 1825-1908, Realist, Italian, *On the Beach,* 1890, Oil on canvas, 69 x 100 cm, Museo Civico Giovanni Fattori, Livorno

702. **Henri de Toulouse-Lautrec,** 1864-1901, Post-impressionism,
French, *At The Moulin Rouge: The Dance,* 1890,
Oil on canvas, 115 x 150 cm, Museum of Art, Philadelphia

703. **Vincent van Gogh,** 1853-1890, Post-impressionism, Dutch,
Church at Auvers, 1890, Oil on canvas, 94 x 74.5 cm,
Musée d'Orsay, Paris

Henri de Toulouse-Lautrec
(1864 Albi – 1901 Château de Malromé)

Lautrec studied with two of the most admired academic painters of the day, Léon Bonnat and Fernand Cormon. Lautrec's time in the studios of Bonnat and Cormon had the advantage of introducing him to the nude as a subject. At that time life-drawing of the nude was the basis of all academic art training in nineteenth-century Paris.

While still a student, Lautrec began to explore Parisian nightlife, which was to provide him with his greatest inspiration, and eventually undermined his health.

Lautrec was an artist able to stamp his vision of the age in which he lived upon the imagination of future generations. Just as we see the English court of Charles I through the eyes of van Dyck and the Paris of Louis-Philippe through the eyes of Daumier, so we see the Paris of the 1890s and its most colourful personalities, through the eyes of Lautrec. The first great personality of Parisian nightlife whom Lautrec encountered – and a man who was to play an important role in helping Lautrec develop his artistic vision – was the cabaret singer Aristide Bruant. Bruant stood out as an heroic figure in what was the golden age of Parisian cabaret.

Among the many other performers inspiring Lautrec in the 1890s were the dancers La Goulue and Valentin-le-Desossé (who both appear in the famous *Moulin Rouge* poster), and Jane Avril and Loïe Fuller, the singers Yvette Guilbert, May Belfort and Marcelle Lender, and the actress Réjane.

Lautrec was, along with Degas, one of the great poets of the brothel. Degas explored the theme in the late 1870s in a series of monotype prints that are among his most remarkable and personal works. He depicts the somewhat ungainly posturing of the prostitutes and their clients with human warmth and a satirical humour that brings these prints closer to the art of Lautrec than anything else by Degas.

However, the truthfulness with which Lautrec portrayed those aspects of life that most of his more respectable contemporaries preferred to sweep under the carpet naturally caused offence. The German critic Gensel probably spoke for many when he wrote: "There can of course be no talk of admiration for someone who is the master of the representation of all that is base and perverse. The only explanation as to how such filth – there can be no milder term for it – as *Elles* can be publicly exhibited without an outcry of indignations being heard is that one half of the general public does not understand the meaning of this cycle at all, and the other is ashamed of admitting that it does understand it."

70

Paul Cézanne
(1839 – 1906 Aix–en–Provence)

Since his death 200 years ago, Cézanne has become the most famous painter of the nineteenth century. He was born in Aix-en-Provence in 1839 and the happiest period of his life was his early youth in Provence, in company with Emile Zolá, another Italian. Following Zolá's example, Cézanne went to Paris in his twenty-first year.

During the Franco-Prussian war he deserted the military, dividing his time between open-air painting and the studio. He said to Vollard, an art dealer, "I'm only a painter. Parisian wit gives me a pain. Painting nudes on the banks of the Arc [a river near Aix] is all I could ask for." Encouraged by Renoir, one of the first to appreciate him, he exhibited with the impressionists in 1874 and in 1877. He was received with derision, which deeply hurt him.

Cézanne's ambition, in his own words, was "to make out of Impressionism something as solid and durable as the paintings of the museums." His aim was to achieve the monumental in a modern language of glowing, vibrating tones. Cézanne wanted to retain the natural colour of an object and to harmonise it with the various influences of light and shade trying to destroy it; to work out a scale of tones expressing the mass and character of the form.

Cézanne loved to paint fruit because it afforded him obedient models and he was a slow worker. He did not intend to simply copy an apple. He kept the dominant colour and the character of the fruit, but heightened the emotional appeal of the form by a scheme of rich and concordant tones. In his paintings of still-life he is a master. His fruit and vegetable compositions are truly dramatic; they have the weight, the nobility, the style of immortal forms. No other painter ever brought to a red apple a conviction so heated, sympathy so genuinely spiritual, or an observation so protracted. No other painter of equal ability ever reserved for still-life his strongest impulses. Cézanne restored to painting the pre-eminence of knowledge, the most essential quality to all creative effort.

The death of his father in 1886 made him a rich man, but he made no change in his abstemious mode of living. Soon afterwards, Cézanne retired permanently to his estate in Provence. He was probably the loneliest of painters of his day. At times a curious melancholy attacked him, a black hopelessness. He grew more savage and exacting, destroying canvases, throwing them out of his studio into the trees, abandoning them in the fields, and giving them to his son to cut into puzzles, or to the people of Aix.

At the beginning of the century, when Vollard arrived in Provence with intentions of buying on speculation all the Cézannes he could get hold of, the peasantry, hearing that a fool from Paris was actually handing out money for old linen, produced from barns a considerable number of still-lifes and landscapes. The old master of Aix was overcome with joy, but recognition came too late. In 1906 he died from a fever contracted while painting in a downpour of rain.

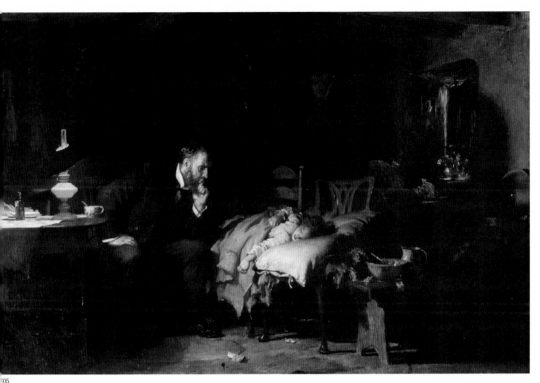

'05

706

'04. **Paul Cézanne,** 1839-1906, Post-impressionism, French, *Bathers,*
1890-1892, Oil on canvas, 60 x 82 cm, Musée d'Orsay, Paris

'05. **Luke Fildes,** 1843-1927, Realism, British, *The Doctor,* 1891,
Oil on canvas, 166.4 x 242 cm, Tate Gallery, London

*This painting was the star attraction when Sir Henry Tate, the British sugar
tycoon (inventor of the sugar cube) and art collector, opened the Tate gallery.*

'06. **Georges Seurat,** 1859-1891, Neo-impressionism, French, *The Circus,* 1891,
Oil on canvas, 185.5 x 152.5 cm, Musée d'Orsay, Paris

*Even though this work remains unfinished, it stands as·one of the greatest
examples of the divisionist touch of the artist. Seurat also depicted the frame of
the painting in the same technique.*

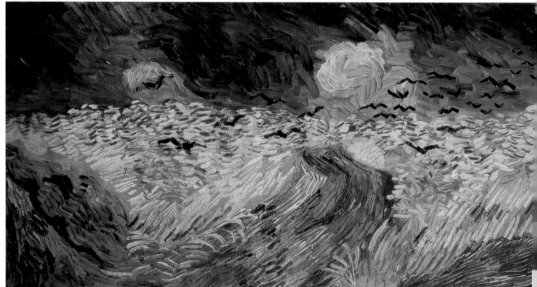

710

07. Paul Gauguin, 1848-1903, Post-impressionism, French, *Aha Oe Feii? What! Are You Jealous?*, 1892, Oil on canvas, 66 x 89 cm, The Pushkin Museum of Fine Arts, Moskow

This picture, painted during Gauguin's first Tahitian period, is one of the earliest examples of his synthetic style as applied to the treatment of Tahitian landscape and figures. The women are depicted on a shore, but the sand and the water are rendered schematically, being reduced to a single screen-like surface enlivened by areas of saturated colour.

Gauguin witnessed this scene in Tahiti and later described it in Noa Noa: "On the shore, two sisters are lying after bathing, in the graceful poses of resting animals; they speak of yesterday's love and tomorrow's conquests. The recollection causes them to quarrel: What! Are you jealous?"

08. Vincent van Gogh, 1853-1890, Post-impressionism, Dutch, *Wheatfield with Crows*, 1890, Oil on canvas, 50.5 x 105 cm, van Gogh Museum, Amsterdam

09. Edvard Munch, 1863-1944, Symbolism/Expressionism, Norwegian, *Spring Evening on Karl Johan Street*, 1892, Oil on canvas, 84.5 x 121 cm, Private collection, Bergen

10. Henri de Toulouse-Lautrec, 1864-1901, Post-impressionism, French, *Aristide Bruant in his Cabaret*, 1892, Colour Lithograph, 150 x 100 cm, Private collection

711

712

711. **James Ensor,** 1860-1949, Symbolism/Expressionism,
Belgian, *Skeletons Fighting over a Hanged Man,* 1891,
Oil on canvas, 59 x 74 cm,
Koninklijk Museum voor Schone Kunsten, Antwerp

712. **Paul Gauguin,** 1848-1903, Post-impressionism, French,
Tahitian Women (On the Beach), 1891,
Oil on canvas, 69 x 91.5 cm, Musée d'Orsay, Paris

713. **Frederic Remington,** 1861-1909, Realism, American,
The Rock of the Signature, 1891,
Oil on canvas, Private collection

714. **Giovanni Segantini,** 1858-1899, Symbolism, Italian,
The Punishment of Lust, also known as *The Punishment*
Luxury, 1891, Oil on canvas, 235 x 129.2 cm,
Walker Art Gallery, Liverpool

3

4

716

Isaak Levitan
(1860 Kibartai – 1900 Moscow)

One of the greatest and best-known landscape painters among the
Itinerants, Isaak Levitan had the advantage of studying under both
Savrasov and Polenov. Although his art is perhaps less epic than
Shishkin's, his style and subject matter are more varied – perhaps
surprisingly, since he died at a comparatively early age.

Levitan, like Shishkin, was a supreme master of the use of colour,
composition, light and shade. The seasons of the year, the different
times of day, and the infinite variety of nature figure in Levitan's
canvases. But, unlike Shishkin, who had a preference for summer
landscapes, Levitan preferred the fresh colours of spring and the muted
cadences of autumn. When he painted summer scenes, such as *Secluded
Monastery*, he preferred to work in the evening, when the light was
softer, or even at dusk.

Levitan joined the Society of Itinerant Exhibitions. He was a
contemporary of Nesterov, Korovin, Stepaniv, Bakcheev and Arkhipov.
He was friends with Ostroukhov and Serov.

Summing up Levitan's mature work, Chekhov (who was a friend) said,
"Nobody before him achieved such astonishing simplicity and clarity of
purpose... and I don't know whether anyone after him will ever achieve the
same."

718

*15. **Isaak Levitan,** 1860-1900, Realism, Russian, *The Vladimirka Road,* 1892, Oil on canvas, 79 x 123 cm, The State Tretyakov Gallery, Moscow

Levitan's paintings are in effect a hymn to nature. Autumn Day: Solniki and Summer Evening: Fence both express the vastness and emptiness of the Russian landscape. The Vladimirka Road is a typical Russian plain that stretches out on the canvas and disappears in the distance. The sky is heavy, grey and cloudy, like a lid that weighs on the entire tract of land crossed by a road alongside of which run paths made by many feet. If the painting is marked by a certain feeling of sadness, an impression of solemnity also emanates from this empty space. The silhouette placed in the painting accentuates even further the feeling of solitude. On the subject of the road, Levitan said (remarks later recounted by the painter Kouvchinnikova), "It's the Vladimirka road, the Vladimirka along which convoys of countless unhappy souls with chained feet formerly made their way toward the prisons of Siberia."

16. **Paul Signac,** 1863-1935, Neo-impressionism, French, *Women at the Well,* 1892, Oil on canvas, 210 x 146 cm, Musée d'Orsay, Paris

17. **Henri de Toulouse-Lautrec,** 1864-1901, Post-impressionism, French, *La Goulue, Dance at the Moulin Rouge,* 1891, Colour Lithograph, 191 x 117 cm, Private collection

18. **Henri de Toulouse-Lautrec,** 1864-1901, Post-impressionism, French, *Jane Avril in the Paris Garden,* 1893, Colour Lithograph poster, 130 x 95 cm, Private collection

19. **Frederic Leighton,** 1830-1896, Neoclassicism, English, *Garden of the Hesperides,* 1892, Oil on panel, Tondo, dia. 169 cm, Lady Lever Art Gallery, Port Sunlight

Victorian painter Leighton illustrates the classical academic art of the end of the nineteenth century.

719

720

721

720. Jan Toorop, 1858-1928, Symbolism, Dutch, *The Three Brides*, 1893, Oil on canvas, 78 x 97.8 cm, Rijksmuseum Kröller-Müller, Otterlo

Leading artist of the Symbolist movement, Toorop developed a style wi[th] curvilinear figures that prefigured the Art Nouveau.

721. Pierre Bonnard, 1867-1947, Nabis, French, *Nursemaids' Promenade, Frieze of Carriages,* 1894, Tempera on canvas, 147 x 54 cm, Private collection

22. Henri de Toulouse-Lautrec, 1864-1901, Post-Impressionism, French,
At The Salon Rue des Moulins, 1894, Black chalk and oil on canvas,
115.5 x 132.5 cm, Musée Toulouse-Lautrec, Albi

In Toulouse-Lautrec's ambitious and monumental painting of a brothel At the Salon in the Rue des Moulins of 1894, the atmosphere is solemn and joyless. The colloquial term 'filles de joie' seems singularly inappropriate. The prostitutes loll in attitudes of boredom on plushly upholstered divans under the watchful eye of the severe-looking madame. On the right, we glimpse the half-seen figure of a prostitute lifting her skirts to display what she has to sell to prospective clients.

724

23. Maurice Denis, 1870-1943, Nabis/Symbolism, French,
The Muses, 1893, Oil on canvas, 171.5 x 137.5 cm,
Musée d'Orsay, Paris

725

Member of the Nabis, Maurice Denis published his first definition of Neo-traditionalism in 1890: "Remember that a picture – before being a war horse or a nude woman or an anecdote – is essentially a flat surface covered with colours assembled in a certain order."
Paul Sérusier and a group of young painters launched the Nabis movement in 1888. Under the influence of Gauguin, the painters only kept the essential subject through a symbol, replacing the representation of reality by the interpretation of an idea. Maurice Denis, the group's theorist, developed a technique exalting pure colour, and simplifying the outline in order to bring out the subject's features. This was a reaction against the allegiance of Impressionism and its depiction of nature.

24. Mary Cassatt, 1844-1926, Impressionism, American,
The Boating Party, 1893-1894,
Oil on canvas, 90 x 117.3 cm,
The National Gallery of Art, Washington, D.C.

25. William Merritt Chase, 1849-1916, Impressionism,
American, *Leisure,* 1894, Oil on canvas,
64.8 x 90.2 cm, Amon Carter Museum, Fort Worth

E. Munch

727

728

Edvard Munch
(1863 Løten – 1944 Ekely)

dvard Munch, born in 1863, was Norway's most popular artist. His
rooding and anguished paintings, based on personal grief and
osessions, were instrumental in the development of Expressionism.
uring his childhood, the death of his parents, his brother and sister,
nd the mental illness of another sister, were of great influence on his
onvulsed and tortuous art. In his works, Munch turned again and
gain to the memory of illness, death and grief.

During his career, Munch changed his idiom many times. At first,
fluenced by Impressionism and Post-impressionism, he turned to a
ghly personal style and content, increasingly concerned with images of
ness and death. In the 1892s, his style developed a 'Synthetist' idiom
seen in *The Scream* (1893) which is regarded as an icon and the
ortrayal of modern humanity's spiritual and existential anguish. He
ainted different versions of it. During the 1890s Munch favoured a
allow pictorial space, and used it in his frequently frontal pictures. His
ork often included the symbolic portrayal of such themes as misery,
ckness, and death. and the poses of his figures in many of his portraits
ere chosen in order to capture their state of mind and psychological
ondition. It also lends a monumental, static quality to the paintings. In
392, the Union of Berlin Artists invited Munch to exhibit at its
ovember exhibition. His paintings invoked bitter controversy at the
ow, and after one week the exhibition closed. In the 1930s and 1940s,
e Nazis labeled his work "degenerate art", and removed his works
om German museums. This deeply hurt the anti-fascist Munch, who
d come to feel Germany was his second homeland. In 1908 Munch's
xiety became acute and he was hospitalized. He returned to Norway
n 1909 and died in Oslo in 1944.

726. Edvard Munch, 1863-1944, Symbolism/Expressionism, Norwegian,
Madonna, 1894, Oil on canvas, 90 x 68.5 cm, Munch-Museet, Oslo

727. Edvard Munch, 1863-1944, Symbolism/Expressionism, Norwegian,
The Scream, 1893, Tempera on board, 83.5 x 66 cm,
Stolen from the Munch-Museet, Oslo, on the 22nd August 2004, Oslo

*The name of Edvard Munch conjures up, for most people, one irresistibly
memorable picture: The Scream, a shriek of stomach-churning terror uttered by
a cringing figure with a skull-like face outlined against a fiery, blood-red sunset.
This iconic image has come to epitomise the angst embodied in the
Expressionism of the late nineteenth century. Yet its creator, a gentle soul given
to introspection and self-analysis, lived to see his eightieth birthday and
witnessed the world-wide critical acceptance of the Expressionist movement
which he had been largely instrumental in initiating.*

728. Franz von Stuck, 1863-1928, Symbolism/Expressionism, German,
The Sin, 1893, Oil on canvas, 94.5 x 59.5 cm, Neue Pinakothek, Munich

Claude Monet
(1840 Paris –1926 Giverny)

For Claude Monet the designation 'impressionist' always remained a source of pride. In spite of all the things critics have written about his work, Monet continued to be a true impressionist to the end of his very long life. He was so by deep conviction, and for his Impressionism he may have sacrificed many other opportunities that his enormous talent held out to him. Monet did not paint classical compositions with figures, and he did not become a portraitist, although his professional training included those skills. He chose a single genre for himself, landscape painting, and in that he achieved a degree of perfection none of his contemporaries managed to attain.

Yet the little boy began by drawing caricatures. Boudin advised Monet to stop doing caricatures and to take up landscapes instead. The sea, the sky, animals, people, and trees are beautiful in the exact state in which nature created them – surrounded by air and light. Indeed, it was Boudin who passed on to Monet his conviction of the importance of working in the open air, which Monet would in turn transmit to his impressionist friends. Monet did not want to enrol at the Ecole des Beaux-Arts. He chose to attend a private school, L'Académie Suisse, established by an ex-model on the Quai d'Orfèvres near the Pont Saint-Michel. One could draw and paint from a live model there for a modest fee. This was where Monet met the future impressionist Camille Pissarro.

Later in Gleyre's studio, Monet met Auguste Renoir Alfred Sisley, and Frédéric Bazille. Monet considered it very important that Boudin be introduced to his new friends. He also told his friends of another painter he had found in Normandy. This was the remarkable Dutchman Jongkind. His landscapes were saturated with colour, and their sincerity, at times even their naïveté, was combined with subtle observation of the Normandy shore's variable nature. At this time Monet's landscapes were not yet characterized by great richness of colour. Rather, they recalled the tonalities of paintings by the Barbizon artists, and Boudin's seascapes. He composed a range of colour based on yellow-brown or blue-grey.

At the Third Impressionist Exhibition in 1877 Monet presented a series of paintings for the first time: seven views of the Saint-Lazare train station. He selected them from among twelve he had painted at the station. This motif in Monet's work is in line not only with Manet's *Chemin de fer* (*The Railway*) and with his own landscapes featuring trains and stations at Argenteuil, but also with a trend that surfaced after the railways first began to appear.

In 1883, Monet had bought a house in the village of Giverny, near the little town of Vernon. At Giverny, series painting became one of his chief working procedures. Meadows became his permanent workplace. When a journalist, who had come from Vétheuil to interview Monet, asked him where his studio was, the painter answered, "My studio! I've never had a studio, and I can't see why one would lock oneself up in a room. To draw, yes – to paint, no". Then, broadly gesturing towards the Seine, the hills, and the silhouette of the little town, he declared, "There's my real studio."

Monet began to go to London in the last decade of the nineteenth century. He began all his London paintings working directly from nature, but completed many of them afterwards, at Giverny. The series formed an indivisible whole, and the painter had to work on all his canvases at one time.

A friend of Monet's, the writer Octave Mirbeau, wrote that he had accomplished a miracle. With the help of colours he had succeeded in recreating on the canvas something almost impossible to capture: he was reproducing sunlight, enriching it with an infinite number of reflections.

Alone among the impressionists, Claude Monet took an almost scientific study of the possibilities of colour to its limits; it is unlikely that one could have gone any further in that direction.

72

729. Claude Monet, 1840-1926, Impressionism, French, *Rouen Cathedral, Portral of Saint-Romain's Tower (Full Sun)*, 1894, Oil on canvas, 107 x 73 cm, Musée d'Orsay, Paris

Monet liked to use one and the same motif repeatedly. Thus between 189 *and 1895 he produced the famous series of twenty paintings devoted* *Rouen Cathedral. The most remarkable work in that series dates from 189* *Monet arrived at Rouen in February 1892 and boarded in a house oppos* *Rouen Cathedral. From this viewpoint, at close range, the main paintings* *the Cathedral series were executed. The view from the window determin* *the design of all the pictures in the series; the facade of the cathedr* *occupies almost the entire canvas, the soaring towers cut off by the top edg* *of the picture.*

In his desire to capture all the wealth and variety of lighting effects on t *cathedral's surface the artist passed quickly from one canvas to another as t* *lighting changed with the movement of the sun. The Cathedral series can* *regarded as the culmination of the impressionist method in Monet's work. T* *entire set was first displayed in the year of its completion, 1895; later it w* *often exhibited both in France and abroad. At present the canvases making* *the Rouen Cathedral series are in different museums of the world, the Mus* *d'Orsay in Paris boasting five of them.*

30

31

732

30. **Paul Gauguin,** 1848-1903, Post-impressionism,
French, *Where Do We Come From? Who Are We?
Where Are We Going?*, 1897, Oil on canvas,
139.1 x 374.6 cm, Museum of Fine Arts, Boston

31. **Fernand Khnopff,** 1858-1921, Symbolism, Belgian,
The Caresses, 1896, Oil on canvas, 50 x 151 cm,
Musées Royaux des Beaux Arts, Brussels

32. **Camille Pissarro,** 1830-1903, Impressionism, French,
Place du théâtre français à Paris, 1898,
Oil on canvas, 65.5 x 81.5 cm,
The State Hermitage Museum, St. Petersburg

7.

Edouard Vuillard
(1868 Cuiseaux – 1940 La Baule)

As a ten-year-old at the Lycée Condorcet, Vuillard made friends with Roussel, who persuaded the young Edouard to enter the *Ecole des Beaux-Arts*. At home and in the small dressmaker's studio which Vuillard's mother ran after her husband's death, the future artist was surrounded from an early age by the unusual patterns and combinations of colours presented by jumbled off-cuts of fabric. Moreover, Vuillard's father, mother, and brother were all fabric designers. Like all in the Nabis group, Vuillard was very well-read. He was fond of Baudelaire, Giraudoux and Valéty, and adored Mallarmé. The Nabis' desire to paint "icons" took an unexpected turn in Vuillard's small paintings of 1890-91. They were put together from a few small areas of colour that are completely flat and very bright. Their boldness anticipates Fauvism. Immediately afterwards Vuillard returned to calmer colours and abandoned absolute flatness without, however, resorting to the modelling devices used by the Old Masters. His painting became an ornamental pattern with a very complex rhythm. Impressions of Japanese woodcuts or old French *mille-fleurs* suggest themselves as possible inspirations. But the most probable source of Vuillard's inspiration was contemporary cheap fabrics.

Vuillard endows the painting with an inner significance. The artist did not have to resort to an unusual or exotic theme to achieve a rich decorative effect. His subject-matter was always at hand: mainly the lives of his nearest and dearest. By the end of his life, Vuillard's paintings became somehow drier, more "natural", and quite often fell into repetition, especially in his society portraits.

733. **Edouard Vuillard**, 1868-1940, Nabis, French, *In a Room*, 1899, Oil on cardboard, 52 x 79 cm, The State Hermitage Museum, St. Peters

734. **Frederic Remington**, 1861-1909, Realism, American, *The Fall of the Cowboy*, 1895, Oil on canvas, 63.5 x 89 cm, Amon Carter Museum, Fort Worth

735. **Paul Cézanne**, 1839-1906, Post-impressionism, French, *Boy in a Red Waistcoat*, 1890-1895, Oil on canvas, 79.6 x 64 cm, E.G Bührle Foundation, Zurich

734

735

Frederic Remington
(1861 Canton –1909 Ridgefield)

It is impossible to reflect upon Frederic Remington's art without thinking of the merely human elements. Remington became interested in the American Indian, probably because he became interested in the active, exciting life of the American Great Plains. The Indian appealed to him not in any histrionic way, not as a figure stepped out from the pages of *Hiawatha*, but just as a human subject. Remington hit upon this truth when he travelled west. What he found there was majesty that he did not make, solely, an affair of Indians in war paint and feathers.

Remington knew how the light of the moon or of the stars is diffused, how softly and magically it envelops the landscape. There is a sort of artistic honesty in his nocturnal studies. He never set out to be romantic or melodramatic, just to develop his affinity and closeness to nature. The beauty of the painter's motive, too, has communicated itself in his technique. His grey-green tones fading into velvety depths take on transparency, and in his handling of form he uses a touch as firm as need be. The determining influence in his career was that of the creative impulse, urging him to deal in the translation of visible things into pictorial terms.

736

"I am not interested in myself as a subject for painting, but in others, particularly women..."

Beautiful, sensuous and above all erotic, Gustav Klimt's paintings speak of a world of opulence and leisure, which seems aeons away from the harsh, post-modern environment we live in now. The subjects he treats – allegories, portraits, landscapes and erotic figures – contain virtually no reference to external events, but strive rather to create a world where beauty, above everything else, is dominant. His use of colour and pattern was profoundly influenced by the art of Japan, ancient Egypt, and Byzantium.

Ravenne, the flat, two-dimensional perspective of his paintings, and the frequently stylised quality of his images form an oeuvre imbued with a profound sensuality and one where the figure of woman, above all, reigns supreme.

Klimt's very first works brought him success at an unusually young age. Gustav, born in 1862, obtained a state grant to study at *Kunstgewerbeschule* (the Vienna School of Arts and Crafts) at the age of fourteen. His talents as a draughtsman and painter were quickly noticed, and in 1879 he formed the *Künstlercompagnie* (Artists' Company) with his brother Ernst and another student, Franz Matsch.

The latter part of the nineteenth century was a period of great architectural activity in Vienna. In 1857, the Emperor Franz Joseph had ordered the destruction of the fortifications that had surrounded the medieval city centre. The Ringstrasse was the result, a budding new district with magnificent buildings and beautiful parks, all paid for by public expenses. Therefore the young Klimt and his partners had ample opportunities to show off their talents, and they received early commissions to contribute to the decorations for the pageant organised to celebrate the silver wedding anniversary of the Emperor Franz Joseph and the Empress Elisabeth.

In 1894, Matsch moved out of their communal studio, and in 1897 Klimt, together with his closest friends, resigned from the *Künstlerhausgenossenschaft* (the Cooperative Society of Austrian Artists) to form a new movement known as the Secession, of which he was immediately elected president. The Secession was a great success, holding both a first and second exhibition in 1898. The movement made enough money to commission its very own building, designed for it by the architect Joseph Maria Olbrich. Above the entrance was its motto: "To each age its art, to art its freedom."

From around 1897 onward, Klimt spent almost every summer on the Attersee with the Flöge family. These were periods of peace and tranquillity in which he produced the landscape paintings constituting almost a quarter of his entire oeuvre. Klimt made sketches for virtually everything he did. Sometimes there were over a hundred drawings for one painting, each showing a different detail – a piece of clothing or jewellery, or a simple gesture.

Just how exceptional Gustav Klimt was is perhaps reflected in the fact that he had no predecessors and no real followers. He admired Rodin and Whistler without slavishly copying them, and was admired in turn by the younger Viennese painters Egon Schiele and Oskar Kokoschka, both of whom were greatly influenced by Klimt.

736. **Nicolae Grigorescu**, 1838-1907, Realism, Romanian,
Cheerful Young Peasant, 1894, Oil on canvas, 134 x 65 cm,
National Museum of Romania, Bucarest

737. **Gustav Klimt**, 1862-1918, Art Nouveau, Austrian, *Nuda Veritas*, 1899,
Oil on canvas, 252 x 55 cm, Österreichische National Library, Vienna

738. **Lawrence Alma-Tadema**, 1836-1912, Neoclassicism, English,
A Coign of Vantage, 1895, Oil on canvas, 64.2 x 45 cm, Private collection

739. **Henri Rousseau (Le Douanier Rousseau)**, 1844-1910,
Naive Art, French, *The Sleeping Gypsy*, 1897,
Oil on canvas, 129.5 x 200.7 cm, The Museum of Modern Art, New York

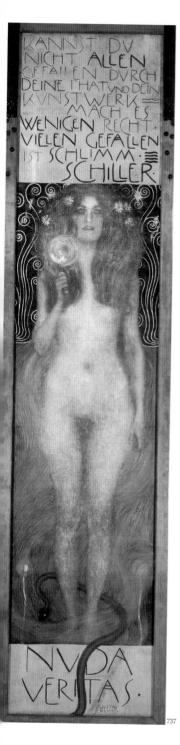

738

739

20th CENTURY

Following the tremendous industrialisation of the nineteenth century, the start of the twentieth century witnessed the emergence of international, industrial capitalism on an unprecedented scale. Mechanisation impacted not only society and the arts, but it also created an ethos of efficiency in technological warfare that was unknown in previous conflicts. Aerial bombardment, rapid-fire machine guns, chemical warfare, genocide, and atomic bombs marked the global conflagrations of the two world wars.

The rise of nationalism and imperialism of the nineteenth century was seen on a larger scale as centres of contestation burst forth everywhere, as for instance, in Russia with the 1917 Bolshevik Revolution epitomising the birth of Communism, and the death of an absolute monarchy.

This rush for power, combined with bad governance and great rivalries, triggered the first landmark event of the century: World War I. This first global war from 1914 to 1918 redistributed power, spurred the collapse of several monarchies, and prepared the way for new totalitarian powers throughout Europe and Russia.

With the close of World War I and the rejection of Wilson's proposals – among them the establishment of a League of Nations and the refusal of reconciliation between Germany and the rest of Europe – nationalism became uncompromising in Spain, Italy, and Germany.

On 24 October, 1929, or "Black Thursday", the United States' stock market crashed, causing international economic collapse, and the world endured the Great Depression until the beginning of World War II. In those harsh depression years, the difficult economic and social situation made many countries vulnerable to the rise of Fascism, and while Roosevelt's New Deal was providing jobs and putting new energy into the American art world, thanks to state patronage through the Federal Art Project, in Hitler's Germany "degenerate" art works were being destroyed. In Nazi Germany, as well as in other totalitarian regimes of the era, art was used as an instrument of propaganda. World War I was to be "the war to end all wars", but when German troops invaded Poland in 1939, humanity found itself in the middle of the Second World War, the largest and deadliest continuous war in history.

The Second World War ended with the capitulation of Germany and the atomic bombing of Japan. The trauma of the war redistributed power across the world. The post-1945 world would be quite different. Indeed Europe progressively lost all its colonies and thus its presence across borders and oceans. In the aftermath of the war, the world observed the rise of two radically opposed superpowers, the United States – embodying the spirit of capitalism – and its allies on the one hand, and the Soviet Union – the communist state – and its allies on the other. Both parties endured the Cold War, leading to the escalation of military build-ups and several outbursts of armed violence such as the Vietnam War, the symbol of the antagonism between the capitalist United States and the communist Soviet Union. Gradually, the Cold War led to the Détente in 1991 when the Soviet Union collapsed, putting an end to communism as a global model.

The wars thus changed the face of the world, and also imposed an evolution on the modern human psyche. As men were mobilised to the front during Second World War, women became increasingly empowered throughout the century. Women fought for their advancement, producing feminist art and literature, among other developments, from then onwards. The emancipation of women from the traditional patriarchal order of society brought with it the freeing of social and sexual behaviour. At all levels of society, a turning point occurred in the mid-twentieth century. In the United States, the Civil Rights movement gave new rights to blacks and gradually put an end to segregation. Globally, mentalities changed.

The radical destruction of human lives and social structures throughout the century created a significant period of social alienation. People began to believe that civilisation itself was in jeopardy. Enlightenment notions about the perfectibility of humankind seemed radically misplaced and defunct alongside the horrors of mechanised warfare and genocide. Artists, however, embraced these destabilising notions and sought to overturn many classical ideals.

140. **Claude Monet**, 1840-1926, Impressionism, French,
Houses of Parliament, London, Stormy Sky, 1904, Oil on canvas, 81 x 92 cm,
Musée des Beaux-Arts de Lille.

741

744

745

741. Gustav Klimt, 1862-1918, Art Nouveau, Austrian,
Portrait of Emilie Flöge, 1902, Oil on canvas, 181 x 84 cm,
Historisches Museum, Vienna

742. Pablo Picasso, 1881-1973, Cubism, Spanish,
Life, 1903, Oil on canvas, 196.5 x 128.8 cm,
Cleveland Museum of Art, Cleveland

743. Pierre Bonnard, 1867-1947, Nabis, French,
Siesta, The Artist's Studio, 1900, Oil on canvas, 109 x 132 cm,
National Gallery of Victoria, Melbourne

744. Claude Monet, 1840-1926, Impressionism, French, *Waterlilies*,
1903, Oil on canvas, 81.5 x 101.5 cm, Art Institute, Dayton

745. Paul Cézanne, 1839-1906, Post-Impressionism, French,
Mont Sainte-Victoire, View from Lauves, 1904,
Oil on canvas, 70 x 92 cm, Museum of Art, Philadelphia

746

747

746. Maurice Denis, 1870-1943, Symbolism, French,
Homage to Cézanne, 1900, Oil on canvas, 180 x 240 cm, Musée d'Orsay, Paris

In 1901 Denis exhibited a large canvas called Homage to Cézanne *at the Salon de
Société Nationale des Beaux-Arts, which could be regarded as a manifesto of the new
art. It was a full-length group portrait of himself, Redon, Sérusier, Bonnard, Rousse*
Vuillard and Vollard standing round a still-life by the then little-known artist. The
Nabis were enthusiastic admirers of Cézanne, and Denis was among his fir
advocates and expounders, although his own art owes little to Cézanne. He was muc
closer to Gauguin, not only when he was first impressed by his Talisman, *but als*
years later. Incidentally, the Cézanne still-life on the easel in the Homage *belonged t*
Gauguin, a fact appreciated only by those "in the know".

747. Paula Modersohn-Becker, 1876-1907, Expressionism, German,
Trumpeting Girl in a Birch Wood, 1903, Oil on canvas,
Paula Modersohn-Becker Museum, Bremen

748. Théo van Rysselberghe, 1862-1926, Neo-Impressionism, Belgian,
The Woman in White, 1904, Oil on canvas,
Musée d'Art Moderne et d'Art Contemporain, Liège

749. Gustav Klimt, 1862-1918, Art Nouveau, Austrian,
Island in the Attersee, 1901, Oil on canvas, 100 x 100 cm, Private collection

750. Franz von Stuck, 1863-1928, Symbolism/Expressionism, German,
Fighting for a Woman, 1905, Oil on panel, 90 x 117 cm,
The State Hermitage Museum, St. Petersburg

749

750

751

752

751. Henri Matisse, 1869-1954, Fauvism, French,
Luxe, calme et volupté, 1904-05, Oil on canvas, 98.5 x 118.5 cm
Musée National d'Art Moderne, Centre Georges Pompidou, Paris

Matisse painted his first Fauve paintings in southern France. As
pupil of Gustave Moreau at the School of Fine Arts, Matisse met Du
and Rouault in the master's workshop.
*   Harmony comes out of this picture. Matisse is looking for ide*
beauty, and here he depicts the Mediterranean Eden of Saint-Trope
He carries on a tradition commenced by Poussin and Puvis
Chavanne with characters expressing happiness and an out-of-tin
scenery. The painting betrays a neo-impressionist technique, throu
the little brush strokes, inspired by Signac.

752. Maurice de Vlaminck, 1876-1958, Fauvism, French,
Houses at Chatou, c. 1905, Oil on canvas, 81.3 x 101.6 cm,
The Art Institute of Chicago, Chicago

753

754

Ferdinand Hodler, 1853-1918,
Art Nouveau, Swiss, *Day*, 1904-
1906, Oil on canvas, 163 x 358 cm,
Kunsthaus, Zurich

André Derain, 1880-1954,
Fauvism, French, *Fishing Boats*,
1905, Oil on canvas, 82 x 101 cm,
Pushkin State Museum of Fine Arts,
Moscow

755

756

755. André Derain, 1880-1954, Fauvism, French, *Hyde Park*, c. 1906, Oil on canvas, 66 x 99 cm, Musée d'Art Moderne, Troyes

756. Albert Marquet, 1875-1947, Fauvism, French, *14 July at Le Havre*, 1906, Oil on canvas, 81 x 65 cm, Musée Léon Alègre, Bagnols-sur-Cèze

757. Henri Matisse, 1869-1954, French, Fauvism. *Game of Bowls*, 1908. Oil on canvas, 115 x 147 cm. The State Hermitage Museum, St. Petersburg.

In 1908, Matisse created the Ball game in which he tried to solve seven problems: that of the decorative generalisation, that of the concentration colour - blue, green, and yellow ocre- as well as that of building, on the surface of the canvas, a balanced construction that would have a class triangle for a base. Matisse introduced in such a pyramid, curved lines dynamic and laconic at the same time, the solving the problem of balance a painting representing forms in movement.

757

HENRI MATISSE
(1869 LE CATEAU-CAMBRÉSIS – 1954 NICE)

"Fauvism is when there is a red," said Henri Matisse concisely putting into words the most straightforward notion held of Fauvism. Matisse has in fact become Fauvism's leader over the years as a result of his contemporaries and researchers persistently perpetuating such an idea. Consequently Matisse's œuvre has been scoured through in a search for the ultimate Fauvist painting. Matisse never pretended or aspired to such a role, and on the question of what Fauvism represents in theory and in practice, he never came to a final conclusion.

Matisse started to take lessons at the Académie Julian in 1891, working as a law tutor to help pay his way. In 1892 he abandoned Bouguereau's totally uninspiring lessons and transferred to Gustave Moreau's classes at the Ecole des Beaux-Arts. During the evenings Matisse also attended classes in applied art and there he made friends with Albert Marquet, who soon also became a pupil of Moreau. It was at these classes that a group of artists came together and formed friendships that would endure all the trials and tribulations of their respective lives. This group consisted of the "Three M's" – Matisse, Marquet and Manguin – as well as Georges Rouault, Charles Camoin and Louis Valtat. Working in Léon Bonnat's studio, which was just across the corridor, was another future member, Othon Friesz. And he would later be joined by Raoul Dufy. In 1901 Matisse and his friends started to exhibit their work at the Salon des Indépendants and in Berthe Weill's gallery. In 1903 they were involved in the founding of the Salon d'Automne, where two years later Vauxcelles would see their work and dub them "les fauves". The Salon d'Automne scandal over *Woman with a Hat* in 1905 brought Matisse fame and glory at a time when the preceding generation of artists were only just beginning to receive theirs. Matisse, as a natural inheritor of the French tradition, showed himself more than respectful of his elders. Renoir, whom he often met whilst in the south in 1917-18, always remained a teacher figure for him. The paintings Matisse produced between 1897 and 1901 demonstrate the mastery of his predecessors' techniques, from the Impressionists through to Cézanne. Matisse began this process around the time of Gustave Moreau's death. Unlike Derain and Vlaminck he was never troubled by the "museum issue" since he learnt to appreciate exhibits and their influence under Moreau's guidance. Fauvism shaped all Matisse's creative work and he himself defined it so well as: "The courage to find the purity of means".

758

758. Henri Matisse, 1869-1954, French, Fauvism,
Woman at window, 1905. Oil on canvas, 32 x 30 cm. Private collection

759. Max Liebermann, 1847-1935, Impressionism, German,
Papageienallee, 1902, Oil on canvas, 88.1 x 72.5 cm, Kunsthalle, Bremen

760

760. Maurice de Vlaminck, 1876-1958, Fauvism, French,
View of the Seine, 1905-06, Oil on canvas, 54.5 x 65.5 cm,
The State Hermitage Museum, St. Petersburg

*View of the Seine depicts the river bank near the Chatou Bridge (
spot where Vlaminck often worked before moving to Bougiva
and is reminiscent of August Renoir's Oarsmen at Chatou (1879
National Gallery, Washington), which Renoir painted at the sam
place during the Impressionist period. Renoir's red boat, cuttin
diagonally across the surface of the water, possesses a resonance
which seems impossible for the age of Impressionism. Vlaminck
painting, constructed on the parallel, almost horizontal lines of th
boats and bank, looks quieter and there are no figures in th
foreground adding life. Yet, to use Vlaminck's mode of expression
colour makes his painting a "fanfare" in contrast to Renoir's "pian
music!" His red comma of a boat burns in the centre against a rive
of shimmering blue, red, ochre and white vertical strokes; touche
of red on the shore repeat the main melody and red reflections o
the white sails echo it again diminuendo. The drawing of object
here is very generalised; the outlines of the trees and the house
are highly abstracted and the sail is inaccurately portrayed, thoug
Vlaminck as an experienced waterman no doubt knew what sai
really look like. Vlaminck subordinates everything to the power o
colour in his desire to recreate on canvas his vital energy and joi
de vivre. In his enthusiasm to capture his momentary responses
Vlaminck often squeezed paint directly from the tube withou
stopping to mix it. The resulting effect is so powerful that afte
many decades the pictures evoke the same feelings of impatience
and trepidation which gripped the artist himself. The brush move
freely, temperamentally, laying rich patches of ochre on popla
crowns, and daubing heavy streaks of cobalt blue and white int
the sky. Within this apparently irregular patchwork of colour i
pre-dominance of red – and it is not by chance that it is enhance
by the only green patch – and the white of the sail standing ou
sharply against the saturated colour scheme. There are smudge
horizontal lines clearly visible under the first layer of paint – th
result of Vlaminck either scraping the paint off with a palette knife
or, perhaps, as he said, wiping the freshly painted picture on th
grass in his haste to begin another on the same canvas.*

763

Kees van Dongen, 1877-1968, Fauvism, Dutch, *The Red Dancer*, 1907,
Oil on canvas, 99.7 x 81 cm, The State Hermitage Museum, St. Petersburg

*The Red Dancer was bought in 1909 by the publisher Nikolai Riabushinsky at the
Golden Fleece Salon in Moscow. A sea of orange-red flames floods half the canvas
which is sharply divided along one diagonal. Laid broadly and coarsely on the
ochrous foundation are dabs of colour in varying shapes and sizes tracing the motion
of the twirling skirt. One small feature – a tiny particle of pure green on the white
garter – is testimony to van Dongen's far from indifferent attitude to the science of
colour. Yet this is a merely subtle nuance just like the green shadow on the face. The
blazing red has no need for support for it is borne in the freedom of the painterly
texture and the intensity of pure colour applied straight from the tube. Colour
decides everything here; it determines the work's design, motion, and space. The
wavy contours of the skirt contrast with the abstracted, simplified outlines of the face,
neck and shoulder. The line in a graphical sense is replaced by a fading of colour
from the figure to the background, which creates an impression of depth, breaching
the flatness of the canvas. By the character of the image and the painterly manner,
The Red Dancer is closest of all to a portrait of the Dutch male soprano Modjesco
performing a woman's role (Museum of Modern Art, New York) in which a critic in
1908 saw a new manner.*

762. André Derain, 1880-1954, Fauvism, French, *London Bridge*, 1906,
Oil on canvas, 66 x 99.1 cm, The Museum of Modern Art, New York

*Using the divisionism technique, Derain applied a sophisticated range of
colours. The painter worked on the complementary colours to define the space
and the depth of the painting.*

763. Paula Modersohn-Becker, 1876-1907, Expressionism, German,
Self-Portrait with Amber Necklace, 1906, Oil on wood, 61.5 x 30.5 cm,
Museum Folkwang, Essen

764. Pablo Picasso, 1881-1973, Cubism, Spanish, *Les Demoiselles d'Avignon*, 1906-1907, Oil on canvas, 243.9 x 233.7 cm, The Museum of Modern Art, New York

Thirty years before painting his masterpiece Guernica, *Picasso showed his early interest in Cubism. In 1907, after being impressed with the almond-shaped eyes an elongated egg-shaped faces of African masks, he returned to a recent work and repainted the faces of its five figures. The blend of the mask shapes with his desire t reduce visual realities to abstract forms and to simultaneously show multiple points-of-view resulted in the breakthrough work that moved the artist from his Africa period to his most dominant period in pure Cubism. The challenge of evolving this new art form would possess the artist for several years of his long life. The landscape of Cézanne, and works such as his* Boy in a Red Vest *(1893-5), were influences on how Picasso presented the jagged planes of the work so as to give the figures continu motion. The "Avignon" referred to in the title refers to a street in Barcelona's commercial sex district.*

The painting betrays the influence of the Bathers *by Cézanne. The faces of the women (especially the two on the right) are also clearly inspired by African art. Th exhibition of "art nègre" given in Paris in 1906 had a great impact on the artist. Initially, Picasso had depicted men (sailors and students) in his first drawings. He late excluded them so that it is the spectator who becomes the intruder in the scene.*

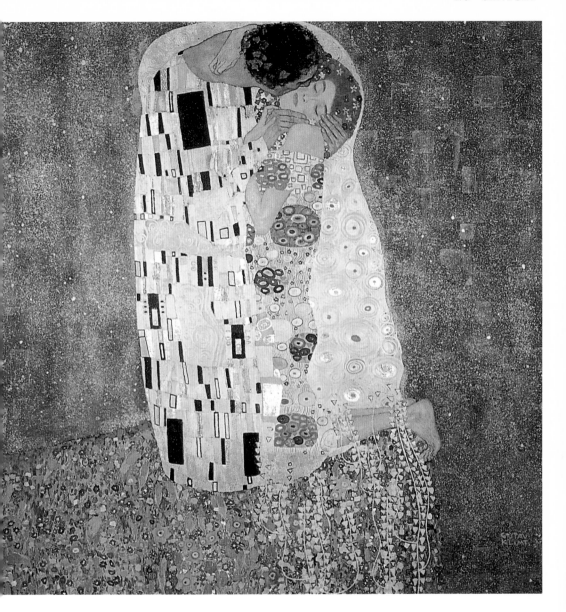

65. **Gustav Klimt**, 1862-1918, Art Nouveau, Austrian, *The Kiss*, 1907-08, Oil on canvas, 180 x 180 cm, Österreichische Galerie, Vienna

Klimt's The Kiss *of 1908, which has become his best-known picture, was preceded by two other famous versions of the subject by Rodin and Munch. All three show a pre-occupation with Eros and the troubled sexual relations between man and woman that was characteristic of the turn of the century's Western culture. Klimt's Kiss is less pessimistic and less misogynistic than Munch's puddle of melted human flesh and less pretentious than Rodin's heroically nude pair of marble lovers.*

Of the three though, Klimt's image is the most explicitly sexual with its use of symbolic and erotically charged ornament. The embracing lovers whose combined forms suggest that the moment of climactic ecstasy has just passed. Despite Klimt's not so oblique treatment of a sexual theme, The Kiss *with its sumptuously decorative qualities must have looked reassuringly beautiful beside the harshly expressionistic works of Schiele and Gerstl that were shown with it in the 1908 Kunstschau. For once, Klimt's work was received with enthusiasm, and it was bought directly from the exhibition by the Austrian state.*

Félix Vallotton
(1865 Lausanne – 1925 Paris)

The "foreign Nabi" stood out among the members of the Nabis group, not so much because of his non-French extraction but because of his manner of painting which was quite unlike that of his fellow artists. For this reason some critics have regarded his affiliation with the Nabis as purely formal.

Vallotton displayed his talent to the full at the very outset of his career. As a boy of sixteen, he amazed his teachers in Lausanne with a study of an old man's head, executed with a sure hand. Soon afterwards he moved to Paris.

As far back as 1885, when Vallotton first showed his works at the Salon des Artistes Français, he drew the attention of art critics. However, both at that time and for years to come, progressive artists who advocated the supremacy of pictorial effect and the unrestrained use of colours looked on his manner as something retrograde. Signac, who could not bear smoothness and "blew up" his surfaces with divided strokes, regarded Vallotton's brushwork as the complete antithesis of his own style and, indeed, of everything that derived from Impressionism. But the young Swiss, who had arrived in Paris when the Impressionists were still striving for recognition, did not know them, or at least had no wish to do so. That was not because he was wholly "indoctrinated" by Jules Lefebvre, Bouguereau and Boulanger at the Académie Julian; in fact, he preferred going to the Louvre and making copies of Antonello da Messina, Leonardo da Vinci and Albrecht Dürer.

Vallotton's art is indispensable for any student of life in that period: the accuracy of his details never needs to be questioned; the design, mood and, with rare exception, bitter astringency of his work set him apart, not only among the Nabis, but among other contemporaries too. His deliberate objectivity and emphatically dispassionate observation, expressed in meticulous draughtsmanship and inexpressive texture, link him not only with the Naturalism of the nineteenth century, but also with the tendencies of the twentieth. It is natural, therefore, that public interest in his work has tended to grow whenever there was a turn towards the concrete, material aspect in the arts, be it the 1920s, with their renewed materialism, or the 1970s, with their hyper-realism and other semi-naturalistic trends.

766

767

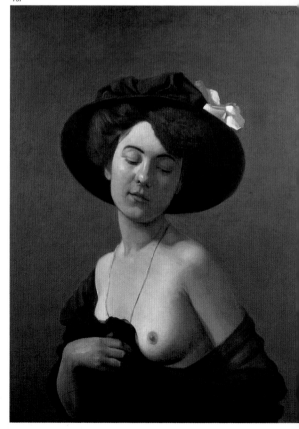

766. **Emil Nolde**, 1867-1956, Expressionism, German,
Autumn Sea XI, 1910, Oil on canvas, 73 x 88 cm, Kunsthaus Zurich, Zurich

767. **Félix Vallotton**, 1865-1925, Nabism, Swiss,
Woman with Black Hat, 1908, Oil on canvas, 81.3 x 65 cm, The State Hermitage Museum, St. Petersburg

Vallotton's Woman with Black Hat *(Woman Wearing a Hat) is undoubtedly a parody, combining the almost uncombinable: the striking turn of the half-clothed figure and a plain, dull face topped with an elaborate flowery hat. The painter's eye seems dispassionate, yet something personal comes across in his attitude toward the woman. Annette Vaillant recollected that Vallotton's Calvinist exterior concealed a strange Ingres-like sensuality. But the intimate effect of the portrait is extinguished by mockery which is noticeable even in the range of colours he uses. His palette is limited here and clearly imitates that of Salon journeyman painters.*

38

68. Valentin Serov, 1865-1911, World of Art group, Russian,
Portrait of Ida Rubinstein, 1910, Tempera and charcoal on paper,
147 x 233 cm, The State Russian Museum, St. Petersburg

*Portrait of Ida Rubinstein can be said to conform to the new style in
every way. The famous ballerina posed for Serov in the nude, and this
obliged the artist to forestall any associations of the future portrait with
reality. Serov did not portray Ida Rubinstein: he created an image out
of the boundless possibilities presented by the model. In doing so he
sought to combine the abstract with the real, something typical of the
Art Nouveau, as such, and also typical of almost all of Serov's
portraits. The curving lines of the contours are traced directly onto the
canvas. Only three hues are present in the colour scheme – blue,
green, and brown – without any gradations or combinations. Each
colour is isolated and local. The spatial environment is not designed,
be it by colour or compositional arrangement or perspective. She
seems not to be seated, but sprawled, pressed to the canvas, which,
for all her beguiling and extravagant features, creates and impression
of weakness and vulnerability. Serov regarded Ida Rubinstein with
admiration, although he did not stress the characteristic aspect of her
image at the expense of the ideal. In a number of other portraits,
however, his treatment of the models borders on the grotesque. This
tendency attained its peak in the very last years of his life and, above
all, in the* Portrait of Olga Orlova *(1911).*

Valentin Serov
(1865 St. Petersburg – 1911 Moscow)

Among the "young peredvizhniki" who joined the World of Art
group, the most brilliant portraitist was Valentin Serov. Like many of
his contemporaries, he delighted in painting out of doors, and some
of his most appealing portraits – such as *Girl with Peaches*, *Girl in
Sunlight* and *In Summer* - owe their naturalness to their setting or to
the interplay of sunlight and shadows. Indeed, Serov regarded them
as "studies" rather than portraits, giving them descriptive titles that
omitted the sitter's name. The subject of *Girl with Peaches* – painted
when Serov was only twenty-two – was in fact Mamontov's daughter
Vera. The model for *In Summer* was Serov's wife.

When only six years old, Serov began to display signs of artistic
talent. At nine years old, Repin acted as his teacher and mentor,
giving him lessons in his studio in Paris, then let Serov work with
him in Moscow, almost like an apprentice. Eventually Repin sent him
to study with Pavel Chistiakov – the teacher of many of the World of
Art painters, including Nesterov and Vrubel. Chistiakov was to
become a close friend. Because Serov's career spanned such a long
period, his style and subject matter vary considerably, ranging from
voluptuous society portraits (the later ones notable for their grand
style and sumptuous dresses) to sensitive studies of children. Utterly
different from any of these is the famous nude study of the dancer Ida
Rubinstein, in tempera and charcoal on canvas, which he painted
towards the end of his life. Although Serov's early style has much in
common with the French Impressionists, he did not become
acquainted with their work until after he had painted pictures such as
Girl with Peaches.

769

771

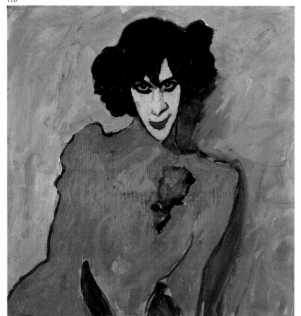

770

769. **Marie Laurencin**, 1883-1956, French, *Head of a Woman*, Oil on canva
pasted on cardboard, 35 x 27 cm, Pushkin State Museum of Fine Arts, N

770. **Alexei von Jawlensky**, 1864-1941, Expressionism, Russian,
Portrait of the Dancer Alexander Sakharov, 1909, Oil on canvas,
Städtische Galerie im Lenbachhaus, Munich

*Russian dancer Alexander Sakharov was captured in an extraordinary po
his friend Alexei von Jawlensky. The dancer visited the painter one
before a performance, already made up and in costume, which cr
particularly androgynous effect. Quickly and spontaneously – reportedl
than half an hour – Jawlensky produced this free, vigorous and
memorable image.*

771. **Kees van Dongen**, 1877-1968, Fauvism, Dutch,
Woman in a Black Hat, 1908, Oil on canvas, 100 x 81.5 cm,
The State Hermitage Museum, St. Petersburg

*Woman in a Black Hat was a continuation, as it were, of van L
reflections on beauty. This is one more aspect of that reflection. It is that
image which in van Dongen's words is not a photograph of life but be
the realm of the daydream. The wide-brimmed hat and green raincoat
model a timeless character, taking us away from the sphere of observed
slightly vibrant background is radiant, the contours softened. The mass
just like the large black patch of the hat, are present on the canvas so as
the warm pink tones of the face with its huge dark eyes to light up tend
precisely at this time that the foundations were laid for that idealisatio
society people expected when commissioning a portrait from van Dong*

772. **Natalia Goncharova**, 1881-1962, Primitivism, Russian-French,
Street in Moscow, 1909, Oil on canvas, 65 x 79 cm, Private collection

LE DOUANIER ROUSSEAU (HENRI ROUSSEAU)
(1844 Laval – 1910 Paris)

Henri Rousseau served as a customs officer at the Gate of Vanves in Paris. In his free time he painted, sometimes on commission for his neighbours and sometimes in exchange for food. Year after year from 1886 to 1910 he brought his work to the Salon des Indépendants for display. (In 1884 the Salon des Indépendants was launched. It had no selection committee and was set up specifically to put on show the works of those artists who painted for a living but were yet unable or unwilling to meet the requirements of the official salons.) Year after year his work was exhibited despite its total lack of professional worth. Nevertheless he was proud to be numbered among the city's artists, and thoroughly enjoyed the right they all had to see their works shown to the public like the more accepted artists in the better salons.

Rousseau was among the first in his generation to perceive the dawn of a new era in art in which it was possible to grasp the notion of freedom – the freedom to be an artist irrespective of a specific style of painting or the possession professional qualifications. Discussion and appreciation of Rousseau's works inevitably led to discussion and (sometimes) appreciation of the works of others in a similar vein. Accordingly, some perhaps not so talented but undoubtedly original artists were noticed and even encouraged to come forward. A chain of "discoveries" ensued. "Primitive" and "naïve" art was suddenly all around. Professional artists were also becoming heavily involved.

773

774

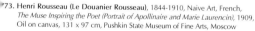

73. Henri Rousseau (Le Douanier Rousseau), 1844-1910, Naive Art, French, *The Muse Inspiring the Poet (Portrait of Apollinaire and Marie Laurencin)*, 1909, Oil on canvas, 131 x 97 cm, Pushkin State Museum of Fine Arts, Moscow

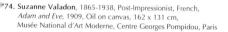

74. Suzanne Valadon, 1865-1938, Post-Impressionist, French, *Adam and Eve*, 1909, Oil on canvas, 162 x 131 cm, Musée National d'Art Moderne, Centre Georges Pompidou, Paris

775

776

775. **Henri Matisse**, 1869-1954, French, Fauvism, *Conversation*, 1908-12.
Oil on canvas, 177 x 217 cm. The State Hermitage Museum, St. Petersburg.

776. **Georges Braque**, 1882-1963, Cubism, French,
Houses at L'Estaque, 1908, Oil on canvas, 73 x 60 cm, Kunstmuseum, Berne

Georges Braque
(1882 Argenteuil-sur-Seine – 1963 Paris)

The French painter Georges Braque, born at Argenteuil, near Paris, was one of the major painters of the twentieth century. Together with Picasso he was the founder of Cubism. In addition to the pioneering work in Analytical Cubism that he shared with Picasso, he may also be credited with the development of a thoroughly original and exciting version of Cubism intertwined with Fauve colour effects. The association of Braque and Picasso was so mutual and their association so intense that in many instances only experts can distinguish Braque's paintings of 1910-12 from those of Picasso. The paintings of this period are all executed in muted greens, greys, ochre, and browns. The objects are fragmented, as though seen from multiple viewpoints. Eventually, Picasso and Braque went separate ways.

Braque served in World War I, and was seriously injured in 1916. He devoted the rest of his career to the exploration of Cubism. Active until the end of his life, Braque produced an oeuvre that includes sculpture, graphics, book illustration, and decorative art. He certainly was the most consistent of the original Cubist painters and one of the half-dozen greatest painters of the century.

778

779

Pierre Bonnard, 1867-1947, Nabis, French,
The Bathroom Mirror, 1908, Oil on canvas, 125 x 110 cm,
Pushkin State Museum of Fine Arts, Moscow

This painting is one of the most wide-ranging of Bonnard's works in terms of genre as well as one of the most captivating for its visual harmony. A painting as complex as this required not only daring, but also the considerable experience accumulated over twenty years of work. Bonnard's earliest still-lifes, including student pieces dating back to 1888, were far removed from the solution of complex issues of genre and space.

The juxtaposition of two women, one naked, the other clothed, has about it an element of irony, which was highly characteristic of Bonnard. A somewhat unusual feature of this painting is the inclusion of the mirror. A detail of this kind occurred quite often in the work of the Old Masters, most frequently as an element in vanitas compositions, which through the idiom of juxtaposed objects, spoke of the transitory nature of life and of human vanity. Sometimes a mirror was depicted in combination with a statuette of a half-naked woman which symbolised Art. However, this kind of object symbolism had lost its original meaning as early as the eighteenth century. In their still-lifes, Bonnard's immediate predecessors, the Impressionists, hardly ever used a mirror as a compositional element.

The basic structural elements of The Bathroom Mirror *had formed long before 1908. For example, in 1894 the artist painted* The Cup of Coffee *which depicts a girl at a little table holding a coffee-cup. The following year, in response to a commission for the decoration of a bathroom and boudoir, Bonnard produced a series of grisaille and red-chalk nudes in which we can detect the influence of Degas.*

Vasily Kandinsky, 1866-1944, Lyrical Abstraction/ Der Blaue Reiter, Russian, *Improvisation II*, 1910, Oil on canvas, The State Russian Museum, St. Petersburg

Mikhail Larionov, 1881-1964, Rayonnism, Russian,
Bread, c. 1910, Oil on canvas, 102 x 84 cm, Private collection, Paris

A pyramid of round and oblong loaves of bread takes up the entire surface of this monumental painting. The poet Maximilien Volochine, after having visited the Knave of Diamonds exhibition in late 1910, noted, "Larionov is the most naïve and most spontaneous of our Knaves'. His painting Bread *is nothing more than bread: good bread, well baked, that would have been the pride of any bakery had it been in its tinplate sign". While drawing inspiration from signs, Larionov was not content to simply imitate. His approach to the subject is a study in contrariness: weighty and serious for the sign painter, ironic and full of good humour here.*

781

781. Vladimir Tatlin, 1885-1953, Constructivism, Russian, *The Sailor*, 1911-12, Tempera on canvas, 71.5 x 71.5 cm, The State Russian Museum, St. Petersburg

Tatlin is the founder of Constructivism. In 1917, after the October revolution, he was commissioned to design the monument to the Third International, a huge spiral tower in iron and glass. Thirty-one years later, the Soviet government declared him an "enemy of the people".

780. Henri Matisse, 1869-1954, Fauvism, French, *The Music*, 1910, Oil on canvas, 260 x 389 cm, The State Hermitage Museum, St. Petersburg

The paintings The Music *and* The Dance *are inseparable parts of a sing decorative concept. The intense wild rhythm of* The Dance, *which confronte visitors to Shishkin's house on the first-floor landing, was supplanted by th conciliating peace of the second panel which hung on the next landing.*

In The Music *the level of the horizon is higher and the relative weight the green surface has been increased. The construction is reduced to primitive pattern – the canvas is cut by a diagonal line of orange figures frame by two vertical lines. In reducing composition to a bare minimum, Matis made changes directly on the canvas without the use of many prelimina sketches. What is remarkable in these paintings is that the alterations of on single element – the proportional relationship in the configuration of areas colour – results in dynamic motion in* The Dance *and a diametrically oppose stasis in* The Music.

782. Oskar Kokoschka, 1886-1980, Expressionism, Austrian, *Adolf Loos*, 1909, Oil on canvas, 74 x 91 cm, Staatliche Museen, Berlin

Without a doubt, Kokoschka's greatest achievements in the pre-war years we his portraits. They rank among the most remarkable not only of Expressionis but of the history of art itself. In the German context, at least until the arrival Otto Dix, only Lovis Corinth's portraits come close to Kokoschka's capacity f revealing the inner nature of his sitters. But in his extraordinary painting of th aristocratic aesthete Count Keyserling, for example, Corinth did on surreptitiously what Kokoschka was to do as his very raison d'être. Kokoschka friend, patron and mentor, the architect Adolf Loos, seems instinctively to hav known that the young artist had a unique ability to draw out an individua most essential (and hence most elusive) characteristics. He encourage Kokoschka, in spite of the fact that he had painted almost no portraits to dat and his prior training had only been in the applied arts.

Loos believed so fervently in Kokoschka's potential for portraiture th he not only procured a string of wealthy sitters, but also assured the (though he could barely afford to) that he would personally buy any portrai that they rejected.

783. George Wesley Bellows, 1882-1925,
Ashcan School, American, *Stag at Sharkey's*, 1909,
Oil on canvas, 92 x 122.6 cm,
Cleveland Museum of Art, Cleveland

George Wesley Bellows is thought of as a member of the Ashcan School of Realism, although he was not one of its charter members. The observation by Bellows of the everyday life of ordinary people, without commenting on the broader socialist unrest of the time, is captured in his masterpiece, which alone qualifies him for the realism movement.

The viewer is placed near ringside at an all male "stag" event. He is slightly elevated above ring, above the heads of the spectators, where Bellows still manages to capture the rawness and the noise of the crowd and the fight taking place.

The atmosphere of the event, which is clearly not just a spontaneous moment, is caught by the artist. The top rope of the ring is adjusted conveniently so as not to obscure the view of the central subject.

784

785

784. Henri Rousseau (Le Douanier Rousseau), 1844-1910,
Naive Art, French, *Tiger Attacking a Bull*, 1908-09, Oil on canv
46 x 55 cm, The State Hermitage Museum, St. Petersburg

785. Albert Marquet, 1875-1947, Fauvism, French,
Harbour at Honfleur, c. 1910, Oil on canvas, 65 x 81 cm,
Pushkin State Museum of Fine Arts, Moscow

786

787

786. Fernand Léger, 1881-1955, Cubism/ Purism, French, *Nudes in the Forest*, 1909-10, Oil on canvas, 120 x 170.2 cm, Rijksmuseum Kröller-Müller, Otterlo

According to Léger, these figures are "a battle of volumes" overlapping and with syncopated rhythm. Unified by the cold light they are "at the antipodes of Impressionism". To a certain extent, this work is an anticipation of Italian Futurism.

787. André Lhote, 1885-1962, Cubism, French, *Landscape with Houses*, after 1911, Oil on canvas, 65 x 50 cm, Pushkin State Museum of Fine Arts, Moscow

788

788. Umberto Boccioni, 1882-1916, Futurism, Italian, *The City Rises*, 1910, Oil on canvas, 199.3 x 301 cm, The Museum of Modern Art, New York

789. Umberto Boccioni, 1882-1916, Futurism, Italian, *The Street Penetrates the House*, 1911, Oil on canvas, 100 x 100 cm, Sprengel Museum, Hannover

789

790

790. Alberto Magnelli, 1888-1971, Abstraction, Italian, *The Workers on the Cart*, 1914, Oil on canvas, 100 x 75.5 cm, Musée National d'Art Moderne, Centre Georges Pompidou, Paris

791

Oskar Kokoschka
(1886 Pöchlarn – 1980 Montreux)

Oskar Kokoschka painted some of the major works of Expressionism and set a new standard for modern portraiture. Towards the end of his long life, his work was described as "eternal Expressionism". Yet there has long been a strong tendency among critics and curators to regard his earliest work, particularly from the "Vienna years" of 1909-1914, as his best. Certainly Kokoschka created some of his most stunningly original visual and literary work during this period. However, he continued to explore the means for powerful expression in painting throughout his life.

Kokoschka was also a significant writer and active in cultural politics — as an outspoken opponent of the Nazi oppression — in his later career.

Kokoschka was born in Lower Austria and emerged from a milieu still under the thrall of Klimt and Viennese Secessionism. He made his name while still a student at the 1908 Kunstschau in Vienna with works he produced under the aegis of the stylish Wiener Werkstätte. The already radical and unsettling qualities of his work were recognised early. He was dubbed *Oberwildling* or "Chief Savage". Kokoschka did not train as a painter. He studied other techniques at the Kunstgewerbeschule (School of Applied Arts). Yet he had barely graduated when he began his intensive engagement with the portrait genre. Loos recognised the young artist's raw, precocious talent and encouraged him, particularly in his portraiture. It is therefore fitting that one of Kokoschka's first great portraits was of his mentor, painted in 1909.

791. **Oskar Kokoschka**, 1886-1980, Expressionism, Austrian, *The Tempest (The Bride of the Winds)*, 1914, Oil on canvas, 71 x 86 cm, Kunstmuseum, Basle

The painting for which Kokoschka is perhaps best known emerged from a passionate love affair he had, which has also become legendary. Die Windsbraut (The Tempest) is a large painting, worked over many times. Its evocative title, which literally means "Bride of the Winds," came from the poet Georg Trakl – Kokoschka had originally envisaged the couple as the Wagnerian lovers Tristan and Isolde. At an early stage the painting was dominated by the red tones suggestive of burning passion. In its final state, however, it is a testimony to the artist's own experience of love and longing crystallised in cold, dreamlike hues of greens, blues, greys and pale pinks. No victim of false modesty, Kokoschka described it as "my strongest and greatest work, the masterpiece of all Expressionist endeavours". The figures, elevated above earthly reality and tossed on the storms of love even as they embrace, are Kokoschka and the woman who possessed his work and his thoughts for many years, his lover Alma Mahler.

792. Franz Marc, 1880-1916, Expressionism, German, *Blue Horse I*, 1911,
Oil on canvas, 112.5 x 84.5 cm, Städtische Galerie im Lenbachhaus, Munich

Egon Schiele
(1890 Tulln – 1918 Vienna)

Egon Schiele's work is so distinctive that it resists categorisation. Admitted to the Vienna Academy of Fine Arts at just sixteen, he was an extraordinarily precocious artist, whose consummate skill in the manipulation of line, above all, lent a taut expressivity to all his work. Profoundly convinced of his own significance as an artist, Schiele achieved more in his abruptly curtailed youth than many other artists achieved in a full lifetime. His roots were in the *Jugendstil* of the Viennese Secession movement. Like a whole generation, he came under the overwhelming influence of Vienna's most charismatic and celebrated artist, Gustav Klimt. In turn, Klimt recognised Schiele's outstanding talent and supported the young artist, who within just a couple of years, was already breaking away from his mentor's decorative sensuality.

Beginning with an intense period of creativity around 1910, Schiele embarked on an unflinching exposé of the human form – not the least his own – so penetrating that it is clear he was examining an anatomy more psychological, spiritual and emotional than physical.

He painted many townscapes, landscapes, formal portraits and allegorical subjects, but it was his extremely candid works on paper, which are sometimes overtly erotic, together with his penchant for using under-age models that made Schiele vulnerable to censorious morality. In 1912, he was imprisoned on suspicion of a series of offences including kidnapping, rape and public immorality. The most serious charges (all but that of public immorality) were dropped, but Schiele spent around three despairing weeks in prison.

Expressionist circles in Germany gave a lukewarm reception to Schiele's work. His compatriot, Kokoschka, fared much better there. While he admired the Munich artists of *Der Blaue Reiter*, for example, they rebuffed him. Later, during the First World War, his work became better known and in 1916 he was featured in an issue of the left-wing, Berlin-based Expressionist magazine *Die Aktion*. Schiele was an acquired taste. From an early stage he was regarded as a genius. This won him the support of a small group of long-suffering collectors and admirers but, nonetheless, for several years of his life his finances were precarious. He was often in debt and sometimes he was forced to use cheap materials, painting on brown wrapping paper or cardboard instead of artists' paper or canvas. It was only in 1918 that he enjoyed his first substantial public success in Vienna. Tragically, a short time later, he and his wife Edith were struck down by the massive influenza epidemic of 1918 that had just killed Klimt and millions of other victims, and they died within days of one another. Schiele was just twenty-eight years old.

793. Egon Schiele, 1890-1918, Expressionism, Austrian,
The Poet (Self-Portrait), 1911, Oil on canvas, 80.1 x 79.7 cm, Private collection

This is generally considered to be one of Schiele's early masterpieces and an example of Expressionist portraiture. The title reminds us of Schiele's notion that artistic forms are inter-related. Here he states that the artist is a condemned creature who, by virtue of his true vision of the world, sees more and is, therefore, condemned to suffer more. An unusual feature of this painting is that the genitals appear to be almost hermaphrodite-like, with feminine detail being pierced red violently by a red-tipped phallic image.

This, too, suggests that all artists are as one, whether female or male. It also at sexual ambiguities and cross-gender issues which were both fashionable and slightly outrageous at this time. The notion of the hermaphrodite, however, leads to the idea that Schiele is both a creator of art and a mother of all creation. He is outside the common sexual and social taboos of society and thus aligned his fellow artists, but he also contains within himself an almost mythical force, a super-sexual ability to create and procreate.

Marc Chagall
(1887 Vitebsk – 1985 Saint-Paul-de-Vence)

Marc Chagall was born into a strict Jewish family for whom the ban on representations of the human figure had the weight of dogma. A failure in the entrance examination for the Stieglitz School did not stop Chagall from later joining that famous school founded by the Imperial Society for the Encouragement of the Arts and directed by Nicholas Roerich. Chagall moved to Paris in 1910. The city was his "second Vitebsk". At first, isolated in the little room on the Impasse du Maine at La Ruche, Chagall soon found numerous compatriots also attracted by the prestige of Paris: Lipchitz, Zadkine, Archipenko and Soutine, all of whom were to maintain the "smell" of his native land. From his very arrival Chagall wanted to "discover everything". And to his dazzled eyes painting did indeed reveal itself. Even the most attentive and partial observer is at times unable to distinguish the "Parisian", Chagall from the "Vitebskian". The artist was not full of contradictions, nor was he a split personality, but he always remained different; he looked around and within himself and at the surrounding world, and he used his present thoughts and recollections. He had an utterly poetical mode of thought that enabled him to pursue such a complex course. Chagall was endowed with a sort of stylistic immunity: he enriched himself without destroying anything of his own inner structure. Admiring the works of others he studied them ingenuously, ridding himself of his youthful awkwardness, yet never losing his authenticity for a moment.

At times Chagall seemed to look at the world through magic crystal — overloaded with artistic experimentation — of the *Ecole de Paris*. In such cases he would embark on a subtle and serious play with the various discoveries of the turn of the century and turned his prophetic gaze like that of a biblical youth, to look at himself ironically and thoughtfully in the mirror. Naturally, it totally and uneclectically reflected the painterly discoveries of Cézanne, the delicate inspiration of Modigliani, and the complex surface rhythms recalling the experiments of the early Cubists (*See-Portrait at the Easel*, 1914). Despite the analyses which nowadays illuminate the painter's Judaeo-Russian sources, inherited or borrowed but always sublime, and his formal relationships, there is always some share of mystery in Chagall's art. The mystery perhaps lies in the very nature of his art, in which he uses his experiences and memories. Painting truly is life, and perhaps life is painting.

794. Gino Severini, 1883-1966, Futurism, Italian,
Dynamic Hieroglyphic of the Bal Tabarin, 1912, Oil on canvas with sequins, 161.6 x 156.2 cm, The Museum of Modern Art, New York

Marc Chagall, 1887-1985, Surrealism, Russian born French, *I and the Village*, 1911, Oil on canvas, 191.2 x 150.5 cm, The Museum of Modern Art, New York

In I and the Village, Chagall's compositional logic is hidden behind an apparently improvisational quality. Of course, Chagall was, above all, guided by intuition. It was not natural for him "to verify harmony through algebra". But the harmony he created can, in the final analysis and in the unconsciously achieved result, also be analysed like some sort of rational model. However, his picture is undoubtedly far richer than any such model.

The centre, clearly set off by the intersecting diagonals; the plastic likeness of an hourglass running along the middle vertical of the picture (the motif of time!); the flowers in the lower part of the hourglass and in the upper part the fantastical vision of Vitebsk; the sense of ever greater colouristic tranquillity which results from contemplation of the picture and is achieved by fine colour caesurae between splashes of saturated tones: all these together form a compositional unity.

In such a fantastical picture, where the subject alone does not concentrate the attention of the spectator, the absence of such a unity can be fatal; the canvas could really become a chaotic visual stream, deprived of all harmony, and consequently deprived of full artistic merit. Here we can also sense Chagall's links with the traditions of primitive art, even of the lubok, in which intuitive compositional unity (as in a fairytale or bylina) is natural and essential.

796. **Robert Delaunay**, 1885-1941, Orphism, French, *Tour Eiffel (Eiffel Tower)*, 1911, Oil on canvas, 195.5 x 129 cm, Kunstmuseum, Basle

797. **Natalia Goncharova**, 1881-1962, Rayonism, Russian-French, *The Cyclist*, 1913, Oil on canvas, 78 x 105 cm, The State Russian Museum, St. Petersburg

798. **Amedeo Modigliani**, 1884-1920, Expressionism, Italian, *Caryatide*, 1912, Oil on canvas, 81 x 46 cm, Sogetsu Museum of Art, Tokyo

799

800

801

Ernst Ludwig Kirchner, 1880-1938, Expressionism,
German, *Circus Rider*, 1912, Oil on canvas,
120 x 100 cm, Staatsgalerie Moderne Kunst, Munich

Marcel Duchamp, 1887-1968, Dada, French,
Nude Descending a Staircase (No. 2), 1912,
Oil on canvas, 146.8 x 89.2 cm,
Philadelphia Museum of Art, Philadelphia

Karl Schmidt-Rottluff, 1884-1976,
Expressionism, German, *Pharisees*, 1912,
Oil on canvas, 75.9 x 102.9 cm,
The Museum of Modern Art, New York

802

Giacomo Balla
(1871 Turin – 1958 Rome)

As a child, Giacomo Balla studied music before focusing on painting. Following his studies of academic art in Turin he settled in Rome. In 1912, alongside Fillipo Tomasso Marinetti, Balla was one of the originators of Futurism. He contributed to both the political and ideological bases of the movement, which was particularly involved in the depiction of light and movement. Simultaneously, he attempted to capture the modern age of sound and energy in paintings such as *Automobile and Noise* (1912).

Dynamism of a Dog on a Leash appeared in the same year as Duchamp's *Nude Descending the Staircase* (1912) and revealed his interest for the representation of movement and speed. In the 1930s, his art had moved towards abstraction and eventually returned to academic realism.

802. Giacomo Balla, 1871-1958, Futurism, Italian, *Dynamism of a Dog on a Leash*, 1912, Oil on canvas, 89.9 x 109.9 cm, Albright-Knox Art Gallery, Buffalo

Like other followers of the poet Filippo Tomasso Marinetti at the start of the twentieth century, Balla wanted to give birth to an art praising modern society (Futurism). He was fascinated with expressing movement and energy. The viewer may notice here the animation given to the dog's feet, tail and leash. He and other early Modernists, including Duchamp were also influenced by "chronophotography" that dated back to 1886. He was interested especially in recent advances, such as the motion studies of Etienne-Jules Marey that was then passed on to Frank Gilbreth, a student of Frederick Winslow Taylor, and his campaign to use chronophotography to improve industrial productivity.

803. Egon Schiele, 1890-1918, Expressionism, Austrian, *Agony*, 1912, Oil on canvas, 70 x 80 cm, Neue Pinakothek, Munich

This is an image with deeply religious overtones made explicit by the monk-like attire of the two figures. The precise identity of these figures is not important. What matters is the way that Schiele has used their strangely held poses to create an entirely expressionistic image from a patchwork of linear patterns, colours and shapes. Schiele has used everything he learnt from Klimt and his thesis that decorative patterning is extremely useful for filling empty spaces, and has incorporated this information into the body of the picture itself, bringing the background of the painting right into the foreground and thus merging life with itself. The lines take the viewer both out to the edges of the image and then straight back into its heart. This use of a pattern which stretches from one edge of the image to the other lies in direct contrast to Schiele's specifically religious-themed paintings where the holy images have to hold centre stage in order to emphasise their sanctity.

804. Franz Marc, 1880-1916, Expressionism, German, *Red Deers II*, 1912, Oil on canvas, 70 x 100 cm, Franz Marc Museum, Kochel am See

In Red Deers II of 1912, the painter's concern is no longer primarily with the naturalistic rendition of the deer and their movements. Marc's vision has become much more subjective. The natural subject itself is now more distilled. Incidental details are eliminated in favour of a synthesis of essential elements. In contrast to the naturalistic earth tones of the earlier painting, this work is now a finely tuned composition in colour.

A common misconception about Expressionism is that it simply involved artists spewing forth onto the canvas or page emotional gestures or instinctive impulses. These kinds of outpourings can be found within Expressionism of course. However, works like Marc's Red Deers II was a product of several years of intensive experimentation, theorisation, and reflection on the symbolic properties of colours and their effect in juxtaposition.

805. Georges Braque, 1882-1963, Cubism, French, *Woman with Guitar or Young Girl with Guitar*, 1913, Oil and charcoal on canvas, 130 x 73 cm, Musée National d'Art Moderne, Centre Georges Pompidou, Paris

803

804

805

FRANZ MARC
(1880 Munich – 1916 Verdun)

During his lifetime Franz Marc was widely regarded as one of the most promising German painters of his generation. His death in the First World War was mourned as a bitter loss for the art world. It was also a deep personal loss for his surviving friends, Klee and Kandinsky - his other close friend from the *Der Blaue Reiter* circle, Macke, had died before him on the battlefield. As a young student, Marc had intended to study philosophy and theology. Then, in 1900, he decided to become a painter instead, and registered at the Munich Art academy.

Marc's early work was relatively naturalistic, but it showed evidence of his admiration for van Gogh and Gauguin, whose works he had seen at first hand in Paris. He painted and made some prints and small sculptures. Most of his subjects came from nature. They were landscapes, a few nudes and, increasingly, the animals that would become so central and distinctive in his work. By around 1908 he was starting to intensify his exploration of the movement, behaviour and character of animals. He would spend hours observing and sketching cows and horses in the Bavarian pastures, and watching deer in the wild.

As he matured as an artist, in keeping with Expressionism's tendency to deal in universals – fundamental ethical issues and philosophies – Marc's intellectual concerns were with a future age of "the spiritual" and with the redemptive function of art in the modern society that he and his friends found so shallow and materialistic. Seeking a deeper experience of the ineffable, Marc verbalised it once to his friend Kandinsky: "I want to try to think the thoughts that dance behind a black curtain".

806

807

806. Wasily Kandinsky, 1866-1944, Lyrical Abstraction/ Der Blaue Reiter, Russian
Composition VII, 1913, Oil on canvas, 200 x 300 cm,
The State Tretyakov Gallery, Moscow

This work appeared about the same time as his main writing, On the Spiritu
in Art, albeit the Russian artist had written that book two years before. Short
before that, he was the founding influence on The Blue Rider group (Der Blau
Reiter). While he had not yet given up representational painting entirely at th
time of this series, there is no objective content in it. It is only after he left Russ
in 1922 that intentional geometric shapes appear in his work, as in Accente
Corners (1823). Like Gauguin, he wanted to have a spiritual reservoir fro
which to draw and not to be merely a channel for the beauty of nature.
Distinct from his "Improvisations", more spontaneous works, Kandinsky
"Compositions" are more elaborate. Also the influence of music upo
Kandinsky's work was major. The artist drew a parallel between the use
colours and musical composition, with the same interactions betwee
harmonies and dissonances.

807. Francis Picabia, 1879-1953, Dada/ Orphism, French,
Catch as Catch Can, 1913, Oil on canvas, 100.6 x 81.6 cm,
Philadelphia Museum of Art, Philadelphia

After meeting Marcel Duchamp, Picabia became a master of Orphism an
represented space and movement through fragmented colours.

432

Wasily Kandinsky
(1866 Moscow – 1944 Neuilly-sur-Seine)

Kandinsky's art does not reflect and is not burdened by the fate of other Russian avant-garde masters. He left Russia well before the semi-official Soviet aesthetic turned its back on modernist art.

He had been to Paris and Italy, even giving Impressionism its due in his earliest works. However, it was only in Germany that he aspired to study. It is obvious that in his preference for Munich over Paris, Kandinsky had been thinking more about schools than about artistic milieu. The qualities of salon Impressionism, a hint of the dry rhythms of modernism (*Jugendstil*), a heavy "demiurgic stroke" reminiscent of Cézanne, the occasionally significant echoes of Symbolism and much more can be found in the artist's early works. Kandinsky began working in Murnau in August, 1908. The intensity with which he worked during this period is stunning. In his early Murnau landscapes it is not hard to recognise a Fauvist boiling of colours and an abruptness in their juxtapositioning, the dramatic tension of Expressionism, which was gathering strength at that time, and the insistent texture of Cézanne.

Kandinsky was leaving behind the earthly gravitational field of objects for the weightlessness of the abstract world, where the principal coordinates of being up and down, space and weight are lost. According to the myths of the twentieth century, by leaving reality behind, Kandinsky renounced illusion and, therefore, drew closer to a higher reality. In 1911, Kandinsky participated in the foundation of the group *Der Blaue Reiter* (Blue Rider). Kandinsky had already acquired a name in his Russian homeland. His *On the Spiritual in Art* (1912) was known from lectures and other accounts. When, with the "Improvisations" and "Compositions" of 1915-20, Kandinsky made his final break with the object world, he preserved until the early 1930s the feeling of dynamic, even organic, life in his paintings. In the summer of 1922, Kandinsky began teaching at the Weimar Bauhaus. It was then, in the first Bauhaus years, that he began working on his "Worlds", works in which he quite directly contrasted the grandeur of the great and the small. Kandinsky's fame grew with that of the Bauhaus.

Kandinsky determined the essence of what was happening to him in the context of his environment. On the one hand, the presence of surrealistic overtones in his art is unquestionable. Those splendid carnivals of the subconscious, those "landscapes of the soul," realised in his simultaneously menacing and festive paintings from the 1910s, had already been in partial contact with the poetics of Surrealism.

In Russia he had come to know himself as an artist: Russian motifs and sensations nourished his brush for a long time. In Germany he had become a professional and a great master; a transnational master. In France, where he was already welcomed as a world celebrity, he completed brilliantly and a bit dryly what he had begun in Russia and Germany.

808

808. Pablo Picasso, 1881-1973, Cubism, Spanish,
Violin and Guitar, c. 1912, Oil on canvas, 65.5 x 54.3 cm,
The State Hermitage Museum, St. Petersburg

809. Lovis Corinth, 1858-1925, Impressionism, German,
Walchen Lake, 1912, Oil on canvas, Neue Pinakothek, Munich

809

810

Emil Nolde
(1867 Schleswig-Holstein – 1956 Seebüll)

Emil Nolde was born Emil Hansen. His attachment to the land of the northern German countryside, and especially to the sea, was given philosophical meaning and a kind of portentousness through the filter of the *völkisch* ideas he gleaned from writers such as Julius Langbehn. Nolde often spoke of the struggle for what he called "*das Heimische*" (roughly translated, the "native regional") in art. However, he also knew and loved his northern region from first-hand experience. His paintings of the sea and landscapes of Schleswig-Holstein therefore emerged from close familiarity as well as the vividness of Nolde's imagination.

As an artist, Nolde saw himself as an outsider. Yet his highly coloured, original and richly imaginative work appealed to the much younger *Die Brücke* artists when they saw it. They responded with enthusiasm and revered, in particular, Nolde's "storms of colour". They asked him to become a member of *Die Brücke*, and Nolde exhibited with them in 1906 and 1907. Schmidt-Rottluff came to the Baltic island of Alsen, where Nolde and his wife Ada had made a home, to paint for a few months, but such collaborative projects and group activities did not come naturally to Nolde. From his own copious writings, the image of the artist that emerges, indeed that these texts construct, is that of a lone visionary.

Some of Nolde's most spectacular paintings are seascapes. The sea, especially at times and seasons on the cusp of change – sunset, sunrise, autumn – was an enduring, yet endlessly changing subject. Nolde painted it, without the need for anecdotal detail, in a vast range of moods and weather effects. It has been argued that only Turner before him had ever painted such dramatic and sensitive evocations of the sea. Nolde created a series of thirteen autumn seascapes in 1910 alone. This series continued the following year.

812

813

0. **Emil Nolde**, 1867-1956, Expressionism, German, *Young Men from Papua*, 1913-14, Oil on canvas, 70 x 103.5 cm, Staatliche Museen, Berlin

1. **Ernst Ludwig Kirchner**, 1880-1938, Expressionism, German, *Street, Berlin*, 1913, Oil on canvas, 120.6 x 91.1 cm, The Museum of Modern Art, New York

Part of the Die Brucke group, Kirchner's search for simplified form of expression was strongly influenced by the hectic life in Berlin. His work was considered by the Nazis as "degenerate art". Distressed and overcome by anxiety, he shot himself in 1938.

2. **Juan Gris**, 1887-1927, Cubism, Spanish, *Landscape at Céret*, 1913, Oil on canvas, 92 x 60 cm, Moderna Museet, Stockholm

3. **Roger de La Fresnaye**, 1885-1925, Cubism, French, *The Conquest of the Air*, 1913, Oil on canvas, 235.9 x 195.6 cm, The Museum of Modern Art, New York

814

815

814. Karl Schmidt-Rottluff, 1884-1976, Expressionism, German,
Summer, 1913, Oil on canvas, 88 x 104 cm, Sprengel Museum, Hannover

815. Maurice Utrillo, 1883-1955, Post-Impressionist, French,
La Rue du Mont-Cenis, 1914-15, Oil on canvas, 48 x 63 cm,
Pushkin State Museum of Fine Arts, Moscow

*Born to unwed painter Suzanne Valadon, Utrillo is characterized by a dark
and thick manner. Although his Parisian street scenes were grouped with
the Impressionists, Utrillo is an autodidact and his style can hardly be
categorised. Original in his rendering of space and perspective, he mainly
depicted views of Montmartre in Paris.*

816. David Bomberg, 1890-1957, Abstraction, British,
The Mud Bath, 1914, Oil on canvas, 152.4 x 226.9 cm,
Tate Gallery, London

*Little known and appreciated, Bomberg's reputation is now
excellent, thanks to a major exhibition at the Tate Gallery in 1988.
One of the major artists of London avant-garde, he elaborated
a visual language between Cubism and Futurism, approaching
Abstraction, and expressing his perception of the modern urban
environment.*

817. Juan Gris, 1887-1927, Cubism, Spanish,
Figure of Woman, 1917, Oil on canvas, 116 x 73 cm,
Private collection

818. Sonia Delaunay-Terk, 1895-1979, Orphism, Russian,
*Prose du Transsibérien et de la Petite Jehanne de France
(Prose of the Trans-Siberian and of the Little Jehanne of France)*,
1913, Oil on canvas, 193.5 x 18.5 cm,
Musée National d'Art Moderne, Centre Georges Pompidou, Paris

819

820

819. August Macke, 1887-1914, Expressionism, German, *Girls Under Trees*, 1914, Oil on canvas, 119.5 x 159 cm, Staatsgalerie moderner Kunst, Munich

820. Robert Delaunay, 1885-1941, Orphism, French, *Hommage à Blériot* (Homage to Blériot), 1914, Watercolour on paper, 250.5 x 251.5 cm, Kunstsammlung, Basle

This painting celebrates the first time that Louis Blériot crossed the Channel in 1909. This is a preliminary sketch for a bigger collage displayed in the Kunstmuseum in Basle.

822

823

821. Marsden Hartley, 1877-1943, Semi-Abstraction, American,
Portrait of a German Officer, 1914, Oil on canvas, 173.4 x 105.1 cm,
The Metropolitan Museum of Art, New York

822. Giorgio de Chirico, 1888-1978, Surrealism, Italian, *The Song of Love*, 1914,
Oil on canvas, 73 x 59.1 cm, The Museum of Modern Art, New York

*The artist was one of the signers of the Dada manifesto of 1920. He was born
in Greece of Italian parents in 1888. Not yet twenty years old, he studied
mystical romanticism in Munich, then lived in Milan, Florence and, finally,
Paris, where he met Picasso and Apollinaire. Here, in The Song of Love, we are
cold, distant and surrealistic elements that seem unrelated to each other or to
the title. The artist eventually gave up the metaphysical style, but not before
playing a decisive role in modern art. Describing his landscapes, the artist said:
"Sometimes the horizon is defined by a wall behind which rises the noise of a
disappearing train".*

823. Walter Richard Sickert, 1860-1942, Impressionism, British,
Ennui, 1914, Oil on canvas, 152.4 x 112.4 cm, Tate Gallery, London

*Born in Germany of a Danish-German father and an Anglo-Irish mother, his
family came to England where he became one of the most important British
artists of his time. The author Virginia Woolf imagined a whole story behind
these figures, referring to the man as a pub landlord "looking out of his shrewd
little pig's eyes at the intolerable wastes of desolation in front of him".*

824

Kasimir Malevitch
(1878 Kiev – 1935 Leningrad)

Pioneer of geometric abstract art and one of the most important members of the Russian Avant-garde, Malevitch experimented with various modernist styles. In reaction to the influence of Cubism and Futurism on artists in Russia, Malevitch in his art reduced the world of nature to basic elements and colours, such as in his *Red Square* (1915). He introduced his abstract, non-objective geometric patterns in a style and artistic movement he called Suprematism. One of the important names of the twentieth century, he however turned back to Primitivism once Russia's communist leaders forced him to do so.

824. **Kasimir Malevitch**, 1878-1935, Abstraction/ Suprematism, Russian, *Red Square*, 1915, Oil on canvas, 53 x 53 cm, The State Russian Museum, St. Petersburg

825. **Albert Gleizes**, 1881-1953, Cubism, French, *Brooklyn Bridge*, 1915, Oil on canvas, Private collection

826. **Kasimir Malevitch**, 1878-1935, Abstraction/ Suprematism, Russian, *Suprematist Painting*, 1915, Oil on canvas, 101.5 x 62 cm, Stedelijk Museum, Amsterdam

825

826

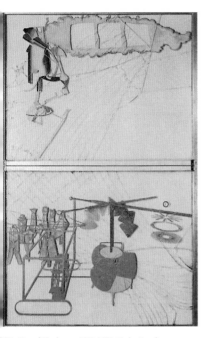

327. Marcel Duchamp, 1887-1968, Dada, French,
The Bride Stripped Bare by her Bachelors, 1915-23,
Oil, varnish, lead foil, lead wire, and dust on two glass
panels, 277.5 x 176 cm, Museum of Art, Philadelphia

328. Francis Picabia, 1879-1953, Dada/Orphism, French,
Very Rare Picture on Earth, 1915, Oil and metallic paint
on board, and silver and gold leaf on wood,
125.7 x 97.8 cm, Peggy Guggenheim Collection, Venice

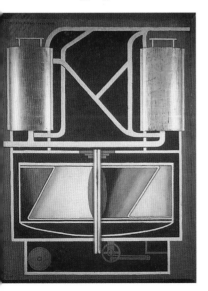

MARCEL DUCHAMP
(1887 Blainville – 1968 Neuilly sur Seine)

Marcel Duchamp came from an artistic family. He lived in Paris, in Montparnasse and studied at the Julian Academy. He and his brother, Raymond, often organised meetings with such artists as Fernand Leger, Francis Picabia, and Robert Delaunay. Eventually, they called themselves the Putteaux group. Duchamp was attracted by Futurism but mainly was influenced by Cubism. His work, either his experiments to Cubism or to Dadaism and Surrealism, definitely change the observer's vision of art. Actually, he seemed to simply find, sign, and display everyday objects, proclaiming them *object d'art*. One such object was a porcelain urinal, which he signed R. Mutt and titled *Fountain* (1917). He mounted a bicycle wheel upside-down on a kitchen stool as one of his "ready-made" artefacts. Duchamp lived also in the United States. His most famous work is *Nude Descending a Staircase #2* (1912) – the centre of attention in the Armory Show of 1913, which was called the most significant exhibition in American art history. This is testimony to the influence of Duchamp's work, and the mark he has left on the art world. As an artist he was in revolt against the established art system and coveted his artistic freedom. In his absurd objects the observer can see his sense of humour and his personal philosophy.

829

829. Kasimir Malevitch, 1878-1935, Abstraction/ Suprematism, Russian,
Suprematist Composition: White on White, 1918, Oil on canvas, 79.4 x 79.4 cm,
The Museum of Modern Art, New York

The Russian artist's most famous work is also his most minimalist. However, three years before he did present a black canvas simply with a white border. The work involves only a few components, breaking each down to a basic quality. The irony of the title is misleading. This is a work of nearly identical entities: the colours are nearly white; the shapes are nearly square; and the areas are nearly on the same plane, albeit at slightly different angles. This may be the logo work of Suprematism, the early twentieth-century movement in Russia interested in reducing painting to geometry, the science that was considered the "supreme" reality. It might then, in effect, be stating that oneness is an illusion.

830

831

Amedeo Modigliani
(1884 Livorno – 1920 Paris)

Amedeo Modigliani was born in Italy in 1884 and died in Paris at the age of thirty-five. From an early age he was interested in nude studies and in the classical notion of ideal beauty. In 1900-1901 he visited Naples, Capri, Amalfi, and Rome, returning by way of Florence and Venice, and studied first-hand many Renaissance masterpieces. He was impressed by *trecento* (thirteenth century) artists, including Simone Martini (c. 1284-1344), whose elongated and serpentine figures, rendered with a delicacy of composition and colour, and suffused with tender sadness, were a precursor to the sinuous line and luminosity evident in the work of Sandro Botticelli (c. 1445-1510). Both artists clearly influenced Modigliani, who used the pose of Botticelli's Venus in *The Birth of Venus* (1482) in his *Standing Nude (Venus)* (1917) and *Red-Haired Young Woman with Chemise* (1918), and a reversal of this pose in *Seated Nude with Necklace* (1917).

Modigliani's debt to the art of the past was transformed by the influence of ancient art (ancient Greek Cycladic figures essentially), the art of other cultures (African for example) and Cubism. Their balanced circles and curves, despite having a voluptuousness, are carefully patterned rather than naturalistic. Their curves are precursors of the swinging lines and geometric approach that Modigliani later used in such nudes as *Reclining Nude*. Modigliani's drawings of caryatids allowed him to explore the decorative potential of poses that may not have been possible to create in sculpture. For his series of nudes, Modigliani took compositions from many well-known nudes of High Art, including those by Giorgione (c. 1477-1510), Titian (c. 1488-1576), Jean-Auguste-Dominique Ingres (1780-1867), and Velázquez (1599-1660), but avoided their romanticisation and elaborate decorativeness. Modigliani was also familiar with the work of Francisco de Goya y Lucientes (1746-1828) and Edouard Manet (1832-1883), who had caused controversy by painting real, individual women as nudes, breaking the artistic conventions of setting nudes in mythological, allegorical, or historical scenes.

832

833

30. Amedeo Modigliani, 1884-1920, Expressionism, Italian,
Reclining Nude, 1917, Oil on canvas, 60 x 92 cm, Collection Gianni Mattioli

Reminiscent of Goya's Naked Maja (1800), this painting bears many of the hallmarks of Modigliani's nude work during the years 1917-19. It is an overtly sexual picture: the model lies on her back, propped up on a cushion, one breast in profile, arms behind her head; the torso is elongated, the pelvis twisted towards the viewer. The legs are cut off around the thigh so that all the emphasis is on the sexual elements of the woman's body. The hair and lips are depicted in some detail and the eyes, although black and blank, look made-up, giving a modern look to the woman's face. The blankness of the eyes effectively depersonalises her so that, although she looks at us provocatively, sexually, there is no expression of her individual personality in the gaze. Modigliani's affinity with sculpture is clear here, inviting us to examine the sheer physicality and mass of the body through the medium of paint.

31. Amedeo Modigliani, 1884-1920, Expressionism, Italian,
Portrait of Chaïm Soutine, 1916, Oil on canvas, 100 x 65 cm, Private collection

832. Egon Schiele, 1890-1918, Expressionism, Austrian,
Sitting Woman with Bent Leg, 1917, Gouache, watercolour and black crayon, 46 x 30.5 cm, Národní Galerie, Prague

833. Amedeo Modigliani, 1884-1920, Expressionism, Italian,
Portrait of Jeanne Hébuterne, 1918, Oil on canvas, 100.3 x 65.4 cm, Norton Simon Art Foundation, Pasadena

There are many different portraits of Jeanne, and they differ enormously in terms of style and mood. Typically, however, she is depicted with extreme elongation of the neck and arms. Here she is shown during her pregnancy, languidly posed upon a chair. The graceful, elegant curves of her arms and neck are almost Baroque in style, and the warm palette of colours suggest, that this may have been painted in the south of France. However, there is little in the portrait to tell us much about Jeanne's character. Her blue eyes are blank and she sits with rather passive elegance, a subject for a painting rather than a person in her own right.

443

834

835

George Grosz
(1893 – Berlin 1959)

George Grosz, who spent much of his childhood in a small town in the German province of Pomerania, was fascinated by big cities. Those that gripped his imagination most were the biggest and most frenetic – above all, Berlin and New York. He made Berlin his home until the rise of Nazism made Germany unbearable, but he dreamt of America, his youthful imagination fired by stories of cowboys and gold-diggers. Grosz's early work, made during the First World War, is his most "Expressionist". His drawings and paintings of alienated individuals, rioting masses, furtive criminals, prostitutes and (very real) brutal mass violence are staged in the streets, tenements and back alleys of Berlin. He also absorbed some of the Italian Futurists' dynamic, energy-laden compositional devices so well suited to conveying the more spectacular effects of modernity – electric lighting, mass transport and the surging movement of urban crowds.

Described by a Dadaist colleague, Hans Richter, as a "savage boxer, fighter and hater," Grosz became a key figure in the Berlin Dada movement. His pugnacious nature, his fearlessly irreverent sense for the absurd, and dark humour were fuel for Dada's political momentum as well as its anti-art stance. These aspects of Grosz, which infuse much of his work, made him resistant to many of the more literary, romantic and utopian aspects of Expressionism.

However, what Grosz undeniably shares with Expressionist contemporaries is a fascinating sensitivity to the intoxicating life-pulse and dynamism of the city. In 1933, to escape Nazi persecution, he emigrated with his wife to America. In 1959 he finally returned to Berlin, only to die barely a month later after a high-spirited night out on the town.

834. George Grosz, 1893-1959, Expressionism, German, *Metropolis*, 1916-17, Oil on canvas, 100 x 102 cm, Thyssen-Bornemisza collection, Lugano

835. Mark Gertler, 1891-1939, Modernism, British, *Merry-Go-Round*, 1916, Oil on canvas, 189.2 x 142.2 cm, Tate Gallery, London

Gertler, a conscientious objector to military service, painted this work at the height of the First World War. The fairground ride becomes here a metaphor of a military machine.
The failure of an exhibition in London at the Lefevre Gallery 1939 caused him acute distress and, overcome by mental anxiety he committed suicide.

836

837

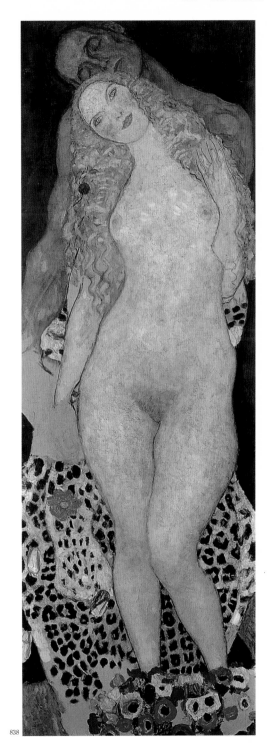

36. Marc Chagall, 1887-1985, Surrealism, Russian, *The Promenade*, 1917,
Oil on canvas, 170 x 163.5 cm, The State Russian Museum, St. Petersburg

The famous Promenade *(1917) is a large canvas, almost square (rare for Chagall), in which two basic colours – green and violet-pink – are boldly combined. Old Vitebsk, emerald-green, magical, is barely recognisable in the refined build up of Cubist syncopated volumes in which Bella, wearing a lilac dress, hovers in the air, holding her husband by the hand so as not to fly away into the heavens. The artist himself smiles like a genial, happy clown who has created both his own happiness and this radiant world. And, as always, the mysterious and imposing painting of the sky, melting in the summer haze and signifying the cosmic elements, peacefully co-exists with purely earthly symbols, the carafe and glass on the red shawl which seems to burn against the green grass. The cosmic quality in Chagall's work grows out of everyday life. For a time the artist seems to forget about dramatic "ends" and "beginnings". Birth becomes only a reason for serene happiness. He completely stops recalling death. Clocks do not beat out fatal time but stop it and do not hurry. The artist is, as before, in a state of unceasing flight.*

37. Wyndham Lewis, 1882-1957, Camden Town Group, British,
A Battery Shelled, 1919, Oil on canvas, 152.5 x 317.5 cm,
Imperial War Museum, London

38. Gustav Klimt, 1862-1918, Art Nouveau, Austrian, *Adam and Eve*, 1917-18,
Oil on canvas, 173 x 60 cm, Österreichische Galerie, Vienna

838

445

839

840

839. Ernst Ludwig Kirchner, 1880-1938, Expressionism, German,
Animals Returning Home, 1919, Oil on canvas, 120 x 167 cm
Collection SWK, Berne

840. Tom Thomson, 1877-1917, Group of Seven (landscape
painter), Canadian, *Jack Pine*, 1917, Oil on canvas,
127.9 x 139.8 cm, National Gallery of Canada, Ottawa

*Tom Thomson is one of the principal founders of the Canadian
school of painting. His life ended tragically when he was
drowned in Algonquin Park. Probably because of the mystery
that surrounds his death, Thomson has become a legend in
Canada.*

841. Paul Klee, 1879-1940, Expressionism, German-Swiss,
Villa R, 1919, Oil on panel, 26 x 22 cm,
Öffentliche Kunstsammlung, Basle

842. Giorgio de Chirico, 1892-1964, Surrealism, Italian,
The Disquieting Muses, 1916,
Oil on canvas, Private collection, Milan

843. Pablo Picasso, 1881-1973, Cubism, Spanish,
Mother and Child, 1921, Oil on canvas, 142 x 172 cm,
The Art Institute of Chicago, Chicago

446

842

843

Ernst Ludwig Kirchner
(1880 Aschaffenburg – 1938 Frauenkirch)

The self-appointed "leader" of the artists' group *Die Brücke* (Bridge), founded in Dresden in 1905, Ernst Ludwig Kirchner was a key figure in the early development of German Expressionism. His first works show the influence of Impressionism, Post-impressionism and *Jugendstil*, but by about 1909, Kirchner was painting in a distinctive, expressive manner with bold, loose brushwork, vibrant and non-naturalistic colours and heightened gestures. He worked in the studio from sketches made very rapidly from life, often from moving figures, from scenes of life out in the city or from the *Die Brücke* group's trips to the countryside. A little later he began making roughly-hewn sculptures from single blocks of wood. Around the time of his move to Berlin, in 1912, Kirchner's style in both painting and his prolific graphic works became more angular, characterized by jagged lines, slender, attenuated forms and often, a greater sense of nervousness. These features can be seen to most powerful effect in his Berlin street scenes. With the outbreak of the First World War, Kirchner became physically weak and prone to anxiety. Conscripted, he was deeply traumatised by his brief experience of military training during the First World War. From 1917 until his death by suicide in 1938, he lived a reclusive, though artistically productive life in the tranquillity of the Swiss Alps, near Davos.

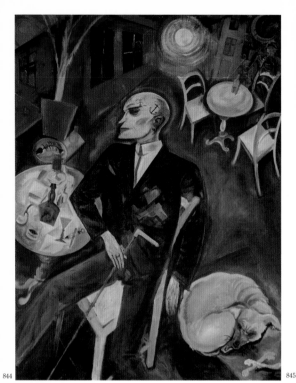

844. George Grosz, 1893-1959, Expressionism, German,
Lovesick, 1916, Oil on canvas, 100 x 78 cm,
Kunstsammlung Nordrhein-Westfalen, Dusseldorf

*In a period of reprise from army service which he so hated,
in a canvas reeking of Gothic melodrama, Grosz painted a
gaunt and deathly pale figure. Loosely based on his ill-
nourished wartime self, Grosz called it Liebeskranker
(Lovesick). The palette is that of cold, moon lit, gangrenous,
black-and-blue night, and congealed blood. The figure is
one of Grosz's alter-ego types – an adventurer dandy. His
bearing and silver-handled cane mark him as an aristocratic
rogue. The anchor tattoo on his skull and gold earring show
him as a rootless, pirate figure of the high seas. The
crossbones before the dog curled up on the ground are the
pirate pendent to the figure's white skull. At the centre of the
composition is the pistol and blood-red heart beating at his
breast. Morbidly, they suggest a crime of passion –
committed (murder?), or yet being contemplated (suicide?).
The accessories for intoxication litter the table – drink and
drugs. Grosz was a heavy and enthusiastic drinker.*

*The exaggeratedly steep, angular perspective and lack of
horizon is typical of many Expressionist visualisations of
urban space. Equally striking here, is the way that Grosz
elides the distinction between outside and inside, exterior
and interior space. In this nocturne, Grosz collapses the
objects and ambience of a café interior into the architecture
of the street, so that a disorientation – the visual equivalent
of the subject queasy intoxication by love and liquor –
ensues. We cannot know if the glowing white orb is the
moon, a night-club spot or the beam of a search-light. Are
we looking in or out of the walls and windows?*

845. Otto Dix, 1891-1969, Expressionism, German,
Prager Street, 1920, Oil and collage on canvas, 100 x 80 cm,
Galerie der Stadt, Stuttgart

Otto Dix
(1891 Untermhaus – 1969 Singen)

Dix was born near Gera but gained his first experience and training in art in the venera[ble]
Baroque city of Dresden. He would return there in 1927 to take up a position as profes[sor]
at the Academy. However, Dix's first important work was produced in the midst of [the]
violence of the First World War.

Slightly younger than the original Expressionists, he had a long and prolific career in wh[ich]
his work went through significant changes. Loosely, these changes followed the
developments in the German avant-garde, from Expressionism to Dada and then, from ab[out]
1923, the so-called *Neue Sachlichkeit* (New Objectivity). However, Dix's work was so va[ried]
that it cannot easily be reduced to simple formulae. Although he was one of German[y's]
foremost modern artists, underlying much of his best work, especially from the mid-1920s [on]
was a close engagement with the Old German Masters – Cranach, Dürer and Baldung Gr[ien].

When the war was over, Dix became involved in Expressionist and socialist circles s[uch]
as the Berlin-based *Novembergruppe* and another group in Dresden, which also included [the]
precociously gifted Felixmüller. Dix described himself many times as a "realist". In his spe[ech]
and behaviour he was blunt and had little time for idealistic dreams of revolution. *Pra[ger]
Street* was one of Dix's most innovative and memorable responses to the aftermath of w[ar].
As with his group of crippled war veterans playing cards of the same year, Dix used the bl[unt]
juxtaposition of artificial materials, fragments of everyday objects and oil paint to reconst[ruct]
a chaotic reality of broken bodies and alienated modernity.

By the time Dix became a professor at the Dresden Academy, he was working with meth[ods]
and materials more commonly associated with the Old Masters of the sixteenth century. [The]
Großstadt (Metropolis) triptych of 1928 was prepared with infinite care and intended a[s a]
modern masterpiece. By this time, Dix had eschewed Expressionism. Nonetheless, the table[au]
of sex in the city, based on the glitter and the squalor of Berlin, with its pungent juxtaposit[ion]
of Eros and death, continues the themes that had preoccupied Dix almost from the start.

847. Giorgio Morandi, 1890-1964, Metaphysical painting, Italian,
Still-Life, 1920, Oil on canvas, 60.5 x 66.5 cm, Private collection, Milan

846. Fernand Léger, 1881-1955, Cubism/ Purism, French, *The City*, 1919,
Oil on canvas, 230.5 x 297.7 cm, Philadelphia Museum of Art, Philadelphia

In this work the French futurist Leger expresses his optimistic trust in the young twentieth century's machine age. He sees conformity as a solution for individuals losing themselves in an idealised Communist system to which he subscribed. In his future city there is a colourful harmony between clean machines and clear communications, all blended without confusion within a variety of popular expressions as seen in the busy metropolis of the future. Ironically, two robotic, faceless comrades on a staircase walk through the maze of hard-edged realities of the city seen as a colourful but ultimately confusing montage. While this is a mid-life expression for the artist, he would eventually favour only three primary colours and show even more simple designs.

848. Egon Schiele, 1890-1918, Expressionism, Austrian, *Embrace (Lovers II)*, 1917,
Oil on canvas, 100 x 70 cm, Österreichische Galerie, Vienna

This is one of Schiele's best known works and a culmination of his new, semi-classical style. The couple lie together affectionately grasping each other and the artist kisses his wife on the ear. At last, he is able to celebrate a union of two people as one harmonious whole. The lines are smooth; the hair of both heads is joined without distinction; the feet disappear into a single conjoined line. The male and female forms seem to hold each other equally and no one is watching or aware of being watched. The sheet is still crumpled but this is now a modest device to cover the female's genitalia, rather than to expose the brutal animal truth. This is not a pornographic painting but a real image of love. It is as if Schiele is no longer hypnotically enthralled by a juvenile idea of sex and is now focused on actually learning to enjoy his relationship with his wife, Edith. They are two contented people within marriage and, unlike in former works, they are not actually having sex but are locked in a mutually loving embrace.

449

849

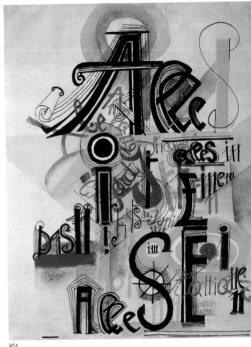

851

850

849. **Wasily Kandinsky**, 1866-1944, Lyrical Abstraction/ Der Blaue Reiter, Rus
Blue Circle, 1922, Oil on canvas, 110 x 100 cm, Guggenheim Museum,
New York

850. **Max Ernst**, 1891-1976, Surrealism, French, German-born,
Celebes, 1921, Oil on canvas, 125.4 x 107.9 cm, Tate Gallery, London

*Ernst, leader of the Dada movement in Cologne, took his inspiration
Sudanese corn-bin for the subject of this painting. The work's title comes
a childish German rhyme that begins: 'The elephant from Celebes has s
yellow bottom grease...' This painting still testifies to the influence e
Chirico (the figure crowning the two-legged monster) as well as annou
Surrealism.*

851. **Johannes Itten**, 1888-1967, Bauhaus, Swiss, *All in One*, 1922,
Ink and watercolour on paper, 29 x 33 cm, Private collection

853

854

852. Maurice Utrillo, 1883-1955, Post-Impressionist, French,
Le Moulin de la Galette, 1922, Oil on canvas, 106 x 81 cm,
Musée d'Art Moderne et Contemporain, Liège

853. Lovis Corinth, 1858-1925, Expressionism, German, *The Red Christ*, 1922,
Oil on canvas, 129 x 108 cm, Neue Pinakothek, Munich

854. Stuart Davis, 1894-1964, Abstraction, American, *Odol*, 1924,
Oil on canvas, 61 x 45.7 cm, The Museum of Modern Art, New York

*Davis led American artists to French Cubism and developed with them the
Abstract Formalism that would become Pop Art. He started with his
participation in the 1913 Armory Show in New York. His Influence then
continued for the next fifty years with many deceptively simple works, such
as Odol. What the product Odol is or does is less important than the medium
that displays it. Marshall McLuhan's maxim, "the medium is the message", is
illustrated with transparent honesty even as there is a typical Madison
Avenue dishonesty or lack of transparency about just what the product is or
does. Such art can point to the driving energy for commercialisation through
art/advertisement to create new needs, rather than satisfy existing needs. The
viewer/customer adjusts his frame of reference to fit the product through
which he sees his orderly checkerboard world. The packaging of the painting
as well as the product within it is functional, even if the actual purpose is not
disclosed. Warhol will later move such artefacts even closer to the product
by presenting only the label or package over and over again.*

855

855. **Chaïm Soutine**, 1893-1943, Expressionism, Lithuanian-born, settled in France,
   Maxim's Groom, 1925, Oil on canvas, 81.9 x 74.9 cm, Private collection

   *Soutine is mostly influenced by Modigliani in his portraits. But he remained
   unsuccessful until he was discovered by the great American collector, Dr. Albert
   C. Barnes, in 1923. He then painted a series of portraits, distinctive through the
   use of colours: white for the bakers, white and red for the hunters (the attributed
   title to this work is* The Hunter*).*

856. **Paul Klee**, 1879-1940, Expressionism, German-Swiss,
   The Goldfish, 1925, Oil and watercolour on paper, mounted on cardboard,
   50 x 69 cm, Kunsthalle, Hamburg

857. **Oskar Schlemmer**, 1888-1943, Bauhaus, German, *Concentri*
   Group, 1925, Oil on canvas, 98 x 62 cm, Staatsgalerie, Stuttga

858. **Joan Miró**, 1893-1983, Surrealism, Spanish,
   Harlequin's Carnival, 1924-5, Oil on canvas, 66 x 93 cm,
   Albright-Knox Art Gallery, Buffalo

   *André Breton stated: " Miró was probably the most Surrealistic of u
   In 1975, a foundation, close to Barcelona, was dedicated to his v*

856

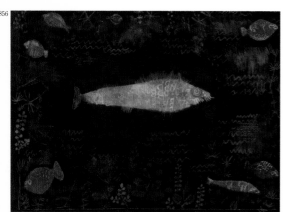

Max Beckmann
(1884 Leipzig – 1950 New York)

As a student in the centre of Germany's Enlightenment, Weimar, Beckmann read avidly the works of Schopenhauer and became interested in Kant, Hegel and Nietzsche. Having graduated in 1903, he painted his early canvases in Paris. He was particularly impressed by Cézanne. Beckmann's own early work was in a broadly impressionist mode and could sometimes be quite traditional in its composition and treatment of historical or monumental subjects. Beckmann retained through his life an instinctive feel for the art of the past, gravitating towards images and epochs in which he saw powerful and simple expression. As his own distinctive style developed, this took the form especially of a creative engagement with the art of the Middle Ages and the Northern Renaissance. Beckmann remained aloof from Expressionism's core groupings and the impassioned programmes they issued. In many ways he was never a true "Expressionist". However, his work between the war years, especially the mid-1920s, constitutes a major contribution to avant-garde German art and to the development, and the decline, of Expressionism.

Beckmann made few public statements about his work, preferring to confine his expression to painting. Precisely because of the scarcity of testimony from the artist, his rare statements, in the form of a "*schöpferische Konfession*" or "creative credo", written in 1918 and published in 1920 by the writer Kasimir Edschmid, has become a central document: "I believe that I particularly love painting so much because it forces one to be objective. There is nothing I hate more than sentimentality. The stronger and more intensive my determination to grasp the unutterable things of the world grows, the deeper and more powerful the emotion about our existence burns in me, the tighter I keep my mouth shut, the colder my will becomes, to capture this monster of vitality and to confine it, to beat it down and to strangle it with crystal-clear, sharp lines and planes. I do not weep, tears are despicable to me and signs of slavery. I always think of the thing".

859

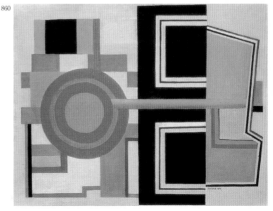

860

859. Max Beckmann, 1884-1950, Expressionism, German, *The Dream*, 1921, Oil on canvas, 182 x 91 cm, Saint Louis Art Museum, St Louis

Painted in 1921, Der Traum, (The Dream) contains many iconographic and compositional elements that were already or would become established in Beckmann's distinctive work: figures crowded into an ambiguous interior, musical instruments and devices, the jester's collar, ambivalent physical postures and gestures, fragments of signage, and the fish. The zig-zag composition draws on the steep, subjective pictorial space and angularity of forms found in Gothic art. In a detailed compositional analysis of the painting in 1924, the critic Wilhelm Fraenger compared Beckmann's consummate ability to order organically the fullness of churning movement in his picture with the old Flemish master Pieter Bruegel's powers of organisation over the forms of tumult. Beckmann himself once spoke of the "mixture of somnambulism and terrible lightness of consciousness" in his art.

860. Fernand Léger, 1881-1955, Cubism/ Purism, French, *Composition*, 1924, Oil on canvas, 73 x 92 cm, The State Hermitage Museum, St. Petersburg

861

863

862

Salvador Dalí
(1904 – 1989 Figueras)

Painter, designer, creator of bizarre objects, author and film maker,
Dalí became the most famous of the Surrealists.

Buñuel, Lorca, Picasso and Breton all had a great influence on
his career. Dalí's film, *An Andalusian Dog*, produced with Buñuel,
marked his official entry into the tightly-knit group of Parisian
Surrealists, where he met Gala, the woman who became his lifelong
companion and his source of inspiration. But his relationship soon
deteriorated until his final rift with André Breton in 1939.
Nevertheless Dalí's art remained surrealist in its philosophy and
expression and a prime example of his freshness, humour and
exploration of the subconscious mind. Throughout his life, Dalí was
a genius at self-promotion, creating and maintaining his reputation
as a mythical figure.

861. Otto Dix, 1891-1969, Expressionism, German, *Portrait of the Journalist
Sylvia von Harden*, 1926, Mixed medium on wood, 121 x 89 cm,
Musée National d'Art Moderne, Centre Georges Pompidou, Paris

*In the 1920s, it was Dix's reputation as a portraitist that secured him the most
success and financial gain. His razor-sharp painting of this ultramodern
woman, with a whiff of decay about her, is exemplary of his best works in the
unflinching style of so-called* Neue Sachlichkeit *(New Objectivity).*

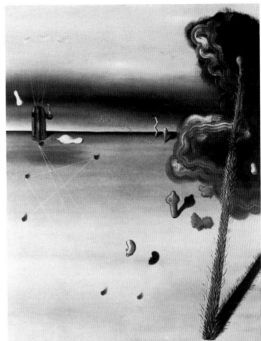
865

866
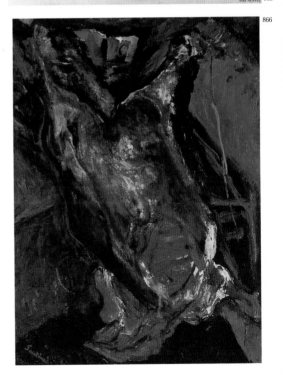

862. Hans Arp, 1886-1966, Dada, French,
Clock, 1924, Painted Wood, Private collection

863. Salvador Dalí, 1904-1989, Surrealism, Spanish,
Woman at the Window, 1925, Oil on canvas, 103 x 75 cm,
Museo Nacional Centro de Arte Reina Sofia, Madrid

864. Lyonel Feininger, 1871-1956, Cubism, American,
Gelmeroda IX, 1926, Oil on canvas, 108 x 80 cm, Museum Folkwang, Essen

The Bauhaus school, founded in 1919, influenced painting as well as architecture, directing it to be closer to Cubism than to the radically abstract. Feininger taught at the Bauhaus right from the beginning, although he was an American citizen. He expressed the challenge in romantic and colourful works that show the Cubist respect for basic shapes, yet find a decorative rendering. He brought to the German school warmth that some found otherwise especially lacking in the pragmatism of Bauhaus architecture. Klee and Kandinsky joined Feininger in teaching, probably more to influence the school than to be influenced by it.

865. Yves Tanguy, 1900-1955, Surrealism, French-born, American,
Mama, Papa is Wounded!, 1927, Oil on canvas, 92.1 x 73 cm,
The Museum of Modern Art, New York

866. Chaïm Soutine, 1893-1943, Expressionism, Lithuanian-born, settled in
France, *Slaughtered Ox*, c. 1925, Oil on canvas, 166.1 x 114.9 cm,
Albright-Knox Art Gallery, Buffalo

867

869

868

870

871

872

Raoul Dufy
(1877 Le Havre – 1953 Forcalquier)

Raoul Dufy was born in Le Havre, France, in 1877. He attended the evening classes at the school of Fine Arts where he developed his innate gift for drawing. At the beginning of his career he was significantly influenced by the Fauve movement and his colourful works with bold contours reflect this approach. After a brief phase with Cubism, he enjoyed painting flowers, fashionable tennis courts, views of the French Riviera and elegant parties. In 1938, Dufy created one of the largest frescos in the world, *La Fée Electricité*.

867. **George Grosz**, 1893-1959, Expressionism, German, *The Agitator*, 1928, Oil on canvas, 108 x 81 cm, Stedelijk Museum, Amsterdam

868. **Georgia O'Keeffe**, 1887-1986, Modernism, American, *Jack-in-the-Pulpit n° V*, 1930, Oil on canvas, 122 x 76.2 cm, The National Gallery of Art, Washington, D.C.

In Madison High School the school's art teacher gave Georgia her first insight into the mysteries and detail of the Jack-In-The-Pulpit flower. In her autobiography, O'Keeffe says: "I had seen many Jacks before, but this was the first time I remember examining a flower… I was a little annoyed at being interested because I did not like the teacher… But maybe she started me looking at things – looking very carefully at details".

869. **Kurt Schwitters**, 1887-1949, Dada, German, *Maraak, Variation I*, 1930, Oil and assemblage on cardboard, 46 x 37 cm, Peggy Guggenheim Collection, Venice

870. **Kasimir Malevitch**, 1878-1935, Abstraction/ Suprematism, Russian, *Two Peasants in the Field*, 1928-1932, Oil on canvas, 53.5 x 70 cm, The State Russian Museum, St. Petersburg

871. **Raoul Dufy**, 1877-1953, Fauvism, French, *The Paddock*, 1926, Oil on canvas, 81 x 125 cm, Private collection

872. **John Steuart Curry**, 1897-1946, Regionalism, American, *Baptism in Kansas*, 1928, Oil on canvas, Whitney Museum of American Art, New York

874

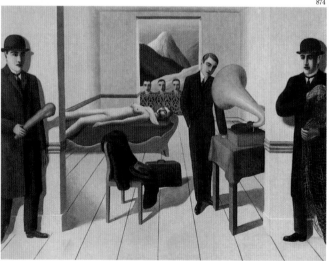

873. Salvador Dalí, 1904-1989, Surrealism, Spanish,
The Great Masturbator, 1929, Oil on canvas, 110 x 150 cm
Museo Nacional Centro de Arte Reina Sofia, Madrid

874. René Magritte, 1898-1967, Surrealism, Belgian,
The Menacing Assassin, 1927, Oil on canvas, 150.4 x 195.
The Museum of Modern Art, New York

Magritte was probably one of the most powerful Surrealist pa
whose disturbing combinations of the erotic, strange, extraor
and ordinary always surprise. Here this scene combines ero
and sadism in the surrealist provocative tradition of repres
positive aspects of horror scenes.

875. Lyonel Feininger, 1871-1956, Cubism, American, *Sailing*
1929, Oil on canvas, 43 x 72 cm, The Institute of Art, Detro

876. Edward Hopper, 1882-1967, Realism, American,
The Lighthouse at Two Lights, 1929, Oil on canvas,
74.9 x 109.9 cm, The Metropolitan Museum of Art, New Yo

JOAN MIRÓ
(1893 BARCELONA – 1983 PALMA DE MALLORCA)

Joan Miró was born in a room with stars painted on the ceiling. He grew up in the city of Barcelona, where rugged independence and creativity go hand in hand. In 1907, he enrolled in art classes at La Escuela de la Lonja, an academic and professionally oriented school of applied arts where a young man named Picasso had impressed the teachers ten years earlier. Then he entered Gali's private classes. Unlike the Lonja School, it offered a setting where Miró's distinctive ways of seeing were rewarded. At Gali's academy, Miró met some of the men who would become not only fellow artists but intimate friends. He and Enric Cristòfol Ricart soon rented a studio together near the Barcelona Cathedral. Later identified as a Surrealist, Miró never really espoused any school or established style of art. "It was clear in his mind," as one critic has put it, "that he had to go beyond all categories and invent an idiom that would express his origins and be authentically his own". Over the course of his career, he even worked hard not to follow his own traditions. Clearly Miró had studied Cubism's broken forms and had learned to admire the strident colours of the Fauves. But he had an eye of his own, and his paintings combined twisted perspectives, heavy brushwork, and surprises in colour. He was finding ways to merge the stylish two-dimensionality of the times with inspirations taken from Catalan folk art and Romanesque church frescos. Joan Miró began to recognise that, like Picasso, if he was going to become an artist in earnest, he needed to move to Paris. For a while he rented a studio at 45 rue Blomet, next door to the painter André Masson. Masson was just the first link in an entire community of artists with which Miró found a home, just as they were beginning to coalesce in the movement of art and sensibility they called "Surrealism". It was a movement of thought that at once extolled the individual and the imagination and at the same time flaunted tradition, rationality, and even common sense. Influenced by the practitioners of surrealism, Miró never really joined their ranks. The joyful freedom espoused by the Dadaists was more to his liking than the manifestos and dogma of the Surrealists. His naïve originality drew the attention and admiration of them all, however, and he was soon the favoured illustrator for the magazine *La Révolution Surréaliste*.

In his last years, Joan Miró spoke to his grandson of his lifelong love of Catalonian folk art - the natural forms, the independent spirit, the naiveté that is both beautiful and surprising. "Folk art never fails to move me," he said. "It is free of deception and artifice. It goes straight to the heart of things". In speaking of the art from the countryside that had nourished him, Joan Miró found the best words to describe himself. With his honesty, spontaneity, and childlike enthusiasm for shape, texture, and colour, he created a universe of artworks sure to delight, puzzle, and reward.

878

877. Joan Miró, 1893-1983, Surrealism, Spanish, *Dutch Interior I*, 1928, Oil on canvas, 91.8 x 73 cm, The Museum of Modern Art, New York

After travels to Belgium and Holland, Miró embarked on a fascinating series of paintings that he called Dutch Interiors – distinctively Miróesque reinterpretations of the Dutch masters, guided by museum postcards he brought home. Pencil studies show how he transformed the realistic paintings into fantastical cartoons of their underlying structures, while the final paintings reflect his characteristic transformation of a shaded world into large, flat shapes of bright, bold colour. The counterpoint between realism and fantasy continues throughout the career of Joan Miró – it is the genius of his art, which makes it both accessible and mysterious.

878. André Masson, 1896-1987, Surrealism, French, *The Maze*, 1928, Oil on canvas, 120 x 61 cm, Musée National d'Art Moderne, Centre Georges Pompidou, Paris

879

880

879. Grant Wood, 1891-1942, Regionalism, American, *American Gothic*, 1930,
Oil on beaverboard, 78 x 65.3 cm, The Art Institute of Chicago, Chicago

Although the American artist Wood was from the mid-western state of Iowa, hi
studio was in the eastern state of Connecticut. When this, by far his most famou
work, was first seen by the residents of Iowa, some of them were offended, thinkin
the work was ridiculing their simple ways and the typically plain appearance o
authentic country folk. Wood explained that the elongated faces (mirrored in th
cameo and pitchfork) modelled by his sister and his dentist, were shaped to carry ou
the vertical theme of the American Gothic *farmhouse in a realistic style. The Woo*
work became and remains one of the most popular of all paintings by an American

880. Georges Rouault, 1871-1958, Expressionism, French, *The Holy Face (Christ)*,
1933, Oil and gouache on paper mounted on canvas, 91 x 65 cm,
Musée National d'Art Moderne, Centre Georges Pompidou, Paris

881. Tamara de Lempicka, 1898-1980, Art Deco, Polish-Russian, *Self-portrait*
(Tamara in the Green Bugatti), 1929, Oil on wood, 35 x 27 cm, Private collection

Over the past quarter century this has become a very famous and widely reproduce
picture. It is not a portrait in the sense of being a likeness of an individual woman.
is unlikely that anyone would have recognised de Lempicka in the street from th
highly stylised image. It is more a portrait of an era and in particular of a type o
woman who came to the fore in that era.

By the drastic means of slaughtering a generation of young men the First Worl
War probably did more for the advancement and emancipation of women than an
event in history. In the "Roaring Twenties" the ultimate symbol of femal
emancipation for those who could afford it was an automobile. De Lempicka's ow
account of how she picked up the beautiful Rafaela in the Bois de Boulogne an
drove her back to her studio is an example of how useful the motor car could be a
an aid to sexual independence.

883

882. Thomas Hart Benton, 1889-1975, Regionalism, American, *City Activities*, 1930-31, Egg Tempera on wood, 19.6 x 66.2 cm, New School of Social Research, New York

883. Diego Rivera, 1886-1957, Social Realism, Mexican, *Detroit Industry*, north wall, 1932, Fresco, Detroit Institute of Art, Detroit

After getting around the Impressionists and Divisionists, Rivera is attracted by Synthetic Cubism such as the one practised by Juan Gris. During a journey in Italy in 1920-1921, he discovered the frescos by Giotto and adopted the technique of monumental decoration with a borrowing of pre-columbian elements. Rivera was commissioned by Edsel Ford, president of the Arts Commission as well as of Ford Motor Company, and Dr. William Valentiner, director of the DIA, to create two murals for the museum in its Garden Court.

885

884

884. Salvador Dalí, 1904-1989, Surrealism, Spanish, *The Persistance of Memory*, 1931,
Oil on canvas, 24.1 x 33 cm, The Museum of Modern Art, New York

*Dalí discusses the genesis of the painting in his autobiography. He writes, "Having
concluded our dinner with a very strong Camembert and after the others had gone, I
remained sitting quietly at the table for a long time considering the philosophical problem
of "Super-Softs" that the cheese had brought to my attention. I stood up, went into my
atelier and turned on the light to take one last look at the picture I was presently working
on, as was my habit. This picture depicts the landscape at Port Lligat; the cliffs lie in a
transparent, melancholy dusk light and an olive-tree with severed branches devoid of
leaves stands in the foreground. I knew that the atmosphere which I had been able to create
with this landscape was the background for an idea that would serve to create a surprising
picture but I didn't know in the slightest what it would be. I was just about to turn off the
light when I suddenly 'saw' the answer. I saw two melting watches, one hanging
pathetically over the branch of the olive-tree. Although my headache had become so
strong that I was suffering, I readied my palette impatiently and got down to work".*

885. René Magritte, 1898-1967, Surrealism, Belgian,
Red Model, 1935, Oil on canvas mounted on cardboard, 56 x 46 cm,
Musée National d'Art Moderne, Centre Georges Pompidou, Paris

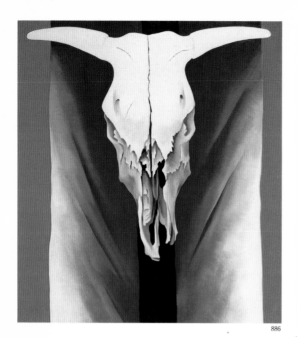

GEORGIA O'KEEFFE
(1887 SUN PRAIRIE, WISCONSIN – 1986 SANTA FE)

In 1905 Georgia travelled to Chicago to study painting at the Art Institute of Chicago. In 1907 she enrolled at the Art Students' League in New York City, where she studied with William Merritt Chase. During her time in New York she became familiar with the 291 Gallery owned by her future husband, photographer Alfred Stieglitz. In 1912, she and her sisters studied at university with Alon Bement, who employed a somewhat revolutionary method in art instruction originally conceived by Arthur Wesley Dow. In Bement's class, the students did not mechanically copy nature, but instead were taught the principles of design using geometric shapes. They worked at exercises that included dividing a square, working within a circle and placing a rectangle around a drawing, then organising the composition by rearranging, adding or eliminating elements. It sounded dull and to most students it was. But Georgia found that these studies gave art its structure and helped her understand the basics of abstraction.

During the 1920s O'Keeffe also produced a huge number of landscapes and botanical studies during annual trips to Lake George. With Stieglitz's connections in the arts community of New York – from 1923 he organised an O'Keeffe exhibition annually – O'Keeffe's work received a great deal of attention and commanded high prices. She, however, resented the sexual connotations people attached to her paintings, especially during the 1920s when Freudian theories became a form of what today might be termed "pop psychology". The legacy she left behind is a unique vision that translates the complexity of nature into simple shapes for us to explore and make our own discoveries. She taught us there is poetry in nature and beauty in geometry. Georgia O'Keeffe's long lifetime of work shows us new ways to see the world, from her eyes to ours.

886. Georgia O'Keeffe, 1887-1986, Modernism, American, *Red, White and Blue*, 19 Oil on canvas, 101.3 x 91.1 cm, The Metropolitan Museum of Art, New York

With her Red, White and Blue, *Georgia O'Keeffe wanted to call people's attent... to the country she loved by adding the red stripes on either side. But while brilliant red, white and blue background is distracting, the eye is still drawn to lacelike edges of the fragments where the bone has worn away. There is a life facet to the tiny staring "eye holes" giving the skull a macabre quality.*

887. Stanley Spencer, 1891-1959, Late Pre-Raphaelite, British, *St Francis and the Birds*, 1935, Oil on canvas, 66 x 58.4 cm, Tate Gallery, London

St Francis of Assisi, the founder of the Franciscans (here shown as an old man popularly known for his ability to talk to birds, and pray with them. Stanley Sper intended to exhibit this work in his ideal gallery, called 'Church House', but it never built.

888. Diego Rivera, 1886-1957, Social Realism, Mexican, *Mexico Today and Tomorrow*, 1935, Fresco, 7.49 x 8.85 m, National Palace, Mexico City

889

890

889. Raoul Dufy, 1877-1953, Fauvism, French, *The Spirit of Electricity*, 1937, Oil on wood, 10 x 60 cm (panel), Musée d'Art Moderne de la ville de Paris, Paris

890. Max Ernst, 1891-1976, Surrealism, French, German-born, *The Entire City*, 1936, Oil on canvas, 97 x 145 cm, Kunsthaus, Zurich

891

892

THOMAS HART BENTON
(1889 Neosho, Missouri – 1975 Kansas City)

Thomas Hart Benton refused to follow a political career, as his father and grandfather had done, and studied, instead, at the Art Institute School of Chicago. After studying in Paris, where he was interested in Impressionism and Pointillism, he rejected European influences and became a regionalist. His work idealised the traditional American rural world. Leader of "The American Scene," he was the teacher of the brothers Charles and Jackson Pollock at the Art Students' League, and friend of the latter throughout life. He is known almost entirely for his murals, especially those at the New School for Social Research of New York.

893

894

894. Roland Penrose, 1900-1984, Surrealism, British, *Winged Domino*, 1938,
Oil on canvas, 60 x 46 cm, Penrose Collection, Chiddingly

891. Thomas Hart Benton, 1889-1975, Regionalism, American,
Cradling Wheat, 1938, Tempera and oil on wood,
78.7 x 96.5 cm, Saint Louis Art Musem, St Louis

892. Otto Dix, 1891-1969, Expressionism, German,
Metropolis, 1938, Mixed medium on wood, 181 x 101 cm,
Staatliche Museen, Berlin

893. Pablo Picasso, 1881-1973, Cubism, Spanish,
Portrait of Marie-Thérèse Walter, 1937,
Oil on canvas, 100 x 81 cm, Musée Picasso, Paris

895. Frida Kahlo, 1907-54, Surrealism, Mexican,
The Two Fridas, 1939, Oil on canvas, 170.2 x 170.2 cm,
Museo de Arte Moderno, Mexico City

895

The six-foot square The Two Fridas would become Frida
Kahlo's signature masterpiece. A mirror had long played a
central role in her paintings, at first from necessity due to her
bed-ridden state. Later, the mirror became a reflection of
reality that could be manipulated and translated into a fantasy
vision of her very personal verité. In The Two Fridas, the
mirror duality becomes a schizophrenic visualisation of
Frida's personal dilemma, the European woman (Frida) in
white with lace and appliqués befitting a chaste Catholic girl,
and the Tehuana woman of darker skin and colourful costume
– the earthy peasant persona encouraged by Diego Rivera.
Both hearts are exposed and a vine-like blood vessel connects
a small amulet that is a miniature portrait of Diego as a child.
The two hearts are the "Fridas". The European "Frida's" heart
is ripped and savaged while she grips the end of the shared
artery with a surgical clamp. But blood still drips from its end
onto her snow white dress.

471

896

897

Paul Klee was born in 1879, in München buchsee, Switzerland, and grew up within a family of musicians. Instead of following his musical roots he chose to study art at the Munich Academy. However, his childhood love of music always remained important in his life and work.

In 1911 Klee met Alexej Jawlensky, Wasily Kandinsky, August Macke, Franz Marc, and other avant-garde figures and participated in important shows of avant-garde art, including the second Blaue Reiter exhibition at Galerie Hans Goltz, Munich, in 1912.

Klee was difficult to classify as an artist as he did not associate himself with a particular movement. His works were best known for their satirical themes and representation of fantasy and dreams. Primitive art, Surrealism and Cubism, all seem blended into his small-scale, delicate paintings. Klee's art was also distinguished by an extraordinary diversity and technical innovation with one of his most effective techniques being oil transfer. This involved the artist drawing with a sharp point on the reverse of a sheet coated in oil paint and laid down over another sheet. Markings and smudges of pigment appeared as a side-effect of the process but it meant Klee achieved, for many of his works, the effect of a "ghostly" impression. One of Klee's most popular paintings today is *Der Goldfisch* (The Goldfish), (1925) in which a luminescent fish glows brightly in suspension in an aquatic netherworld. Klee was a teacher at the Bauhaus, Germany's most advanced art school, from 1920 to 1931 and immensely productive. Finally, the seizure of power by the National Socialists drove him and his wife to leave Germany for his native Switzerland. Klee's later works, in which simplified, archaic forms dominate, show a preoccupation with mortality. Klee died in 1940, after a long period of illness.

896. Paul Klee, 1879-1940, Expressionism/Blaue Reiter, German-Swiss, *New Harmony*, 1936, Oil on canvas, 92.7 x 66 cm, Guggenheim Museum, New York

898

7. **Stuart Davis**, 1894-1964, Cubism, American,
Swing Landscape, 1938, Oil on canvas, 217 x 440 cm,
Indiana University Art Museum, Bloomington

3. **Pablo Picasso**, 1881-1973, Cubism, Spanish,
Guernica, 1937, Oil on canvas, 349.3 x 776.5 cm,
Museo Nacional Centro de Arte Reina Sofia, Madrid

The bloody historical event that moved Picasso to create this masterpiece in one month took place shortly before its first exhibition at the International Exhibition in Paris in 1937. The images and feelings of the three-hour bombing and destruction of the Basque capital of Guernica by Nazi planes were still fresh in the public consciousness. Today, at least one almanac lists the first showing of the work as a highlight of that year, but ironically doesn't mention the event that killed 1,654 people and inspired the artist (Time Almanac, 2002). The brutally stark monochrome work was controversial both as a reactive political statement and as art. Initially, Picasso had put touches of colours in his work. The black and white must have been inspired by photographs taken of the war (particularly those of Robert Capa). It was a major expression of the cubist movement to disregard the distinction between the profile and the full face view of it subjects. The viewer sees the subject from different angles at the same time.

While the work is secular, it is often compared to religious triptychs in composition as well as in the intensity of its thematic presentation. The vertical line between the left panel and the central might run between the bull and house, cutting through the horse's right rear leg. The right panel cuts vertically through the thigh area of the pleading women in the lower right. The geometric centre of the work runs vertically between symbols of hope (the single flower that has survived beneath the broken sword) and the corner of the building from which the horrified, lamp-carrying victim emerges. The tragedy of the small town is extended to all of Spain by including the bull, a symbol of the nation's obsession with bullfighting at that time, but here the bull has its tail raised in anger. It would seem to show defiance, in contrast to the anguished horse that is dismembered like the fallen victim below it. However, Picasso said the horse "represents the people," while the bull is "the brutality and darkness" of fascism. While the head in the lower left seems to still have some life, the child in the anguished mother's arms appears lifeless. The top central symbol is like an eye with a light bulb as its pupil. It is also like a sun that seems not to enlighten the darkness, leaving humanity to question why such tragedies happen, especially to innocent people. However, Picasso remained very secret on the meanings of Guernica's hidden themes and images.

899. Joan Miró, 1893-1983, Surrealism, Spanish,
Ciphers and Constellations in Love with a Woman, 1941,
Gouache and oil wash on paper, 46 x 38 cm, The Art Institute of Chicago, Chicago.

899

900

902

901

900. **Robert Delaunay**, 1885-1941, Orphism, French,
Rythme 1 (Rythm 1), 1940, Oil on canvas, 529 x 592 cm,
Musée National d'Art Moderne, Centre Georges Pompidou, Paris

901. **Wasily Kandinsky**, 1866-1944, Lyrical Abstraction/ Der Blaue Reiter, Russ
Blue Heaven, 1940, Oil on canvas, 100 x 73 cm,
Musée National d'Art Moderne, Centre Georges Pompidou, Paris

902. **Joan Miró**, 1893-1983, Surrealism, Spanish,
Constellation: Awakening in the Early Morning, 1941, Gouache and oil
wash on paper, 46 x 38 cm, Kimbell Art Museum, Fort Worth

*Miró had begun the paintings collectively called "Constellations" w
staying in the Normandy countryside, in Varengeville-sur-Mer, a tiny vil
near Dieppe where he lived from August 1939 to May 1940. He wa
caught up with his work that he did not understand how that location put
into the path of the escalating war. He was busy creating the techniques
sensibility that would carry through a tight series of twenty-three painting
 He began by moistening his paper, scratching its surface and stirring
texture as background to the firmament he was creating. Familiar imag
floated onto the page – eyes, stars, birds, faces, ribs - but also sin
geometric shapes – triangles, circles, crescents, swashes. Some shapes are
black, others primary colours, but all interconnect within the frame, so
the totality is as much the interest of the painting as its component parts.*

474

903

904

903. Paul Delvaux, 1897-1994, Surrealism, Belgian, *Entry into the City*, 1940, Oil on canvas, 170 x 190 cm, Musée Delvaux, Saint Idesbald

904. Paul Nash, 1889-1946, Surrealism, British, *Totes Meer (Dead Sea)*, 1940-41, Oil on canvas, 101.6 x 152.4 cm, Tate Gallery, London

906

905. Edward Hopper, 1882-1967, Realism, American, *Nighthawks*, 1942,
Oil on canvas, 84.1 x 152.4 cm, The Art Institute of Chicago, Chicago

*Hopper's teacher, Robert Henri (1865-1929), was of the Ashcan School, a re
movement in America shortly before World War I. The influence is seen in the a
frequent choice of ordinary cityscapes (called American vernacular architecture
street subjects (cf. Early Sunday Morning, 1930). However, the artist's treatme
light and shadow, seen dramatically demonstrated in Nighthawks, is distinc
and immediately recognisable as his own. In this quiet view of two people at
night coffee shop, there is a cold distance between the couple, symbolised b
separation of their cups and expressionless faces. The waiter is in an unusual pe
on a lower plane apparently so as not to distract from the main subjects. An ise
customer is not relating to either the couple or the waiter; he even has his ba
the viewer, albeit he is geometrically at the centre. The lighting distracts the v
from him. The viewer is even more distant from the interior, left outside of its w
and more secure world. Referring to American cinema in the setting, the ligh
the characters' attitudes, Hopper reflects the Great Depression of America
1930s. The loneliness and melancholy mood and dramatic lighting is typi
Hopper's work, in sharp contrast to the optimistic jingoism of either the A
School or later the contemporary American illustrator Norman Rockwe
example. Yet, there is a universal appeal for Hopper's work, or at least an imm
familiarity with the bleakness he frequently expressed.*

906. Max Ernst, 1891-1976, Surrealism, French, German-born, *Attirement of the B*
1940, Oil on canvas, 129.6 x 96.3 cm, Peggy Guggenheim Collection, Venice

907. Edward Hopper, 1882-1967, Realism, American,
Gas, 1940, Oil on canvas, 66.7 x 102.2 cm, The Museum of Modern Art, Nev

908. Rufino Tamayo, 1899-1991, Mexican, *Animals*, 1941,
Oil on canvas, 76.5 x 101.6 cm, The Museum of Modern Art, New York

907

908

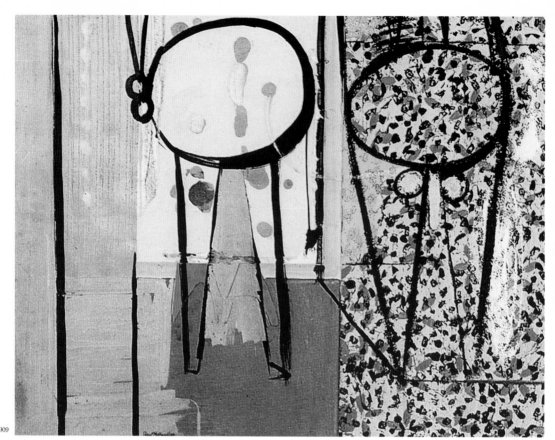

909

910

909. Robert Motherwell, 1915-1991, Abstract Expressionism, American,
Pancho Villa, Dead and Alive, 1943, Gouache and oil, collage on cardboard,
71.1 x 91.1 cm, The Museum of Modern Art, New York

910. Jean Fautrier, 1898-1964, Art Informel, French,
Hostage Head n°2, 1943, Private collection, Paris

911

912

911. Jackson Pollock, 1912-1956, Abstract Expressionism,
American, *The She-Wolf*, 1943,
Oil, gouache and plaster on canvas,
106.4 x 170.2 cm, The Museum of Modern Art, New York

*Pollock's nickname was: "Jack the Dripper". She-Wolf is an
earlier painting of Pollock's, brimming over with archetypal
Jungian imagery. This painting shows the beginnings of his
'drip and pour' technique.*

912. Wifredo Lam, 1902-1982, Surrealism, Cuban,
The Jungle, 1943, Gouache on paper mounted on canvas,
239.4 x 229.9 cm, The Museum of Modern Art, New York

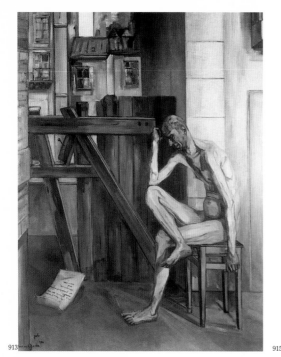

913

915

914

913. Francis Gruber, 1912-1948, Miserabilism, French,
Job, 1944, Oil on canvas, 162 x 130 cm, Tate Gallery, London

*This painting was exhibited at the Salon d'Automne in 1944 which was called
"Salon of the Liberation" because of the German occupation of Paris. This
painting symbolises oppressed people, suffering like Job, and is an allegory of
the survival of hope under the Occupation. Because of this and other works,
Gruber is considered the father of the Miserabiliste variety of French painting.*

914. Pierre Bonnard, 1867-1947, Nabis, French, *Self-Portrait in the Mirror*, 1945,
Oil on canvas, 73 x 51 cm, Musée National d'art Moderne,
Centre Georges Pompidou, Paris

915. Norman Rockwell, 1894-1978, Realism, American,
Freedom from Want, 1943, Oil on canvas, 117.3 x 91 cm,
Norman Rockwell Art Collection Trust, Stockbridge, Massachusetts

916

16. Arshile Gorky, 1904-1948, Abstract Expressionism,
American, *The Engagement II*, 1947,
Oil on canvas, 71.1 x 90.1 cm,
Whitney Museum of American Art, New York

17. Clyfford Still, 1904-1980, Abstract Expressionism,
American, *Jamais*, 1944, Oil on canvas, 165.2 x 82 cm,
Guggenheim Museum, New York

917

481

918

918. Salvador Dalí, 1904-1989, Surrealism, Spanish,
The Temptation of St Anthony, 1946, Oil on canvas, 89.5 x 119.5 cm,
Musées Royaux des Beaux-Arts de Belgique, Brussels

919. Jean Dubuffet, 1901-1985, Art Brut (Raw Art), French,
Jazz Band (Dirty Style Blues), 1944, Oil on canvas, 97 x 130 cm,
Musée National d'Art Moderne, Centre Georges Pompidou, Paris

920. André Masson, 1896-1987, Surrealism, French, *Pasiphaë*, 1945,
Pastel on black paper, 69.8 x 96.8 cm, The Museum of Modern Art, New York

919

921

922

921. **Wolfgang Wols**, 1913-1951,
Art Informel, German-born,
active in France,
Yellow Composition, 1947,
Oil on canvas, 73 x 92 cm,
Neue Nationalgalerie, Berlin

922. **Bernard Buffet**, 1928-1999, French,
La Ravaudeuse de Filet, 1948,
Oil on canvas, 200 x 308 cm,
Private collection, Paris

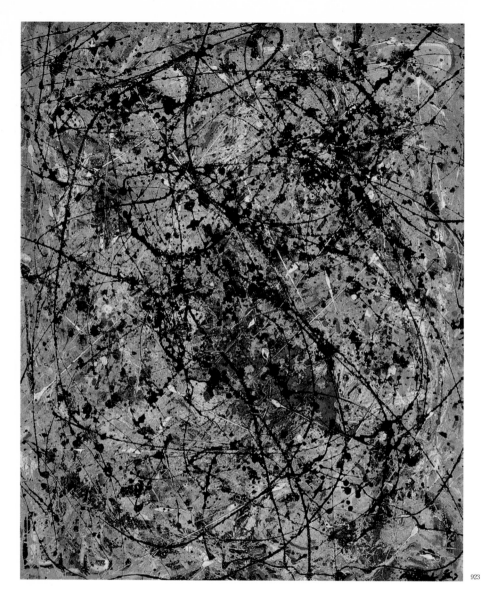

923

923. Jackson Pollock, 1912-1956, Abstract Expressionism, American,
Reflection on the Big Dipper, 1947, Oil on canavs, 111 x 92 cm,
Stedelijk Museum, Amsterdam

924. Graham Sutherland, 1903-1980, Semi-abstraction, British,
Somerset Maugham, 1949, Oil on canvas, 137.2 x 63.5 cm,
Tate Gallery, London

*From 1940 to 1945 Sutherland worked as an official war artist. Then from 1947
through the mid-1960s he moved to the south of France where he painted a
number of new motifs. During this period, Sutherland painted his first portrait
commission,* Somerset Maugham, *which proved to be such a success that he
received numerous commissions.*

925. Henri Michaux, 1899-1984, Art Informel, French,
Untitled, 1948, Watercolour on paper, 50 x 31.5 cm,
Musée National d'Art Moderne, Centre Georges Pompidou, Paris

926. Roger Bissière, 1886-1964, Non-figuration, French,
Great Composition, 1947, Oil on paper mounted on canvas, 41 x 27 cm,
Private collection

924

925

926

927

Andrew Wyeth
(1917 Chadds Ford, Pennsylvania)

Andrew Wyeth, the youngest of five children, sprang from an unusually artistic family. His father, Newell Convers Wyeth (1882-1945), a distinguished illustrator, gave him a rigorous artistic training. Two of Andrew's siblings were noted artists as well as his own son James. Early in his career, Andrew was noted for his impressionistic watercolours. His mature style was characterized by realistic interpretations, overt beauty and an almost photographic exactitude. For over fifty years his landscapes and interiors were consistently realistic and succeeded to convey a strong emotional current. His later works often contained symbolic elements, such as his most famous work, *Christina's world* (1948) which depicts his wife Betsy Merle James. Wyeth's most important subjects were his neighbours and their farms, his wife and her family. Consequently, he is referred to as the 'painter of the people.' According to *Webster's American Biographies* (1984), he is one of the best-known American painters of the 20th century.

927. **Andrew Wyeth**, *1917, Realism, American,
Christina's World, 1948,
Tempera on gessoed panel, 81.9 x 121.3 cm,
The Museum of Modern Art, New York

928

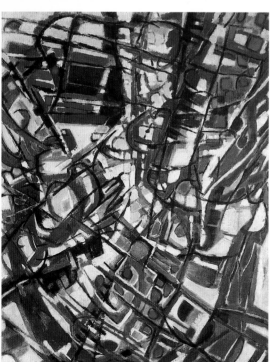

929

928. Alberto Giacometti, 1901-1966, Surrealism, Swiss, *Head of a Man*, 1951, Oil on canvas, 73.3 x 60.3 cm, Private collection

Both a painter and a sculptor, Giacometti concentrated essentially on the representation of human figures. His drawings and paintings often inspired him in the special representation of his sculptural works.

929. Jean René Bazaine, 1904-2001, Non-figuration, French, *The Diver*, 1949, Oil on canvas, 114 x 115 cm, Ludwig Museum, Cologne

930. Maria Helena Vieira da Silva, 1908-1992, Non-figuration, Portuguese, *Summer*, Oil on canvas, 81 x 99 cm, Musée Fabre, Montpellier

Central figure of the Ecole de Paris after the Second World War, Vieira da Silva's paintings are extremely elaborate and the use of a complex game of colours is characteristic of her work.

931. Willem De Kooning, 1904-1997, Abstract Expressionism, American, Dutch-born, *Woman I*, 1950-52, Oil on canvas, 192.7 x 147.3 cm, The Museum of Modern Art, New York

The artist unexpectedly changed his style after decades of development and perfection seen in his masterpiece Excavation *(1950).* Woman I *is not a portrait, but a personal and obviously negative comment on his relationship with women. De Kooning once mentioned that he intended to paint a beautiful woman, but that in the process she changed into a monster. A reading of the artist's life reveals several possible roots of his hostility to women. Ironically, he was friends with some of the most beautiful women in the city at the time. The authors of the Pulitzer Prize-winning biography of the artist note that* Woman I *is "personally, socially, culturally, and artistically fraught with uncertainty. Its anxiety is irreducible. It breaks all rules of safety, even those of the avant-garde". (Mark Stevens and Annalyn Swan: De Kooning: An American Master. Knopf. 2004. Page 338.)*

Willem De Kooning
(1904 Rotterdam – 1997 East Hampton, Long Island)

Willem De Kooning lived in the Netherlands before going to Belgium and then to the USA where he began to work as a house painter. His studies at the Rotterdam Academy of Fine Art gave him a strong knowledge of painting especially in abstract art. His work done under the auspices of the WPA Federal Art Project shows the great influence that Picasso and Cubism had on him. Under the influence of Gorky, one of his closest friends, he introduced male reproductions but his paintings are almost all centred on the female figure. De Kooning alternated between representative and abstract painting. He is considered, nowadays, as one of the leaders of abstract expressionism with Pollock, Rothko and Clyfford Still. Action painting characterizes his work.

Jackson Pollock

(1912 Cody Wyoming – 1956
East Hampton, New York)

Born in 1912, in a small town in Wyoming, Jackson Pollock embodied the American dream as the country found itself confronted with the realities of a modern era replacing the fading nineteenth century. Pollock left home in search of fame and fortune in New York City. Thanks to the Federal Art Project he quickly won acclaim, and after the Second World War became the biggest art celebrity in America. For De Kooning, Pollock was the "icebreaker". For Max Ernst and Masson, Pollock was a fellow member of the European Surrealist movement. And for Motherwell, Pollock was a legitimate candidate for the status of the Master of the American School. During the many upheavals in his life in Nez York in the 1950s and 60s, Pollock lost his bearings · success had simply come too fast and too easily. It was during this period that he turned to alcohol and disintegrated his marriage to Lee Krasner. His life ended like that of 50s film icon James Dean behind the wheel of his Oldsmobile, after a night of drinking.

932. **Alberto Burri**, 1915-1995, Arte Povera, Italian,
Sack 5P, 1953, Mixed media and collage, 150 x 130 cm,
Fondazione Palzzo Albizzini, Città di Castello

Burri was a doctor in the Italian army. He was captured and his works reflect the horrors of war. The use of sacking characterizes his works of the 1950s. His use of red paint is reminiscent of blood.

933. **Jackson Pollock**, 1912-1956, Abstract Expressionism, American,
Number 1, 1950 (Lavender Mist), 1950, Oil, enamel and aluminium on canvas, 221 x 299.7 cm, The National Gallery of Art, Washington, D.C.

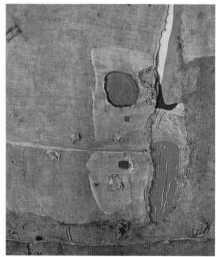

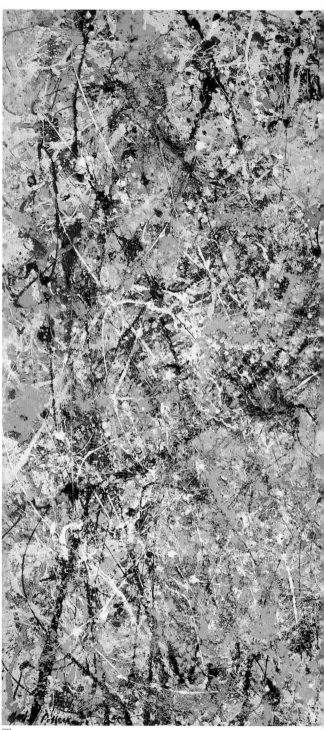

934

936

935

934. **Frantisek Kupka**, 1871-1957, Abstraction, Czech,
   Cathedral, 1951, Oil on canvas, 180 x 150 cm, Private collection

935. **Willem De Kooning**, 1904-1997, Abstract Expressionism, American,
   Dutch-born, *Woman II*, 1952, Oil on canvas, 149.9 x 109.3 cm,
   The Museum of Modern Art, New York

936. **Alfred Manessier**, 1911-1993, Non-Figuration, French,
   Crown of Thorns, 1951, Oil on paper mounted on canvas, 38.8 x 49.8 cm,
   Museum Folkwang, Essen

938

939

. **Salvador Dalí**, 1904-1989, Surrealism, Spanish,
Christ of Saint John the Cross, 1951, Oil on canvas, 205 x 116 cm,
The Glasgow Art Gallery, Glasgow

. **Mark Rothko**, 1903-1970, Abstract Expressionism, Russian-born, American,
Number 10, 1950, Oil on canvas, 229.6 x 145.1 cm, The Museum of
Modern Art, New York

*Colour field painting in America in the late 1940s was partly an identity-
seeking reaction to the action painting of Pollock in particular and Abstract
Expressionism in general. Large works showing soft edged areas of colour
washes dominated his output. In this typical Rothko work, shades of
uplifting blue separated by a central and dominating earthy and pedestrian
brown might reflect what ultimately proved to be the artist's melancholy
and pessimism about life itself. He committed suicide.*

. **Helen Frankenthaler**, *1928, Abstract Expressionism, American,
Mountains and Sea, 1952, Oil on canvas, The National Gallery of Art,
Washington, D.C.

*Frankenthaler is one of the important figures of post-war American painting.
She was married to Robert Motherwell.*

940

941

942

943

940. Nicolas de Staël, 1914-1955, Abstraction, Russian-French,
Seaside Railway Line in the Setting Sun, 1955,
Oil on canvas, 70 x 100 cm, Private collection

941. Karel Appel, *1921, COBRA, Dutch, *Phantom with Mask*, 1952,
Oil on canvas, 116 x 89 cm, Private collection

*Karel Appel was the founder of COBRA. This movement is characterized by
an energetic manner in the execution of the paintings, and spontaneous
expression.*

942. Willi Baumeister, 1889-1955, Abstraction, German, *Martaruru with Red
Overhead*, 1955, Oil on board, 100 x 81 cm, Private collection

*Baumeister belonged to those painters that the Nazis declared "degenerate"
and he had to leave his position as a professor of the Städel School in Frankfurt.*

943. Nicolas de Staël, 1914-1955, Abstraction, Russian-French, *The Beach at
Agrigento*, 1954, Oil on canvas, 81 x 99.8 cm, Private collection

*In the 1950s Nicolas de Staël travelled frequently in southern France and
depicted more and more elementary landscapes in vivid colours.*

944

944. Ad Reinhardt, 1913-1967,
Abstract Expressionism,
American, *Abstract Painting,
Red*, 1952, Oil on canvas,
274.4 x 102 cm,
The Museum of Modern Art,
New York

Marc Chagall 1954-55

946

947

FRANCIS BACON
(1909 Dublin – 1992 Madrid)

The British painter of Irish birth, Francis Bacon, is probably one of England's most controversial and disturbing artists. Marked by Picasso and later by the Surrealists, his work was expressionist in style. Bacon nevertheless remained an independent artist. Obsessed by pictures of diseases of the mouth, Bacon set out to capture expression without total abstraction and specifically tried to represent corrupt and disgusting humanity, intolerable pain or panic, seen in the faces of the damned in the painting of Michelangelo's *The Last Judgment* (1536-1541) and particularly in Edvard Munch's *The Scream* (1893). In works such as *Three Studies for Figures at the Base of a Crucifixion* which portrayed carcass like figures on crosses, he expressed the satirical, horrifying and hallucinatory. Bacon deliberately subverted artistic conventions in painting a series of variations on figural themes such as the famous portrait by Velázquez *Pope Innocent* X into a shockingly grotesque screaming mask.

945. Marc Chagall, 1887-1985, Surrealism, Russian, *Champ de Mars*, 1954-1955, Oil on canvas, 149.5 x 105 cm, Folkwang Museum, Essen

946. Sam Francis, 1923-1994, Abstract Expressionism, American, *In Lovely Blueness*, 1955, Oil on canvas, 300 x 700 cm, Musée National d'Art Moderne, Centre Georges Pompidou, Paris

947. Francis Bacon, 1909-1992, New Figuration, British, *Study after Velázquez's Portrait of Pope Innocent X*, 1953, Oil on canvas, 153 x 118 cm, Des Moines Art Center, Des Moines

948

949

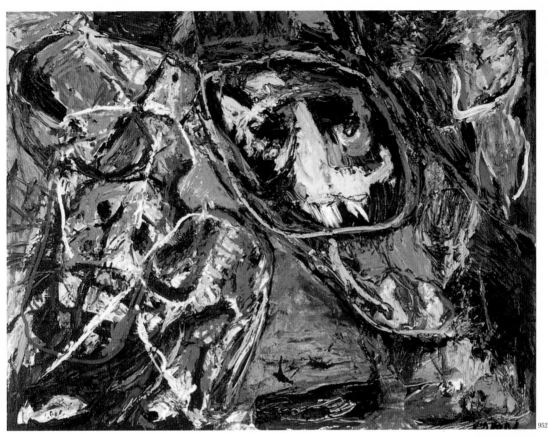

952

953

948. Franz Kline, 1910-1962, Abstract Expressionism, American, *White Forms*, 1955, Oil on canvas, 188.9 x 127.6 cm, The Museum of Modern Art, New York

949. Alberto Magnelli, 1888-1971, Abstraction, Italian, *Dialogue*, 1956, Oil on canvas, 130 x 162 cm, Galleria Nazionale d'Arte Moderna, Rome

950. Mark Tobey, 1890-1976, Tachism, American, *Edge of August*, 1955, Casein on panel, 121.9 x 71.1 cm, The Museum of Modern Art, New York

951. Robert Rauschenberg, *1925, Abstract Expressionism, American, *Monogram*, 1955-59, Angora goat, tyre, paint, collage and metal on canvas, 129 x 186 x 185 cm, Moderna Museet, Stockholm

This is one of Rauschenberg's first and most famous "combines" and it consists of an unlikely set of materials: a stuffed angora goat, a tyre, a police barrier, the heel of a shoe, a tennis ball, and paint. The idea of combining and of noticing combinations of objects and images has remained at the core of Rauschenberg's work.

Rauschenberg is one of the founders of EAT (Experiments in Art and Technology) because he believed he saw in the combination of art and the development of new technologies a new way of expression.

952. Asger Jorn, 1914-1973, COBRA, Danish, *Loss of the Mean*, 1958, Oil on canvas, 141 x 146 cm, Stedelijk Museum voor Actuele Kunst, Gent

953. Francis Bacon, 1909-1992, British, *Figure in a Landscape*, 1956, Oil on canvas, 145 x 128 cm, Tate Gallery, London

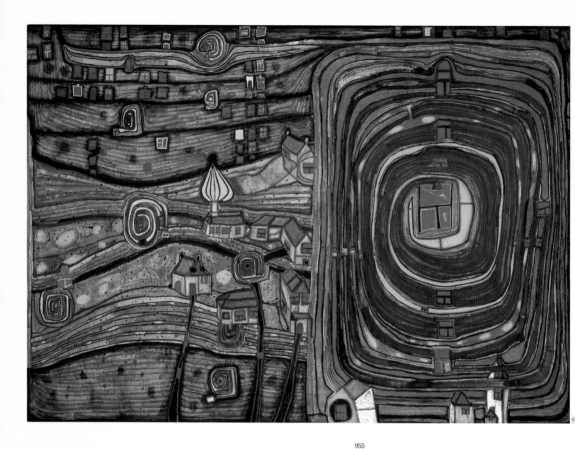

955

954. **Fritz Hundertwasser**, 1928-2000, Austrian,
Grass for Those who Cry, Mixed technique, 65 x 92 cm
Private collection

955. **Lucio Fontana**, 1899-1968, Abstraction, Italian,
Concetto Spaziale – Attese (T 104), 1959, Oil (vinyliqu
on canvas, incisions, 125 x 100.5 cm,
Galleria d'Arte del Naviglio, Milan

956. Ben Nicholson, 1894-1982, Abstraction, British, *August 1956 (Val D'Orcia)*, 1956, Oil, gesso and pencil on board, 122 x 214 cm, Tate Gallery, London

957. Pierre Soulages, *1919, Abstraction, French, *Painting, 14 April*, 1956, Oil on canvas, 195 x 365 cm, Musée National d'Art Moderne, Centre Georges Pompidou, Paris

958. Hans Hartung, 1904-1989, Abstraction, German, *T.*, 1956, Oil on canvas, 180 x 137 cm, Collection Anne-Eva Bergman, Antibes

958

959. Richard Hamilton, *1922, Pop Art, British, *Just what is it that makes today's homes so different, so appealing?*, 1956, Collage on paper, 26 x 25 cm, Kunsthalle, Tübingen

This small collage was a design for the monochrome poster advertising the very first Pop/Mass-Culture Art exhibition ever to be held, namely the 'This is Tomorrow' show mounted at the Whitechapel Art Gallery in London in 1956 by the Independent Group, of which Hamilton was a member. The design demonstrates exactly why its creator is deemed so important to the tradition of Pop/Mass-Culture Art, for it is almost a lexicon of all the themes that would soon be touched upon by both Hamilton and others. Thus the Young Romance comic strip image hanging on the wall points towards things to come from Roy Lichtenstein; the nude on the right coupled with the adjacent tin of ham, bowl of fruit and television set suggests future images by Tom Wesselmann; the word-bearing pointer on the stairs would be paralleled in works by Andy Warhol, just as that selfsame artist would devote a major part of his art to "superstars," as seen here in the form of Al Jolson in The Jazz Singer of 1929; the word "POP" carried on a paddle by the semi-nude male points the way to the future employment of words by Ed Ruscha, Robert Indiana, Allan D'Arcangelo and by Hamilton himself; and the corporate logo appearing on the lampshade anticipates the work of Ashley Bickerton by several decades.

960. Mark Rothko, 1903-1970, Abstract Expressionism, Russian-born, American,
Untitled, 1957, Oil on canvas, 143 x 138 cm, Private collection

961

962

961. Serge Poliakoff, 1906-1969, Abstraction, Russian born, active in Paris,
Composition, 1959, Oil on canvas, 130 x 96.5 cm,
Museum Moderner Kunst, Vienna

962. Sam Francis, 1923-1994, Abstract Expressionism, American,
Around the World, 1958, Oil on canvas, 274.3 x 321.3 cm,
Private collection

963. Jean-Michel Atlan, 1913-1960, Abstraction, French,
La Kahena, 1958, Oil on canvas, 146 x 89 cm,
Musée National d'Art Moderne, Centre Georges Pompidou, Paris

965

966

964. Yves Klein, 1928-1962, New Realism, French, *Untitled, Blue Monochrome (IKB 82)*, 1959, Dry pigment in synthetic resin on canvas, mounted on board, 92.1 x 71.8 cm, Guggenheim Museum, New York

Klein began to exhibit his monochromes in the mid-1950s. Klein patented "The International Klein Bleu" in 1960, a deep blue colour that is kept intact when being mixed with a synthetic resin.

965. Jasper Johns, *1930, Pop Art, American, *Flag on Orange Field*, 1957, Oil on canvas, 167.6 x 124.5 cm, Ludwig Museum, Cologne

966. Maurice Estève, 1904-2001, Non-Figuration, French, *Fressiline*, 1960, Oil on canvas, 46 x 38 cm, Henie-Onstad Art Center, Hovikodden

968

96

968

967. James Rosenquist, *1933, Pop Art, American,
President Elect, 1960-61, Oil on masonite, 228 x 366 cm,
Musée National d'Art Moderne, Centre Georges Pompidou, Paris

*John F. Kennedy was elected President of the United States on
8 November 1960, and this painting was begun very soon afterwards.
It was one of two pictures created in 1960-1961 that proved to be
Rosenquist's breakthrough works in artistic terms. The other painting
is entitled 47, 48, 50, 61 and it shows three men's ties above the dates
1947, 1948 and 1950, thereby implicitly commenting upon fashion
and history. The present painting seems no less meaningful, given the
happy visage of one of America's most famous, youthful and
handsome presidents, from whose head emerges two perfect female
hands holding some pieces of appetising cake placed in front of a
shining car. With merely a hint of irony — for everything is just a little
too faultless — Rosenquist alludes to the perfect consumer society as
projected by its ever-optimistic politicians.*

*The work was developed from a three-part collage Rosenquist
had made using an old magazine photo of Kennedy and ads for cake
and a 1949 Chevrolet. The study reveals more of the vehicle than
seen here, and includes two figures standing behind the car, looking
at it admiringly.*

968. Larry Rivers, 1923-2002, Pop Art, American,
Africa I, 1961-62, Oil on canvas, 185.4 x 165.1 cm, Private collection

969

970

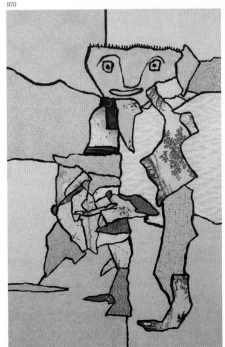

Morris Louis, 1912-1962, Abstract Expressionism, American,
K S I, 1959, Acrylic on canvas, 264 x 438 cm, Museum Folkwang, Essen

Gaston Chaissac, 1910-1964, Art Brut (Raw Art), French, *Untitled: Character*, 1961-62,
Wall-paper collage, ink and gouache on paper mounted on canvas, 95 x 65.5 cm,
Musée National d'Art Moderne, Centre Georges Pompidou, Paris

Jasper Johns, *1930, Pop Art, American, *Map*, 1961, Oil on canvas, 198.2 x 307.7 cm,
The Museum of Modern Art, New York

In his *Flags, Targets* and *Numbers* series of paintings, Johns employed encaustic paint in order to build up the surfaces patiently, and thus prevent any excess emotionalism entering the images. For the Maps paintings, however, he moved in the opposite direction and used oil paint for its dynamism, a gesturality normally associated with Abstract Expressionism. This enacted a clever paradox, for the flurried surfaces go against the grain of most true maps, which are almost always pictorially flattened, diagrammatic affairs, totally devoid of any expression whatsoever.

Naturally, the emphatic marks used by Johns often blur or totally obliterate the boundaries of individual states, thereby possibly commenting upon the increasing political irrelevance of such divisions within an America that had grown enormously in political coherence and wealth since the Second World War. At a time of growing transcontinental air and road travel, national television coverage, the countrywide distribution of mass-produced goods, and nationwide advertising campaigns for those products, such a breakdown or disregard of local boundaries seems highly relevant.

Johns's use of stencilled lettering invokes exactly the same associations of mass-production it had when employed after 1911 by Picasso and Braque, for it is very "low culture" indeed, being primarily found on the sides of packing crates and the like where identifications need to be effected quickly and without any refinement. As employed by Johns, the use of such a uniform type of lettering says much about the blurring of local individuality, the increasing homogeneity of national identity, and the growth of consumerism everywhere.

971 ▶

972

972. Francis Bacon, 1909-1992, Expressionism, British,
Three Studies for a Crucifixion, 1962, Oil with sand on canvas,
198.1 x 144.8 cm, Guggenheim Museum, New York

973. Ellsworth Kelly, *1923, Minimal Art, American,
Red Blue Green, 1963, Oil on canvas, 213.4 x 345.4 cm,
Museum of Contemporary Art, San Diego

973

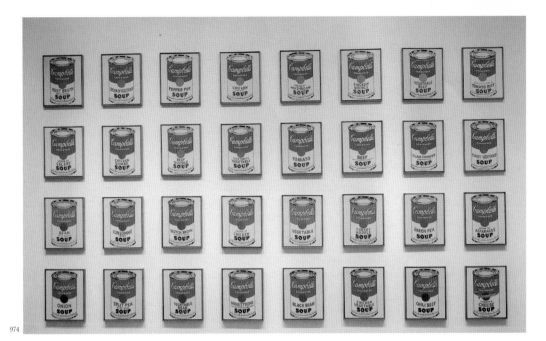

974

Andy Warhol
(1928 Pittsburgh – 1987 New York)

Andy Warhol was an artist who undoubtedly put his finger on the pulse of modern culture. Through pioneering a variety of techniques, but principally by means of the visual isolation of imagery, its repetition and enforced similarity to printed images, and the use of garish colour to denote the visual garishness that is often encountered in mass culture, he threw much direct or indirect light upon modern anomie or world-weariness, nihilism, materialism, political manipulation, economic exploitation, conspicuous consumption, media hero-worship, and the creation of artificially-induced needs and aspirations. Moreover, in his best paintings and prints he was a very fine creator of images, with a superb colour sense and a brilliant feel for the visual rhythm of a picture which resulted from his intense awareness of the pictorial potentialities inherent in forms. Initially, his images might appear rather simple. Yet because of that very simplicity they not only enjoy a high degree of immediate visual impact, but also possess the rare power of projecting huge implications through the mental associations they set in motion. For example, the visual repetition that Warhol employed within a great many of his images was intended, associatively, to parallel the vast repetition of images that are employed in a mass-culture in order to sell goods and services. This includes vehicles of communication such as movies and TV programmes. By incorporating into his images the very techniques of mass production that are central to a modern industrial society, Warhol directly mirrored larger cultural uses and abuses, while emphasising, to the point of absurdity, the complete detachment from emotional commitment that he saw everywhere around him. Moreover, in addition to employing imagery derived from popular culture in order to offer a critique of contemporary society, Warhol also carried forward the assaults on art and bourgeois values that the Dadaists had earlier pioneered; by manipulating images and the public persona of the artist he was able to throw back in our faces the contradictions and superficialities of contemporary art and culture. Ultimately, it is the trenchancy of his cultural critique, as well as the vivaciousness with which he imbued it, that will surely lend his works their continuing relevance long after the particular objects he represented – such as Campbell's Soup cans and Coca-Cola bottles – have perhaps become technologically outmoded, or the outstanding people he depicted – such as Marilyn Monroe, Elvis Presley and Mao Zedong, have come to be regarded merely as the superstars of yesterday.

974. **Andy Warhol**, 1928-1987, Pop Art, American,
32 Soup Cans, 1961-62, Oil on canvas, each 50.8 x 40.6 cm,
The Museum of Modern Art, New York

This is the seminal work in Warhol's oeuvre. It was developed from an idea sold to the painter for fifty dollars by Muriel Latow in December 1961, although the visual realisation of the concept was entirely Warhol's own. The group of canvases formed the artist's first one-man exhibition, held at Irving Blum's Ferus Gallery in Los Angeles in July 1962, where the works were displayed in a single line around the gallery walls, rather than in four rows of eight canvases, as here. The original display maximised the repetition of the imagery by being so spatially extended, given that it filled the gallery. Then, too, any art exhibition necessarily creates a finite world of its own. The show must, therefore, have ultimately projected the fearsome notion that the entire visible universe was filled with Campbell's soup.

This work was equally the first of Warhol's largescale iconic projections. The painter developed the notion of taking an image familiar to millions and presenting it frontally, without painterly qualities, and with a flat surround (as though it were some kind of holy icon) from the Flags paintings of Jasper Johns which were well known to him. In the Flags, Johns treated the holiest of American icons, the national flag, known as the Stars and Stripes, as the starting point for a series of implied painterly and cultural questionings. However, Warhol went much further than Johns in the degree of objectivity with which he projected his icons, for by now an alliance between quasi-abstract expressionist paint-handling and popular cultural imagery in the manner of Johns no longer interested him. Instead, he isolated each of the thirty-two varieties of Campbell's soup so as to emphasise the sterile appearances of mechanically produced objects, and the different varieties of soup as stated on the labels force us to look hard at the images in order to perceive those slight variations, thus making us aware of how we look (or should look) at a work of art. In their subject matter these images both fly in the face of traditional notions of 'art' and, simultaneously, enforce the recognition that no objects are inaccessible to artistic treatment simply because they are familiar or banal.

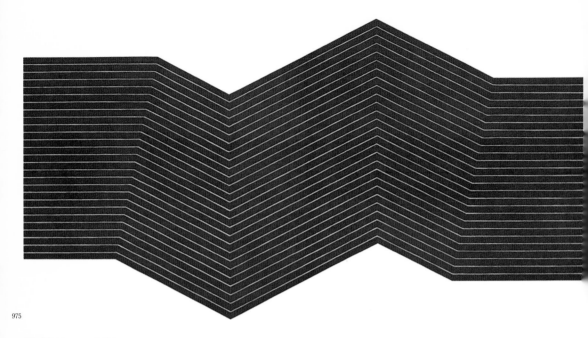

975

976

975. Frank Stella, *1936, Minimal Art, American,
Nunca Pasa Nada, 1964, Metallic polymer on canvas,
279.4 x 558.8 cm, Private collection

976. Andy Warhol, 1928-1987, Pop Art, American,
Triple Elvis, 1962, Aluminium paint and silksreened ink on canvas,
208.3 x 180.3 cm, Virginia Museum of Fine Arts, Richmond

977. Robert Rauschenberg, *1925, Abstract Expressionism,
American, *Retroactive I*, 1964, Oil and silkscreen on canvas,
213 x 152.4 cm, Wadsworth Atheneum, Hartford

*Among its various meanings the word "retroactive" denotes the
extension of things to the past. By the time this work was
created John F. Kennedy was dead, and so a portrait that brings
him back to life is necessarily 'retroactive'. By repeating the
dead president's hand-gesture, Rauschenberg stressed the
man's decisiveness. Clearly the astronaut alludes to the fact that
Kennedy had been largely responsible for expediting the
American space programme, as the artist was well aware. The
nude woman seen walking in multiple positions at the lower-
right might equally serve to remind us that the human drive
towards the exploration of space has its roots in very primal
aspirations indeed: biologically, our species first crawled out of
the swamp, then we stood upright and learned to walk, and as
a result sooner or later we might conquer the stars.*

*This is another of the crowded pictures Rauschenberg
created not long after discovering the visual immediacy
afforded by photo-silkscreen. The apparently arbitrary
organisation of the blocks of imagery strongly parallels the
randomness of life itself, and certainly the density of imagery
parallels the overload we receive daily through the media.
Rauschenberg exploits to the full the graininess that results from
using silkscreen on a fairly open-weave canvas, as well as the
drips that flow from extremely thinned paint. These differing
ways of mark-making add to the vivid sense of spontaneity
throughout.*

977

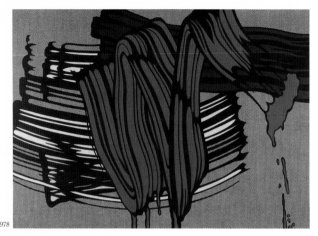

978

980

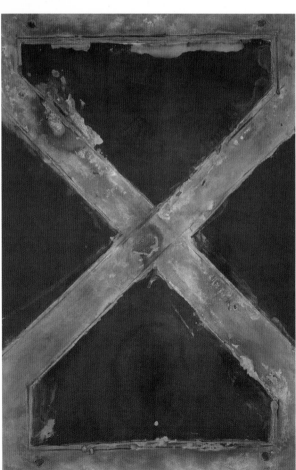

979

978. Roy Lichtenstein, 1923-1997, Pop Art, American,
Great Painting n°6, 1965, Oil and Magna on canvas, 233 x 328 cm,
Kunstsammlung Nordrhein Westfalen, Düsseldorf

979. Antoni Tàpies, *1923, Dau al Set Group, Spanish,
Grand Square, 1962, Mixed medium on canvas, 195 x 130 cm,
Museo de Arte Abstracto Español, Cuenca

980. Josef Albers, 1888-1976, Abstraction, German,
Study for Hommage to the Square: Departing in Yellow, 1964,
Oil on board, 78 x 78 cm, Tate Gallery, London

*Albers, in a very analytical way, preferred to work on an idea by
developing it during a series of paintings, keeping the overview in
mind as he developed each work in that series. The Study for
Hommage to the Square: Departing in Yellow series explored the
possibilities of the geometric form with a variety of colours, giving
optical illusion close to pop art (although Albers is rather related
to abstract art). While he used standard commercial paints, he
developed a complex theory of colour. He distilled the base
colours by adding greys and whites, and the resulting colours
combined into layers that draw the viewer forward and back
within the work. The size of the squares interplays with the
juxtaposed colours, with no two works in the series identical.*

982

981. Georg Baselitz, *1938, Neo-Expressionism, German,
The Great Friends, 1965, Oil on canvas, 250 x 300 cm,
Museum Ludwig, Cologne

982. Antonio Saura, 1930-1998, Art Informel, Spanish,
The Great Crucifixion, 1963, Oil on canvas, 195 x 245 cm,
Boijmans Museum, Rotterdam

984

985

983. **Andy Warhol**, 1928-1987, Pop Art, American,
Jackie Kennedy (16 Jackies), 1964, Synthetic paint on silkscreen ink on canvas,
203.2 x 160 cm, The Brant Foundation, Greenwich

984. **Roy Lichtenstein**, 1923-1997, Pop Art, American, *M-Maybe*, 1965,
Oil on canvas, 152 x 152 cm, Wallraf-Richartz Museum, Cologne

985. **Andy Warhol**, 1928-1987, Pop Art, American, *Shot Blue Marilyn*, 1964,
Silkscreen and acrylic on canvas, 101.6 x 101.6 cm,
The Brant Foundation, Greenwich

986. **David Hockney**, *1937, Pop Art, British, *A Bigger Splash*, 1967,
Acrylic on canvas, 242.5 x 243.9 cm, Tate Gallery, London

986

This is justifiably Hockney's most popular picture, not least of all because the scene depicted typifies the hedonistic lifestyle towards which so many people aspire within contemporary mass-culture. By the time Hockney painted the canvas he had already created two pictures of splashes in swimming pools, one of which he named The Little Splash. That explains the title of the present work.

All is heat and light in the garden of the American Dream. The fairly strident yellow, pink and puce colours of, respectively, the diving board, the patio, and the wall stand at the opposite end of the spectrum to the cool blues of water and sky, thereby generating an immense torridity. That intensity is increased by the climactic white at the heart of the image and by the warm colour of the large, empty surround to the painted area. Hockney created this to reinforce our awareness that we are looking at a fictive space within the enclosure, rather than an actual one. He had already been using this device for some time when he created A Bigger Splash, as can be seen in the Portrait of Nick Wilder of 1966.

On the patio stands a chair, of the type we often associate with Hollywood movie directors. Its presence suggests that the swimmer, who has presumably just vacated it, is a person of some importance. It is not difficult to imagine the sound of the splash breaking the apparent silence. Because we do not see the swimmer, the vacancy of the scene remains intact.

As in the Portrait of Nick Wilder, the influence of Vermeer is apparent, with many lines running parallel to the edges of the image. These create a sense of pictorial rigidity against which the diagonal of the diving board and the free forms of the splash contrast greatly. The unseen swimmer has surely been physically liberated and refreshed by his dive, as, presumably, we all would be in such torrid surroundings.

Bridget Riley
(1931 London)

The English painter Bridget Riley is one of the foremost artists of the late-twentieth century Op Art. After studying at Goldsmiths College and later at the Royal College of Art with Peter Blake and Frank Auerbach, she began exploring the interplay of shape, light and lines. She worked on large canvases with interlocking bands, undulating curves or repeated squares and triangles and mastered particularly well the subtle variations in size, shape or placement of serialized units in an all-over pattern. Her interest in optical effects came partly from her study of Seurat's pointillism. Riley's work has earned attention since the early 1950s when she worked in black and white and used geometric patterns to create the illusion of movement. Her first solo show was in 1962 and four years later, she began to use a full range of colours in order to add depth and tone to her images. Riley's international reputation was established in 1968 when she won the International Prize for Painting, the highest honour at the 1968 Venice Biennale.

987. Bridget Riley, *1931, Op Art, British, *Late Morning III*, 1967, PVA emulsion on canvas, 221.9 x 222.9 cm, British Council, London

988. Bram van Velde, 1895-1981, Abstraction, Dutch, *Untitled: Composition*, 1966, Oil on canvas, 130 x 195 cm, Musée National d'Art Moderne, Centre Georges Pompidou, Paris

989

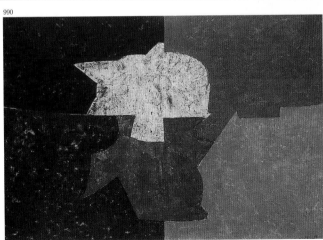

990

989. **Balthasar Balthus**, 1908-2001, French, *Katia Reading*,
1968-1976, Casein and tempera on canvas,
Private collection, New York

990. **Serge Poliakoff**, 1906-1969, Abstraction, Russian-born,
active in Paris, *Abstract Composition*, 1969, Oil on
canvas, 89 x 130 cm, Archives Serge Poliakov, Paris

991

992

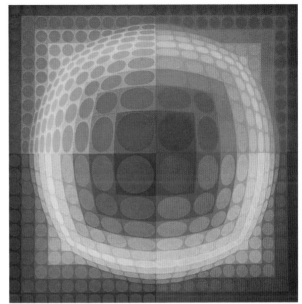

993

994

995

991. **Barnett Newman**, 1905-1970, Minimal Art, American,
Who's Afraid of Red, Yellow, and Blue IV, 1969-1970,
Oil on canvas, 274 x 603 cm, Neue Nationalgalerie, Berlin

992. **Robert Motherwell**, 1915-1991, Abstract Expressionism, American,
Elegy to the Spanish Republic, 1969, Acrylic on canvas, 237.5 x 300 cm,
Graham Gund Collection, Cambridge

993. **Tom Wesselmann**, 1931-2004, Pop Art, American,
Mouth #18 (Smoker #4), 1968, Oil on canvas, 224.8 x 198.1 cm,
Courtesy Sidney Janis Gallery, New York

994. **Victor Vasarely**, 1908-1997, Op Art, French, *Pal-Ket*, 1973-74,
Acrylic on canvas, 151.2 x 150.8 cm, Museo de Bellas Artes, Bilbao

995. **Georg Baselitz**, *1938, Neo-Expressionism, German, *The Forest Upside
Down*, 1969, Oil on canvas, 250 x 190 cm, Museum Ludwig, Cologne

996

Pablo Ruiz Picasso
(1881 Málaga – 1973 Mougins)

Picasso was born a Spaniard and, so they say, began to draw before he could speak. As an infant he was instinctively attracted to artist's tools. In early childhood he could spend hours in happy concentration drawing spirals with a sense and meaning known only to himself. At other times, shunning children's games, he traced his first pictures in the sand. This early self-expression held out promise of a rare gift.

Málaga must be mentioned, for it was there, on 25 October 1881, that Pablo Ruiz Picasso was born and it was there that he spent the first ten years of his life. Picasso's father was a painter and professor at the School of Fine Arts and Crafts. Picasso learnt from him the basics of formal academic art training. Then he studied at the Academy of Arts in Madrid but never finished his degree. Picasso, who was not yet eighteen, had reached the point of his greatest rebelliousness; he repudiated academia's anemic aesthetics along with realism's pedestrian prose and, quite naturally, joined those who called themselves modernists, the nonconformist artists and writers, those whom Sabartés called "the élite of Catalan thought" and who were grouped around the artists' café Els Quatre Gats. During 1899 and 1900 the only subjects Picasso deemed worthy of painting were those which reflected the "final truth"; the transience of human life and the inevitability of death. His early works, ranged under the name of "Blue Period" (1901-1904), consist in blue-tinted paintings influenced by a trip through Spain and the death of his friend, Casagemas. Even though Picasso himself repeatedly insisted on the inner, subjective nature of the Blue Period, its genesis and, especially, the monochromatic blue were for many years explained as merely the results of various aesthetic influences. Between 1905 and 1907, Picasso entered a new phase, called "Rose Period" characterised by a more cheerful style with orange and pink colours. In Gosol, in the summer of 1906 the nude female form assumed an extraordinary importance for Picasso; he equated a depersonalised, aboriginal, simple nakedness with the concept of "woman". The importance that female nudes were to assume as subjects for Picasso in the next few months (in the winter and spring of 1907) came when he developed the composition of the large painting, *Les Demoiselles d'Avignon*.

Just as African art is usually considered the factor leading to the development of Picasso's classic aesthetics in 1907, the lessons of Cézanne are perceived as the cornerstone of this new progression. This relates, first of all, to a spatial conception of the canvas as a composed entity, subjected to a certain constructive system. Georges Braque, with whom Picasso became friends in the autumn of 1908 and together with whom he led Cubism during the six years of its apogee, was amazed by the similarity of Picasso's pictorial experiments to his own. He explained that: "Cubism's main direction was the materialisation of space." After his Cubist period, in the 1920s, Picasso returned to a more figurative style and got closer to the surrealist movement. He represented distorted and monstrous bodies but in a very personal style. After the bombing of Guernica during 1937, Picasso made one of his most famous works which starkly symbolises the horrors of that war and, indeed, all wars. In the 1960s, his art changed again and Picasso began looking at the art of great masters and based his paintings on ones by Velázquez, Poussin, Goya, Manet, Courbet and Delacroix. Picasso's final works were a mixture of style, becoming more colourful, expressive and optimistic. Picasso died in 1973, in his villa in Mougins. The Russian Symbolist Georgy Chulkov wrote: "Picasso's death is tragic. Yet how blind and naïve are those who believe in imitating Picasso and learning from him. Learning what? For these forms have no corresponding emotions outside of Hell. But to be in Hell means to anticipate death. The Cubists are hardly privy to such unlimited knowledge".

997

998

996. Pablo Picasso, 1881-1973, Cubism, Spanish,
Self-portrait, 1972, Black crayon and colour crayon on paper,
Fuji Television Gallery, Tokyo

997. Lucian Freud, *1922, New Realism, British,
Naked Portrait with Reflection, 1980,
Oil on canvas, 225.2 x 225.2 cm, Private collection

998. Corneliu Baba, 1906-1997, Realism, Romanian,
The Mad King, 1981, Oil on canvas, 49 x 33 cm, Artist's collection

999

999. Andy Warhol, 1928-1987, Pop Art, American,
Last Supper, 1986, Polymer on canvas, 101 x 101 cm,
The Andy Warhol Museum, Pittsburgh

1000. Frank Stella, *1936, Minimal Art, American, *Kastura*, 1979,
Oil and epoxy on aluminium and wire mesh with metal tubing,
292.1 x 233.7 cm, The Museum of Modern Art, New York

CHRONOLOGY

see legends on page 536

	1300-1349	1350-1399
IBERIC PENINSULA	1309: First portulan (navigation map)	
	1232–1492: The Nasrid dynasty rules Granada	
ITALY	1308: Dante writes the Divine Comedy. Flourishing of vernacular literature 1348: The plague (known as the Black Death) arrives in Europe	1378: Two popes are elected, one in Italy, one in France. Beginning of the great schism
	1349-1353: Boccaccio writes the *Decameron*	
FRANCE	1309: Avignon becomes residence of the Pope (Clement V) 1320s: Endemic wars and development of sea trade	1378: Two popes are elected, one in Italy, one in France. Beginning of the great schism.
	1309-1423: Avignon becomes the residence of the Pope, starting by Clement V 1337-1453: England and France start the Hundred Years' War	
BRITISH ISLES	1346: Canon powder arrives in Europe and used for the first time at the battle of Crecy	1382: John Wycliffe finishes translating the latin Bible into English
	1337-1453: England and France start the Hundred Years' War	
CENTRAL EUROPE (INCLUDING GERMANY)	1310: Experiments on reflection and refraction of light	1356: Emperor Charles IV issues the Golden Bull. Prague center of learning and culture
FLANDERS (BELGIUM; NETHERLANDS)		1369: Marriage of Philip the Bold, duke of Burgundy, to Margaret of Flanders, beginning of Burgundian rule in the Low Countries
AMERICA		
RUSSIA		

see legends on page 536

	1400-1449	1450-1499
IBERIC PENINSULA	Early 15th c.: Galions, particularly used by Spanish to carry precious materials from the americas 15th c. - 16th c.: Navigation with caravels	1469: Reign of the Catholic Monarchs (Ferdinand of Aragon and Isabella of Castille) 1478: Sixtus IV issues the Bull establishing the Spanish Inquisition 1492: Moors driven out of Spain. End of 800 years of Islamic presence in Spain 1492: Columbus reaches the New World (claims the land for the kings of Spain)
ITALY	1407: Bank of St George established in Genoa as the first public bank 1413: Brunelleschi invents the pictorial perspective 1417: End of the Great Schism	1453: Turkish conquest of Constantinople 1498: Vasco de Gama discovers sea route to India
FRANCE	1429: Saint Joan of Arc leads the French to victory against the English	
BRITISH ISLES		1455: War of the Roses
CENTRAL EUROPE (INCLUDING GERMANY)	1445: Invention of the moveable type (first printer)	1456: Gutenberg produces the first printed Bible 1493: Maximilien I establishes the Habsburg family as a major international power Late 15th c.: Invention of the art of etching (with Daniel Hopfer)
FLANDERS (BELGIUM; NETHERLANDS)	1445: Invention of the moveable type (first printer)	
AMERICA		1492: Columbus reaches the New World (claims the land for the kings of Spain)
RUSSIA		

528

see legends on page 536

	— 16TH CENTURY —	
	1500-1549	**1550-1599**
IBERIC PENINSULA	1500: First Portuguese explorers disembark in Brasil 1506: Hernán Cortés, conquistador, arrives in the New World 1513: Pacific Ocean discovered by Vasco Nuñez de Balboa 1520: Magellan sails across the Pacific Ocean 1521: The Spanish defeat the Mexicans. A 300 year colonial period starts 1543: First scientific study of human anatomy (Andreas Vesalius) 1549: Francis Xavier establishes the first Christian mission in Japan	1571: Battle of Lepanto, Ottomans defeated by the Venetian and the Spanish 1588: Spanish Armada defeated by England. End of Spanish commercial supremacy
	1519-1555: Charles V, Holy Roman Emperor	
ITALY	1494-1559: Italian wars 1545-1563: Council of Trent. Counter-Reformation	
FRANCE	1515-1547: Francis I, King of France	1552: Ambroise Paré practices the first vessel ligature 1598: Edict of Nantes proclaimed by French king Henry IV. End of the Religious wars 1562-1598: Wars of Religion
	1494-1559: Italian wars	
BRITISH ISLES	1533: Henry VIII is excommunicate by the Pope	1558: Protestantism established in the Church of England 1558-1603: Elizabeth I, Queen of England
CENTRAL EUROPE (INCLUDING GERMANY)	1517: Luther posts his 95 theses. Protestant Revolt, Reformation 1529: Turkish invasions, Siege of Vienna 1543 :Copernican Revolution with the theory of heliocentrism	1560: Spreading of Calvinism
FLANDERS (BELGIUM; NETHERLANDS)		1581: Creation of the Dutch Republic (Independence of the Northern provinces from Spain)
	1519-1555: Charles V, Holy Roman Emperor	
AMERICA	1500: First Portuguese explorers disembark in Brasil 1506: Hernán Cortés, conquistador, arrives in the New World 1521: The Spanish defeat the Mexicans. A 300 year colonial period starts 1531-1534: Pizarro conquers the Inca Empire	1588: Spanish Armada defeated by England. End of Spanish commercial Supremacy
RUSSIA	1533-1584: Ivan IV of Russia (Ivan the Terrible) first ruler of Russia to assume the title of tsar	

see legends on page 536

	17TH CENTURY	
	1600-1649	1650-1699
IBERIC PENINSULA	1598-1621: Philip III rules Spain, Naples, Sicily, Southern Netherlands and Portugal 1621: Victories against the French and Dutch 1648: Defeat of Spain against France, peace of Westphalia, concession of the Flanders' territories	
ITALY	1610: Galileo Galilei first uses the telescope 1616: Galileo forbidden by the Church to further scientific work 1644: Evangelista Torricelli invents the barometer	
FRANCE	1610-1643: Louis XIII, King of France 1618-1648: The Thirty Years War 1648: Defeat of Spain against France, peace of Westphalia, concession of the Flanders' territories	1661-1715: Louis XIV, King of France. Castle of Versailles transformed 1685: Revocation of the Edict of Nantes (Protestantism declared illegal in France)
BRITISH ISLES	1640-1660: English Revolution. Led by Oliver Cromwell (1599-1658)	1666: Great fire in London 1687: Isaac Newton's theories of the law motion and principle of gravity 1698: Invention of the steam engine by Thomas Savery
CENTRAL EUROPE (INCLUDING GERMANY)		
FLANDERS (BELGIUM; NETHERLANDS)	1608: Hans Lippershey invents the telescope	
AMERICA	1607-1675: British colonization of North America 1624: Dutch set in Manhattan and around	1681: King Charles II of England grants a land charter to William Penn for the area that now includes Pennsylvania
RUSSIA		

see legends on page 536

	1700-1749	1750-1799
IBERIC PENINSULA	1701-1713: War of the Spanish Succession and Treaty of Utrecht	
ITALY	1709 and 1748: Discovery of the ruins of Herculaneum and Pompeii	
FRANCE		1756-1763: Seven Years War 1763: Treaty of Paris. France ceded Canada and all its territory east of the Mississippi River to England 1770: Nicolas-Joseph Cugnot built the first automobile 1783: First flight in hot air balloon 1789: Lavoisier publishes studies of chemistry 1789: Beginning of the French Revolution 1793-94: Reign of Terror led by Robespierre 1792-1804: First Republic established 1793: Louis XVI executed 1793: Opening of the Musée du Louvre 1798-1799: Expedition of Bonaparte in Egypt
BRITISH ISLES		1768-79: James Cook explores the Pacific 1768: The Royal Academy is founded, with the painter Joshua Reynolds
CENTRAL EUROPE (INCLUDING GERMANY)	1738: Vienna Treaty. End of the war of Polish Succession	1796: Aloys Senefelder invents lithography
FLANDERS (BELGIUM; NETHERLANDS)		1794: Southern Netherlands conquered by the French
AMERICA	Early 18th c.: Benjamin Franklin invents the bifocal lens and performs studies on electricity	1763: Treaty of Paris. France cedes Canada and all its territory east of the Mississippi River to England. 1775: American war of Independence 4th July 1776: Official founding of the United States, declaration of Independence from Great Britain 1789: Election of George Washington
RUSSIA	1703: Foundation of St Petersburg	1762: Catherine II, Empress of Russia

see legends on page 536

	1800-1810	1811-1820	1821-1830	1831-1840	1841-1850
IBERIC PENINSULA	1810-1826: The Spanish colonies of America, except for Cuba and Puerto Rico, conquered their independence				
ITALY					
FRANCE	1804: Napoleon I crowned emperor	1814: Abdication of Napoleon defeated by the armies of Britain, Russia and Austria. Louis XVIII ascends the throne	1822: Champollion studies Egyptian hieroglyphics	1839: Nicéphore Niepce and Louis Daguerre invent the daguerrotype (early process of photography)	1848: Napoléon III is sacred Emperor of the 2nd Em
BRITISH ISLES	1802: Treaty of Amiens (end of the wars with France)	1811-1820: Regency period. Flowering of the arts and literature 1815: George Stephenson invents the railroad locomotive		1834: A furnace destroys most of Wesminster Palace	
CENTRAL EUROPE (INCLUDING GERMANY)					
FLANDERS (BELGIUM; NETHERLANDS)		1815: Defeat of the french army againt Prussia and England at Waterloo		1831: Belgian independence from the Netherlands	
AMERICA	1803: Louisiana sold to the United States by Napoleon	1812: War with Great Britain	1823: Monroe Doctrine	1834: Thomas Davenport makes the first electric motor commerically successful	1848: James W. Marshall disc Gold in California
	1810-1826: The Spanish colonies of America, except for Cuba and Puerto Rico, conquered their independence				
RUSSIA	1801: Assassination of Tsar Paul I. Alexander I is brought to power	1812: Napoleon invades Russia	1825-1855: Nicolas I, Tsar of Russia, enforces military discipline, censorship an traditions of the Orthodox Church.		

532

see legends on page 536

1851-1860	1861-1870	1871-1880	1881-1890	1891-1900
	1861: Italian Kingdom is proclaimed. Victor-Emmanuel II is crowned.			
856: n War, United Kingdom ance declare war on	1869: Charles Cros invents a process for colour photography (based on three colours)	1871: Repression of the Commune in Paris	1885: First use of vaccine for rabies invented by Louis Pasteur	1895: August and Louis Lumière invent the first motion-picture projector
				1898: Marie Curie discovers radium
	1870: French defeated by Prussian. Fall of Second Empire	1871-1914: Expansion of French Colonial Empire (Indochina and Africa)		
		1875-1940: Third Republic		
856: Crimean War, Kingdom and France war on Russia.	1867: Publication of the fist volume of Karl Marx'Capital.			
tion of Darwin's Origin ies				
1837-1901: Victoria, Queen of Great Britain. India under control of the British Empire (1857-1947)				
		1871: Proclamation of the German Empire	1890s: Discovery of psychoanalysis with Sigmund Freud in Vienna	
		1877: Heinrich Hertz discovers electromagnetic radiation, first radio emission		
	1862: Emancipation Proclamation (end of slavery)	1876: Alexandre Graham Bell invents the telephone	1890: Halifax first city to be totally lit up with electricity	1897: New York Journal publishes the first comic strip
n of Abraham Lincoln	1861-1865: American Civil War	1879: First incandescent lamp (Thomas Alva Edison and Joseph Wilson Swan)		1898: Spanish-American War
	1868: Christopher Latham Sholes develops the typing machine			
	1848-1896: Gold rushes toward West America.			
856: Crimean War, Kingdom and France e war on Russia	1861: Emancipation of the serfs			
Russian populist ment (the narodniki)				
	1855-1881: Tsar Alexander II of Russia			

see legends on page 536

	1900-1910	1911-1920	1921-1930	1931-1940
IBERIC PENINSULA		1914-1918: First World War		1931: Attempted coup by Fr and Spanish civil war (1936- 1939-1945: Second World War
ITALY		1915: Vittorio Emanuel III declares war to Austria-Hungary 1914-1918: First World War	1922-1943: Mussolini leads Italy, creation of a fascist state 1929: Lateran Treaties, creation of the State of Vatican	1939-1945: Second World War
FRANCE	1907: Louis Lumière develops a process for colour photography 1908: First cartoon shown (invention of cellulos)	1914-1918: First World War 1919: Treaty of Versailles (Official end of World War I)		1939-1945: Second World W
BRITISH ISLES	1903: Woman's right to vote	1914-1918: First World War	1925: John Baird invents the television	1939-1945: Second World War
CENTRAL EUROPE (INCLUDING GERMANY)		1912-1913: Balkan Wars 1914: Assassination of the archiduke François-Ferdinand and his wife the duchess of Hohenberg at Sarajevo 1914-1918: First World War 1915: Einstein works out the theory of relativity 1916: Freud. Introduction to psychoanalysis	1925-1926: Heisenberg and Schrödinger theories of quantum mechanics 1919-1933: Weimar Republic	1933-1945: Hitler, chancellor of Germany
FLANDERS (BELGIUM; NETHERLANDS)		1914-1918: First World War		1939-1945: Second World War
AMERICA	1900: First flight on a biplane of Wilbur et Orville Wright 1910: Dunwoody and Pickard invent the crystal detector (used for receiving radio broadcast)	1914: Henry Ford mechanizes mass-production 1914: Inauguration of the Panama canal 1917: U.S.A. enter World War One		1939-1945: Second World War
RUSSIA	1904-1905: Russo-Japanese War. Rivalry for dominance in Korea and Manchuria	1914-1918: First World War 1917: Russian Revolutions. Abdication of Tzar Nicolas II	1922-1953: Stalin General Secretary of the Communist Party of the Soviet Union	1939-1945: Second World W

see legends on page 536

1941-1950	1951-1960	1961-1970	1971-1980	1981-1990	1991-2000
			1975: Death of Franco. Restauration of the Spanish monarchy		
Execution of Mussolini. f fascist state.					
	1958: Fifth Republic	1969: First flight of the Concorde between France and Great Britain			
-1960: Conflicts and Decolonization. Algeria (1945-1947), hina (1946-1954), Africa (1956-1960), Maghreb (1954-1962)					
India gains its endence from the British e	1953: James Watson and Francis Crick discover the structure of DNA		1973: First babies born through in-vitro fertilization		
	1955: First radio telescope by Jodrell Bank				
		1947-1991: Cold War			
939-1945: Second World War		1961: Erection of the Berlin Wall		1989: Fall of the Berlin Wall	
Attack of Pearl Harbor e Japanese	1950-1953: War of Korea				
First nuclear fission	1951: First nuclear reactor	1969: Neil Amstrong and Edwin Aldrin walk on the moon	1972-1976: Vietnam War	1981: First space shuttle launched by the States	
Fisrt computer at the ersity of Pennsylvania	1960: Theodore Maiman invents the laser				
Atomic bombing of shima	1960: First satellite for telecommunication created by the NASA				
	1953: Khrushchev, leader of Soviet Union, starts destalinization	1961: First cosmonaute Youri Gagarine flies around the world			
	1957: Sputnik, first satellite launched				

see legends on page 536

LEGENDS

13th century

- Byzantine
- Gothic
- Roman

14th century

- Byzantine
- Gothic

15th century

- Byzantine
- Renaissance

16th century

- High Renaissance
- Mannerism

17th century

- Baroque

18th century

- Baroque
- Neoclassicism
- Rococo
- Romanticism

19th century

- Art & Crafts
- Art Nouveau
- Hudson River School
- Impressionism
- Naïve Art
- Naturalism
- Neoclassicism
- Post-Impressionism
- Pre-Raphaelite Brotherhood
- Realism
- Romanticism
- School of Barbizon
- Symbolism

20th century

- Abstract Expressionism
- Abstraction
- American scene
- Art Déco
- Art Informel
- Art Nouveau
- Arte Povera
- Ashcan School
- Bauhaus
- Camden Town group
- COBRA
- Constructivism
- Cubism
- Dadaism
- Expressionism
- Fauvism
- Free Figuration
- Futurism
- New Realism
- Minimal Art
- Pop Art
- Post-Impressionism
- Rayonnism
- Regionalism
- Social Realism
- Surrealism
- Symbolism

GLOSSARY

A

Abstraction:
International, 20th century, see works by Kandinsky, Kupka, Pollock, and De Kooning.
Art style, begun in 1910 with Kandinsky. Renunciation of naturalistic representation, art without reference to any figurative reality. The term is also used for different movements that are part of Abstraction such as Geometric Abstraction, Abstract Expressionism and Lyrical Abstraction.

Academism (or *art pompier*):
International, mid-19th century, see works by Bouguereau or Cabanel.
Official style influenced by the standards of the French Académie des Beaux-Arts (in particular pretentious history paintings).

Acrylic painting:
International, 20th century.
Fast-drying synthetic paint made with a resin derived from acrylic resin. Can be diluted in water but becomes resistant to water when dry.

Action painting:
USA, Post-World War II movement, see works by Pollock
Generally associated with Abstract Expressionism. Manner in which paint is spontaneously splashed onto a surface. Generally, the term is given to the process of creation rather than to the achieved work.

Art Brut (literally translates as *raw art*):
France, c. 1950, term coined by Jean Dubuffet.
Outsider art, refers to art forms created outside the mainstream of conventional art culture, developed from solitude and from pure and authentic creative impulses.

Art Déco:
International, early-1920s, style in painting, sculpture, architecture, and design.
Paintings influenced by contemporary sculpture, synthetic cubism and futurism. Epitomized in the stream lived works of Tamara de Lempicka.

Art Informel:
Europe, 1950s, see works by Tàpies.
Refers to anti-compositional, formal preoccupations related to Abstract Expressionism.

Art Nouveau:
International, late-19th century to early-20th century. A style in painting, sculpture, architecture, and design.
Style typified in Klimt's paintings, characterized by the use of decorative motifs, vegetal derived patterns, sinuous curves, simple compositions, and denial of volume.

Arte Povera:
Italy, late 1960s, see works by Burri, .
Politically involved art, rejecting consumer society. Use of minimal, ephemeral or worthless materials, both organic and industrial.

Ashcan School:
USA, early-20th century, see works by Bellows, Hopper.
Characterized by the depiction of urban subject matter, focus on the daily life in neighbourhoods.

Atticism:
France, mid-17th century, see works by Le Sueur, La Hyre and Bourdon.
Movement calling for the return to original, classical simplicity, in reaction to the works of Vouet and the seducing aesthetic of works by Vignon.

B

Baroque:
Europe, 17th to mid-18th centuries, see works by Caravaggio, Carracci, Tiepolo, Rubens, Murillo and Vouet.
In contrast with the intellectual qualities of Mannerism, the Baroque displays a more immediate iconography, Characterized by dramatic effects of light, dynamics, contrasts or forms, and illusionist pictorial space.

Byzantine:
Europe, 5th to 15th centuries.
Style derived from Paleo-Christian iconography, characterized by frontal representation, hieratic expression, stylization, and standardized flat figures. Typical of the Byzantine art is the Icon.

C

Camden Town group:
England, 1911-1913, see works by Lewis.
Post-Impressionist group of sixteen artists, inspired by Sickert, and active in Camden Town, a working-class area of London. The group mainly depicted realist urban scenes and some landscapes.

Camera obscura:
Dark box or chamber with a small hole or a lens on one side, through which light comes in. On the opposite side, an invented image reflected on a mirror appears on a glass panel that can be reproduced. It was used for instance by Vermeer and Canaletto to help.

Casein painting:
Painting with pigments bound with a milk precipitate. Generally applied on rigid surfaces such as walls, cardboard, wood or plaster.

Chiaroscuro (from Italian: bright-dark):
Europe, 16th to 18th centuries, see works by Caravaggio, de La Tour, Rembrandt.
Technique existing before Caravaggio but made definitive by the artist. Based on high contrasts of light and shade, suggesting three-dimensional volumes and bringing high-drama to the subjects.

Classicism:
Europe, 17th century, see works by Carracci, Poussin, and Lorrain.
Style referring to an ideal beauty inspired by the antique Greco-roman model. Developed in Italy with Carracci, brought to France by Poussin and Lorrain. Praises the perfection of drawing and the superiority of historical painting.

COBRA (derived from Copenhagen, Brussels and Amsterdam):
France, 1948, see works by Jorn.
Avant-garde movement of expressionists painters focused on semi-abstract paintings and on the return to natural, primitive and instinctive values.

Constructivism:
Russia, c.1920, founded by Tatlin.
Movement praising an industrial art based on a dynamic rhythm, and proposing the conjunction of painting, sculpture and architecture. Works mainly geometric and non-representational, using materials such as plastic and glass.

Cubism:
France, 1907-14, born with Picasso and Braque.
Refers to broken up and reassembled works. Depiction of the object from multiple angles represented simultaneously, as an reduce nature to its geometric elements.

D

Dadaism:
International, 1915-22, see works by Duchamp and Picabia.
Movement created in reaction against bourgeois values and World War I, putting emphasis on the absurd and ignoring aesthetics. Found its expression in the ready-made.

Divisionism:
See Neo-Impressionism.

E

Expressionism:
Germanic countries, early-20ᵗʰ century, see works by Kirchner, Dix and Kokoschka.
Works of expressive emotion with bold contours, crude colours, and anatomical and spatial distortions. Associated with *Der Blaue Reiter and Die Brücke* groups.

F

Fauvism:
France, 1905-1907, see works by Matisse, Derain, Vlaminck, van Dongen.
The first definite revolt against Impressionism and academic rules of art. Movement emerging from Pointillism and influenced by Gauguin's paintings. Use of vibrant patches of colour of extreme intensity to build a picture. The movement initiated the eruption of Modernity.

Fresco:
Technique of painting on wet lime plaster with pigments laid on the fresh wet plaster. The complete design for the fresco was pounced from a cartoon on the dry plaster. Over this was laid each day a thin coat of wet plaster and the paint made out of mineral pigments mixed in water laid on this wet surface.

Futurism:
Italy, early-20ᵗʰ century, see works by Balla or Boccioni.
Movement celebrating the machine age, glorifying war, and often associated with Fascism. Characterized by the expression of dynamism and the repetition of forms to suggest movement.

G

Gothic:
Europe, 13ᵗʰ to early-16ᵗʰ centuries, see works by Monaco or Francke.
Style characterized by well organised space and more dynamic representations. An International Gothic style developed in Burgundy, Bohemia and Italy (fourteenth to fifteenth century) with rich, stylistic features and decorative colouring.

H

Hudson River School:
USA, 1825-1875, see works by Cole.
Group of American landscape painters, inspired y the beauty of America's wilderness with particular effects of light.

I

Impressionism:
France, late-nineteenth century, see works by Monet, Renoir, Manet, and Degas (the core of the group).
A manner in painting that attempts to capture the subjective impression of the effects of light and colour in a scene. Most commonly landscapes painted "en plein-air".

M

Magna paint:
A line of acrylic paints containing pigments in an acrylic resin that dries rapidly to a matt finish. It was often used by Lichtenstein.

Mannerism:
Europe, 1525-1600, see works by Parmigianino, Pontormo, Tintoretto.
Elegant and refined style dominated by profane subjects, complex compositions, muscular and elongated figures in complex poses, with qualities of grace, sophistication and precious details.

Minimal art:
USA, late 1960s, see works by Newman and Stella.
Based on the reduction of the historical and expressive content of an object to an absolute minimum. Large, simplified, and often geometric, forms.

N

Nabism:
France, late 19ᵗʰ – early 20ᵗʰ century, see works by Bonnard and Vuillard.
Post-Impressionist avant-garde movement whose driving force was Sérusier. Characterized by flat colouring of the surface, colours taken straight from the tube and often esoteric in spirit.

Naïve Art:
France, late-19ᵗʰ century, see works by H. Rousseau.
Style developed out of the institutional teaching by artists lacking conventional expertise. Characterized by primitive aspect of the paintings, unusual perspective, use of pattern and cheerful colours.

Naturalism:
Europe, 1880-1900.
Extension of Realism, Naturalism aims at an even more realistic depiction of nature.

Nazarene:
Germanic countries, early-19ᵗʰ century, see works by Overbeck.
Artistic movement that was established in Vienna aiming to revive honesty and spirituality in Christian art.

Neoclassicism:
Europe, 1750-1830, see works by David, Mengs and Ingres.
Movement based on J. Winckelmann's theories on Ancient Greek art and showing a new interest for simplicity and moral values. Art of balance and elegant precision, far from the former expressions of passion.

Neo-Expressionism:
International, 1970s, see works by Baselitz.
Large and rapidly executed figurative painting with aggressive colours.

Neo-Impressionism:
France, late-19ᵗʰ century, works by Seurat and Signac.
Movement part of Post-Impressionism based on a style of painting, Pointillism, in which non-primary colours are generated by the visual mixing of points of juxtaposed primary colours.

New Realism:
Europe, 1960s, co-founded by Klein and the critic Pierre Restany
Artistic movement criticizing mass-produced commercial objects.

Non-Figuration:
France, 1930 to late-20ᵗʰ century, see works by Bazaine, Manessier, da Silva and Estève.
Art taking its inspiration in nature without imitating it.

O

Oil painting:
The colours used in painting are ground to a powder which requires some binding vehicle in order to bring them to a sufficient consistency. The brothers van Eyck are generally known to have been the first to mix their colours with oil.

Op Art:
International, 1960s, see works by Riley and Vasarely. Geometric abstract art dealing with geometrical illusion.

Orphism:
France, 1912, see works by Robert Delaunay. Visionary and lyrical paintings.

P

Perspective/Linear perspective:
Paolo Uccello discovered perspective of which he made a kind of mathematical poetry, a system to create the illusion of space and distance on a flat surface. The first scientific study of perspective can be read in Alberti's treaties *De Pictura* (1435).

Pop Art:
England, USA, 1950s, see works by Warhol, Hamilton or Johns.
Movement characterized by the incorporation of popular mass culture, as opposed to elitist culture, into artistic technique, style and imagery.

Post-Impressionism:
France, late-19th century, see works by Seurat, Cézanne, van Gogh, Gauguin, Utrillo, Valadon, and Toulouse-Lautrec.
Young artists and movement reacting in different ways against Impressionism, which had become the official style of the end of the century.

Pre-Raphaelite Brotherhood:
English, mid-19th century, see works by Millais, Rossetti, and Hunt.
A group of artists that believed the classical compositions of Raphael had corrupted the academic teaching of art. They developed a naturalistic style in pictures of religious and medieval subjects.

Primitivism:
Europe, late-19th century, see works by Gauguin, Picasso and Nolde.
Refers to a style focusing on the tribal arts of Africa, Oceania and North America, believed at the time to be less-developed.

Purism:
France, 1920s, see works by Ozenfant.
The principles of Purism were the purification of the plastic language and the selection of forms and colours. Purism departed from Cubism and sought to determine the ideas and sentiments naturally associated with forms and colours.

R

Rayonnism:
Russia, early-20th century, founded by Larionov.
One of the first expressions of abstract painting. Depicts spatial forms with intersections of rays of colour.

Realism:
France, mid-19th century, see works by Coubet.
The rendering of everyday characters, subjects and events in a manner close to reality, in contrast to classical, idealized forms. It inspired Corot, Millet and the Barbizon School painters.

Regionalism:
USA, 1930s, see works by Curry, Benton and Wood.
A humble, anti-modernist style of painting depicting mid-western rural scenes.

Renaissance:
Europe, c. 1400-c. 1520, see works by Botticelli, Leonardo da Vinci, Dürer.
Period of great creative and intellectual activity, breaking away from the restrictions of Byzantine Art. Study of anatomy and perspective through the understanding of the natural world.

Rococo:
Europe, 1700-1770, see works by Watteau, Boucher or Fragonard.
An exuberant style that began in France, characterized by great displays of ornamentation, tumultuous compositions and light, delicate colours, and curving forms.

Romanticism:
Europe, 1750-1850, see works by Friedrich, Delacroix.
Anti-classical aesthetics bearing emotional content, often depicting melancholic and poetic landscapes, or exotic contents.

S

School of Barbizon:
France, 1830-1870, see works by T.Rousseau, Corot, Courbet, and Millet.
Landscape painters, or painters of peasant scenes, gathered near forest of Fontainebleau. Contributed to realism and inspired by Romanticism.

Semi-Abstraction:
International, 20th century, see works by Hartley or Sutherland. Art directed toward abstraction.

Social Realism:
America, 1930s, see works by Diego Rivera.
Naturalistic realism depicting working class activities or contemporary social or political issues.

Silk screening:
Printmaking technique based on stencilling on a porous fabric. Adopted by American graphic artists in the 1930s, it was popularized by Pop Artists in the 1960s.

Surrealism:
Europe, 1923 to mid-19th century, see works by Ernst, Dalí or Magritte. Artistic exploration of dreams, the intimate, and the imagery of the subconscious mind. Use of the technique of psychic automatism.

Symbolism:
Europe, late-19th century, see works by Moreau or Redon.
Movement taking inspiration in poetry, mythology, legends or in the Bible, characterized by flattened forms, undulating lines, and search of aesthetical harmony.

T

Tachism:
Europe, 1950s, see works by Tobey.
Part of the "Art Informel" movement.

Tempera:
Tempera is the name given to the painting processes in which the medium employed is an albuminous gelatinous or colloidal material. Practically, this is the equivalent to saying that any painting process in which a vehicle or binding material, other than oil is employed is tempera. In constant use during the Renaissance, it was overtaken by oil painting in the fifteenth century.

Trompe-l'œil:
Painting technique that the viewer cannot distinguish from reality (often architectural or scenic detail). Frequent in roof paintings such as Mantegna's works.

INDEX